Infant & Toddler Health Sourcebook
Infectious Diseases Sourcebook
Injury & Trauma Sourcebook
Learning Disabilities Sourcebook, 2nd Edition
Leukemia Sourcebook
Liver Disorders Sourcebook
Lung Disorders Sourcebook
Medical Tests Sourcebook, 2nd Edition
Men's Health Concerns Sourcebook, 2nd Edition
Mental Health Disorders Sourcebook, 3rd Edition
Mental Retardation Sourcebook
Movement Disorders Sourcebook
Muscular Dystrophy Sourcebook
Obesity Sourcebook
Osteoporosis Sourcebook
Pain Sourcebook, 2nd Edition
Pediatric Cancer Sourcebook
Physical & Mental Issues in Aging Sourcebook
Podiatry Sourcebook, 2nd Edition
Pregnancy & Birth Sourcebook, 2nd Edition
Prostate Cancer Sourcebook
Prostate & Urological Disorders Sourcebook
Public Health Sourcebook
Reconstructive & Cosmetic Surgery Sourcebook
Rehabilitation Sourcebook
Respiratory Diseases & Disorders Sourcebook
Sexually Transmitted Diseases Sourcebook, 3rd Edition
Sleep Disorders Sourcebook, 2nd Edition
Smoking Concerns Sourcebook
Sports Injuries Sourcebook, 2nd Edition
Stress-Related Disorders Sourcebook
Stroke Sourcebook
Substance Abuse Sourcebook
Surgery Sourcebook
Thyroid Disorders Sourcebook
Transplantation Sourcebook
Tr[illegible]
Urinary Tract & Kidney Diseases & Disorders Sourcebook, 2nd Edition
Vegetarian Sourcebook
Women's Health Concerns Sourcebook, 2nd Edition
Workplace Health & Safety Sourcebook
Worldwide Health Sourcebook

Teen Health Series

Alcohol Information for Teens
Allergy Information for Teens
Asthma Information for Teens
Cancer Information for Teens
Complementary & Alternative Medicine Information for Teens
Diabetes Information for Teens
Diet Information for Teens, 2nd Edition
Drug Information for Teens, 2nd Edition
Eating Disorders Information for Teens
Fitness Information for Teens
Learning Disabilities Information for Teens
Mental Health Information for Teens, 2nd Edition
Sexual Health Information for Teens
Skin Health Information for Teens
Sports Injuries Information for Teens
Suicide Information for Teens
Tobacco Information for Teens

Eating Disorders SOURCEBOOK

Second Edition

Health Reference Series

Second Edition

Eating Disorders SOURCEBOOK

Basic Consumer Health Information about Anorexia Nervosa, Bulimia Nervosa, Binge Eating, Compulsive Exercise, Female Athlete Triad, and Other Eating Disorders, Including Facts about Body Image and Other Cultural and Age-Related Risk Factors, Prevention Efforts, Adverse Health Effects, Treatment Options, and the Recovery Process

Along with Guidelines for Healthy Weight Control, a Glossary, and Directories of Additional Resources

Edited by
Joyce Brennfleck Shannon

615 Griswold Street • Detroit, MI 48226

Edited by Joyce Brennfleck Shannon

Health Reference Series

Karen Bellenir, *Managing Editor*
David A. Cooke, M.D., *Medical Consultant*
Elizabeth Collins, *Research and Permissions Coordinator*
Cherry Stockdale, *Permissions Assistant*
EdIndex, Services for Publishers, *Indexers*

* * *

Omnigraphics, Inc.

Matthew P. Barbour, *Senior Vice President*
Kay Gill, *Vice President—Directories*
Kevin Hayes, *Operations Manager*
David P. Bianco, *Marketing Director*

* * *

Peter E. Ruffner, *Publisher*

Frederick G. Ruffner, Jr., *Chairman*

ISBN 978-0-7808-0948-2

Library of Congress Cataloging-in-Publication Data

Eating disorders sourcebook : basic consumer health information about anorexia nervosa, bulimia nervosa, binge eating, compulsive exercise, female athlete triad, and other eating disorders, including facts about body image and other cultural and age-related risk factors, prevention efforts, adverse health effects, treatment options, and the recovery process; along with guidelines for healthy weight control, a glossary, and directories of additional resources / edited by Joyce Brennfleck Shannon. -- 2nd ed.

p. cm. -- (Health reference series)

Summary: "Provides basic consumer health information about risk factors, recovery from, and prevention and treatment of various eating disorders. Includes index, glossary of related terms, and other resources"--Provided by publisher.

Includes bibliographical references.

ISBN 978-0-7808-0948-2 (hardcover : alk. paper) 1. Eating disorders. 2. Consumer education. I. Shannon, Joyce Brennfleck.

RC552.E18E287 2007

616.85'26--dc22

2007000861

This book is printed on acid-free paper meeting the ANSI Z39.48 Standard. The infinity symbol that appears above indicates that the paper in this book meets that standard.

Printed in the United States

Table of Contents

Visit www.healthreferenceseries.com to view *A Contents Guide to the Health Reference Series*, a listing of more than 13,000 topics and the volumes in which they are covered.

Part III: Health Effects of Eating Disorders

Part IV: Eating Disorders: Treatment and Recovery

Part V: Healthy Weight Control and Dieting

Part VI: Additional Help and Information

Preface

About This Book

Eating disorders are serious, long-term, potentially life-threatening illnesses, and the number of people affected is growing. In fact, the incidence of eating disorders in the United States has doubled since the 1960s, and currently more than eight million Americans are affected each year. Ninety percent are adolescents and young women, but increasingly young men, younger age groups—including children as young as five years of age—and even seniors are being diagnosed. The battle against eating disorders can be lifelong. Without treatment, as many as twenty percent of people with serious eating disorders die. With early recognition and treatment, however, many sufferers can recover.

Eating Disorders Sourcebook, Second Edition provides updated information about anorexia nervosa, bulimia nervosa, binge eating, and other eating disorders. Symptoms, body image issues, and cultural factors that impact eating disorders for children, adolescents, men, women, and seniors are described. Information is included about the physical and psychological effects of eating disorders, and guidelines for treatment, recovery, and prevention are presented. This book also offers facts about healthy ways of controlling weight, a glossary of related terms, and directories of additional resources.

How to Use This Book

This book is divided into parts and chapters. Parts focus on broad areas of interest. Chapters are devoted to single topics within a part.

Part I: Eating Disorders: Types and Prevalence describes and provides statistical information about the various kinds of eating disorders, including anorexia nervosa, binge eating, bulimia nervosa, emotional eating, compulsive exercising, female athlete triad, and pica.

Part II: Risk Factors, Causes, and Prevention of Eating Disorders discusses genetics, body image perceptions, ethnic and cultural perspectives, and life stages that may contribute to the development of eating disorders. It explains the warning signs and offers prevention tips and guidelines for parents, school personnel, and coaches.

Part III: Health Effects of Eating Disorders describes diagnostic procedures and psychological and medical complications of eating disorders, including malnutrition, osteoporosis, and diabetes. Information is also included about health-related concerns of special significance among people with eating disorders. These include dental health, pregnancy, and the abuse of such substances as alcohol, laxatives, ipecac, and dietary supplements.

Part IV: Eating Disorders: Treatment and Recovery describes behavioral and nutrition therapies used in the care of people with eating disorders. It offers tips for getting treatment and provides information about health insurance benefits. Recovery stages, relapse prevention, and the value of support groups are also explained.

Part V: Healthy Weight Control and Dieting provides guidelines for eating in a healthy manner, exercising appropriately, and determining a suitable calorie intake level. It also describes principles of safe weight management and debunks commonly encountered nutrition myths.

Part VI: Additional Help and Information includes a glossary of related terms and directories of organizations able to provide more information.

Bibliographic Note

This volume contains documents and excerpts from publications issued by the following U.S. government agencies: Agency for Healthcare Research and Quality (AHRQ); National Heart, Lung, and Blood Institute (NHLBI); National Institute of Diabetes and Digestive and Kidney Diseases (NIDDK); National Institute of Mental Health

(NIMH); National Institute on Alcohol Abuse and Alcoholism (NIAAA); National Institute on Drug Abuse (NIDA); National Institutes of Health (NIH); National Institute of Mental Health (NIMH); National Women's Health Information Center; NIDDK Weight-control Information Network (WIN); NIH Office of Rare Diseases; NIH Osteoporosis and Related Bone Diseases National Resource Center; Office on Women's Health; Substance Abuse and Mental Health Services Administration (SAMHSA); U.S. Department of Agriculture (USDA); U.S. Department of Health and Human Services (HHS); and the U.S. Food and Drug Administration (FDA).

In addition, this volume contains copyrighted documents from the following organizations and individuals: Academy for Eating Disorders; A.D.A.M., Inc.; American Association for Clinical Chemistry; American Dental Association; American Medical Association; American Psychological Association; Anorexia Nervosa and Related Eating Disorders (ANRED); Center for Healthy Aging; Nancy Clark; Center for Science in the Public Interest; Cleveland Clinic; Eating Disorders Anonymous; Eating Disorders Association (UK); Eating Disorders Coalition for Research, Policy & Action; Eating Disorder Referral and Information Center; ECRI (formerly known as Emergency Care Research Institute); Patricia Edmonds; Elsevier Health Sciences Publications; Gurze Books; HealthDay/ScoutNews, LLC; King's College London–Institute of Psychiatry; Klarman Eating Disorders Center at McLean Hospital; Lifespan; Lippincott Williams and Wilkins; MBL Communications; National Association of Anorexia Nervosa and Associated Disorders; National Eating Disorders Association; National Eating Disorder Information Centre (Canada); National Institute on Media and the Family; Nemours Foundation; New Orleans Center for Eating Disorders; Ontario Prevention Clearinghouse; Overeaters Anonymous; Roche Diagnostics Canada; Screening for Mental Health, Inc.; Society for Adolescent Medicine; Students Against Destructive Decisions (SADD); Dr. Marika Tiggemann; and the University of Pittsburgh School of Medicine.

Full citation information is provided on the first page of each chapter or section. Every effort has been made to secure all necessary rights to reprint the copyrighted material. If any omissions have been made, please contact Omnigraphics to make corrections for future editions.

Acknowledgements

In addition to the listed organizations, agencies, and individuals who have contributed to this *Sourcebook*, special thanks go to managing editor Karen Bellenir, research and permissions coordinator Liz Collins, and document engineer Bruce Bellenir for their help and support.

About the Health Reference Series

The *Health Reference Series* is designed to provide basic medical information for patients, families, caregivers, and the general public. Each volume takes a particular topic and provides comprehensive coverage. This is especially important for people who may be dealing with a newly diagnosed disease or a chronic disorder in themselves or in a family member. People looking for preventive guidance, information about disease warning signs, medical statistics, and risk factors for health problems will also find answers to their questions in the *Health Reference Series*. The *Series*, however, is not intended to serve as a tool for diagnosing illness, in prescribing treatments, or as a substitute for the physician/patient relationship. All people concerned about medical symptoms or the possibility of disease are encouraged to seek professional care from an appropriate health care provider.

Locating Information within the Health Reference Series

The *Health Reference Series* contains a wealth of information about a wide variety of medical topics. Ensuring easy access to all the fact sheets, research reports, in-depth discussions, and other material contained within the individual books of the *Series* remains one of our highest priorities. As the *Series* continues to grow in size and scope, however, locating the precise information needed by a reader may become more challenging.

A Contents Guide to the Health Reference Series was developed to direct readers to the specific volumes that address their concerns. It presents an extensive list of diseases, treatments, and other topics of general interest compiled from the Tables of Contents and major index headings. To access *A Contents Guide to the Health Reference Series*, visit www.healthreferenceseries.com.

Medical Consultant

Medical consultation services are provided to the *Health Reference Series* editors by David A. Cooke, M.D. Dr. Cooke is a graduate of Brandeis University, and he received his M.D. degree from the

University of Michigan. He completed residency training at the University of Wisconsin Hospital and Clinics. He is board-certified in Internal Medicine. Dr. Cooke currently works as part of the University of Michigan Health System and practices in Brighton, MI. In his free time, he enjoys writing, science fiction, and spending time with his family.

Our Advisory Board

We would like to thank the following board members for providing guidance to the development of this *Series*:

- Dr. Lynda Baker,
  Associate Professor of Library and Information Science,
  Wayne State University, Detroit, MI
- Nancy Bulgarelli,
  William Beaumont Hospital Library, Royal Oak, MI
- Karen Imarisio,
  Bloomfield Township Public Library, Bloomfield Township, MI
- Karen Morgan,
  Mardigian Library, University of Michigan-Dearborn,
  Dearborn, MI
- Rosemary Orlando,
  St. Clair Shores Public Library, St. Clair Shores, MI

Health Reference Series *Update Policy*

The inaugural book in the *Health Reference Series* was the first edition of *Cancer Sourcebook* published in 1989. Since then, the *Series* has been enthusiastically received by librarians and in the medical community. In order to maintain the standard of providing high-quality health information for the layperson the editorial staff at Omnigraphics felt it was necessary to implement a policy of updating volumes when warranted.

Medical researchers have been making tremendous strides, and it is the purpose of the *Health Reference Series* to stay current with the most recent advances. Each decision to update a volume is made on an individual basis. Some of the considerations include how much new information is available and the feedback we receive from people who use the books. If there is a topic you would like to see added to the update list, or an area of medical concern you feel has not been adequately addressed, please write to:

Editor
Health Reference Series
Omnigraphics, Inc.
615 Griswold Street
Detroit, MI 48226
E-mail: editorial@omnigraphics.com

Part One

Eating Disorders: Types and Prevalence

Chapter 1

Eating Disorders Overview

Eating is controlled by many factors, including appetite, food availability, family, peer, and cultural practices, and attempts at voluntary control. Dieting to a body weight leaner than needed for health is highly promoted by current fashion trends, sales campaigns for special foods, and in some activities and professions. Eating disorders involve serious disturbances in eating behavior, such as extreme and unhealthy reduction of food intake or severe overeating, as well as feelings of distress or extreme concern about body shape or weight. Researchers are investigating how and why initially voluntary behaviors, such as eating smaller or larger amounts of food than usual, at some point move beyond control in some people and develop into an eating disorder. Studies on the basic biology of appetite control and its alteration by prolonged overeating or starvation have uncovered enormous complexity, but in the long run have the potential to lead to new pharmacologic treatments for eating disorders.

Eating disorders are not due to a failure of will or behavior; rather, they are real, treatable, medical illnesses in which certain maladaptive patterns of eating take on a life of their own. The main types of eating disorders are anorexia nervosa and bulimia nervosa.[1] A third type, binge eating disorder, has been suggested but has not yet been approved as a formal psychiatric diagnosis.[2] Eating disorders

---

"Eating Disorders: Facts about Eating Disorders and the Search for Solutions," National Institute of Mental Health (NIMH), NIH Publication No. 01-4901, updated February 17, 2006.

frequently develop during adolescence or early adulthood, but some reports indicate their onset can occur during childhood or later in adulthood.[3]

Eating disorders frequently co-occur with other psychiatric disorders such as depression, substance abuse, and anxiety disorders.[1] In addition, people who suffer from eating disorders can experience a wide range of physical health complications including serious heart conditions and kidney failure which may lead to death. Therefore, recognition of eating disorders as real and treatable diseases is critically important.

Females are much more likely than males to develop an eating disorder. Only an estimated 5–15 percent of people with anorexia or bulimia[4] and an estimated 35 percent of those with binge eating disorder[5] are male.

Anorexia Nervosa

An estimated 0.5 to 3.7 percent of females suffer from anorexia nervosa in their lifetime.[1] Symptoms of anorexia nervosa include the following:

- resistance to maintaining body weight at or above a minimally normal weight for age and height
- intense fear of gaining weight or becoming fat, even though underweight
- disturbance in the way in which one's body weight or shape is experienced, undue influence of body weight or shape on self-evaluation, or denial of the seriousness of the current low body weight
- infrequent or absent menstrual periods (in females who have reached puberty)

People with anorexia nervosa see themselves as overweight even though they are dangerously thin. The process of eating becomes an obsession. Unusual eating habits develop, such as avoiding food and meals, picking out a few foods and eating these in small quantities, or carefully weighing and portioning food. People with anorexia may repeatedly check their body weight, and many engage in other techniques to control their weight, such as intense and compulsive exercise, or purging by means of vomiting and abuse of laxatives, enemas, and diuretics. Girls with anorexia often experience a delayed onset of their first menstrual period.

The course and outcome of anorexia nervosa vary across individuals: some fully recover after a single episode; some have a fluctuating pattern of weight gain and relapse; and others experience a chronically deteriorating course of illness over many years. The mortality rate among people with anorexia has been estimated at 0.56 percent per year, or approximately 5.6 percent per decade, which is about 12 times higher than the annual death rate due to all causes of death among females ages 15–24 in the general population.[6] The most common causes of death are complications of the disorder, such as cardiac arrest or electrolyte imbalance, and suicide.

Bulimia Nervosa

An estimated 1.1 percent to 4.2 percent of females have bulimia nervosa in their lifetime.[1] Symptoms of bulimia nervosa include the following:

- recurrent episodes of binge eating, characterized by eating an excessive amount of food within a discrete period of time and by a sense of lack of control over eating during the episode
- recurrent inappropriate compensatory behavior in order to prevent weight gain, such as self-induced vomiting or misuse of laxatives, diuretics, enemas, or other medications (purging); fasting; or excessive exercise
- the binge eating and inappropriate compensatory behaviors both occur, on average, at least twice a week for three months
- self-evaluation is unduly influenced by body shape and weight

Because purging or other compensatory behavior follows the binge eating episodes, people with bulimia usually weigh within the normal range for their age and height. However, like individuals with anorexia, they may fear gaining weight, desire to lose weight, and feel intensely dissatisfied with their bodies. People with bulimia often perform the behaviors in secrecy, feeling disgusted and ashamed when they binge, yet relieved once they purge.

Binge Eating Disorder

Community surveys have estimated that between two percent and five percent of Americans experience binge eating disorder in a six-month period.[5, 7] Symptoms of binge eating disorder include the following:

- recurrent episodes of binge eating, characterized by eating an excessive amount of food within a discrete period of time and by a sense of lack of control over eating during the episode
- The binge eating episodes are associated with at least three of the following:
    - eating much more rapidly than normal
    - eating until feeling uncomfortably full
    - eating large amounts of food when not feeling physically hungry
    - eating alone because of being embarrassed by how much one is eating
    - feeling disgusted with oneself, depressed, or very guilty after overeating
- marked distress about the binge eating behavior
- the binge eating occurs, on average, at least two days a week for six months
- the binge eating is not associated with the regular use of inappropriate compensatory behaviors (for example purging, fasting, excessive exercise)

People with binge eating disorder experience frequent episodes of out-of-control eating, with the same binge eating symptoms as those with bulimia. The main difference is that individuals with binge eating disorder do not purge their bodies of excess calories. Therefore, many with the disorder are overweight for their age and height. Feelings of self-disgust and shame associated with this illness can lead to bingeing again, creating a cycle of binge eating.

Treatment Strategies[1]

Eating disorders can be treated and a healthy weight restored. The sooner these disorders are diagnosed and treated, the better the outcomes are likely to be. Because of their complexity, eating disorders require a comprehensive treatment plan involving medical care and monitoring, psychosocial interventions, nutritional counseling, and when appropriate, medication management. At the time of diagnosis, the clinician must determine whether the person is in immediate danger and requires hospitalization.

Treatment of anorexia calls for a specific program that involves three main phases: (1) restoring weight lost to severe dieting and purging; (2) treating psychological disturbances such as distortion of body image, low self-esteem, and interpersonal conflicts; and (3) achieving long-term remission and rehabilitation, or full recovery. Early diagnosis and treatment increases the treatment success rate. Use of psychotropic medication in people with anorexia should be considered only after weight gain has been established. Certain selective serotonin reuptake inhibitors (SSRIs) have been shown to be helpful for weight maintenance and for resolving mood and anxiety symptoms associated with anorexia.

The acute management of severe weight loss is usually provided in an inpatient hospital setting where feeding plans address the person's medical and nutritional needs. In some cases, intravenous feeding is recommended. Once malnutrition has been corrected and weight gain has begun, psychotherapy (often cognitive-behavioral or interpersonal psychotherapy) can help people with anorexia overcome low self-esteem and address distorted thought and behavior patterns. Families are sometimes included in the therapeutic process.

The primary goal of treatment for bulimia is to reduce or eliminate binge eating and purging behavior. To this end, nutritional rehabilitation, psychosocial intervention, and medication management strategies are often employed. Establishment of a pattern of regular, non-binge meals, improvement of attitudes related to the eating disorder, encouragement of healthy but not excessive exercise, and resolution of co-occurring conditions such as mood or anxiety disorders are among the specific aims of these strategies. Individual psychotherapy (especially cognitive-behavioral or interpersonal psychotherapy), group psychotherapy that uses a cognitive-behavioral approach, and family or marital therapy have been reported to be effective. Psychotropic medications, primarily antidepressants such as the SSRIs, have been found helpful for people with bulimia, particularly those with significant symptoms of depression or anxiety, or those who have not responded adequately to psychosocial treatment alone. These medications also may help prevent relapse. The treatment goals and strategies for binge eating disorder are similar to those for bulimia, and studies are currently evaluating the effectiveness of various interventions.

People with eating disorders often do not recognize or admit that they are ill. As a result, they may strongly resist getting and staying in treatment. Family members or other trusted individuals can be helpful in ensuring that the person with an eating disorder receives needed care and rehabilitation. For some people, treatment may be long term.

Research Findings and Directions

Research is contributing to advances in the understanding and treatment of eating disorders.

- NIMH-funded scientists and others continue to investigate the effectiveness of psychosocial interventions, medications, and the combination of these treatments with the goal of improving outcomes for people with eating disorders.[8, 9]
- Research on interrupting the binge eating cycle has shown that once a structured pattern of eating is established, the person experiences less hunger, less deprivation, and a reduction in negative feelings about food and eating. The two factors that increase the likelihood of bingeing—hunger and negative feelings—are reduced, which decreases the frequency of binges.[10]
- Several family and twin studies are suggestive of a high heritability of anorexia and bulimia,[11, 12] and researchers are searching for genes that confer susceptibility to these disorders.[13] Scientists suspect that multiple genes may interact with environmental and other factors to increase the risk of developing these illnesses. Identification of susceptibility genes will permit the development of improved treatments for eating disorders.
- Other studies are investigating the neurobiology of emotional and social behavior relevant to eating disorders and the neuroscience of feeding behavior.
- Scientists have learned that both appetite and energy expenditure are regulated by a highly complex network of nerve cells and molecular messengers called neuropeptides.[14, 15] These and future discoveries will provide potential targets for the development of new pharmacologic treatments for eating disorders.
- Further insight is likely to come from studying the role of gonadal steroids.[16, 17] Their relevance to eating disorders is suggested by the clear gender effect in the risk for these disorders, their emergence at puberty or soon after, and the increased risk for eating disorders among girls with early onset of menstruation.

References

1. American Psychiatric Association Work Group on Eating Disorders. Practice guideline for the treatment of patients

with eating disorders (revision). *American Journal of Psychiatry*, 2000; 157(1 Suppl): 1–39.

2. American Psychiatric Association. *Diagnostic and Statistical Manual for Mental Disorders, fourth edition (DSM-IV)*. Washington, DC: American Psychiatric Press, 1994.

3. Becker AE, Grinspoon SK, Klibanski A, Herzog DB. Eating disorders. *New England Journal of Medicine*, 1999; 340(14): 1092–8.

4. Andersen AE. Eating disorders in males. In: Brownell KD, Fairburn CG, eds. *Eating disorders and obesity: a comprehensive handbook*. New York: Guilford Press, 1995; 177–87.

5. Spitzer RL, Yanovski S, Wadden T, Wing R, Marcus MD, Stunkard A, Devlin M, Mitchell J, Hasin D, Horne RL. Binge eating disorder: its further validation in a multisite study. *International Journal of Eating Disorders*, 1993; 13(2): 137–53.

6. Sullivan PF. Mortality in anorexia nervosa. *American Journal of Psychiatry*, 1995; 152(7): 1073–4.

7. Bruce B, Agras WS. Binge eating in females: a population-based investigation. *International Journal of Eating Disorders*, 1992; 12: 365–73.

8. Agras WS. Pharmacotherapy of bulimia nervosa and binge eating disorder: longer-term outcomes. *Psychopharmacology Bulletin*, 1997; 33(3): 433–6.

9. Wilfley DE, Cohen LR. Psychological treatment of bulimia nervosa and binge eating disorder. *Psychopharmacology Bulletin*, 1997; 33(3): 437–54.

10. Apple RF, Agras WS. *Overcoming eating disorders. A cognitive-behavioral treatment for bulimia and binge-eating disorder.* San Antonio: Harcourt Brace & Company, 1997.

11. Strober M, Freeman R, Lampert C, Diamond J, Kaye W. Controlled family study of anorexia nervosa and bulimia nervosa: evidence of shared liability and transmission of partial syndromes. *American Journal of Psychiatry*, 2000; 157(3): 393–401.

12. Walters EE, Kendler KS. Anorexia nervosa and anorexic-like syndromes in a population-based female twin sample. *American Journal of Psychiatry*, 1995; 152(1): 64–71.

13. Kaye WH, Lilenfeld LR, Berrettini WH, Strober M, Devlin B, Klump KL, Goldman D, Bulik CM, Halmi KA, Fichter MM, Kaplan A, Woodside DB, Treasure J, Plotnicov KH, Pollice C, Rao R, McConaha CW. A search for susceptibility loci for anorexia nervosa: methods and sample description. *Biological Psychiatry*, 2000; 47(9): 794–803.

14. Frank GK, Kaye WH, Altemus M, Greeno CG. CSF oxytocin and vasopressin levels after recovery from bulimia nervosa and anorexia nervosa, bulimic subtype. *Biological Psychiatry*, 2000; 48(4): 315–8.

15. Elias CF, Kelly JF, Lee CE, Ahima RS, Drucker DJ, Saper CB, Elmquist JK. Chemical characterization of leptin-activated neurons in the rat brain. *Journal of Comparative Neurology*, 2000; 423(2): 261–81.

16. Devlin MJ, Walsh BT, Katz JL, Roose SP, Linkei DM, Wright L, Vande Wiele R, Glassman AH. Hypothalamic-pituitary-gonadal function in anorexia nervosa and bulimia. *Psychiatry Research*, 1989; 28(1): 11–24.

17. Flanagan-Cato LM, King JF, Blechman JG, O'Brien MP. Estrogen reduces cholecystokinin-induced c-Fos expression in the rat brain. *Neuroendocrinology*, 1998; 67(6): 384–91.

Chapter 2

Disordered Eating Behaviors

Parents play a leading role in their children's lives. As a parent or other caregiver, you are in a unique position to educate your children about nutrition and help them maintain a positive body image as they enter their teenage years. This chapter provides basic information on eating disorders, how to detect them, and how to discourage disordered eating.

> "Most parents will not be faced with the enormous challenges of dealing with an anorexic or bulimic...Many, however, will face the challenges of children who have poor body images or eating problems like excessive dieting, which are associated with lesser, but still unhealthy, outcomes."[1] Julia A. Graber, Ph.D., associate director, Adolescent Study Program at Columbia University

Eating Disorder or Disordered Eating Behavior?

Your child may not have an eating disorder, but she or he could be engaging in disordered eating behaviors. Pre-adolescence and adolescence are times of tremendous physical and psychological change. The rate of most rapid weight gain for girls is from age 9 to 14. By the time a girl reaches 18 years, it is likely she will nearly double her weight.[2] This is also a time when young people seek more independence from their parents and approval from their peers. As body image

---

"BodyWise: Parents and Other Caregivers," Office on Women's Health, October 2005.

becomes more important, your child may begin to pay more attention to media images that portray the female body ideal as thin and the male ideal as muscular.

These changes and the pressures they bring can affect how your child relates to food. Instead of eating normally—eating when hungry and stopping when satisfied—your child may engage in disordered eating behaviors. For example, she or he may skip meals, binge one day and eat very little on the next day, use diet pills, laxatives, or diuretics, or try the latest diet fad. If your child is involved in sports or other athletic activities that emphasize low weight and thin body shape, she or he may be particularly likely to restrict food and/or exercise in unhealthy ways to lose weight. Stressful situations like moving or losing a family member can also contribute to disordered eating behaviors among children.

Disordered Eating Behaviors Can Harm Developing Bodies and Minds

Disordered eating behaviors can be very harmful to children's developing bodies and minds. Children who are restricting food can have a hard time concentrating on their school work and often report feeling tired or having headaches. They may fail to get all of the nutrients their bodies need to grow and develop into healthy adults. As a result, their growth can be stunted and menstrual cycles of girls disrupted. Restricting calories over time can also decrease bone density and increase their risks of experiencing bone fractures and osteoporosis. For some children, disordered eating behaviors can precede full-blown eating disorders, such as anorexia nervosa or bulimia nervosa, which require intensive treatment.

In a society obsessed with thinness, children may engage in a number of disordered eating behaviors which may not be identified as eating disorders according to established diagnostic criteria. However, these behaviors can have very harmful consequences for children's health. If disordered eating persists, parents should consider consulting with a nutritionist and/or a therapist.

Signs and Symptoms of Eating Disorders

The early detection of an eating disorder can increase the likelihood of successful treatment and recovery. In your interactions with your child, you may notice one or more of the physical, behavioral, and emotional signs and symptoms of eating disorders.

Physical

- weight loss or fluctuation over a short period of time
- abdominal pain and discomfort
- feeling full or bloated
- feeling faint, cold, or tired
- dry hair or skin, dehydration, blue hands/feet
- lanugo hair (fine body hair)
- headaches

Behavioral

- dieting or chaotic food intake
- pretending to eat, throwing away food
- exercising for long periods of time
- showing concern with food, weight, or body size
- wearing baggy clothes to hide a very thin body
- making frequent trips to the bathroom
- avoiding food in social situations

Emotional

- complaints about appearance, particularly about being or feeling fat
- sadness or comments about feeling worthless
- perfectionist attitude
- always listening to friends' problems; never sharing one's own

All Ethnic and Cultural Groups Are Vulnerable

Children of all ethnic and cultural groups are vulnerable to developing eating disorders. Although rates of anorexia are higher among White girls, eating disorders occur among girls of all ethnic and cultural groups. Many immigrant girls, especially those isolated from their own culture, engage in disordered eating behaviors as they become exposed to social norms that value thinness. In addition, hundreds of thousands of boys and men are also experiencing this problem, and they may have difficulty seeking help because it is considered a girl's problem.

Family Attitudes Contribute to Disordered Eating Behaviors

Although it may not always seem so, your child pays a lot of attention to what you say and do. If you are constantly complaining about your weight or feel pressured to exercise in order to lose weight or change the shape of your body, your child may learn that losing weight is an important concern. If you are always on the lookout for the new miracle diet, your child may learn that restrictive dieting is a good way to lose weight. And if you tell your child she would be much prettier if she lost a few pounds, she will learn that the goal of weight loss is attractiveness and acceptance.

Questions that can help you consider your own attitudes and behaviors:

- Am I unhappy with my body size and shape?
- Am I always on a diet or going on a diet?
- Do I make fun of overweight people?
- Do I tease my child about body shape or weight?
- Do I focus on exercise for body size and shape control or for health?[2]

Parents Do Not Cause Eating Disorders

While parents can contribute to their children's eating disorders, they are not the cause of these disorders. Eating disorders are associated with emotional problems and are closely related to many other health issues, such as depression, low self-esteem, physical and sexual abuse, substance abuse, and problems at home or with friends. Many factors, including genetics, can increase the likelihood that a child will develop an eating disorder.

Talk with Your Child

Have a talk with your child if you are concerned about her or him. Pay attention to your child's eating habits. If you notice an intense preoccupation with food, weight, and exercise, especially if it affects different parts of her or his life, it may signal a deeper problem.

Have a talk with your child to gauge what's going on. Ask specific questions about food amounts (too little or too much) and exercise. If she or he becomes angry or defensive, you may consider seeing a professional with expertise in eating disorders. Be sure to validate your child's feelings and encourage discussion.

Things You Can Do

As a parent or other caregiver, you can help your child develop a positive body image and relate to food in a healthy way. Here are some ideas:

1. Make sure your child understands that weight gain is a normal part of development, especially during puberty.
2. Avoid negative statements about food, weight, and body size or shape.
3. Allow your child to make decisions about food, while making sure that plenty of healthy and nutritious meals and snacks are available.
4. Compliment your child on her or his efforts, talents, accomplishments, and personal values.
5. Restrict television viewing and watch television with your child and discuss the media images presented.
6. Encourage your school to enact policies against size and sexual discrimination, harassment, teasing, and name calling; support the elimination of public weigh-ins and fat measurements.
7. Keep the communication lines with your child open.

   "...if a father agrees with our culture's shared fantasy that all your problems will be solved if you have a perfect body, he will be contributing to the development of an eating disorder. However, a father can give his daughter other messages about beauty, self-worth, and body image that can counteract these strong cultural influences. Girls need a male adult to give corrective feedback and to balance the cultural pressures about being thin, sexy, and successful."[2]
   Margo Maine, PhD, in *Father Hunger*

End Notes

1. Eller D. Detecting Eating Disorders. *Parents*, August 1998, p.115.
2. Centers for Disease Control and Prevention. CDC Growth Charts: United States. Developed by the National Center for Health Statistics in Collaboration with the National Center for Chronic Disease Prevention and Health Promotion, 2000.
3. Maine, M. *Father Hunger: Fathers, Daughters & Food.* Carlsbad, CA: Gürze Books, 1991, p.9.

Definitions

Anorexia nervosa is self-starvation. People with this disorder eat very little even though they are thin. They have an intense and overpowering fear of body fat and weight gain.

Binge eating disorder means eating large amounts of food in a short period of time, usually alone, without being able to stop when full. The overeating or bingeing is often accompanied by feeling out of control and followed by feelings of depression, guilt, or disgust.

Bulimia nervosa is characterized by cycles of binge eating and purging, either by vomiting or taking laxatives or diuretics (water pills). People with bulimia have a fear of body fat even though their size and weight may be normal.

Disordered eating refers to troublesome eating behaviors, such as restrictive dieting, bingeing, or purging, which occur less frequently or are less severe than those required to meet the full criteria for the diagnosis of an eating disorder.

Over-exercising is exercising compulsively for long periods of time as a way to burn calories from food that has just been eaten. People with anorexia or bulimia may overexercise.

Additional Information

Eating Disorders Coalition
611 Pennsylvania Ave., SE #423
Washington, DC 20003-4303
Phone: 202-543-9570
Website: http://www.eatingdisorderscoalition.org

GirlsHealth.gov
8270 Willow Oaks Corporate Drive, Suite 301
Fairfax, VA 22031
Website: http://www.4girls.gov

National Association of Anorexia Nervosa and Associated Disorders
Box 7
Highland Park, IL 60035
Phone: 847-831-3438
Fax: 847-433-4632
Website: http://www.anad.org

National Eating Disorders Association
603 Stewart St., Suite 803
Seattle, WA 98101
Toll-Free Referral Hotline: 800-931-2237
Phone: 206-382-3587
Website: http://www.nationaleatingdisorders.org
E-mail: info@NationalEatingDisorders.org

Office on Women's Health
Department of Health and Human Services
200 Independence Avenue, SW Room 712E
Washington, DC 20201
Toll-Free: 800-994-9662
Toll-Free TDD: 888-220-5446
Phone: 202-690-7650
Fax: 202-205-2631
Website: http://www.4woman.gov

Chapter 3

Anorexia Nervosa

Anorexia Nervosa: Signs, Symptoms, Causes, Effects, and Treatments

What is anorexia?

Eating habits lie on a continuum, from healthy eating habits on one end, to serious eating disorders like anorexia and bulimia on the other end. We are saturated with messages from the media that advise us to eat a healthy diet and exercise regularly. However, an obsession with losing weight, counting calories, and exercising can lead to an eating disorder with serious emotional and physical consequences.

According to Ohio State University, the defining signs and symptoms of anorexia are:

- an intense and irrational fear of body fat and weight gain
- a determination to become thinner and thinner
- a misperception of body weight and shape to the extent that the person feels fat even when underweight

---

This chapter includes: Excerpts from "Anorexia Nervosa: Signs, Symptoms, Causes, Effects, and Treatments," reprinted with permission from http://www.helpguide.org. And, "Anorexia Nervosa: 11 Areas of Advancement," by Arnold E. Andersen, M.D. Reprinted with permission from *Eating Disorders Review*, March/April 2003.

The person with anorexia loses weight and does not realize the dangers of denying food to the body.

What are the signs and symptoms of anorexia?

People who have anorexia try to hide their condition, so others may not notice the signs and symptoms of the eating disorder. The warning signs and symptoms of anorexia include:

- dramatic weight loss
- refusal to maintain the minimal normal body weight for one's age and height
- basing self-worth on body weight and body image
- frequent skipping of meals, with excuses for not eating
- eating only a few foods, especially those low in fat and calories
- making meals for others, but not eating the meals themselves
- frequent weighing of oneself and focusing on tiny fluctuations in weight
- wearing baggy clothing to cover up thinness
- excessive focus on an exercise regimen
- frequent looking in the mirror for flaws
- avoidance of social gatherings where food is involved
- even when thin, complaining about being overweight
- in females, missing three consecutive menstrual periods
- in males, decreased sexual desire

What are the types of anorexia?

There are two types of anorexia, based on whether the anorexia is combined with bulimia.

Classic anorexia (restricting anorexia). The person eats very little and loses weight through self-starvation or excessive exercise. Calories consumed are insufficient to support bodily functions and activities.

Binge eating and purging anorexia. In addition to cutting the intake of calories, this person also binges and purges (self-induced vomiting, or misuse of laxatives, diuretics, or enemas). The person has symptoms of both anorexia and bulimia. About 50% of people with anorexia also develop bulimia.

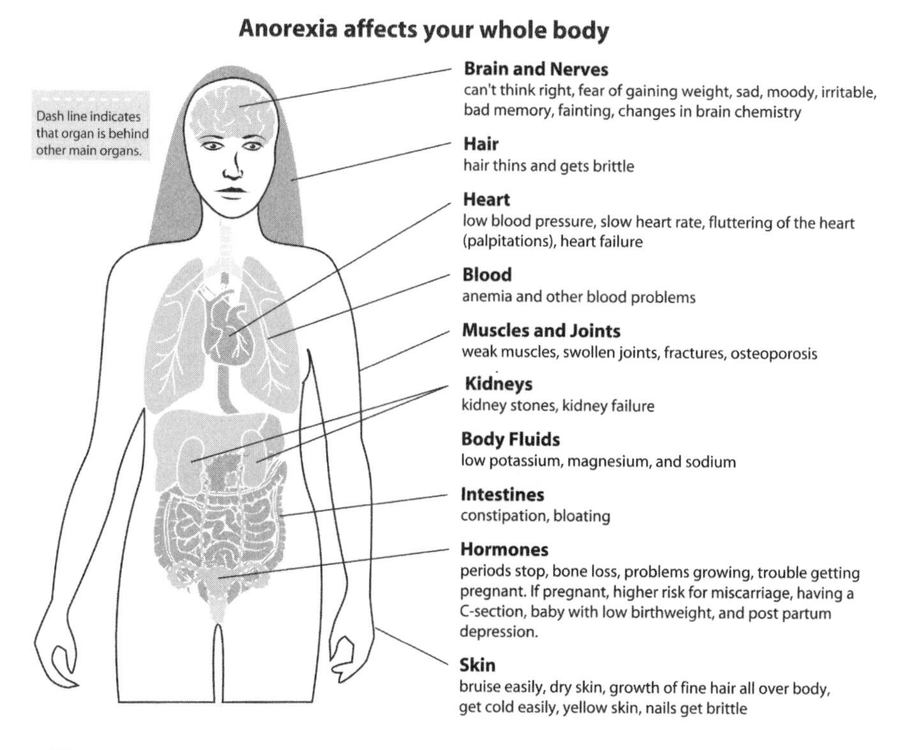

Figure 3.1. *Anorexia Affects the Entire Body (Source: National Women's Health Information Center, August 2004)*

What are the physical effects of anorexia?

In addition to the wide-ranging physical effects of anorexia that are noted in Figure 3.1, the following can occur:

- hair loss
- lowered resistance to illness

- hypersensitivity to heat
- less need for sleep than normal eaters
- severe dehydration, which can result in kidney failure
- fatigue and overall weakness
- in severe cases: heart trouble, low blood pressure, low heart rate, low body temperature, poor circulation, anemia, stunted growth, and even death

What are the emotional and behavioral effects of anorexia?

In addition to the depression, irritability, and bad memory noted under "Brain and Nerves" in Figure 3.1, the following emotional and behavioral effects of anorexia can occur:

- difficulty in concentrating on anything else except weight
- isolation from family and friends
- emotional regression to a child-like state
- feelings of guilt
- dependence upon alcohol or drugs to handle the negative outlook

What are causes and risk factors for anorexia?

A constellation of risk factors seem to cause anorexia. Sociocultural factors have an especially strong influence. Our culture rewards thinness, and societal approval can be so important that a person will starve to match that cultural ideal.

Social and cultural causes of anorexia. A culture that equates thinness with attractiveness and success pushes people to try to meet that ideal. The media present the ideal woman as ultrathin, and women respond by emulating that vision. However, eating disorders have been around for centuries, so the cultural ideal of thinness is not the only contributing factor to anorexia.

Psychological and emotional causes of anorexia. An individual's inner feelings, personality characteristics, and personal history can contribute to anorexia. For example:

- Personality traits that are associated with anorexia include perfectionism, obsessiveness, approval-seeking, low self-esteem, withdrawal, irritability, and black-or-white (all-or-nothing) thinking.

- Major events in a person's life history such as critical transitions or emotional upsets can contribute to anorexia. Relational or early life trauma (sometimes called developmental trauma) affects the brain which in turn can impact both biology and psychology. Symptoms of trauma can include low self-esteem and obsessive-compulsive eating disorders like anorexia. Physical or sexual abuse can trigger anorexia.
- Interpersonal or relationship problems can trigger an eating disorder such as anorexia.
- Other conditions such as depression, anxiety, and attention deficit hyperactivity disorder (ADHD) may contribute to anorexia.
- According to mental health experts, the feelings during adolescence of being overwhelmed and powerless can bring about a desire to maintain control in some realm of life, such as control of body weight. Being in total control of what enters the mouth can give an adolescent a feeling of powerfulness. Thus, the period of adolescence may be when anorexia first arises.

Biological causes of anorexia. Studies of the families of people with anorexia suggest that a predisposition to anorexia may be genetically based. When experts have looked at how the brain works in people with anorexia, they see higher levels of the neurotransmitter serotonin (a brain chemical), which makes the individual withdraw socially and have less desire for food. However, the higher level of serotonin may be a result of the anorexia, rather than a cause.

How is anorexia diagnosed?

When you consult a doctor for a possible diagnosis of anorexia, the doctor first makes sure that endocrine, metabolic, and central nervous system disorders do not explain your apparent weight loss. If you do have anorexia, your physical problems are usually the result of not eating.

In addition to diagnosing for anorexia, your doctor may also assess damage already done to the body, with the following tests:

- a physical exam, including a physical history
- laboratory tests, such as a blood test and urinalysis
- other specialized tests, such as an electrocardiogram and an x-ray

- a psychological evaluation

The medical profession uses the following criteria for the diagnosis of anorexia.

- Your weight is 15% or more below normal for your age and height.
- You have an intense fear of being fat or gaining weight, even though you are underweight.
- You have a distorted image of your body and deny being underweight.
- (For women) You have missed at least three menstrual periods in a row.

What are the common treatments for anorexia?

Treatment for anorexia is multi-faceted and individualized according to your specific problems. The first priority of treatment is to regain physical health; all other treatment follows from that. A treatment program for anorexia commonly involves the following steps:

- address physical effects of the anorexia
- gain weight
- implement a plan for healthy eating
- adjust to the new eating habits and increased body weight
- address the psychological underpinnings of the anorexia

Regaining physical health is essential for working toward psychological health: you can devote yourself to developing a healthier mental state when your body is in a stable, healthy condition.

Psychotherapy as Treatment for Anorexia

Because a poor body image and low self-esteem underlie anorexia, psychotherapy is an important aspect of treatment for anorexia.

Individual psychotherapy addresses the emotional underpinnings of anorexia. Therapy helps you to identify concerns, solve problems, overcome fears, and test new skills. Each kind of therapist approaches discussions about anorexia differently, according to specialty.

- **Cognitive behavior therapy** focuses on the thoughts that envelop food and eating. One of the main goals is for you to become more self-aware of your relationship to food. Your therapist may ask you to keep a food diary or a journal of your thought processes about food.
- **Behavior therapy** uses rewards and repercussions to change the behavior of self-starvation. The behavior therapist teaches you to substitute relaxation and other coping strategies for the excessive exercising or fasting of anorexia.
- **Other types of psychotherapy** focus on social and emotional conditions in your life that can lead to low self-esteem, which may in turn contribute to your anorexia. Therapists may include massage or relaxation exercises in your mental health treatment.
- **Family therapy** looks at the family dynamics that may contribute to your anorexia and often includes some therapy sessions without you. Family therapy may be the solution when the person with anorexia denies the eating disorder.
- **Group therapy** led by a psychotherapist allows you to talk in a supervised setting with other people who have anorexia. Group therapy helps to reduce the isolation you may feel about your disorder, and group members can support each other in their quest for wellness.
- **Support groups** are led by trained volunteers or health professionals and can play an effective part in your anorexia treatment plan.

Medical Care and Monitoring for Treatment of Anorexia

A medical doctor assesses the physical effects of anorexia on your body, helps you to regain physical health, and monitors vital signs, hydration level, and electrolytes during the course of your treatment.

Nutritional Counseling for Treatment of Anorexia

A dietitian helps you to develop and follow through on a diet that will sustain you. To increase your weight, the dietitian designs balanced meal plans that include the right number of calories for you to gain weight and restore health.

Medications as Treatment for Anorexia

Medication alone is not effective for the treatment of anorexia, but a medical doctor or psychiatrist may prescribe drugs to help with the symptoms or results of anorexia. Antidepressant drugs treat the depression and anxiety that often accompany (or cause) anorexia. Other drugs for treating anorexia may help you to gain weight or to curb obsessive-compulsive behaviors. Inpatient treatment centers for anorexia.

If the physical effects of anorexia become life-threatening, or the psychological problems are severe, your mental health practitioner or medical doctor may recommend residential, inpatient treatment for anorexia. This may be in a hospital or in an eating disorders treatment center. After the initial, urgent care in a residential center, you will continue anorexia treatment on an outpatient basis.

Anorexia Nervosa: Eleven Areas of Advancement

Although the origin, treatment, course, and outlook of anorexia nervosa (AN) have remained a puzzle, advances in at least eleven areas have helped to better understand this disease.

1. Genetic Links

Important multicenter studies on the genetics of anorexia nervosa are underway to compare vulnerable patients with their siblings and parents, and to sort out clusters of genes that increase vulnerability to anorexia nervosa. For example, unlike Huntington disease, the genetics of AN do not determine whether one gets the disease. However, genetics probably do provide a crucial predisposition to AN through abnormalities of serotonin and metabolism and their effects on personality, reactivity, perseverance, and perhaps weight control, hunger, and satiety.

2. The Brain as a Mirror

The brain is clearly affected structurally and functionally as a consequence of AN. Several studies have confirmed the significant effects of self-starvation on the brain. With starvation, the ventricles of the brain increase in size and the cortical mass decreases. One matter of concern is the fact that there is improvement, but not complete normalization, of gray and white matter as long as six to twelve months after weight restoration. The very powerful imaging tools of functional magnetic resonance imaging (MRI) and positron emission tomography (PET) scans are demonstrating a change in the interaction between the prefrontal cortex and components of the limbic system in regard to the sensing and perpetuation of emotional distress in active AN. These tools will not only demonstrate the effects of eating disorders but will also document the relative benefits of a variety of treatments.

3. Critical Diagnostic Criteria

In another development, diagnostic criteria for anorexia are being reviewed with a goal of sorting out the critical features and introducing more flexibility for traditional but perhaps out-of-date criteria. Including amenorrhea as a criterion for AN is less useful than noting abnormalities of reproductive hormone function in general. Even more useful is broader recognition of medical consequences of starvation not limited to levels of reproductive hormones. The key concept here is that AN involves self-starvation to a substantial degree below the individual's usual or healthy weight. Some people may be semi-starved even if their hormone levels are normal and they are at their normal weight. This means that amenorrhea is not as important as are general measures of self-starvation, and that a final, lowest weight of 85% of normal healthy weight is not as crucial as is a significant decline in weight from an initial healthy weight.

4. Men Also Develop Anorexia Nervosa

A recent large epidemiologic study has substantiated that males are probably underrepresented in both epidemiologic and clinical studies. While earlier studies reported ratios of as many as ten females to one male, a ratio of one male to three or four females may be more accurate. This raises concerns that males are underrepresented in clinical programs, and calls for better understanding of the factors that may be keeping them from seeking treatment.

5. Axis I Comorbidities

The recognition that AN usually has associated comorbidities on Axis I or II has been confirmed with awareness that AN seldom presents by itself but there is a high probability of Axis I diagnoses, including comorbid depression, anxiety, and substance use disorders. On Axis II, there is an overrepresentation of cluster C for restricting AN and a mixture of clusters B and C for AN binge-purge subtype. Studies from Denmark have highlighted the especially deadly combination of AN with insulin-dependent diabetes mellitus in young individuals. These studies spell out an approximately tenfold increase in mortality with this combination compared to having either of these disorders alone.

6. The Rise of Neuroleptics

A number of trials are underway using atypical neuroleptics such as risperidone and olanzapine. The hope is that they will have an effect on the core psychopathology of AN rather than merely stimulating weight gain, as was the case with chlorpromazine in the 1960s.

7. An Excellent Outcome May Be Possible for Many

Although AN is often considered a chronic disorder with a poor prognosis, in fact the duration of AN is quite variable, and more than 75% of patients will have an excellent outcome. This is especially true for adolescent anorexics who are treated comprehensively to full weight restoration with associated cognitive behavioral psychotherapy and careful follow-up. A 10-year follow-up study at University of California–Los Angeles (UCLA) documented complete improvement with absence of any diagnostic features for any eating disorder in 76% of patients.

8. Insurance Limitations

Despite improvements in outcome with modern treatment modalities, many patients cannot get access to treatment because of irrational insurance limitations. Decreasing length of hospital stays—an increasingly common occurrence with restrictive and irrational insurance limitations—is leading to more frequent relapse and less sustained improvement. Groups such as the Eating Disorders Coalition have been working to change this.

9. Arguments Over Effectiveness of Prevention Efforts

Controversy exists between clinicians, between treatment centers, and between countries on the possible effectiveness of preventive efforts in AN. Several studies are now suggesting there is a decrease in the prevalence or severity of AN in vulnerable individuals when pressure to lose and maintain an abnormal body weight is removed. For example, there is evidence that the number of cases of eating disorders declines when a strict ballet school refuses to let a dancer participate below a certain weight or when a collegiate wrestler is barred from participating below a certain percent body fat or absolute weight. The more adventurous approach toward empowering young people with media skepticism, with assertiveness, and with improved body image has not yet been tried on a broad-enough population to comment on its effectiveness. But the approach to "inoculating" the vulnerable subgroup of young people with techniques to make their way through a society obsessed with thinness merits continued work.

10. A Disease That Stands on Its Own

There has been some attempt to subsume AN into other diagnostic categories, such as obsessive-compulsive disorder (OCD), major depression, or psychosis. In fact, AN "breeds true," with evidence that the core syndrome has not changed in hundreds of years. There is ongoing discussion about the presentation in different cultures in regard to the content of the core psychopathology. There is support for the concept that overvalued beliefs are part of the core psychopathology of AN, and that the overvalued beliefs vary from culture to culture. For example, in the West, we overvalue thinness. To further clarify this, overvalued beliefs are defined as culturally normative beliefs that have been assigned disproportionate values in a particular individual and which demonstrate that individual's thinking, emotional life, and behavior. Nor are they the type of ego dystonic thoughts or behaviors required for obsessive-compulsive disorders. Although overvalued beliefs are not abnormal themselves, what is abnormal is the excessive value assigned to them. This diagnostic criterion is less frequently used than it should be and helps to differentiate the AN psychopathology from OCD or psychosis and also explains some of the chronicity of the disease. It also offers hope for change through stopping the abnormal behavior and challenging the core overvalued belief with cognitive behavioral techniques.

11. Family Therapy

There is exciting evidence that the families of young anorexics may be able to be empowered through teaching techniques to keep the patient from ever being hospitalized, even when very starved, when parents practice a stepwise approach toward changing the self-starvation with caring but firm techniques.

Chapter 4

Binge Eating Disorder

Binge eating disorder is a condition that millions of Americans may have. People with binge eating disorder often eat large amounts of food and feel that they cannot control their eating.

How do I know if I have binge eating disorder?

Most of us overeat from time to time, and some of us often feel we have eaten more than we should have. Eating a lot of food does not necessarily mean that you have binge eating disorder. Experts generally agree that most people with serious binge eating problems often eat an unusually large amount of food and feel their eating is out of control. People with binge eating disorder also may:

- eat much more quickly than usual during binge episodes;
- eat until they are uncomfortably full;
- eat large amounts of food even when they are not really hungry;
- eat alone because they are embarrassed about the amount of food they eat;
- feel disgusted, depressed, or guilty after overeating.

"Binge Eating Disorder," Weight-Control Information Network (WIN) of the National Institute of Diabetes and Digestive and Kidney Diseases (NIDDK), NIH Publication No. 04–3589, September 2004.

Binge eating also occurs in another eating disorder called bulimia nervosa. Persons with bulimia nervosa, however, usually purge, fast, or do strenuous exercise after they binge eat. Purging means vomiting or using a lot of diuretics (water pills) or laxatives to keep from gaining weight. Fasting is not eating for at least 24 hours. Strenuous exercise, in this case, means exercising for more than an hour just to keep from gaining weight after binge eating. Purging, fasting, and over-exercising are dangerous ways to try to control your weight.

How common is binge eating disorder, and who is at risk?

Binge eating disorder is probably the most common eating disorder. Most people with this problem are either overweight or obese, but normal-weight people also can have the disorder. The 1998 National Institutes of Health (NIH) *Clinical Guidelines on the Identification, Evaluation, and Treatment of Overweight and Obesity in Adults* define overweight as a body mass index (BMI) of 25 to 29.9 and obesity as a BMI of 30 or more. BMI is calculated by dividing weight (in kilograms) by height (in meters) squared.

About two percent of all adults in the United States (as many as 4 million Americans) have binge eating disorder. About 10 to 15 percent of people who are mildly obese and who try to lose weight on their own or through commercial weight loss programs have binge eating disorder. The disorder is even more common in people who are severely obese.

Binge eating disorder is a little more common in women than in men; three women for every two men have it. The disorder affects blacks as often as whites. No one knows how often it affects people in other ethnic groups.

People who are obese and have binge eating disorder often became overweight at a younger age than those without the disorder. They might also lose and gain back weight (yo-yo diet) more often.

What causes binge eating disorder?

No one knows for sure what causes binge eating disorder. As many as half of all people with binge eating disorder are depressed or have been depressed in the past. Whether depression causes binge eating disorder or whether binge eating disorder causes depression is not known.

It is also unclear if dieting and binge eating are related. Some people binge eat after dieting. Dieting here means skipping meals, not eating enough food each day, or avoiding certain kinds of food. These are unhealthy ways to try to change your body shape and weight.

Studies suggest that people with binge eating may have trouble handling some of their emotions. Many people who are binge eaters say that being angry, sad, bored, worried, or stressed can cause them to binge eat.

Certain behaviors and emotional problems are more common in people with binge eating disorder. These include abusing alcohol, acting quickly without thinking (impulsive behavior), not feeling in charge of themselves, not feeling a part of their communities, and not noticing and talking about their feelings.

Researchers are looking into how brain chemicals and metabolism (the way the body uses calories) affect binge eating disorder. Other research suggests that genes may be involved in binge eating, since the disorder often occurs in several members of the same family. This research is still in the early stages.

What are the complications of binge eating disorder?

People with binge eating disorder are usually very upset by their binge eating and may become depressed. Research has shown that people with binge eating disorder report more health problems, stress, trouble sleeping, and suicidal thoughts than people without an eating disorder do. People with binge eating disorder often feel bad about themselves and may miss work, school, or social activities to binge eat.

People with binge eating disorder may gain weight. Weight gain can lead to obesity, and obesity puts people at risk for many health problems, including the following:

- type 2 diabetes
- high blood pressure
- high blood cholesterol levels
- gallbladder disease
- heart disease
- certain types of cancer

Most people who binge eat, whether they are obese or not, feel ashamed and try to hide their problem. Often they become so good at hiding it that even close friends and family members do not know they binge eat.

Should people with binge eating disorder try to lose weight?

Many people with binge eating disorder are obese and have health problems because of their weight. They should try to lose weight and keep it off; however, research shows that long-term weight loss is more likely when a person has long-term control over his or her binge eating.

People with binge eating disorder who are obese may benefit from a weight loss program that also offers treatment for eating disorders. However, some people with binge eating disorder may do just as well in a standard weight loss program as people who do not binge eat.

People who are not overweight should avoid trying to lose weight, because it sometimes makes their binge eating worse.

How can people with binge eating disorder be helped?

People with binge eating disorder should get help from a health professional such as a psychiatrist, psychologist, or clinical social worker. There are several different ways to treat binge eating disorder.

- Cognitive-behavioral therapy teaches people how to keep track of their eating and change their unhealthy eating habits. It teaches them how to change the way they act in tough situations. It also helps them feel better about their body shape and weight.
- Interpersonal psychotherapy helps people look at their relationships with friends and family and make changes in problem areas.
- Drug therapy, such as antidepressants, may be helpful for some people.

The treatment methods mentioned seem to be equally helpful. Researchers are still trying to find the treatment that is the most helpful in controlling binge eating disorder. Other therapies being tried include dialectical behavior therapy, which helps people regulate their emotions; drug therapy with the anti-seizure medication topiramate; weight loss surgery (gastrointestinal surgery); exercise used alone or in combination with cognitive-behavioral therapy; and self-help. Self-help books, videos, and groups have helped some people to control their binge eating.

Getting Help

If you think you might have binge eating disorder, it is important to know that you are not alone. Most people who have the disorder have tried but failed to control it on their own. You may want to get professional help. Talk to your health care provider about the type of help that may be best for you. The good news is that most people do well in treatment and can overcome binge eating.

Programs for Patients with Binge Eating Disorder or Compulsive Over Eating

Center for Brief Therapy

Department of Clinical Psychology
Philadelphia College of Osteopathic Medicine
4190 City Avenue
Rolland Hall, Suite 530
Philadelphia, PA 19131
Phone: 215-871-6487
Website: http://www.pcom.edu/Department_Web_Pages/Department_of_Psychology/Center_for_Brief_The/Center_for_Brief_The.html

Child and Adolescent Eating Disorders Program

Menninger Clinic
2801 Gessner Drive
P.O. Box 809045
Houston, TX 77280-9048
Toll-Free: 800-351-9058
Phone: 713-275-5000
Fax: 713-275-5107
Website: http://www.menningerclinic.compeatingdisorders/index.htm

Eating Disorder Program

Centers for Women at Strong
610 Elmwood Avenue
Rochester, NY 14642
Phone: 585-341-8138
Website: https://www.stronghealth.com/services/womenshealth/womenshealth_hospitals/eatingdisorders.cfm

Eating Disorder Program at the University of Chicago Hospitals

Department of Psychiatry, MC 3077
The University of Chicago
5841 S. Maryland Avenue
Chicago, IL 60637
Toll-Free: 888-824-0200
Phone: 773-834-5677
Website: http://www.uchospitals.edu/specialties/psychiatry

New York State Psychiatric Institute
Columbia University Medical Center
1051 Riverside Drive, NYSPI Unit 98
New York, NY 10032
Phone: 212-543-5739
Website: http://www.nyspi.org

Rutgers Eating Disorders Clinic GSAPP
Rutgers University
41 Gordon Road, Suite C
Piscataway, NJ 08854-5972
Phone: 732-445-2292
Website: http://gsappweb.rutgers.edu/EDC

Weight and Eating Disorders Program
University of Pennsylvania
3535 Market Street, Suite 3108
Philadelphia, PA 19104
Phone: 215-898-7314
Fax: 215-898-2878
Website: http://www.med.upenn.edu/weight
E-mail: weight@uphsnet.med.upenn.edu

Western Psychiatric Institute and Clinic
University of Pittsburgh Medical Center
200 Lothrop St.
Pittsburgh, PA 15213
Phone: 412-624-2100
Website: http://wpic.upmc.com

Yale Center for Eating Disorders Program
Yale University, Department of Psychology
P.O. Box 208205
New Haven, CT 06520-8205
Phone: 203-432-4610
Website: http://www.yale.edu/ycewd
E-mail: ycewd@yale.edu

Chapter 5

Bulimia Nervosa

Risk Factors and Causes of Bulimia Nervosa

Bulimia nervosa is an eating disorder in which a person binge eats followed by some type of behavior intended to prevent weight gain from the calories consumed. The disorder, first described in modern medical literature in 1979 by a physician named Russell, seriously affects mental and physical health. Bulimia nervosa can even lead to death if untreated.

Binge eating is defined as eating more food than most people would eat in a similar timeframe and associating that consumption with a

---

This information is excerpted from "ECRI's Bulimia Nervosa Resource Guide," For additional information, visit www.bulimiaguide.org or www.ecri.org. This resource guide was produced by ECRI, a 40-year-old international non-profit health services research agency. ECRI's mission is to improve the quality, safety, and cost-effectiveness of healthcare. Recognized by the healthcare community worldwide as a trusted source of highly credible information with very strict conflict-of-interest rules, ECRI is designated as an Evidence-based Practice Center by the U.S. Agency for Healthcare Research and Quality, and as a Collaborating Center of the World Health Organization for Patient Safety, Risk Management, and Health Technology Assessment. This resource guide was funded in large part by the Hilda and Preston Davis Foundation and is available in print and online: www.bulimiaguide.org (free); in print (for a nominal shipping/handling cost) at National Eating Disorders Association online store www.nationaleatingdisorders.org. The guide is part of ECRI's National Patient Library™ of evidence-based healthcare guides for consumers.

feeling of a loss of control. The behavior to prevent weight gain is called "compensatory behavior." The compensatory behavior usually takes one of the following forms: purging by self-induced vomiting, or excessive use of enemas or laxatives; or non-purging by excessive exercise, fasting for long periods before binge eating again, or in the case of a person with diabetes, omitting insulin intake.

Bulimia nervosa is listed as a mental health disorder in the *Diagnostic and Statistical Manual of Mental Disorders Volume IV (DSM-IV)*. This manual is the 4th edition of a diagnostic reference book by the American Psychiatric Association that lists mental disorders and describes the characteristics or criteria used to diagnose each disorder. Individuals with a diagnosis of bulimia nervosa often have a co-existing disorder such as obsessive-compulsive disorder (OCD), major depressive disorder, or substance abuse. People who fit many, but not all, of the criteria may be given a diagnosis of "eating disorder, not otherwise specified" or EDNOS, which is also listed in the manual.

The clinical terms used for the disorder and the criteria listed in the manual have changed several times over the past 25 years. At times the disorder was called just bulimia, but now is clinically referred to as bulimia nervosa, which is used throughout this resource guide.

Who develops bulimia nervosa?

The disorder affects females and males, and people as young as eight years old and as old as 60 years, people who appear thin and people who appear overweight. Research has shown that bulimia nervosa is most common in females—about 90% of diagnoses are made in females. Recent studies suggest that up to 7% of females in the United States have had bulimia nervosa at some time in their life. An estimated 1% of young women in the United States are believed to be affected at any given time.

Yet, many myths exist about who develops bulimia nervosa and why, and what a person with the disorder looks like. While people with the disorder have several traits in common, it does not discriminate by race, socioeconomic, or education level. In Westernized cultures, bulimia nervosa has been diagnosed in Asians, African Americans, Latinos, Caucasians and other ethnic and racial groups and in all socioeconomic classes. However, high-quality studies are not available to tell us for sure how many cases occur each year in a given group or people, or how many bulimic people there are overall. The reason that it is hard to find out, according to researchers, is that people with eating disorders are less likely to admit to having a problem than people without the disorder. They are also less likely to respond openly to questions a doctor asks about it and are less likely to fill out an eating disorder symptom survey than people without the disorder. However, researchers believe that a two-stage process is the best approach to try to determine how many people have an eating disorder. The process involves screening people by using a questionnaire first and then using those results to follow-up and confirm suspected cases through personal interviews.

One myth about who develops the disorder is the stereotype of thin young white women from higher socioeconomic classes. Older published studies of bulimia nervosa reported that this group was more likely than any other group to develop the disorder. Now researchers think these older data are inaccurate because the people in those studies did not reflect the general population. These studies came from universities and clinics where white women in higher socioeconomic classes were overrepresented. One result of this stereotype was that doctors generally did not believe that bulimia nervosa occurred in other types of people, such as those previously described. So, doctors did not consider a diagnosis of bulimia nervosa in such people even when the signs and symptoms suggested a person might have the disorder.

More recent published studies that include these other groups have found a higher incidence of eating disorders in males and minority females than has previously been reported. Bulimia nervosa is thought to be increasing among males in Westernized societies as more pressure comes to bear on boys and men to achieve and maintain a trim and fit body.

Bulimia nervosa is also more common than previously thought among women in their 40s and 50s in Western cultures. Some reasons given for this are pressures that in combination can create high stress levels. These pressures include career, family, children growing up, changes in personal health and body size and shape with aging, and divorce. With age, a woman's body can also look less like the idealized women seen in much product advertising. Changing metabolisms and weight gain are changes that women face with aging. Today women have generally become more conscious about appearance over a longer time span than women from previous generations—in part because more women are out in the workforce and are living longer. Thus the expectation is to maintain a youthful body and appearance for a longer time.

Athletes comprise another group affected by bulimia nervosa. As expectations for peak performance rise in top male and female athletes, so does the pressure to maintain that level of performance. This can lead to compulsive exercising and dieting. Some sports like gymnastics, wrestling, ice skating, and diving promote a certain body image. Some believe that participants in these sports may be at higher risk of developing disordered eating as a coping mechanism to try to maintain their performance level and appearance. Maintaining weight limits is important in many of these sports. For example, wrestlers may use drastic means to stay in their wrestling weight class—means that are similar to the compensatory practices used by people with bulimia nervosa. However, study results on whether certain groups of athletes are actually at higher risk of developing bulimia nervosa are mixed.

The National College Athletic Association (NCAA) carried out studies on the incidence of eating-disordered behavior among athletes in the 1990s. NCAA reported that of those athletes who were reported to have an eating disorder, 93% were female. Women's sports reporting the highest rates of eating disorders were cross country running, gymnastics, swimming, and track and field. Male sports reporting the highest rates of eating disorders were wrestling and cross country running. However, a later NCAA study reported that the rate of eating disorders among college athletes was no higher than the rates reported for the general population.

What causes bulimia nervosa?

Researchers have several theories about the causes of bulimia nervosa; yet no single theory accounts for all possible causes and symptoms. Most of the current theories about the disorder relate to self-perceptions about body image (size, shape, and weight), mood and depression, and genetics, but researchers and clinicians do not know why one particular person develops the disorder while another person with a very similar profile does not. Researchers are studying possible cause-and-effect relationships between bulimia nervosa and other mental disorders commonly associated with it. Pinpointing the causes of bulimia nervosa has proven difficult because the disorder has both mental and physical components, and it develops in many age groups, races, socioeconomic classes, and both sexes.

What are the risk factors?

Traits common to people with bulimia nervosa have led researchers to identify certain risk factors for developing the disorder. Issues about body shape and size can arise especially during physical developmental phases when bodies change rapidly. For example, girls who enter puberty early may be uncomfortable about changes in their body size and shape because of rapid weight gain and sexual maturation that occur sooner than their peers. Women in middle age approaching menopause may also experience body shape changes, along with changes in family and social roles as children grow into adulthood and leave home. Major life role and body changes can lead to stress. Such stresses may contribute to development of bulimia nervosa in people with additional risk factors for the disorder.

Risk factors for developing bulimia nervosa include the following:

- genetics (or family history of eating disorders)
- past physical or sexual abuse
- early onset of menstruation
- past weight issues
- body image (shape and size) issues
- depression
- anxiety
- perfectionism
- obsessive-compulsive disorder
- history of substance abuse

Signs and Symptoms of Bulimia Nervosa

Signs and symptoms are a blend of mental, behavioral, and physical signs and symptoms. Some may be obvious only to a medical professional; others may be more easily noticed by friends and family. The most common signs and symptoms are listed. Other less common symptoms may be present as well.

Binge eating and purging may seem like obvious signs that are hard to miss. But, these behaviors can be, and often are, well-masked by a person with bulimia nervosa. People with bulimia nervosa may hide the behavior because they feel shame and guilt about it. The disorder may progress for some time before anyone else notices because the weight or outward physical appearance of people with bulimia nervosa may not change in the same way that appearance changes with an eating disorder like anorexia nervosa. Even an individual with a severe case bulimia nervosa can appear to be of normal weight, or even be overweight. That is why weight is not used as a criterion in the *DSM-IV* for diagnosing bulimia nervosa.

What are the signs a healthcare professional may be most likely to notice?

Certain healthcare professionals are in a position to observe the first clinical signs of the disorder. Dentists, in particular, may be the first to see signs because tooth, gum, and mouth problems are a common result of frequent purging by vomiting. Stomach acid, vitamin deficiency, and trauma from vomiting can decalcify teeth, erode enamel, cause cavities, and dry out and crack the skin of lips. Dentists may also notice swollen salivary glands in the mouth, a common side effect of frequent vomiting.

Other signs that a dentist or medical doctor may notice include "Russell's sign," named after the researcher who first identified bulimia nervosa. This is a sign in which the backs of the person's finger joints are particularly callused or discolored from using fingers to gag and induce vomiting. Nonprofessionals may notice this, but be unaware that it is a sign of bulimia nervosa. If the disorder is suspected, examination by a doctor using an endoscope to see into the lowest part of the esophagus may reveal slit-like tears from vomiting. Blood tests may also reveal electrolyte imbalances. More specific chemical imbalances that suggest bulimia nervosa may also be noted.

What are the signs and symptoms that family and friends may be most likely to notice?

People with bulimia nervosa may behave strangely around food. They might skip meals, rapidly change food likes and dislikes, avoid social outings that involve consuming food in front of others, or make excuses not to eat. People with bulimia nervosa may drink lots of water and diet soda or cut food into small bites and chew each bite excessively. Doing these things allegedly makes vomiting easier. They may also be excessively impulsive, depressed, or socially isolate themselves by choice from peers, friends, and family.

Purging behavior often is not obvious because the affected person may strive to hide it. Even roommates or spouses of people with bulimia nervosa can be totally unaware of purging behaviors for years because the affected person is extremely effective at hiding the behavior. For example, a person with bulimia nervosa may run water while in the bathroom to obscure the sound of vomiting. An affected person may use mouthwash, gum, and mints frequently, or excuse herself or himself from meals.

The non-purging behavior of excessive exercise can be noticed by friends and family, but if the individual is a bulimic athlete, it is very difficult to draw the line between training and excess exercise. Fasting may be less obvious if the person makes reasonable excuses for not eating in certain situations.

Signs and symptoms health professionals may observe include:

- dental sensitivity;
- dry mouth;
- enamel erosion;
- irregularly-shaped biting edges of teeth;
- bleeding or irritated gums;
- tooth decalcification;
- increase in number of cavities;
- dry, red, cracked lips, especially at corners;
- swollen cheeks and jaw;
- bloodshot eyes;
- swollen salivary glands (sialadenosis);
- callused and/or discolored skin on the finger joints (Russell's sign);
- abnormal blood test results that show metabolic acidosis (blood too acidic); metabolic alkalosis (blood too alkaline); hypochloremia (chloride too low); hypokalemia (potassium too low); hyperamylasemia (amylase too high); or hypercholesterolemia (cholesterol too high).

Signs and symptoms that family and friends may observe include that the individual:

- appears uncomfortable eating around others;
- buys large amounts of food that disappear with no explanation;
- skips meals;
- takes small food portions at regular meals;
- mixes strange foods;
- insists on isolating foods from each other on a plate;
- sudden changes in food likes and dislikes;

- stops eating a particular food or food group;
- eats only a particular food or food group;
- offers excuses for not eating at regular meals with family or friends;
- declines social engagements that involve food;
- isolates self from interactions with family and friends;
- engages in excessive exercise regimens;
- hides body with larger, baggy clothes;
- has distorted perception about body size and shape;
- shows signs of depression (lack of concentration, mood swings, isolation);
- cuts food into small pieces;
- chews each bite excessively;
- drinks excessive amounts of water or soda;
- excuses self from meal before anyone else;
- keeps family out of his or her room;
- excessive requirements for privacy in bedroom and bathroom;
- avoids looking at self in mirrors.

Diagnosing Bulimia Nervosa

A medical or mental health professional who is experienced in recognizing the signs and symptoms of eating disorders can usually make a diagnosis after interviewing a patient and performing a physical examination. Often, a dentist, pediatrician, therapist, or family physician—the doctors who see the patient most often—are the first healthcare professionals with the opportunity to recognize the signs and symptoms of bulimia nervosa. The patient may not willingly describe symptoms and may be unwilling to acknowledge the observations made by a dentist or family doctor. The key to making a diagnosis is that the dentist or physician seeing the patient has to be aware of the signs and symptoms of bulimia nervosa so they recognize a possible case when they see it. They should then refer to the *DSM* to see if the signs and symptoms they observed fit the criteria.

Since first being described in 1979, the criteria used to make an official diagnosis of bulimia nervosa have changed several times. These changes reflect ongoing debate among medical and psychological professionals over the criteria that define the disorder. Early definitions focused on binge eating and the purging/non-purging activity, irresistible urges to overeat, and a morbid fear of becoming fat. Later definitions defined binge eating and purging/non-purging more specifically in terms of numbers of episodes within a timeframe, and added some psychiatric components. These criteria are also used to define remission and recovery from the disorder.

According to the latest edition of the *DSM*, the diagnostic criteria that must be met before a clinician applies a diagnosis of bulimia nervosa to a patient require that the person must have binged and engaged in purging or non-purging compensatory behavior at least twice weekly for three months, and evaluate, or judge, self according to body size and shape.

Can bulimia nervosa be prevented?

No one knows any sure way to prevent bulimia nervosa. Adhering to some lifestyle guidelines may reduce the risk of a person developing the disorder, but so many factors may influence the development of the disorder, including genetics, that it is difficult to know what can prevent it. Nonetheless, a healthy attitude toward eating and self-perceptions about body size and share are important, as is maintaining good mental health. Education and awareness of eating disorders may help identify problems early and offer the best chance for appropriate treatment and recovery.

Ways to reduce the risk of bulimia nervosa include:

- education about and awareness of the disorder and associated risk factors;
- early intervention if risk factors are identified;
- knowledge and maintenance of healthy eating habits;
- cultivation of a positive self-image of the body;
- maintenance of good mental health;
- counseling as needed to identify and resolve areas of conflict and stress;
- balancing school, work, social life, rest, and exercise;

- encouraging the at-risk person to develop close relationships with trusted friends, mentors (teachers, coaches), and family where possible.

Can bulimia nervosa be cured?

There is some controversy about the use of the term cure for bulimia nervosa. Some clinicians prefer the terms remission and recovery because the risk factors for the behavior are often still present and relapse can occur. Nonetheless, treatment for bulimia nervosa can reduce and even halt binge eating and purging/non-purging behavior in many patients. The amount and type of treatment required to achieve a successful long-term outcome and the chances of relapse vary widely among individuals. Also, the definitions that different clinicians use to define remission may vary, and these variations affect the reported rates of remission, according researchers from the University of Toronto in Canada who recently studied the impact of different definitions on reported relapse rates. They proposed using standard definitions for partial and full relapses: partial relapse would be two symptom episodes per month for two months (which by *DSM-IV* standards would be considered a diagnosis of ED-NOS); full relapse would be defined as meeting the full *DSM-IV* diagnostic criteria for the disorder. Thus, from this definition, the implied definition of remission is less than two episodes per month.

The published scientific data on remission rates is scarce, since few long-term studies have been done on patients who have received treatment for bulimia nervosa. The available data from several studies shows that about 52%–74% of patients who received treatment for bulimia nervosa and achieved a remission were in remission five years later. For shorter time periods, the remission rates reported in published studies varied more widely. Some clinicians have reported anecdotally that self-recovery is possible, although little scientific evidence from well-conducted studies is available to really indicate the effectiveness of self-recovery.

What are the positive and negative indications for recovery?

Researchers have identified some indicators that may predict chances for a successful recovery. Individuals who are self-confident, realistic, goal-oriented, and make early progress in therapy usually respond well to the overall treatment plan. Individuals who begin treatment with a low body mass index, have a history of obesity, and show signs of depression may not respond well to therapy.

Bulimia nervosa may also evolve into "eating disorder–not otherwise specified" (ED-NOS) if the symptoms occur infrequently after treatment and only some of the criteria for bulimia nervosa are met. Few people with bulimia nervosa develop anorexia, although this does occur. A slang term for this condition is "bulimarexia."

What triggers a bulimic episode?

Many situations and feelings can trigger bulimic behavior: extreme emotional distress, anxiety, depression, dieting, exposure to certain foods (especially high-sugar or high-fat foods), or sudden dissatisfaction with body image. People with bulimia nervosa have reported extreme mood changes before, during, and after binge eating and purging or non-purging compensatory behavior. They have also reported feeling depressed or anxious before binge eating, and then feeling temporary relief or even euphoria afterwards. These feelings are often followed by feelings of guilt, shame, and self-loathing. Then purging or excessive exercise occurs to regain feelings of self-control.

Treatments Used for Bulimia Nervosa

Standard bulimia nervosa treatments include medications (prescription drugs), various psychotherapies, nutrition therapy, other non-drug therapies and supportive or adjunct interventions such as yoga, art, massage, and movement therapy. Some novel treatments are currently under research, such as implantation of a device called a vagus nerve stimulator implanted at the base of the neck. This stimulator is currently in use to treat some forms of depression, and it is under research for treating obesity.

The most commonly used treatments—psychotherapy and medication—are delivered at various levels of inpatient and outpatient care, and in various settings depending on the severity of the illness and the treatment plan that has been developed for a particular patient. Bulimia nervosa can often be treated on an outpatient basis, although more severe cases may require inpatient residential treatment. The treatment plan should be developed by a multidisciplinary team in consultation with the patient and family members as deemed appropriate by the patient and his or her team.

What types of prescription drug therapy are used?

Biochemical abnormalities in the brain and body have been associated with bulimia nervosa. Many types of prescription drugs have been used in treatment of bulimia nervosa, however, only one prescription drug (fluoxetine) actually has a labeled indication for bulimia nervosa. [This means that the manufacturer requested the U.S. Food and Drug Administration (FDA) for permission to market the drug specifically for treatment of bulimia nervosa, and that FDA approved this request based on the evidence the manufacturer provided about the drug's efficacy for bulimia nervosa.]

Most prescription drug therapy used for treatment of the disorder is aimed at alleviating major depression, anxiety, or obsessive-compulsive disorder (OCD), which often co-exist with bulimia nervosa. Some prescription drug therapies are intended to make individuals feel full to try to prevent binge eating.

Anti-depressants are intended to try to reduce a patient's urge to binge and purge by treating depression, anxiety, and OCD. Some of anti-depressants also can exert other effects. SSRIs alleviate depression but may also play a role in making an individual feel full and possibly prevent binge eating.

What are the complications of bulimia nervosa?

The complications of bulimia nervosa are serious and can adversely affect teeth, the esophagus, the reproductive cycle and hormones, and electrolyte balances which in turn can affect the heart. Some of the complications can be life threatening. In addition, patients with underlying depression may be at risk of suicide.

Stomach acid can erode the enamel of teeth, exposing soft dentin and making the teeth more susceptible to cavities. This erosion may be prevented by using fluoride applications, taking mineral supplements, and rinsing with water or a baking soda solution after purging. Brushing the teeth after vomiting is harmful because it rubs off the weakened enamel. Dentists have many ways to repair eroded enamel, including fillings, composites, root canals, crowns, and dentures. However, most dentists advise against performing these restorative procedures until the patient is in recovery from bulimia nervosa.

Electrolyte imbalances are common in patients with more severe bulimic symptoms, occurring in up to 49% of patients. These imbalances occur when ionized salt concentrations (commonly sodium and potassium) are at abnormal levels in the body. Potentially fatal irregular heart rhythms can occur as a result, so testing patients for these imbalances is very important. Certain electrolyte imbalances—hypokalemia (potassium too low), metabolic alkalosis (blood too alkaline), and hypochloremia (chloride too low) occur more often in patients who purge through vomiting or abuse diuretics.

The menstrual cycles of females with bulimia nervosa can be altered, although few patients have long-term cessation of menses, and many patients maintain their normal level of sexual activity. Some studies show that bulimic symptoms and behaviors improve during pregnancy in many women, but few recover totally. Also, bulimic pregnant women can experience complications during pregnancy directly associated with the bulimic behavior.

A number of medical tests may be ordered during the course of diagnosing, treating, and monitoring the patient during treatment of bulimia nervosa. Many of these tests are also used for other eating disorders. Which, if any, tests are used will depend on each patient's medical status.

Medical tests that diagnose bulimia nervosa and monitor treatment include:

- complete blood count with differential;
- urinalysis;
- complete metabolic profile: sodium, chloride, potassium, glucose, blood urea;
- nitrogen, creatinine, total protein, albumin, globulin, calcium, carbon dioxide, aspartate aminotransferase (AST), alkaline phosphates, total bilirubin;
- serum magnesium;
- thyroid screen (T3, T4, TSH);
- electrocardiogram.

Tests used if the patient is 15% to 20% or more below ideal body weight (usually applies to anorexia, but some bulimia patients can also be underweight) include:

- chest x-ray;
- complement activity;
- 24-hour creatinine clearance;
- uric acid.

For low weight lasting six months or longer, tests may include:

- bone mineral density scan;
- estradiol level in females or testosterone in males;
- echocardiogram;
- brain scan, if neurologic signs.

Which treatments work best?

Many different treatment approaches are used for bulimia nervosa. To know what really works best requires analyzing results of all the clinical trials that have been published on each treatment. Then, doctors and patients have the best information available to decide about treatment.

ECRI's analysis of all the available evidence found that medication used to treat bulimia nervosa reduced the frequency of binge eating and purging. Medication also lessened anxiety, depression, and eating disorder psychopathology (abnormal behavior). Cognitive behavioral therapy (CBT) reduced the frequency of purging, and it did so more effectively than medication. However, the effect of CBT on binge eating itself and on anxiety, depression, and eating disorder psychopathology is not clear from the available evidence. The effectiveness of other kinds of psychotherapy is also unclear at this time. More clinical research of high quality is needed to answer the questions that remain about how well CBT and other kinds of psychotherapy, and medications work for bulimia nervosa.

Trials on complementary therapies and alternative therapies for bulimia nervosa either did not exist or were of such poor quality that they could not be analyzed—so it was not possible to determine whether or not they work.

Chapter 6

Emotional Eating

Description of Emotional Eating

Emotional eating is characterized by episodes of binge eating, grazing, and/or eating when not hungry to soothe feelings.

Binge eating is characterized by uncontrollable eating followed by guilt and feelings of shame about the behavior. Dieting is mistakenly seen as the solution and is undertaken with strenuous effort. Feelings of deprivation result from rigid dieting. These feelings are assuaged by eating foods that produce more guilt, ultimately leading to defeat of the diet and demoralization. The problem becomes cyclic because diets address symptoms rather than issues.

Emotional eaters have a pattern of eating to cope with stress, emotional conflicts, and problems of daily life. Whether overeating or dieting, the emotional eater is still engaged in an unremitting problem with food.

An emotional eater may or may not be obese. Obesity is defined as weighing more than 25% above expected normal body weight. Not all overweight people are emotional eaters.

Recognizing Emotional Eating

Emotional eating may include the following:

- obsessive thoughts about food
- episodic binge eating with awareness that the pattern is abnormal
- fear of not being able to stop voluntarily
- feeling out of control
- self-deprecating thoughts following binges
- depressed mood
- eating little in public
- hiding evidence of having eaten
- cycling through dieting, bingeing, and remorse
- specific foods labeled "good" or "bad"
- disconnection from signals of hunger or satiety
- weight frequently fluctuates
- preoccupation with body image
- restricting activities due to embarrassment about weight and/or eating habits
- difficulty identifying feelings and needs
- intense fear of anger and conflict
- impulsivity in other areas of life
- food is used for reward, nurturing, and excitement

Associated Issues

Other issues that may be associated with emotional eating include the following:

- low self-esteem based on weight and control of eating
- fantasizing about being happier, more outgoing when thin
- intense fear of rejection related to weight
- social withdrawal and isolation increases
- putting off taking risks in life until thin
- feeling tormented by eating habits
- professional failures attributed to weight
- weight becomes the focus of life

Medical Consequences

Physical effects of emotional eating may include these symptoms:

- hypertension
- depression and/or fatigue
- gastrointestinal disorders
- diabetes and/or hypoglycemia
- high cholesterol
- heart disease
- gallbladder disease
- mobility problems
- hormonal imbalances
- fertility problems
- certain types of cancer
- sleep apnea and other sleep disorders

The Story of Emotional Eaters

Many emotional eaters began eating secretively during their youth. They eat when they are not physically hungry in an attempt to manage feelings of despair, fear, sadness, and loneliness. As time goes by, eating behaviors worsen. Some people resort to binge eating, hiding while eating, and stealing food. Once a binge commences, emotional eaters are unable to stop. Control is lost. To manage body weight, they diet and berate themselves. As their lives are increasingly focused on food and weight, they become depressed, isolated, and their self-esteem plummets. They may feel unworthy, unlovable, and rejected. Help is needed and diets do not work.

Could This Be You?

Typically graced with intelligence and talent, many emotional eaters become so engaged with their eating disorder that they bypass opportunities to take the necessary steps required to fulfill dreams and succeed in life. Sometimes, potential is unrealized as they become progressively more preoccupied with food. Feelings are suppressed and needs denied. They may be unable to recognize and identify their emotions. Depression often sets in; leading to feeling more isolated and hopeless. Eating becomes a way to squelch feelings of shame and the disappointments of life. Food is used in an unsuccessful attempt to meet deep emotional needs. Emotional eating cannot be stopped until the person finds and practices more satisfying ways to meet their emotional needs.

Recovery

1. Starts with willingness to be honest.
2. Typically requires professional help and group support.
3. Requires facing and dealing with emotions openly and responsibly.

There is no diet or magic pill that will make emotional eaters better. Recovery is hard work. Emotional eating is not about food; it is a coping tool for handling life. Many people are deeply negative and unable to distinguish negative thought patterns from reality; their perspective is distorted. Many emotional eaters are caretakers who are out of touch with their own needs. Because their needs went unmet, they may be deeply resentful. In recovery, emotional eaters learn to recognize their needs and take responsibility for getting them met.

More on Recovery

Recovery means rebuilding trust, listening, validating feelings, and trying to understand needs and get them met. Changing thinking makes it possible to change feelings and behavior; developing willingness and learning new skills is a process, not an event. It takes time to develop an eating disorder. It takes time and effort to rebuild trust and gain back the power of choice. Many people waste a lot of time trying to recover by self-help. Recovery requires great support and motivation. There are bound to be setbacks and moments of fear and frustration; support helps to get through these trials safely. Support groups provide necessary examples, inspiration, and opportunity for turning deeply painful and humbling experiences to useful purpose. Eating Disorders Anonymous is one such support group.

Additional Information

Eating Disorders Anonymous
P.O. Box 55876
Phoenix, AZ 85078-5876
Website: http://www.eatingdisordersanonymous.org
E-mail: info@eatingdisordersanonymous.org

Chapter 7

Compulsive Exercising

Melissa has been a track fanatic since she was 12 years old. She has run the mile in meets in junior high and high school, constantly improving her times and winning several medals. Best of all, Melissa truly loves her sport.

Recently, however, Melissa's parents have noticed a change in their daughter. She used to return tired but happy from practice and relax with her family, but now she's hardly home for 15 minutes before she heads out for another run on her own. On many days, she gets up to run before school as well. When she's unable to squeeze in her extra runs, she becomes irritable and anxious. And she no longer talks about how much fun track is, just how many miles she has to run today and how many more she should run tomorrow.

Melissa is living proof that even though exercise has many positive benefits, too much can be harmful. Teens, like Melissa, who exercise compulsively are at risk for both physical and psychological problems.

What Is Compulsive Exercise?

Compulsive exercise (also called obligatory exercise and anorexia athletica) is best defined by an exercise addict's frame of mind: He or

---

This information was provided by KidsHealth, one of the largest resources online for medically reviewed health information written for parents, kids, and teens. For more articles like this one, visit www.KidsHealth.org, or www.TeensHealth.org.

she no longer chooses to exercise but feels compelled to do so and struggles with guilt and anxiety if he or she doesn't work out. Injury, illness, an outing with friends, bad weather—none of these will deter those who compulsively exercise. In a sense, exercising takes over a compulsive exerciser's life because he or she plans life around it.

Of course, it's nearly impossible to draw a clear line dividing a healthy amount of exercise from too much. The government's 2005 dietary guidelines, published by the U.S. Department of Agriculture (USDA) and the U.S. Department of Health and Human Services (HHS), recommend at least 60 minutes of physical activity for kids and teens on most—if not all—days of the week.

Experts say that repeatedly exercising beyond the requirements for good health is an indicator of compulsive behavior, but because different amounts of exercise are appropriate for different people, this definition covers a range of activity levels. However, several workouts a day, every day, is overdoing it for almost anyone.

Much like with eating disorders, many people who engage in compulsive exercise do so to feel more in control of their lives, and the majority of them are female. They often define their self-worth through their athletic performance and try to deal with emotions like anger or depression by pushing their bodies to the limit. In sticking to a rigorous workout schedule, they seek a sense of power to help them cope with low self-esteem.

Although compulsive exercising doesn't have to accompany an eating disorder, the two often go hand in hand. In anorexia nervosa, the excessive workouts usually begin as a means to control weight and become more and more extreme. As the person's rate of activity increases, the amount he or she eats may also decrease. A person with bulimia may also use exercise as a way to compensate for binge eating.

Compulsive exercise behavior can also grow out of student athletes' demanding practice schedules and their quest to excel. Pressure, both external (from coaches, peers, or parents) and internal, can drive the athlete to go too far to be the best. He or she ends up believing that just one more workout will make the difference between first and second place, then keeps adding more workouts.

Eventually, compulsive exercising can breed other compulsive behavior, from strict dieting to obsessive thoughts about perceived flaws. Exercise addicts may keep detailed journals about their exercise schedules and obsess about improving themselves. Unfortunately, these behaviors often compound each other, trapping the person in a downward spiral of negative thinking and low self-esteem.

Why Is Exercising Too Much a Bad Thing?

We all know that regular exercise is an important part of a healthy lifestyle. But few people realize that too much can cause physical and psychological harm.

- Excessive exercise can damage tendons, ligaments, bones, cartilage, and joints, and when minor injuries aren't allowed to heal, they often result in long-term damage. Instead of building muscle, too much exercise actually destroys muscle mass, especially if the body isn't getting enough nutrition, forcing it to break down muscle for energy.
- Girls who exercise compulsively may disrupt the balance of hormones in their bodies. This can change their menstrual cycles (some girls lose their periods altogether, a condition known as amenorrhea) and increase the risk of premature bone loss (a condition known as osteoporosis). And of course, working their bodies so hard leads to exhaustion and constant fatigue.
- An even more serious risk is the stress that excessive exercise can place on the heart, particularly when someone is also limiting how much he or she eats. In extreme cases, the combination of anorexia and compulsive exercise can be fatal.
- Psychologically, exercise addicts are often plagued by anxiety and depression. They may have a negative image of themselves and feel worthless. Their social and academic lives may suffer as they withdraw from friends and family to fixate on exercise. Even if they want to succeed in school or in relationships, working out always comes first, so they end up skipping homework or missing out on time spent with friends.

Is Your Child Exercising Too Much?

If you're concerned that your child may be exercising compulsively, look for these warning signs. There could be a problem if he or she:

- won't skip a workout, even if tired, sick, or injured;
- doesn't enjoy exercise sessions, but feels obligated to do them;
- seems anxious or guilty when missing even one workout;
- does miss one workout and exercises twice as long the next time;

- is constantly preoccupied with his or her weight and exercise routine;
- doesn't like to sit still or relax because of worry that not enough calories are being burnt;
- has lost a significant amount of weight;
- exercises more after eating more;
- skips seeing friends, gives up activities, and abandons responsibilities to make more time for exercise;
- seems to base self-worth on the number of workouts completed and the effort put into training;
- is never satisfied with his or her own physical achievements.

It's important, too, to recognize the types of athletes who are more prone to compulsive exercise because their sports place a particular emphasis on being thin. Ice skaters, gymnasts, wrestlers, and dancers can feel even more pressure than most athletes to keep their weight down and their body toned. Runners also frequently fall into a cycle of obsessive workouts.

Getting Professional Help for Your Child

If you recognize two or more warning signs of compulsive exercise in your child, call your child's doctor to discuss your concerns. After evaluating your child, the doctor may recommend medical treatment and/or other therapy. Because compulsive exercise is so often linked to an eating disorder, a community agency that focuses on treating these disorders might be able to offer advice or referrals. Extreme cases may require hospitalization to get the child's weight back up to a safe range.

Treating a compulsion to exercise is never a quick-fix process—it may take several months or even years. But with time and effort, your child can get back on the road to good health. Therapy can help improve self-esteem and body image, as well as teach your child how to deal with emotions instead of sweating them out. Sessions with a nutritionist can help your child develop healthy eating habits. Once your child knows what to watch out for, he or she will be better equipped to steer clear of unsafe exercise and eating patterns.

Ways You Can Help Your Child at Home

You can do a lot to help your child overcome a compulsion to exercise.

- Involve your child in preparing nutritious meals.
- Combine activity and fun by going for a hike or a bike ride together as a family.
- Be a good body-image role model. In other words, don't fixate on your own physical flaws, as that just teaches your child that it's normal to dislike what he or she sees in the mirror.
- Never criticize another family member's weight or body shape, even if you're just kidding around. Such remarks may seem harmless, but they can leave a lasting impression on kids or teens struggling to define and accept themselves.
- Examine whether you're putting too much pressure on your child to excel, particularly in a sport (because some teens turn to exercise to cope with pressure). Take a look at where your child may be feeling too much pressure. Help your child put it in perspective and help him or her find other ways to cope.

Most importantly, just be there with constant support. Point out all of your child's great qualities that have nothing to do with how much he or she works out—small daily doses of encouragement and praise can help improve your child's self-esteem. If you teach kids to be proud of the challenges they've faced, and not just the first-place ribbons they've won, they will likely be much happier and healthier children now and in the long run.

Chapter 8

Female Athlete Triad

With dreams of Olympic trials and college scholarships in her mind, Hannah joined the track team her freshman year and trained hard to become a lean, strong sprinter. When her coach told her losing a few pounds would improve her performance, she didn't hesitate to start counting calories and increasing the duration of her workouts. She was too busy with practices and meets to notice that her period had stopped—she was more worried about the stress fracture in her ankle slowing her down.

Although Hannah thinks her intense training and disciplined diet are helping her performance, they may actually be hurting her—and her health.

What Is Female Athlete Triad?

There's no doubt about it—playing sports and exercise are part of a balanced, healthy lifestyle. Girls who play sports are healthier; get better grades; are less likely to experience depression; and use alcohol, cigarettes, and drugs less frequently. But for some girls, not balancing the needs of their bodies and their sports can have major consequences. Some girls who play sports or exercise are at risk for a problem called female athlete triad. Female athlete triad—also known

---

This information was provided by TeensHealth, one of the largest resources online for medically reviewed health information written for parents, kids, and teens. For more articles like this one, visit www.TeensHealth.org, or www.KidsHealth.org.

as female athletic triad—is a combination of three conditions: disordered eating, amenorrhea (pronounced: ay-meh-nuh-ree-uh, which means loss of a girl's period), and osteoporosis (a weakening of the bones). A female athlete can have one, two, or all three parts of the triad.

Triad Factor #1: Disordered Eating

Girls who have the disordered eating that accompanies female athlete triad often have many of the signs and symptoms of anorexia nervosa or bulimia nervosa, such as low body weight for their height and age and episodes of binge eating and purging. But girls with female athlete triad try to lose weight primarily to improve their athletic performance. Sometimes the disordered eating that accompanies this condition isn't technically an eating disorder. Many girls with female athlete triad are simply trying to become better at their chosen sports. But like teens with eating disorders, girls with female athlete triad may use behaviors such as calorie restriction, purging, and exercise to lose weight.

Triad Factor #2: Amenorrhea

Because a girl with female athlete triad is simultaneously exercising intensely and reducing her weight, she may experience decreases in estrogen, the hormone that helps to regulate the menstrual cycle. As a result, a girl's periods may become irregular or stop altogether. (In many cases, of course, a missed period indicates another medical condition—pregnancy. If you have missed a period and you are sexually active, you should talk to your doctor.) Some girls who participate intensively in sports may never even get their first period because they've been training so hard—this is called primary amenorrhea. Other girls may have had periods, but once they increase their training and change their eating habits, their periods may stop—this is called secondary amenorrhea.

Triad Factor #3: Osteoporosis

Low estrogen levels and poor nutrition can also lead to osteoporosis, the third aspect of the triad. Osteoporosis is a weakening of the bones due to the loss of bone density and improper bone formation. This condition can ruin a female athlete's career because it may lead to stress fractures and other injuries due to weakened bones. Because of poor nutrition, a girl's body may not be able to repair the injuries efficiently.

Usually, the teen years are a time when girls should be building up their bone mass to their highest levels—called peak bone mass. Female athlete triad can lead to a lower level of peak bone mass and a lot of time on the sidelines. After she becomes an adult, a girl may also develop health problems related to osteoporosis at an earlier age than she would have otherwise.

Who Gets Female Athlete Triad?

Most girls have concerns about the size and shape of their bodies, but girls who develop female athlete triad have certain risk factors that set them apart. Being a highly competitive athlete and participating in a sport that requires you to train extra hard is a risk factor. Girls with female athlete triad often care so much about their sports that they would do almost anything to improve their performances. Martial arts and rowing are examples of sports that classify athletes by weight class, so focusing on weight becomes an important part of the training program and can put a girl at risk for disordered eating.

Participation in sports where a thin appearance is valued can also put a girl at risk for female athlete triad. Sports such as gymnastics, figure skating, diving, and ballet are examples of sports that value a thin, lean body shape. Some girls may even be told by coaches or judges that losing weight would improve their scores.

Even in sports where body size and shape aren't as important for judging purposes, such as distance running and cross-country skiing, girls may be pressured by teammates, parents, partners, and coaches who mistakenly believe that "losing just a few pounds" would improve their performance. Losing those few pounds generally doesn't improve performance at all—people who are fit and active enough to compete in sports generally have more muscle than fat, so it's the muscle that gets starved when a girl cuts back on food. Plus, if a girl loses weight when she doesn't need to, it interferes with healthy body processes such as menstruation and bone development.

In addition, for some competitive female athletes, problems such as low self-esteem, a tendency toward perfectionism, and family stress place them at risk for disordered eating.

What Are the Signs and Symptoms?

If a girl has risk factors for female athlete triad, she may already be experiencing some symptoms and signs of the disorder, such as:

- weight loss;

- no periods or irregular periods;
- fatigue and decreased ability to concentrate;
- stress fractures (fractures that occur even if a person hasn't had a significant injury);
- muscle injuries.

Girls with female athlete triad often have signs and symptoms of eating disorders, such as:

- eating alone;
- preoccupation with food and weight;
- continuous drinking of water and diet soda;
- frequent trips to the bathroom during and after meals;
- using laxatives;
- presence of lanugo hair (fine, soft hair that grows on the body);
- tooth enamel that's worn away from frequent vomiting;
- anemia (fewer red blood cells in the blood than normal);
- sensitivity to cold;
- heart irregularities and chest pain.

What Do Doctors Do?

It may be easy for girls with female athlete triad to keep their symptoms a secret because information about their periods and any damage done to bones usually isn't visible to friends and family. And lots of girls become very skilled at hiding their disordered eating habits.

A doctor may recognize that a girl has female athlete triad during a regular exam. An extensive physical examination is a crucial part of diagnosing the triad. A doctor who suspects a girl has female athlete triad will probably ask questions about her periods, her nutrition and exercise habits, any medications she takes, and her feelings about her body. This is called the medical history. Because poor nutrition can affect the body in many ways, a doctor might also test for blood problems and nutritional imbalances. Because osteoporosis can put a girl at higher risk for bone fractures, a doctor who suspects female athlete triad may also request tests to measure bone density.

Doctors don't work alone to help a girl with female athlete triad—coaches, parents, physical therapists, pediatricians and adolescent medicine specialists, nutritionists and dietitians, and mental health specialists all work together to treat the physical and emotional problems that a girl with female athlete triad faces.

It might be tempting for a girl with female athlete triad to shrug off several months of missed periods, but getting help right away is important. In the short term, a girl with female athlete triad may have muscle weakness, stress fractures, and reduced physical performance. Over the long term, a girl with female athlete triad may suffer from bone weakness, damage to her reproductive system, and heart problems.

A girl who is recovering from female athlete triad may work with a dietitian to help get to and maintain a healthy weight and ensure she's eating enough nutrients for health and good athletic performance. Depending on how much the girl is exercising, she may have to reduce the length of her workouts. Talking to a psychologist or therapist can help a girl deal with depression, pressure from coaches or family members, or low self-esteem, and can help her find ways to deal with her problems other than restricting her food intake or exercising excessively.

Some girls with female athlete triad may need to take hormones to supply their bodies with estrogen so they can get their periods started again. In such cases, birth control pills are often used to regulate a girl's menstrual cycle. Calcium and vitamin D supplementation is also common for a girl who has suffered bone loss as the result of female athlete triad.

What if I Think Someone I Know Has Female Athlete Triad?

A girl with female athlete triad can't just ignore the disorder and hope it goes away—she needs to get help from a doctor and other health professionals. If your friend, sister, or teammate has signs and symptoms of female athlete triad, discuss your concerns with her and encourage her to seek treatment. If she refuses to seek treatment, you may need to mention your concern to her parent, coach, teacher, or school nurse.

Looking for ways to be supportive to your friend with female athlete triad? You may worry about being nosy, but don't: Your concern is a sign that you're a caring friend. Lending an ear may be just what your friend needs.

Tips for Female Athletes

Here are a few tips to help teen athletes stay on top of their physical condition:

- **Keep track of your periods.** It's easy to forget when you had your last visit from Aunt Flo, so keep a little calendar in your gym bag and mark down when your period starts and stops and if the bleeding is particularly heavy or light. That way, if you start missing periods, you'll know right away and you'll have accurate information to give to your doctor.

- **Don't skip meals or snacks.** You're constantly on the go between school, practice, and competitions, so it may be tempting to skip meals and snacks to save time. But eating now will improve your performance later, so stock your locker or bag with quick and easy favorites such as bagels, string cheese, unsalted nuts and seeds, raw vegetables, energy bars, and fruit.

- **Visit a dietitian or nutritionist who works with teen athletes.** He or she can help you get your dietary game plan into gear and can help you determine if you're getting enough key nutrients such as iron, calcium, and protein. And, if you need supplements, a nutritionist can recommend the best choices.

- **Do it for you.** Pressure from teammates, parents, or coaches can turn an activity you took up for fun into a nightmare. If you're not enjoying your sport, make a change. Remember: It's your body and your life. Any damage you do to your body now, you—not your coach or teammates—will have to live with later.

Chapter 9

Pica

Many young children put nonfood items in their mouths at one time or another. They're naturally curious about their environment, and they may, for instance, eat some dirt out of the sandbox. Kids with pica, however, go beyond this innocent exploration of their surroundings. As many as 25% to 30% of kids (and 20% of those seen in mental health clinics) have an eating disorder called pica, which is characterized by persistent and compulsive cravings (lasting one month or longer) to eat nonfood items.

What Is Pica?

The word pica comes from the Latin word for magpie, a bird known for its large and indiscriminate appetite.

Pica is most common in people with developmental disabilities, including autism and mental retardation, and in children between the ages of two and three. Although kids younger than 18 to 24 months can try to eat nonfood items, it isn't necessarily considered abnormal at that age.

Pica is also a behavior that may surface in children who've had a brain injury affecting their development. It can also be a problem for some pregnant women, as well as people with epilepsy.

This information was provided by KidsHealth, one of the largest resources online for medically reviewed health information written for parents, kids, and teens. For more articles like this one, visit www.KidsHealth.org, or www.TeensHealth.org.

People with pica frequently crave and consume nonfood items such as:

- dirt;
- paint chips;
- chalk;
- laundry starch;
- coffee grounds;
- burnt match heads;
- feces;
- glue;
- buttons;
- sand;
- soap.
- clay;
- plaster;
- cornstarch;
- baking soda;
- cigarette ashes;
- cigarette butts;
- ice;
- hair;
- paper;
- toothpaste;

Although consumption of some items may be harmless, pica is considered to be a serious eating disorder that can sometimes result in serious health problems such as lead poisoning and iron-deficiency anemia.

Does My Child Have Pica?

Look for these warning signs that your child may have pica:

- repetitive consumption of a nonfood item, despite efforts to restrict it, for a period of at least one month or longer
- the behavior is considered inappropriate for your child's age or developmental stage (older than 18 to 24 months)
- the behavior is not part of a cultural, ethnic, or religious practice

Why Do Some People Eat Nonfood Items?

The specific causes of pica are unknown, but certain conditions and situations can increase a person's risk for pica:

- nutritional deficiencies, such as iron or zinc, that may trigger specific cravings (however, the nonfood items craved usually don't supply the minerals lacking in the person's body)
- dieting—people who diet may attempt to ease hunger by eating nonfood substances to get a feeling of fullness

- malnutrition, especially in underdeveloped countries, where people with pica most commonly eat soil or clay
- cultural factors—in families, religions, or groups in which eating nonfood substances is a learned practice
- parental neglect, lack of supervision, or food deprivation—often seen in children living in poverty
- developmental problems, such as mental retardation, autism, other developmental disabilities, or brain abnormalities
- mental health conditions, such as obsessive-compulsive disorder and schizophrenia
- pregnancy, but it's been suggested that pica during pregnancy occurs more frequently in women who exhibited similar practices during their childhood or before pregnancy or who have a history of pica in their family

Theories about what causes pica abound. The nutritional theory suggests that nutritional deficiency, such as iron deficiency, trigger specific cravings. Some evidence supports the hypothesis that at least some pica is a response to dietary deficiency—nutritional deficiencies are often associated with pica and correction of that deficiency has improved symptoms. Some pregnant women, for example, have stopped eating nonfood items after they were treated for iron deficiency anemia, a common condition among pregnant women with pica. However, not everyone responds when a nutritional deficiency is corrected, which may be a consequence of the behavior (rather than the cause). But there are also people with pica who don't have a documented nutritional deficiency.

Known as geophagia, eating earth substances such as clay or dirt is a form of pica that can cause iron deficiency. One theory to explain pica is that in some cultures, eating clay or dirt may help relieve nausea (and therefore, morning sickness), control diarrhea, increase salivation, remove toxins, and alter odor or taste perception; some people actually claim to enjoy the taste and texture of dirt or clay. Some people eat clay or dirt as part of a daily habit (just like smoking is a daily routine for others). And some psychological theories explain pica as a behavioral response to stress or an indication that the individual has an oral fixation (is comforted by having things in his or her mouth).

Another explanation is that pica is a cultural feature of certain religious rituals, folk medicine, and magical beliefs. For example, some people in various cultures believe that eating dirt will help them incorporate magical spirits into their bodies.

Despite the wide variety of theories, not one of them explains all forms of pica. A doctor must treat every case individually to try to understand what may be causing the condition.

When to Call Your Child's Doctor

If your child is at risk for pica, talk to your child's doctor. If your child has consumed a harmful substance, seek medical care immediately. If you think your child has ingested something poisonous, call Poison Control at (800) 222-1222.

If your child continues to consume nonfood items, he or she may be at risk for serious health problems, including:

- lead poisoning (from eating paint chips in older buildings with lead-based paint);
- bowel problems (from consuming indigestible substances like hair, cloth, etc.);
- intestinal obstruction or perforation (from eating objects that could get lodged in the intestines);
- dental injury (from eating hard substances that could harm the teeth);
- parasitic infections (from eating dirt or feces).

Medical emergencies and death can occur if the craved substance is toxic or contaminated with lead or mercury, or if the item forms an indigestible mass blocking the intestines. Pica involving lead-containing substances during pregnancy may be associated with an increase in both maternal and fetal lead levels.

What Will the Doctor Do?

Your child's doctor will play an important role in helping you manage and prevent pica-related behaviors. He or she will educate you on teaching your child about acceptable and non-acceptable food substances. The doctor will also work with you to prevent your child from obtaining the nonfood items he or she craves (for example, using child-safety locks and high shelving, and keeping household chemicals and medications out of reach of your child).

Depending on your child's age and developmental stage, your child's doctor will work with your child to teach him or her ways to eat more appropriately. Medication may also be prescribed to help the behavior associated with pica.

If your child has ingested a potentially harmful substance, such as lead, a doctor will screen your child for lead poisoning, anemia, or other biochemical abnormalities, and may order stool testing for parasites or imaging for bowel obstruction.

Fortunately, pica is usually a temporary condition that improves as children get older or following pregnancy. But for individuals with developmental or mental health issues, pica can be a more prolonged concern.

Following treatment, if your child's pica behavior continues beyond several weeks, despite the attempts to intervene, contact your child's doctor again for additional treatment. But it's important to remember that patience is key in treating pica because it may take some time to stop your child from wanting to eat nonfood items.

Chapter 10

Sleep-Related Eating Disorder

There are at least two problems that involve disordered eating primarily at night—nocturnal sleep-related eating disorder, which is discussed in this chapter, and night eating syndrome, both perplexing and distressing problems.

> "When I woke up this morning, there were candy bar wrappers all over the kitchen, and I had a stomach ache. I had chocolate on my face and hands. My husband says I was up eating last night, but I have no memories of doing so. Could he be playing a joke on me?"

Maybe not. You might have nocturnal sleep-related eating disorder, a relatively unknown condition currently being investigated.

What is nocturnal sleep-related eating disorder (NS-RED)?

In spite of its name, NS-RED is not, strictly speaking, an eating disorder. It is thought to be a type of sleep disorder in which people eat while seeming to be sound asleep. They may eat in bed or roam through the house and prowl the kitchen.

These people are not conscious during episodes of NS-RED, which may be related to sleep-walking. They are not aware that they are eating. They have no memories of having done so when they wake, or

---

"Nocturnal Sleep-Related Eating Disorder," used with permission of ANRED: Anorexia Nervosa and Related Eating Disorders, Inc. © 2005 ANRED. For additional information, visit http://www.anred.com.

they have only fragmentary memories. Episodes seem to occur in a state somewhere between wakefulness and sleep.

When people with NS-RED awake and discover the evidence of their nighttime forays, they are embarrassed, ashamed, and afraid they may be losing their minds. Some, when confronted with the evidence by family members, deny that they were the perpetrators. They truly do not believe they could have done such a thing and cannot admit to such dramatic loss of control.

Food consumed during NS-RED episodes tends to be high-fat, high-sugar, comfort food that people deny themselves while awake. Sometimes these folks eat bizarre combinations of food (for example, hotdogs dipped in peanut butter, or raw bacon smeared with mayonnaise) or non-food items like soap that they have sliced like they would slice cheese.

Who gets NS-RED?

One to three percent of the general population (3–9 million people) seems to be subject to this disorder, and ten to fifteen percent of people with eating disorders are affected. The problem may be chronic or appear once or twice and then disappear. Many of these people are severely stressed, anxious individuals who are dismayed and angry at themselves for their nocturnal loss of control. Their behaviors may pave the way to depression and weight gain.

Many of these individuals diet during the day, which leaves them hungry and vulnerable to binge eating at night when their control is weakened by sleep.

People with NS-RED sometimes have histories of alcoholism, drug abuse, and sleep disorders other than NS-RED, problems such as sleep walking, restless legs, and sleep apnea. Their sleep is fragmented, and they are often tired when they wake.

Sleep disorders, including NS-RED, seem to run in families. They may have a genetic component.

Reports have been received by the U.S. Food and Drug Administration (FDA) and the makers of Ambien, a prescription sleep aid, to the effect that some of the people who took this medication discovered that they had eaten or binge eaten while they slept under the influence of the drug. Most had no memory of doing so when they awoke in the morning.

How can people eat and not remember doing so? Are they lying?

No, they are not lying. It seems that parts of their brains are truly asleep, and, at the same time, other parts are awake. The parts that regulate waking consciousness are asleep, so the next day there are no memories of eating the night before.

Is there any treatment for NS-RED? If there is, what is it?

Yes, there is treatment. It begins with a clinical interview and a night or two at a sleep-disorders center where brain activity is monitored. Sometimes medication is helpful, but sleeping pills should be avoided. They can make matters worse by increasing confusion and clumsiness that can lead to injury. Regular use of sleeping pills can also lead to dependency and rebound wakefulness on withdrawal. Instead, ask your doctor about prescription selective serotonin reuptake inhibitors (SSRIs). Also helpful are interventions that reduce stress and anxiety; for example, stress management classes, assertiveness training, counseling, and reducing intake of alcohol, street drugs, and caffeine.

How about self-help techniques? Are there any that work?

Some people find that sleep-eating episodes are fewer and farther between if they play soft, rhythmic music at night. Headsets and earbuds can eliminate annoyance for bed partners, but the volume should be low enough to prevent damage to one's hearing.

Some people enlist the help of family members who lock cupboards and the refrigerator at night and then hide the keys. Others tie one end of a thread or string to a wrist and the other to the bed frame so that they wake themselves if they get up and walk away from the bed. Some have even used baby alarms or burglar alarms that are triggered by motion.

These techniques should be implemented carefully and safely so that a person who is somewhere between sleep and wakefulness does not hurt her/himself during a sleep-walking/eating episode.

Recommendation

If you think you may have NS-RED, before you try self-help, talk to your physician and ask for a referral to a sleep-disorders treatment center. You especially need to talk to your doctor if you are taking, or have taken, the sleep medication Ambien. Help is available. Take advantage of it.

Chapter 11

U.S. Eating Disorders Statistics

Statistics about Eating Disorders from Students Against Destructive Decisions (SADD)

- More than five million Americans experience eating disorders. (Source: Harvard Eating Disorders Center)
- Anorexia nervosa, bulimia nervosa, and binge eating disorder are diseases that affect the mind and body simultaneously. (Source: Harvard Eating Disorders Center)
- Three percent of adolescent and adult women and one percent of men have anorexia nervosa, bulimia nervosa, or binge eating disorder. (Source: Harvard Eating Disorders Center)
- A young woman with anorexia is twelve times more likely to die than are other women her age without anorexia. (Source: Harvard Eating Disorders Center)
- Fifteen percent of young women have substantially disordered eating attitudes and behaviors. (Source: Harvard Eating Disorders Center)

This chapter begins with "Statistics about Eating Disorders from Students Against Destructive Decisions (SADD)" an excerpt from "Statistics," © Students Against Destructive Decisions (SADD), reprinted with permission. It continues with text from "Facts about Eating Disorders," © 2004 Screening for Mental Health, Inc. All rights reserved. Reprinted with permission.

- Between 10% and 15% of those diagnosed with bulimia nervosa are men. (Source: Harvard Eating Disorders Center)
- Forty percent of fourth graders report that they diet either "very often" or "sometimes." (Source: Harvard Eating Disorders Center)
- About half of those with anorexia or bulimia have a full recovery, 30% have a partial recovery, and 20% have no substantial improvement. (Source: Harvard Eating Disorders Center)
- In the United States, conservative estimates indicate that, after puberty, 5–10 million girls and women and one million boys and men are struggling with eating disorders including anorexia, bulimia, binge eating disorder, or borderline conditions. (Source: National Eating Disorders Association)
- Approximately 90–95% of anorexia nervosa sufferers are girls and women. (Source: National Eating Disorders Association)
- Between one and two percent of American women suffer from anorexia nervosa. (Source: National Eating Disorders Association)
- Anorexia nervosa is one of the most common psychiatric diagnoses in young women. (Source: National Eating Disorders Association)
- Anorexia nervosa typically appears in early to mid-adolescence. (Source: National Eating Disorders Association)
- Bulimia nervosa affects one to three percent of middle and high school girls and one to four percent of college age women. (Source: National Eating Disorders Association)
- Approximately 80% of bulimia nervosa patients are female. (Source: National Eating Disorders Association)

Facts about Eating Disorders from Screening for Mental Health

General

- Almost 50% of people with eating disorders meet the criteria for depression.[1]
- Only one in ten men and women with eating disorders receive treatment. Only 35% of people that receive treatment for eating disorders get treatment at a specialized facility for eating disorders.[2]

- Up to 24 million people of all ages and genders suffer from an eating disorder (anorexia, bulimia and binge eating disorder) in the U.S.[3]
- Eating disorders have the highest mortality rate of any mental illness.[4]

Students

- Ninety-one percent of women surveyed on a college campus had attempted to control their weight through dieting with 22% saying they dieted "often" or "always."[5]
- Eighty-six percent report onset of eating disorder by age 20; 43% report onset between ages of 16 and 20.[6]
- Anorexia is the third most common chronic illness among adolescents.[7]
- Ninety-five percent of those who have eating disorders are between the ages of 12 and 25.[8]
- Twenty-five percent of college-aged women engage in bingeing and purging as a weight-management technique.[3]
- The mortality rate associated with anorexia nervosa is twelve times higher than the death rate associated with all causes of death for females 15–24 years old.[4]

Men

- An estimated 10–15% of people with anorexia or bulimia are male.[9]
- Men are less likely to seek treatment for eating disorders because of the perception that they are "woman's diseases."[10]
- Among gay men, nearly 14% appeared to suffer from bulimia and over 20% appeared to be anorexic.[11]

Media, Perception, Dieting

- Ninety-five percent of all dieters will regain their lost weight within five years.[3]
- Thirty-five percent of "normal dieters" progress to pathological dieting. Of those, 20–25% progress to partial or full-syndrome eating disorders.[5]

- The body type portrayed in advertising as the ideal is possessed naturally by only 5% of American females.[3]
- Forty-seven percent of girls in 5th–12th grade reported wanting to lose weight because of magazine pictures.[12]
- Sixty-nine percent of girls in 5th–12th grade reported that magazine pictures influenced their idea of a perfect body shape.[13]
- Forty-two percent of 1st–3rd grade girls want to be thinner.[16]
- Eighty-one percent of ten year olds are afraid of being fat.[17]

For Women

- Women are much more likely than men to develop an eating disorder. Only an estimated 5 to 15 percent of people with anorexia or bulimia are male.[14]
- An estimated 0.5 to 3.7 percent of women suffer from anorexia nervosa in their lifetime.[14] Research suggests that about one percent of female adolescents have anorexia.[15]
- An estimated 1.1 to 4.2 percent of women have bulimia nervosa in their lifetime.[14]
- An estimated two to five percent of Americans experience binge-eating disorder in a six month period.[14]
- About fifty percent of people who have had anorexia develop bulimia or bulimic patterns.[15]

References

1. Mortality in Anorexia Nervosa. *American Journal of Psychiatry*, 1995; 152 (7): 1073–4.
2. Characteristics and Treatment of Patients with Chronic Eating Disorders, by Dr. Greta Noordenbox, *International Journal of Eating Disorders*, Volume 10: 15–29, 2002.
3. The Renfrew Center Foundation for Eating Disorders, "Eating Disorders 101 Guide: A Summary of Issues, Statistics and Resources," 2003.
4. *American Journal of Psychiatry*, Vol. 152 (7), July 1995, p. 1073–1074, Sullivan, Patrick F.

5. Shisslak, C.M., Crago, M., and Estes, L.S. (1995). The Spectrum of Eating Disturbances. *International Journal of Eating Disorders*, 18 (3): 209–219.

6. National Association of Anorexia Nervosa and Associated Disorders 10-year study, 2000.

7. Public Health Service's Office in Women's Health, Eating Disorders Information Sheet, 2000.

8. Substance Abuse and Mental Health Services Administration (SAMHSA), The Center for Mental Health Services (CMHS), offices of the U.S. Department of Health and Human Services.

9. Carlat, D.J., Camargo. Review of Bulimia Nervosa in Males. *American Journal of Psychiatry*, 154, 1997.

10. American Psychological Association, 2001.

11. *International Journal of Eating Disorders 2002*; 31: 300–308.

12. Prevention of Eating Problems with Elementary Children, Michael Levine, *USA Today*, July 1998.

13. Ibid.

14. The National Institute of Mental Health: "Eating Disorders: Facts About Eating Disorders and the Search for Solutions." Pub No. 01–4901. Accessed Feb. 2002. http://www.nimh.nih.gov/publicat/nedspdisorder.cfm.

15. Anorexia Nervosa and Related Eating Disorders, Inc. website. Accessed Feb. 2002. http://www.anred.com/

16. Collins, M.E. (1991). Body figure perceptions and preferences among pre-adolescent children. *International Journal of Eating Disorders*, 199–208.

17. Mellin, L., McNutt, S., Hu, Y., Schreiber, G.B., Crawford, P., and Obarzanek, E. (1991). A longitudinal study of the dietary practices of black and white girls 9 and 10 years old at enrollment: The NHLBI growth and health study. *Journal of Adolescent Health*, 23–37.

Part Two

Risk Factors, Causes, and Prevention of Eating Disorders

Chapter 12

Warning Signs and Causes of Eating Disorders

Warning Signs and Symptoms

Eating disorders can go undetected for several reasons:

- It can be difficult to distinguish a warning sign or symptom from a consequence.
- Eating disorders are secretive by nature.
- Some warning signs (such as moodiness) can be consistent with normal adolescent development, making it difficult to distinguish an eating problem from normal behavior.

Early detection can be improved by being aware of clusters of symptoms from behavioral, physical, social, and emotional or psychological categories. People develop and experience eating disorders differently. Therefore, some people exhibit many of the listed warning signs or symptoms, while others may exhibit only a few.

Emotional and psychological warning signs of eating disorders may include the following:

- preoccupation with body appearance or weight
- moodiness, irritability

Excerpted from "Eating Disorders: Types, Warning Signs, and Treatments," and reprinted with permission from http://www.helpguide.org.

- reduced concentration, memory, and thinking ability
- anxiety, depression, or suicidal thoughts
- anxiety around meal times
- guilt or self-dislike

Behavioral warning signs of eating disorders may include the following:

- dieting or making frequent excuses not to eat
- overeating
- obsessive rituals such as drinking only out of a certain cup, or eating certain foods on certain days
- wearing baggy clothes, or a change in clothing style
- hoarding food
- trips to the bathroom after meals

Social warning signs of eating disorders may include the following:

- social withdrawal or isolation
- avoidance of social situations involving food
- decreased interest in hobbies

Physical warning signs of eating disorders may include the following:

- weight loss or rapid fluctuation in weight
- changes in hair, skin, and nails (dry and brittle)
- dehydration
- edema (retention of body fluid, giving a puffy appearance)
- loss or irregularity of menstrual periods (females)
- reduced metabolic rate (can lead to slow heart rate, low blood pressure, reduced body temperature, and bluish-colored extremities)
- sensitivity to the cold
- hypoglycemia (low blood glucose levels), which can cause confusion, illogical thinking, coma, shakiness, and irritability
- faintness, dizziness, or fatigue
- reduced concentration, memory, and thinking ability

- bowel problems such as constipation, diarrhea, or cramps
- sore throat, indigestion, and heartburn
- easy bruising

Causes of Eating Disorders

Eating disorders are complex conditions caused by a combination of individual, family, interpersonal, biological, sociocultural, and precipitating factors.

Individual factors that can help to cause eating disorders include the following:

- self-esteem issues
- social anxiety
- depression
- feelings of lack of control

Family factors. Weak family dynamics can help to cause an eating disorder or interfere with recovery from an eating disorder:

- poor communication and support within the family
- lack of emotional bonding and dealing with feelings within the family
- family values that magnify the importance of appearance
- sexual or physical abuse
- lack of a focus on the importance of family life
- dysfunctional body image and dieting behavior of parents

Interpersonal factors that may help to cause an eating disorder include the following:

- difficulty expressing feelings
- troubled personal or family relationships
- history of being teased or bullied because of weight or shape
- ineffective coping strategies

Biological factors that may help to cause an eating disorder include the following:

- genetic predisposition to an imbalance in serotonin (a neurotransmitter involved in mood and brain function)

- an imbalance in serotonin that is brought about by severe weight loss, fasting, over-exercise, or vomiting
- reduced blood flow to the temporal lobe

Sociocultural factors. The primary sociocultural factor that may help to cause an eating disorder is a cultural focus on appearance, especially an idealization of thinness.

Precipitating factors. The onset of an eating disorder can be triggered by external factors such as these types of issues:

- a life crisis, such as the loss of a family member or friend; moving to a new home, school, or job; or a major personal disappointment
- an accumulation of stress without adequate coping strategies, which may intensify the impact of other factors
- weight loss, or extreme or frequent dieting

Chapter 13

Eating Disorders Self-Evaluation Quiz

Are You at Risk for an Eating Disorder?

The following questionnaire can help you decide if you have an eating disorder, or if you are at risk of developing one. The easiest way to take the test is to copy it, mark T (True) or F (False) for each item, and then read the explanatory paragraph at the end.

__ Even though people tell me I'm thin, I feel fat.

__ I get anxious if I can't exercise.

__ [Female] My menstrual periods are irregular or absent.

__ [Male] My sex drive is not as strong as it used to be.

__ I worry about what I will eat.

__ If I gain weight, I get anxious and depressed.

__ I would rather eat by myself than with family or friends.

__ Other people talk about the way I eat.

__ I get anxious when people urge me to eat.

__ I don't talk much about my fear of being fat because no one understands how I feel.

"ANRED: Self-Test," used with permission of ANRED: Anorexia Nervosa and Related Eating Disorder, Inc. © 2006 ANRED. For additional information, visit http://www.anred.com.

__ I enjoy cooking for others, but I usually don't eat what I've cooked.

__ I have a secret stash of food.

__ When I eat, I'm afraid I won't be able to stop.

__ I lie about what I eat.

__ I don't like to be bothered or interrupted when I'm eating.

__ If I were thinner, I would like myself better.

__ I like to read recipes, cookbooks, calorie charts, and books about dieting and exercise.

__ I have missed work or school because of my weight or eating habits.

__ I tend to be depressed and irritable.

__ I feel guilty when I eat.

__ I avoid some people because they bug me about the way I eat.

__ When I eat, I feel bloated and fat.

__ My eating habits and fear of food interfere with friendships or romantic relationships.

__ I binge eat.

__ I do strange things with my food (for example, cut it into tiny pieces, eat it in special ways, eat it on special dishes with special utensils, make patterns on my plate with it, secretly throw it away, give it to the dog, hide it, or spit it out before I swallow).

__ I get anxious when people watch me eat.

__ I am hardly ever satisfied with myself.

__ I vomit or take laxatives to control my weight.

__ I want to be thinner than my friends.

__ I have said or thought, "I would rather die than be fat."

__ I have stolen food, laxatives, or diet pills from stores or from other people.

__ I have fasted to lose weight.

__ In romantic moments, I cannot let myself go because I am worried about my fat and flab.

__ I have noticed one or more of the following: cold hands and feet, dry skin, thinning hair, fragile nails, swollen glands in my neck, dental cavities, dizziness, weakness, fainting, rapid or irregular heartbeat.

Discussion and Scoring

As strange as it seems in our thin-obsessed society, none of the listed behaviors is normal or healthy. Because of unhealthy demands for unrealistic thinness, most women—and a lot of men—will check a few of the above items as "true." But remember, the more items you have marked true, the more serious your situation may be. Please consult with your physician or a qualified mental health counselor to prevent medical and psychological problems. You could show the person this questionnaire and the items you have circled as a way to begin the conversation.

People do recover from eating disorders, but almost all of those who do, need professional help to get back on track. This is hard, and you must have courage as you take the first step by calling today to make an appointment with your physician or counselor.

Chapter 14

Genetics Affect Eating Disorders

Refusing Sustenance

In 1996, Walter Kaye (a professor of psychiatry at the University of Pittsburgh's Western Psychiatric Institute and Clinic) embarked on a landmark study—the first ever genetic study of eating disorders. Supported by the Price Foundation, he collaborated with centers all over the world to collect data on families with two or more cases of eating disorders. The primary goal was to see what set these families apart genetically from those without a history of eating disorders.

Important findings trickled out of the study. Kaye and colleagues showed that around 20 percent of fathers of anorexic patients had obsessive, perfectionist traits—very high compared to the general population. One might say this points to family environment as a causal factor, but it points to genetics as well. Women with bulimia were found to have altered levels of the mood-regulating neurotransmitter serotonin, even after they recovered from the eating disorder. Could this biological susceptibility explain why some women developed eating disorders when exposed to cultural influences and others

---

This chapter begins with information excerpted with permission from "Refusing Sustenance," by Chuck Staresinic, *Pitt Med magazine*, University of Pittsburgh School of Medicine, May 2004. © 2004, University of Pittsburgh. It continues with "Recent Scientific Advances in Anorexia Nervosa and Bulimia Nervosa," an excerpt from "Annual Report on the Rare Diseases and Conditions Research Activities," National Institutes of Health (NIH) Office of Rare Diseases, January 27, 2004.

did not? The serotonin reuptake inhibitor Prozac was later found to help patients recovering from anorexia to maintain body weight, strengthening the notion that eating disorders were true biochemical imbalances.

Kaye says that he could not do the genetic studies without the contributions of Bernie Devlin, a University of Pittsburgh PhD associate professor of psychiatry and human genetics. The two bring vastly different skills and personalities to their work. Kaye is soft-spoken and subdued, while Devlin is outgoing and animated. Kaye is an expert in the clinical presentation of eating disorders. Devlin is a statistical geneticist; he crunches numbers, and he crunches nucleotides. When Kaye first came to see him, Devlin could tell that the psychiatrist had been rigorous in gathering data. He recalls that Kaye said, "We have about 100 behavioral co-variables we've assessed on these eating-disordered individuals, but we don't know how to use them efficiently in a genetic analysis. Do you?"

In other words, Kaye and his team had come up with a hundred different characteristics to look for in study subjects with eating disorders (more than 90 percent of whom were women). Was there a history of depression in the family? A history of obsessive behavior? Was this a purely restrictive anorexic patient (who restricts food intake but does not binge and purge)? Or does she binge and purge? Or purge during bouts of intensive exercise? Or display ritual behavior with food? Food obsession? Perfectionism? Kaye's team had compiled the most detailed record ever made of patients with eating disorders—a mountain of data which, according to Devlin, "they knew in their hearts and minds would be useful, but they didn't exactly know how to use."

Devlin says he and his team spent "a year or two" working out the methodology for analyzing this wealth of data. The job required experts in the genetic basis of behavioral characteristics, experts in genetic analysis, and experts in statistical analysis.

In the 1990s, geneticists were beginning to rack up an extensive list of diseases linked to specific genes. They were filled with confidence that if a disease had a genetic component, that component could be uncovered. With the sequencing of the human genome, geneticists became even more confident of future successes.

But when Devlin ran data on eating disorders, he came up with lemons. His lab took 192 families with various eating disorders and processed the data. The links were weak, at best. Then they began using some of Kaye's 100 behavioral co-variables as filters. When they separated out the families in which at least two relatives had restricting anorexia nervosa (AN)—characterized by severe limitation of food and no bingeing or purging—the results clearly pointed to a region of chromosome 1. When they looked at bulimia—characterized by bingeing and purging—the results pointed to chromosome 10.

Their methods may shed light on other complex illnesses. After sequencing the human genome, geneticists around the world have been searching for new ways to mine the data for keys to disease. It's becoming clearer that many diseases with genetic components are not like cystic fibrosis or hemophilia, in the sense that they will not be linked to a single mutation. Devlin calls these "simple genetic diseases," and he does not count eating disorders among them.

"The recognition that complex diseases were going to be so hard to crack really only came within the last decade," he notes. When asked to explain why, he quips, "Optimism," and laughs. With eating disorders, the underlying genetics can't be linked to a single gene, or even to one region of the genome. Many genes are involved, and the linkage signals are much weaker, he explains. "The patterns are more difficult to see. You can't find these chunks of deoxyribonucleic acid (DNA) nearly as easily, and even when you do it's not so clear what genetic variants in that region are responsible for the expression of liability to the disease."

Devlin says that partly as a result of their study, geneticists have been eager to apply similar methods, such as using a large number of secondary characteristics to unravel complex genetic diseases, but most researchers are finding they simply do not have data as detailed as what Kaye and his colleagues have been gathering since the mid-1990s.

Based on their promising results, Devlin and Kaye have won support from the National Institute of Mental Health (NIMH) for a $10 million study of the genetics of anorexia nervosa—the first government-funded study of the genetics of anorexia nervosa. They hope to enlist 400 families with two or more cases of anorexia, a considerable challenge, but one that they expect will lead to more significant discoveries. Nine clinical centers around the world will join with Western Psychiatric Institute and Clinic (WPIC) to recruit families and gather data over the next five years.

Kaye recognizes that it may take a long time for public perception of eating disorders to change. There's a deeply ingrained attitude that if anorexics weren't exposed to images of shockingly thin super models they might cease being so stubborn and begin to eat more. While those images may contribute to the disease, the soft-spoken psychiatrist quietly challenges the facile nature of the assumption that they're the primary culprit: "Anorexia has the highest death rate of any psychiatric illness. Ten to 15 percent of these people will die. People don't starve themselves to death because of purely cultural influences. You try to starve yourself to death. You eat only 200 calories a day for a couple of months. How do you think you'd feel? There's a powerful physiological drive to eat. There's something wrong with that physiologic drive in anorexia."

We once believed that schizophrenia was caused primarily by environment, Kaye points out. Now, it is accepted that culture and family play a role, "but if you don't have certain susceptibilities," the psychiatrist says, "it's not likely that you will develop the illness. The same thing is true of anorexia. It's just that we're 20 years behind in relation to other major psychiatric problems."

Recent Scientific Advances in Anorexia Nervosa and Bulimia Nervosa

Eating disorders are often chronic relapsing disorders that have some of the highest death rates of any psychiatric illness. Recent studies have shown that anorexia nervosa (AN) and bulimia nervosa (BN) run in families, and studies in twins suggest a genetic basis for the high rate of these eating disorders in certain families; that is, 50% to 80% of the factors contributing to the development of eating disorders are genetic. This means that AN and BN may be as heritable as schizophrenia or bipolar disorder, illnesses that have long been regarded as exhibiting a strong degree of genetic vulnerability.

Twin, family, and genetic studies support the possibility that some underlying trait, such as a vulnerability to an imbalance in the serotonin system, place someone at risk for developing an eating disorder. Studies have established that the leptin system also is fundamental in the regulation of energy balance and neuroendocrine function and that the leptin and serotonin systems may interact in an important manner to influence ingestion. Current studies are also examining the role of various hormone levels in the modification of taste signals, which could help us better understand the way ingestion-related information is processed in individuals with AN and BN.

Individuals with AN often exhibit symptoms of other psychiatric disorders, such as major depression and obsessive-compulsive disorder, which respond favorably to medication. It has been somewhat puzzling that medical treatment for AN has been consistently unsuccessful. One possible reason for the lack of medication effectiveness may be the associated neurochemical changes due to starvation.

Currently funded research is under way to examine the utility of medication for patients with AN who have regained body mass into normal range as they leave the hospital. In addition to the cognitive behavior therapy, the effects of fluoxetine, compared to placebo, will be examined with regard to protection again relapse.

Efforts to prevent eating disorders have been limited by difficulties in refining specific risk factors. Two separate randomized prevention trials have identified body image concerns and unhealthy weight control methods as symptoms to target to prevent onset of more severe forms of eating disorders. Each of these trials are school-based (high school and college), target young women, and utilize the Internet as a resource for monitoring attitude and knowledge change, as well as monitoring homework assignments.

Chapter 15

Body Image: A Key Risk Factor in Eating Disorders

Chapter Contents

Section 15.1

Are You Imagining the Wrong Body?

Reprinted with permission from Nancy Clark R.D., Author of *Nancy Clark's Sports Nutrition Guidebook*. © 2005.

In general, women seem more dissatisfied with their appearance than men. Women most commonly complain about their thighs, abdomen, breast, and buttocks while men are dissatisfied with their abdomen, upper body, and balding hair. Sometimes, the problem is imaginary, such as the runner who complains about her fat thighs, or the bikini wearer whose stomach is not absolutely flat. Sometimes, the problem is real and ranges from a mild complaint about cellulite to a major preoccupation with "thunder thighs" that results in relentless dieting and exercise akin to punishment.

More likely than not, you have at least one body part that bothers you. The following body image test may uncover the extent of your concerns:

1. List five body parts in order of dissatisfaction and write exactly what you don't like about their appearance. For example:
   - thighs too fat
   - breasts too small
   - teeth crooked
   - facial skin wrinkled
   - stomach protrudes
2. Write out how you normally describe these parts when you are looking in the mirror (for example, disgusting flabby thighs) and notice if your body talk is negative and self-critical, or objective and neutral.
3. To what extent do you feel embarrassed or self-conscious about your appearance around others? Do you imagine others are checking you out and thinking something negative about you because of your appearance? Do you avoid wearing a bathing suit at beaches and swimming pools?

4. Note the ways you feel ashamed of your body part and have tried to change or improve its appearance (such as liposuction, baggy "cover-up" clothes, rigorous exercise). Have you dieted in an unhealthy way? Smoked cigarettes to control weight? Spent hours at the gym in the name of vanity, not health improvement?
5. Think about how you feel about your appearance. Do any of these emotions come to mind:
   - dissatisfied
   - insecure
   - distressed
   - obsessed
   - embarrassed
6. Is your appearance too far up on the list of factors that define who you are? Do you consider yourself to be fat as opposed to intelligent, caring, a good worker, loving mother, or reliable friend?
7. Take a deep breath and relax. Appearance is only skin deep. Your real worth is the love, caring, and concern you have to offer to your family, friends, and peers. No one is going to comment on the imperfections of your body at your funeral. However, people will remember you for the beauty of your life. Practice loving yourself from the inside out, rather than judging yourself from the outside in.

Body Image and Eating Disorders

Even active, fit people—those who religiously workout at the health club or run in the wee hours of the morning—are not immune from the epidemic of body dissatisfaction. Despite their fitness, many perceive themselves as having unacceptable bodies. Some go on to develop unhealthy eating patterns and eating disorders out of desperation.

According to Dr. James Rosen, body image researcher and psychology professor at the University of Vermont in Burlington, women who develop eating disorders tend to hate their bodies. In fact, the best predictor of who will develop an eating disorder relates to who struggles most with body image. This easily includes women fighting the middle age spread, young dancers experiencing body changes at the time of puberty, runners feeling pressure to be thinner, and group exercise leaders who think every student scrutinizes her every bulge.

How to Find Peace with Your Body

If you are dissatisfied with your body, you might think the solution is to lose weight, pump iron, or do thousands of sit-ups. This external approach to correcting body dissatisfaction tends to be inadequate. The better approach is to learn to love the body you have. After all, so much of what you look like (your height, musculature, and some of your weight) is under genetic influence. Yes, you can slightly redesign the house Mother Nature gave you, but you cannot totally remodel it—at least not without paying a high price.

Weight issues are often self-esteem issues. Concern about what you look like is really a mask for how you feel about yourself, your self-esteem. Given about twenty-five percent of self-esteem is tied-up in how you look, you cannot feel good about yourself unless you like your body and feel confident with your appearance.

Ideally, what you look like on the outside should have little to do with how you feel on the inside. But, in reality, the thinking goes like this:

1. I have a defect that makes me different than others.
2. Other people notice this difference.
3. My looks affect how these people see me—repulsive, ugly.
4. I'm bad, unlovable, and inadequate.

If you are struggling with your body image, Dr. Rosen suggests you identify when you first got the message that something is wrong with your body. Perhaps it was:

- a parent who way-back-when lovingly remarked, "You look good, honey, but if only you'd lose a few pounds, you might get a better job;"
- the siblings who teased you about your "thunder thighs;" or
- the relative who molested you—sexual abuse is a common cause of body-hate.

Next, you need to take steps to be at peace with your body and to like yourself. This includes:

- renaming your disliked body part (for example, "round stomach" is a more loving name than "ugly jelly belly");
- identifying the parts of your body that you do like and giving yourself credit for those with positive body talk (for example, my muscular legs help me enjoy bike rides with my children).

Don't dwell on the negative, but instead love all the good things your body does for you. It bears children; lets you do meaningful work that can make a difference in the world; and lets you have fun. How could you enjoy life without your body?

A Resolution for the New Year

The following contract is taken from the National Eating Disorders Association's Declaration of Independence from Weight Obsessions. Perhaps it will offer you guidelines for a new way to relate to your body.

Contract

I, the undersigned, do hereby declare that from this day forward I will choose to live my life by the following tenets. In doing so, I declare myself free and independent from the pressures and constraints of the weight-obsessed world.

- I will accept my body in its natural shape and size.
- I will celebrate all that my body can do for me each day.
- I will treat my body with respect, give it rest, fuel it with a variety of foods, exercise it moderately, and listen to what it needs.
- I will choose to resist our society's pressures to judge myself and other people on physical characteristics like body weight, shape, or size. I will respect people based on the depth of their character and the impact of their accomplishments.
- I will refuse to deny my body valuable nutrients by dieting or using weight-loss products. I will avoid categorizing foods as good or bad. I will not associate guilt or shame with eating certain foods. Instead, I will nourish my body with a balance of foods, listening and responding to what it needs.
- I will not use food to mask my emotional needs.
- I will not avoid participating in activities that I enjoy (such as swimming, dancing, enjoying a meal) simply because I am self-conscious about the way my body looks. I will recognize that I have the right to enjoy any activities regardless of my body shape or size.
- I will believe that my self-esteem and identity come from within.

Section 15.2

Body Image and Self-Esteem

This information was provided by TeensHealth, one of the largest resources online for medically reviewed health information written for parents, kids, and teens. For more articles like this one, visit www.TeensHealth.org, or www.KidsHealth.org.

I'm fat. I'm too skinny. I'd be happy if I were taller, shorter, had curly hair, straight hair, a smaller nose, bigger muscles, longer legs.

Do any of these statements sound familiar? Are you used to putting yourself down? If so, you're not alone. As a teen, you're going through a ton of changes in your body. And as your body changes, so does your image of yourself. Lots of people have trouble adjusting, and this can affect their self-esteem.

Why Are Self-Esteem and Body Image Important?

Self-esteem is all about how much people value themselves, the pride they feel in themselves, and how worthwhile they feel. Self-esteem is important because feeling good about yourself can affect how you act. A person who has high self-esteem will make friends easily, is more in control of his or her behavior, and will enjoy life more.

Body image is how a person feels about his or her own physical appearance. For many people, especially people in their early teens, body image can be closely linked to self-esteem. That's because as kids develop into teens, they care more about how others see them.

What Influences a Person's Self-Esteem?

Puberty

Some teens struggle with their self-esteem when they begin puberty because the body goes through many changes. These changes, combined with a natural desire to feel accepted, mean it can be tempting for people to compare themselves to others. They may compare themselves to the people around them or to actors and celebs they see on television, in movies, or in magazines.

But it's impossible to compare ourselves to others because the changes that come with puberty are different for everyone. Some people start developing early; others are late bloomers. Some get a temporary layer of fat to prepare for a growth spurt, others fill out permanently, and others feel like they stay skinny no matter how much they eat. It all depends on how our genes have programmed our bodies to act.

The changes that come with puberty can affect how both girls and guys feel about themselves. Some girls may feel uncomfortable or embarrassed about their maturing bodies. Others may wish that they were developing faster. Girls may feel pressure to be thin, but guys may feel like they don't look big or muscular enough.

Outside Influences

It's not just development that affects self-esteem, though. Lots of other factors (like media images of skinny girls and bulked-up guys) can affect a person's body image too.

Family life can sometimes influence a person's self-esteem. Some parents spend more time criticizing their children and the way they look than praising them. This criticism may reduce a person's ability to develop good self-esteem.

People may also experience negative comments and hurtful teasing about the way they look from classmates and peers. Sometimes racial and ethnic prejudice is the source of such comments. Although these comments often come from ignorance on the part of the person who makes them, sometimes they can affect a person's body image and self-esteem.

Healthy Self-Esteem

If you have a positive body image, you probably like and accept yourself the way you are. This healthy attitude allows you to explore other aspects of growing up, such as developing good friendships, growing more independent from your parents, and challenging yourself physically and mentally. Developing these parts of yourself can help boost your self-esteem.

A positive, optimistic attitude can help people develop strong self-esteem. For example, saying, "Hey, I'm human," instead of "Wow, I'm such a loser," when you've made a mistake. Or not blaming others when things don't go as expected.

Knowing what makes you happy and how to meet your goals can help you feel capable, strong, and in control of your life. A positive attitude and a healthy lifestyle (such as exercising and eating right) are a great combination for building good self-esteem.

Tips for Improving Your Body Image

Some people think they need to change how they look or act to feel good about themselves. But actually all you need to do is change the way you see your body and how you think about yourself.

The first thing to do is recognize that your body is your own, no matter what shape, size, or color it comes in. If you are very worried about your weight or size, check with your doctor to verify that things are okay. But it is no one's business but your own what your body is like — ultimately, you have to be happy with yourself.

Next, identify which aspects of your appearance you can realistically change and which you can't. Everyone (even the most perfect-seeming celeb) has things about themselves that they can't change and need to accept—like their height, for example, or their shoe size.

If there are things about yourself that you want to change and can (such as how fit you are), do this by making goals for yourself. For example, if you want to lose weight, make a plan to exercise every day and eat nutritious foods. Then keep track of your progress until you reach your goal. Meeting a challenge you set for yourself is a great way to boost self-esteem.

When you hear negative comments coming from within yourself, tell yourself to stop. Try building your self-esteem by giving yourself three compliments every day. While you're at it, every evening list three things in your day that really gave you pleasure. It can be anything from the way the sun felt on your face, the sound of your favorite band, or the way someone laughed at your jokes. By focusing on the good things you do and the positive aspects of your life, you can change how you feel about yourself.

Where Can I Go if I Need Help?

Sometimes low self-esteem and body image problems are too much to handle alone. A few teens may become depressed, lose interest in activities or friends, and even hurt themselves or resort to alcohol or drug abuse. If you're feeling this way, it can help to talk to a parent, coach, religious leader, guidance counselor, therapist, or an adult friend. A trusted adult—someone who supports you and doesn't bring you down—can help you put your body image in perspective and give you positive feedback about your body, your skills, and your abilities.

If you can't turn to anyone you know, call a teen crisis hotline (check the yellow pages under social services). The most important thing is to get help if you feel like your body image and self-esteem are affecting your life.

Section 15.3

Media's Impact on Body Image

This section begins with: "Media's Effect on Girls: Body Image and Gender Identity," For additional information, visit www.mediafamily.org or call toll-free 1-888-672-KIDS. It continues with excerpts from "Body Image and the Media: What do we know?"

Media's Effect on Girls: Body Image and Gender Identity

Did you know?

Gender identity begins in toddlerhood (identifying self as a girl or boy) with gender roles being assigned to tasks early in the preschool years (Durkin, 1998). A child's body image develops as the result of many influences:

- A newborn begins immediately to explore what her body feels like and can do. This process continues her whole life.
- A child's body image is influenced by how people around her react to her body and how she looks.
- A pre-adolescent becomes increasingly aware of what society's standards are for the "ideal body."

Media's Effect on Body Image

The popular media (television, movies, magazines) have, since World War II, increasingly held up a thinner and thinner body (and now ever more physically fit) image as the ideal for women. The ideal man is also presented as trim, but muscular.

- In a survey of girls nine and ten years old, 40% have tried to lose weight, according to an ongoing study funded by the National Heart, Lung and Blood Institute (*USA Today*, 1996).
- A 1996 study found that the amount of time an adolescent watches soaps, movies, and music videos is associated with their degree of body dissatisfaction and desire to be thin (Tiggemann and Pickering, 1996).
- One author reports that at age thirteen, 53% of American girls are "unhappy with their bodies." This grows to 78% by the time girls reach seventeen (Brumberg, 1997).
- In a study among undergraduates media consumption was positively associated with a strive for thinness among men and body dissatisfaction among women (Harrison and Cantor, 1997).
- Teen-age girls who viewed commercials depicting women who modeled the unrealistically thin-ideal type of beauty caused adolescent girls to feel less confident, more angry, and more dissatisfied with their weight and appearance (Hargreaves, 2002).
- In a study on fifth graders, ten year old girls and boys told researchers they were dissatisfied with their own bodies after watching a music video by Britney Spears or a clip from the television show "Friends" (Mundell, 2002).
- In another study on media's impact on adolescent body dissatisfaction, two researchers found that:
    1. Teens who watched soaps and television shows that emphasized the ideal body typed reported higher sense of body dissatisfaction. This was also true for girls who watched music videos.
    2. Reading magazines for teen girls or women also correlated with body dissatisfaction for girls.
    3. Identification with television stars (for girls and boys), and models (girls) or athletes (boys), positively correlated with body dissatisfaction (Hofschire and Greenberg, 2002).

Media's Effect on Gender Identity

Many children watch between two and four hours of television per day. The presence or absence of role models; how women, men, girls, and boys are presented; and what activities they participate in on the screen powerfully affect how girls and boys view their role in the world. Studies looking at cartoons, regular television, and commercials show that although many changes have occurred and girls, in particular have a wider range of role models, for girls "how they look" is more important than "what they do."

- In a 1997 study designed to study how children described the roles of cartoon characters, children (ages four to nine) "perceived most cartoon characters in stereotypical ways: boys were violent and active and girls were domestic, interested in boys, and concerned with appearances" (Thompson, 1997).

- In another study, three weeks of Saturday morning toy commercials were analyzed. Results found that:

  1. Fifty percent of the commercials aimed at girls spoke about physical attractiveness, while none of the commercials aimed at boys referenced appearance.

  2. Boys acted aggressively in 50% of the commercials aimed at them, while none of the girls behaved aggressively.

  3. With regard to work roles, no boys had unpaid labor roles, and girls were mainly shown in traditional female jobs or roles of unpaid labor (Sobieraj, 1996).

- Dr. Nancy Signorielli, Professor of Communications at the University of Delaware examined the types of media most often viewed by adolescent girls: television, commercials, films, music videos, magazines, and advertisements. While the study did find positive role models of women and girls using their intelligence and acting independently, the media also presented an overwhelming message that girls and women were more concerned with romance and dating (and it follows how they look), while men focus on their occupations (Signorielli, 1997).

Sources

Brumberg, J. J. (1997). *The Body project: An intimate history of American girls*. NY: Random House.

Durkin, K. and Nugent, B. (1998, March). Kindergarten children's gender-role expectations for television actors. *Sex Roles: A Journal of Research*, 38, 387–403.

Hargreaves, D. (2002). Idealized Women in TV Ads Make Girls Feel Bad. *Journal of Social and Clinical Psychology*, 21, 287–308.

Harrison, K. and Cantor, J. (1997). The relationship between media consumption and eating disorders. *Journal of Communication*, 47, 40–67.

Hofschire, L. J., and Greenberg, B. S. (2002). Media's impact on adolescents' body dissatisfaction. In J. D. Brown, J. R. Steele, and K. Walsh-Childers (Eds.), *Sexual Teens, Sexual Media*. NJ: Lawrence Erlbaum Associates, Inc.

Mundell, EJ. (2002, August 26). Sitcoms, Videos Make Even Fifth-Graders Feel Fat. Reuters Health (last visited 9/16/02).

Signorielli, N. (1997, April). Reflections of girls in the media: A two-part study on gender and media. Kaiser Family foundation and Children NOW (last visited 9/6/02).

Sobieraj, S. (1996). Beauty and the beast: toy commercials and the social construction of gender. American Sociological Association, *Sociological Abstracts*, 044.

Thompson, T. and Zerbinos, E. (1997). Television cartoons: Do children notice it's a boy's world? *Sex Roles: A Journal of Research*, 37, 415–433.

Tiggemann, M., and Pickering, A. S. (1996). Role of television in adolescent women's body dissatisfaction and drive for thinness. *International Journal of Eating Disorders*, 20, 199–203.

USA Today, (1996, August 12). p 01D.

Body Image and the Media: What Do We Know?

What do we know about body image?

- There is widespread negative body image among women.
- Body dissatisfaction is increasing among men and boys.
- Negative consequences of body dissatisfaction include the following:
    - decrease in self-esteem
    - increase in dieting
    - increase in cosmetic surgery
    - increase in use of anabolic steroids

- increase in compulsive over-exercise
- increase in eating disorders

What do we know about mass media?

- Mass media are pervasive in Western societies.
    - Most adults read newspapers daily.
    - Many women and girls (up to 83%) read fashion magazines.
    - Television is on seven hours per day with most individuals seeing three or four hours per day.
- Media promote thin ideals for women.
- Media increasingly promote muscular ideals for men.

Results of Correlational Studies of Naturally-Occurring Media Exposure

- Fashion magazine reading is related to body image for girls.
- Total television time is not related to anything for anyone.
- Watching soaps affected body image for boys and girls.
- Internalization of body image was the effect of watching soaps.
- Watching television for social learning or to escape the negative affect related to negative body image.

Longitudinal Studies of Media Exposure

- Very few longitudinal studies of actual media exposure have been done.
- Involvement with media and perceived media pressure to be thin predicts body dissatisfaction (Field et al., 2001; Stice, 2002).
- Free subscription to *Seventeen* magazine had no effect on body dissatisfaction (Stice, Spangler, and Agras, 2001).
- Change in magazine exposure is associated with change in eating disorder symptomatology (Vaughan, and Fouts, 2003).

Experimental Studies of Acute Media Exposure Findings

- Brief exposure to thin ideal images (magazine ads, television commercials, music videos) does result in increased body dissatisfaction.

- Meta-analytic review (Groesz et al., 2002) concluded "a small but relatively consistent" negative effect, with some women being particularly vulnerable.
- Thin idealized media images elicit social comparison, which mediates effects on body dissatisfaction.

Remember: Experiments demonstrate only immediate effects. A small study of 24 girls done by Hargreaves and Tiggemann in 2003 found that media responsiveness to thin-ideal television commercials at age 15 predicted an increase in body dissatisfaction and drive for thinness two years later.

Conclusions

Evidence that suggests that mass media impacts body dissatisfaction includes the following:

- self-reports from women and girls
- correlational studies that show association between media exposure and body dissatisfaction
- experimental studies which show negative effects in body dissatisfaction after acute exposure to media

Further evidence is needed through longitudinal or prospective studies over longer periods of time starting at younger ages.

Section 15.4

Body Dysmorphic Disorder

What is body dysmorphic disorder?

Body dysmorphic disorder (BDD) is a type of somatoform disorder, a mental illness in which a person has symptoms of a medical illness, but the symptoms cannot be fully explained by an actual physical disorder. People with BDD are preoccupied with an imagined physical defect or a minor defect that others often cannot see. People with this disorder see themselves as ugly and often avoid social exposure to others or turn to plastic surgery to try to improve their appearance.

BDD shares some features with eating disorders and obsessive-compulsive disorder. BDD is similar to eating disorders in that both involve a concern with body image. However, a person with an eating disorder worries about weight and the shape of the entire body, while a person with BDD is concerned about a specific body part. BDD is a long-term (chronic) disorder that affects men and women equally. It usually begins during the teen years or early adulthood.

Obsessive-compulsive disorder (OCD) is an anxiety disorder that traps people in endless cycles of thoughts and behaviors. People with OCD have recurring and distressing thoughts, fears, or images (obsessions) that they cannot control. The anxiety (nervousness) produced by these thoughts leads to an urgent need to perform certain rituals or routines (compulsions). With BDD, a person's preoccupation with the defect often leads to ritualistic behaviors, such as constantly looking in a mirror or picking at the skin. The person with BDD eventually becomes so obsessed with the defect that his or her social, work, and home functioning suffers.

The most common areas of concern for people with BDD include the following:

- skin imperfections—wrinkles, scars, acne, and blemishes
- hair—head or body hair or absence of hair
- facial features—very often the nose, but it also might involve the shape and size of any feature

Other areas of concern include the size of the penis, muscles, breasts, thighs, buttocks, and the presence of certain body odors.

What are the symptoms of BDD?

People with BDD have distorted views of themselves, which can lead to harmful or socially avoidant behaviors or repeated attempts to correct perceived problems through surgery. Some of the warning signs that a person might have BDD include the following:

- engaging in repetitive and time-consuming behaviors, such as looking in a mirror, picking at the skin, and trying to hide or cover-up the defect
- constantly asking for reassurance that the defect is not visible or too obvious
- repeatedly measuring or touching the defect
- experiencing problems at work or school, or in relationships due to the inability to stop focusing on the defect
- feeling self-conscious and not wanting to go out in public, or feeling anxious when around other people
- repeatedly consulting with medical specialists, such as plastic surgeons or dermatologists, to find ways to improve his or her appearance

What causes BDD?

The exact cause of BDD is not known. One theory suggests the disorder involves a problem with certain neurotransmitters in the brain. Neurotransmitters are chemicals that help nerve cells in the brain send messages to each other. The fact that BDD often occurs in people with other mental health disorders, such as major depression and anxiety, further supports a biological basis for the disorder.

Other factors that might influence the development of or trigger BDD include the following:

- experience of traumatic events or emotional conflict during childhood
- low self-esteem
- parents and others who were critical of the person's appearance

Pressure from peers and a society that equates physical appearance with beauty and value also can have an impact on the development of BDD.

How is BDD diagnosed?

The secrecy and shame that often accompany BDD make its diagnosis difficult. Most experts agree that many cases of BDD go unrecognized. People with the disorder often are embarrassed and reluctant to tell their doctors about their concerns. As a result, the disorder can go unnoticed for years or never be diagnosed. One red flag to doctors or family members is when patients repeatedly seek plastic surgery for the same or multiple perceived physical defects.

In diagnosing BDD, the doctor will begin his or her evaluation with a complete medical history and physical examination. If the doctor suspects BDD, he or she might refer the person to a psychiatrist or psychologist—health care professionals who are specially trained to diagnose and treat mental illnesses. The psychiatrist or psychologist makes a diagnosis based on his or her assessment of the person's attitude, behavior, and symptoms.

How is BDD treated?

Treatment for BDD likely will include a combination of the following therapies:

- **Psychotherapy:** This is a type of individual counseling that focuses on changing the thinking (cognitive therapy) and behavior (behavioral therapy) of a person with body dysmorphic disorder. The goal is to correct the false belief about the defect and to minimize the compulsive behavior.
- **Medicine:** Certain antidepressant medicines called selective serotonin reuptake inhibitors (SSRIs) are showing promising in treating body dysmorphic disorder.
- **Group and/or family therapy:** Family support is very important to treatment success. It is important that family members understand body dysmorphic disorder, and learn to recognize its signs and symptoms.

What are the complications associated with body dysmorphic disorder?

Social isolation can occur if the person becomes too self-conscious to go out in public. This also can have a negative impact on school or work. People with BDD also are at high risk for developing major depression, and the distress associated with the disorder puts people with BDD at high risk for suicide. Further, people with this disorder might undergo many surgical procedures in an attempt to correct their perceived defect.

What is the outlook for people with BDD?

The outlook is promising for people with BDD who receive and follow their treatment plan. The support of family members and other loved ones can help ensure that the person receives and stays with treatment, and might help to improve outcomes.

Can BDD be prevented?

There is no known way to prevent BDD. However, it might be helpful to begin treatment in people as soon as they begin to have symptoms. Teaching and encouraging healthy and realistic attitudes about body image also might help prevent the development or worsening of BDD. Finally, providing the person with an understanding and supporting environment might help decrease the severity of the symptoms and help him or her better cope with the disorder.

Section 15.5

Negative Body Image Related to Depression, Anxiety, and Suicide

Adolescents with negative body image concerns are more likely to be depressed, anxious, and suicidal than those without intense dissatisfaction over their appearance, even when compared to adolescents with other psychiatric illnesses, according to a study by researchers at Bradley Hospital, Butler Hospital, and Brown Medical School.

Researchers assessed the prevalence and clinical correlates of body image concerns including: body dysmorphic disorder (BDD), eating disorders (ED) such as bulimia or anorexia, and other clinically significant concerns over shape and/or weight in adolescent inpatients at Bradley Hospital, the nation's first psychiatric hospital for children and adolescents. Classic BDD is a preoccupation with an imagined physical defect in appearance or a vastly exaggerated concern about a minimal defect, like a crooked nose or imperfect complexion. Weight-related BDD, however, is classified as distressing and impairing preoccupations with one's weight and shape—for example, thinking one's thighs are too fat or one's waist is too big.

The study found that one-third of inpatient adolescents had problematic body image concerns, and that these patients were more severely ill than other adolescent inpatients in a number of important domains. Specifically, those with BDD and shape and/or weight preoccupations had significantly higher levels of depression, anxiety, and suicidality than other patients with no body image concerns. Those with eating disorders had significantly higher rates of depression than those without body image concerns.

"These findings underscore just how central feelings about one's appearance tend to be in the world of teenagers and how impairing these concerns can be," says lead author, Jennifer Dyl, Ph.D., with Bradley Hospital and Brown Medical School.

This is the first study to show that adolescents with BDD and with shape and/or weight preoccupations display higher levels of symptoms in areas like depression, anxiety, and suicidality, as compared to other adolescents presenting with psychiatric disorders such as behavioral, psychotic, or mood and anxiety disorders who do not have body image concerns.

"This is important because distressing and impairing body image concerns appear to be very prevalent among adolescents with psychiatric illnesses, and are related to a higher degree of distress and impairment," says author Jennifer Kittler, Ph.D. with Bradley Hospital and Brown Medical School.

An additional finding revealed that in addition to higher levels of depression, anxiety and suicidality, patients with shape and/or weight preoccupations expressed higher levels of dissociation (a coping style characterized by blocking out emotions), sexual preoccupation and/or distress, and post-traumatic stress disorder (PTSD), suggesting that such concerns may be related to the experience of past physical or sexual abuse. Interestingly, the authors found that the majority of the adolescents in the study were not actually overweight.

Two hundred and eight consecutively admitted patients (ages 12 to 17) on the adolescent inpatient unit of Bradley Hospital completed the *Body Dysmorphic Disorder Questionnaire* (BDDQ) as part of their admission evaluation. The questionnaire assesses the presence of BDD by asking whether respondents are very worried about how they look, think about their appearance problems a lot, and wish they could think about them less, and whether their main appearance concern is that they are not thin enough, or might become too fat. It also asks for the amount of time that they spend focusing on appearance concerns.

"We found that 6.7 percent of patients on the adolescent inpatient unit at Bradley Hospital met criteria for classic (non-weight-related) BDD, but that a much higher percentage (22.1 percent) exhibited distressing and impairing concerns with their weight and shape," says Kittler.

The study was published in the June 2006 issue of the journal of *Child Psychiatry and Human Development*.

Body Image Concerns Under-Recognized in Teens

These findings are especially concerning for treatment providers and parents, the authors say, because the majority of adolescents in this study were not receiving psychiatric treatment specifically targeted towards their body image problems. They were most commonly being treated for mood disorders, anxiety disorders, and posttraumatic stress disorder, and these body image preoccupations may well have been contributing to the events leading to their hospitalization.

"We have indeed seen a number of teens entering the hospital whose negative feelings about their appearance are a major influence on suicidal thoughts and even suicide attempts, a fact which is often initially not recognized by parents and even professionals," says Dyl.

The authors looked at whether individuals determined to have BDD via a self-report measure were diagnosed with BDD by their clinician. They found that only one of fourteen participants with definite or probable BDD was diagnosed with BDD in the clinical record.

"This is likely due to clinicians' lack of systematic questioning about BDD, as well as patients' embarrassment and reluctance to reveal their symptoms, which may be particularly characteristic of adolescents," they write.

The authors conclude that severe body image disturbances among adolescents are likely to be under-recognized and under-treated, and may be related to other forms of psychological distress (including depression and suicidality). They also note that since many adults presenting in psychiatric settings often report that preoccupation with their appearance first began in adolescence, it is all the more important to recognize and begin to treat body dysmorphic disorder and other body image concerns in the teenage years, to prevent the problem from becoming a more chronic condition.

Even in the absence of an eating disorder, the study finds that body image concerns can be impairing, preoccupying, and distressing for teens, taking up a great deal of mental energy and detracting from their quality of life. "Helping teens verbalize their negative feelings and concerns about their appearance is the first step in getting them to value themselves as individuals and recognize the importance of other non-weight, or non-appearance-based qualities and activities as contributors to their self-esteem and self-worth," Dyl explains.

Section 15.6

Parent's Body Image Affects Child's Body Image

"Body Image and Your Kids," National Women's Health Information Center, January 2006.

Body Image and Your Kids: Your Body Image Plays a Role in Theirs

"On a diet, you can't eat." This is what one five year old girl had to say in a study on girls' ideas about dieting. This and other research has shown that daughters are more likely to have ideas about dieting when their mothers diet. Children pick up on comments about dieting concepts that may seem harmless, such as limiting high-fat foods or eating less. Yet, as girls enter their teen years, having ideas about dieting can lead to problems. Many things can spark weight concerns for girls and impact their eating habits in potentially unhealthy ways including the following:

- having mothers concerned about their own weight
- having mothers who are overly concerned about their daughters' weight and looks
- natural weight gain and other body changes during puberty
- peer pressure to look a certain way
- struggles with self-esteem
- media images showing the ideal female body as thin

Many teenage girls of average weight think they are overweight and are not satisfied with their bodies. Having extreme weight concerns—and acting on those concerns—can harm girls' social, physical, and emotional growth. Actions such as skipping meals or taking diet pills can lead to poor nutrition and difficulty learning. For some, extreme efforts to lose weight can lead to eating disorders such as anorexia or bulimia. For others, the pressure to be thin can actually lead to binge eating disorder—overeating that is followed by extreme guilt. What's more, girls are more likely to further risk their health by trying to lose weight in unhealthy ways, such as smoking.

While not as common, boys are also at risk of developing unhealthy eating habits and eating disorders. Body image becomes an important issue for teenage boys as they struggle with body changes and pay more attention to media images of the ideal muscular male.

What You Can Do

Your children pay attention to what you say and do—even if it doesn't seem like it sometimes. If you are always complaining about your weight or feel pressure to change your body shape, your children may learn that these are important concerns. If you are attracted to new miracle diets, they may learn that restrictive dieting is better than making healthy lifestyle choices. If you tell your daughter that she would be prettier if she lost weight, she will learn that the goals of weight loss are to be attractive and accepted by others.

Parents are role models and should try to follow the healthy eating and physical activity patterns that you would like your children to follow—for your health and theirs. Extreme weight concerns and eating disorders, as well as obesity, are hard to treat. Yet, you can play an important role in preventing these problems for your children.

These steps can help your child develop a positive body image and relate to food in a healthy way:

- Make sure your child understands that weight gain is a normal part of development, especially during puberty.
- Avoid negative statements about food, weight, and body size and shape.
- Allow your child to make decisions about food, while making sure that plenty of healthy and nutritious meals and snacks are available.
- Compliment your child on her or his efforts, talents, accomplishments, and personal values.
- Restrict television viewing, and watch television with your child and discuss the media images you see.

- Encourage your school to enact policies against size and sexual discrimination, harassment, teasing, and name-calling; support the elimination of public weigh-ins and fat measurements.
- Keep the communication lines with your child open.

Chapter 16

Ethnic and Cultural Risks of Eating Disorders

Chapter Contents

Section 16.1

Boys and Girls of All Ethnic Groups Susceptible to Eating Disorders

This section includes: "At Risk: All Ethnic and Cultural Groups," and an excerpt titled "How Adults Can Help," from "African American Girls," Office on Women's Health, updated October 2005.

At Risk: All Ethnic and Cultural Groups

Many people believe that eating disorders commonly occur among affluent white females. Although the prevalence of these disorders elsewhere in the population is much lower, an increasing number of males and minorities are also suffering from eating disorders.[1]

Girls and boys from all ethnic and racial groups may suffer from eating disorders and disordered eating. The specific nature of the most common eating problems, as well as risk and protective factors, may vary from group to group, but no population is exempt.[2] Research findings regarding prevalence rates and specific types of problems among particular groups are limited, but it is evident that disturbed eating behaviors and attitudes occur across all cultures.[3]

Large percentages of African American, American Indian, and Hispanic females are overweight. Being overweight is a risk factor for engaging in disordered eating behaviors. Risk factors and incidence rates for eating disorders can vary dramatically among subgroups of a specific population.

Cultural Norms and Eating Disorders

Cultural norms regarding body size can play a role in the development of eating disorders. In Western cultures, the ideal female body is thin. Membership in ethnic groups and cultures that do not value a thin body may protect girls from body dissatisfaction and weight concerns. However, young people who identify with cultures that prefer larger body sizes may be at risk for becoming overweight or obese. Research also suggests that women who think they are smaller than the body size favored by their cultural group may be at risk for binge eating.[4]

Reporting of Eating Disorders

Eating disorders among ethnically and culturally diverse girls may be underreported due to the lack of population-based studies that include representatives from these groups. The perception that non-white females are at decreased risk may also contribute to the lack of detection. Stereotyped body images of ethnically diverse women (such as petite Asian American, heavier African American) can also deter detection. In addition, for some ethnic and cultural groups, seeking professional help for emotional problems is not a common practice.

Girls of different ethnic and cultural groups often receive treatment for the accompanying symptoms of an eating disorder, such as depression or malnutrition, rather than for the eating disorder itself. When these girls are finally diagnosed as having an eating disorder, the disorder (especially anorexia), tends to be more severe. This problem is exacerbated by the difficulty they may have in locating culturally sensitive treatment centers.

School Personnel Can Help

Here are some ideas for school personnel to promote healthy eating and attitudes:

- Provide students with diverse role models of all shapes and sizes who are praised for their accomplishments, not their appearance.
- Invite community representatives to speak about specific cultural attitudes toward food preferences, dietary practices, and body image.
- Provide students with information on the relationship between nutrition and overall health.
- Gather and disseminate culturally sensitive materials on eating disorders, puberty, and other adolescent health issues.
- Conduct media literacy activities that allow students to examine critically how magazines, television, and other media—including those targeting specific cultural groups—present the concept of beauty.
- Encourage children and adolescents of all ethnic and cultural groups to exercise and participate in sports and other athletic activities.

- Advocate for a safe and respectful school environment that prohibits gender, cultural, and racial stereotyping as well as sexual harassment, teasing, and bullying.

How Adults Can Help

As an adult working with adolescent girls, you can help identify those at risk, promote an environment that discourages negative body image and disordered eating behaviors, and prevent eating disorders among this population. Here are some ideas:

1. Provide adolescents with information on the benefits of healthy eating and regular physical activity.
2. Educate families about eating disorders.
3. Do not tolerate sexual harassment or teasing about another person's body shape or weight.
4. Conduct media literacy activities that explore the images of thinness as beauty in television, magazines, and advertisements targeting girls.
5. Incorporate culturally appropriate materials, curricula, and interventions, as well as ethnically diverse role models.
6. Refer girls who want to achieve a healthy weight to appropriate health professionals for information on healthy weight management strategies.
7. Help girls understand cross-cultural differences regarding body image and weight control.
8. Assist parents in accessing appropriate health care services.

Definitions

Anorexia nervosa is self-starvation. People with this disorder eat very little even though they are thin. They have an intense and overpowering fear of body fat and weight gain.

Binge eating disorder means eating large amounts of food in a short period of time, usually alone, without being able to stop when full. The overeating or bingeing is often accompanied by feeling out of control and then depressed, guilty, or disgusted.

Bulimia nervosa is characterized by cycles of binge eating and purging, either by vomiting or taking laxatives or diuretics (water pills). People with bulimia have a fear of body fat even though their size and weight may be normal.

Disordered eating refers to troublesome eating behaviors, such as restrictive dieting, bingeing, or purging, which occur less frequently or are less severe than those required to meet the full criteria for the diagnosis of an eating disorder.

Over-exercising is exercising compulsively for long periods of time as a way to burn calories from food that has just been eaten. People with anorexia or bulimia may overexercise.

End Notes

1. Practice Guidelines for Eating Disorders. *American Psychiatric Association Practice Guidelines.* Washington, DC: American Psychiatric Press, 1993.
2. Smolak L, Striegel-Moore RH. Challenging the myth of the golden girl: Ethnicity and eating disorders. In RH Striegel-Moore, L Smolak (eds.), *Eating Disorders: Innovative Directions in Research and Practice*. Washington, DC: APA, 2001.
3. Ibid.
4. Perez M, Joiner Jr. TE. Body image dissatisfaction and disordered eating in Black and White women. *International Journal of Eating Disorders*, 33, 342–350, 2003.
5. Thompson, B.W. *A Hunger So Wide and So Deep*. Minneapolis, MN: University of Minnesota Press, 1994, p. 29.
6. Crute, S. (ed). *Health and Healing for African-Americans*. Emmaus, PA: Rodale Press, Inc., 1997, p. 92.

Section 16.2

African American Girls

Office on Women's Health, updated October 2005.

African American girls are at risk. Many people believe that only White girls are affected by eating disorders. In reality, no ethnic or socioeconomic group is immune to the dangers of this disease. Cases of eating disorders among diverse racial ethnic groups, including African Americans, are often underreported because studies typically do not include ethnically diverse populations.

After White Americans, African Americans comprise the ethnic and cultural group about which most studies on eating disorders are available. While there are no incidence or prevalence rates for eating disorders in the African American population, recent studies are providing clinical accounts of eating disorders in African American women.[1]

Numerous studies have documented a high rate of eating disorder behaviors and risk factors, including body dissatisfaction among African American women.[2] More specifically, research demonstrates that binge eating and purging is at least as common among African American women as White women.[3] Unfortunately, little work has been undertaken regarding differences in presentation of symptoms, cultural-specific risk factors, and effective treatment methods for African Americans.

The belief that African American women do not experience eating disorders contributes to the lack of identification of eating disorder problems among this population. Since the early detection of an eating disorder is very important for its successful treatment, this misperception can result in serious health problems for African American girls.

African American Girls Are Not Immune to the Pressure to Be Thin

The African American culture is more accepting of diverse body sizes and seems to favor a broader beauty ideal. This tolerance may help protect some African American girls from body dissatisfaction and low self-image.[4] However, as Black girls approach adolescence, they become more concerned with thinness.[6] Studies indicate that when African American girls experience social pressure to be thin, they express the same type of body dissatisfaction and drive for thinness as White girls.[7]

Adolescents from middle-class African American families may be particularly vulnerable to the influence of the White beauty ideal. *Essence*, a magazine that caters to African American women, regularly runs stories on body size anxiety and eating disorders.[8] A survey of its readers indicated that African American women appear to have at least equal levels of abnormal eating attitudes and behaviors as White women.[9] Studies indicate that Blacks who identify with mainstream culture exhibit more eating problems, including dieting and fear of fat.[10]

Media targeting African Americans and other racial and ethnic and cultural groups in this country are increasingly embracing the beauty as thinness ideal. Black female stars in the music, film, and fashion industries are just as thin as their White counterparts.[11] The influence of these role models may contribute to body dissatisfaction and weight control behaviors among African American girls.

High Rates of Obesity

African American women experience high rates of obesity, a risk factor for eating disorders. Although the preference for a larger body size may help protect African American girls from body dissatisfaction and dieting, it can encourage obesity, which is also a risk factor for eating disorders. Black women are more than three times as likely as White women to be obese. Black women and girls are also less likely to exercise than their White counterparts.[12]

African American families with low incomes are particularly at risk for obesity, due in part to a diet of food that is high in fat.[13] African American girls are not likely to be heavier than White girls during childhood; but after adolescence their body mass index (BMI) surpasses that of White adolescent girls.[14] This increase may be partially due to metabolic differences, since Black women and girls tend to have lower resting expenditures than their White counterparts.[15] Weight gain during adolescence may contribute to body dissatisfaction, disordered eating, and eating disorders.

Black women who consider themselves heavier than the body ideal preferred by their culture, particularly those who are obese, may experience weight dissatisfaction and a desire to be thinner. Overweight women are more likely than women of normal weight to experience teasing, criticism, or discrimination.[16] These pressures may contribute to binge eating, a disorder that is more common among people who have a history of obesity than others.[17] People with this disorder eat a large amount of food in a short period of time and feel a lack of control over their eating.

Women who consider themselves thinner than the ideal may also be at risk for binge eating. These women may experience body dissatisfaction along with a desire to gain weight in order to approximate their cultural ideal.[18]

Binge Eating Rates

African American women have high rates of binge eating. The first large-scale epidemiological study of recurrent binge eating in Black women indicated that Black women were as likely as White women to report that they had engaged in binge eating and self-induced vomiting.[19] More specifically, a greater number of Black women than White women reported that they had used laxatives, diuretics, or fasting to control their weight. Almost twice as many Black women as White women were identified as probable eating disorder cases. Recurrent binge eaters, regardless of race, are overweight and report a greater number of psychiatric symptoms that those who do not binge eat frequently.[20] In addition, some researchers believe that racial prejudice and discrimination toward African Americans result in a sense of isolation that may contribute to binge eating.[21] Health professionals must be prepared to respond to this specific health risk behavior and to address possible eating disorders in African American adolescents.[3]

End Notes

1. Crago, M., Shisslak, C.M., & Estes, L.S. Eating disturbances among American minority groups. *International Journal of Eating Disorders*, 1996, vol. 19, p. 239.

2. Field, A.E., Colditz, G.A., & Peterson, K.E. Racial/ethnic and gender differences in concern with weight and bulimic behavior among adolescents. *Obesity Research*, 1997, vol. 5, p. 239; and Dounchis, J.Z., Hayden, H.A., & Wilfley, D.E. Obesity, eating disorders, and body image in ethnically diverse children and adolescents. In Thompson, J.K., & Smolak, L. (eds.). *Body image, eating disorders, and obesity in youth: Assessment, prevention, and treatment*. Washington, DC: American Psychological Association, 2001, pp. 67–98.

3. Striegel-Moore & Smolak, The influence of ethnicity on eating disorders in women. In Eisler, R.M., & Hersen, M. (eds.). *Handbook of gender, culture, and health*. Mahwah, NJ: Lawrence Erlbaum Associates, 2000, pp. 227–253; and Dounchis et al., 2001.
4. Striegel-Moore, R., & Smolak, L. The role of race in the development of eating disorders. In Smolak, L., Levine, M.P., & Striegel-Moore. *The developmental psychopathology of eating disorders: Implications for research, treatment, and prevention*. Mahwah, NJ: Lawrence Erlbaum, 1996.
5. Crute, S, ed. *Health and healing for African Americans*. Emmaus, PA: Rodale Press, Inc., 1997.
6. Striegel-Moore & Smolak, 1996.
7. Striegel-Moore et al., 2000.
8. Brumberg, J.J. *The body project: An intimate history of American girls*. New York: Random House, 1997.
9. Pumariega, A.J., Gustavson, C.R., Gustavson, J.C., Motes, P.S., & Ayers, S. Eating attitudes in African-American women: The Essence Eating Disorders Survey. Eating Disorders: *The Journal for Treatment and Prevention*, 1994, vol. 2, pp. 5–16.
10. Brumberg, 1997. (Note: The term “Black” is used when the studies cited included groups other than African Americans, such as girls or women from the Caribbean).
11. Pumariega et al., 1994.
12. Striegel-Moore & Smolak, 1996.
13. Dounchis et al., 2001.
14. Kumanyika, S. Obesity in black women. *Epidemiologic Review*, 1987, vol. 9, pp. 31–50.
15. Yanovski, S. Z., Reynolds, J. C., Boyle, A. J., & Yanovski, J. A. Resting metabolic rate in African-American and Caucasian girls. *Obesity Research*, 1997, vol. 5, pp. 321–325.
16. Striegel-Moore & Smolak, 1996.
17. Ibid.
18. Perez, M., Joiner Jr., T. E. Body image dissatisfaction and disordered eating in Black and White women. *International Journal of Eating Disorders*, 2003, vol. 33, pp. 342–350.

19. Striegel-Moore, R.H., Wilfley, D.E., Pike, K.M., Dohm, F., & Fairburn, C.G. Recurrent binge eating in black American women. *Archives of Family Medicine*, January 2000, vol. 9, no. 1, pp. 83–87.

20. Striegel-Moore et al., 2000.

21. In Thompson, B.W. *A hunger so wide and so deep: A multiracial view of women's eating problems*. Minneapolis, MN: University of Minnesota Press, 1994.

Section 16.3

American Indian and Alaska Native Girls

Office on Women's Health, updated October 2005.

Studies indicate that American Indian and Alaska Native adolescents are increasingly exhibiting disturbed eating behaviors and using unhealthy practices to control their weight. Disordered eating has been shown to occur more often among this group than among White, Hispanic, African American, or Asian girls.[1]

In a large study involving 545 Hispanic, American Indian, and White high school students, American Indians consistently scored the highest on each of seven items representing disturbed eating behaviors and attitudes. This study, which included 129 American Indians, also found very high rates of self-induced vomiting and binge eating among this group.[2] Other small studies of American Indian adolescents also indicate high rates of disordered eating, including dieting and purging.[3]

American Indian Youth Express High Levels of Body Dissatisfaction

The largest and most comprehensive survey undertaken to date on the health status of Native American youths living on or near reservations involved 13,454 American Indians and Alaska Natives in grades 7 through 12. Approximately 41% of the adolescents reported feeling overweight, 50% were dissatisfied with their weight, and 44% worried about being overweight.[4]

Among American Indian youth, body dissatisfaction is associated with unhealthy weight control behaviors. In the Indian Adolescent Health Study previously mentioned, almost half of the girls and one-third of the boys had been on weight loss diets in the past year with 27% reporting self-induced vomiting and 11% reporting the use of diet pills. Girls who reported feeling overweight were more likely to engage in unhealthy weight control practices.[5]

Acculturation May Increase Vulnerability

Increased contact with the mainstream culture that equates thinness with beauty seems to contribute to higher rates of disordered eating among American Indian girls. In one study, anorexic Navajo girls from Arizona were more likely to come from upwardly mobile families who moved off the reservation.[6] In a second study, child and adolescent members of a tribe were much more likely to prefer thinner body sizes than elder tribe members.[7] Eating disturbances have also been associated with racism, social isolation, low self-worth, and pressure to look a certain way, which may increase vulnerability to developing eating disorders.[8]

Obesity Is Also a Risk Factor

American Indians have a high prevalence of obesity in all age groups and both sexes.[9] Children who are obese are at risk for developing eating disorders and for becoming obese adults. More specifically, being overweight is a risk factor for eating disturbances in ethnically diverse women.[10] Attention needs to be focused, therefore, on the prevention and treatment of obesity in American Indian adolescents.

Disordered Eating and Other Harmful Behaviors

Among American Indian youth, disordered eating is linked to other harmful behaviors. The Indian Adolescent Health Study indicates that disordered eating behaviors are related to other health compromising behaviors.[11] Frequent dieting and purging among American Indian girls was associated with a wide range of risk factors, such as high emotional stress, binge eating, alcohol and tobacco use, thoughts and attempts of suicide, delinquent behaviors, and physical and sexual abuse.[12] The early identification of disordered eating behaviors may help uncover risk factors for other unhealthy and possibly more serious behaviors among these adolescents.

End Notes

1. Crago, M., Shisslak, C.M., & Estes, L.S. Eating disturbances among American minority groups: a review. *International Journal of Eating Disorders* 1996, vol. 19, pp. 239–248.
2. Smith, J.E., & Krejci, J. Minorities join the majority: eating disturbances among Hispanic and Native American youth. *International Journal of Eating Disorders* 1991, vol. 10, pp. 179–186.
3. Snow, J.J., & Harris, M.B. Disordered eating in Southwestern Pueblo Indians and Hispanics. *Journal of Adolescence* 1989, vol. 12, pp. 329–336; and Rosen, L.W., Shafer, C.L., Drummer, G.M., Cross, L.K., Deuman, G.W., & Malmberg, S.R. Prevalence of pathogenic weight-control behaviors among Native American women and girls. *International Journal of Eating Disorders* 1988, vol. 7, pp. 807–811.
4. Story, M., French, .SA., Neumark-Sztainer, D., Downes, B., Resnick, M.D., & Blum, R.W. Psychosocial and behavioral correlates of dieting and purging in Native American adolescents. *Pediatrics* April 1997, vol. 99, no. 4, p. e8.
5. Ibid.
6. Yates, A. Current perspectives on the eating disorders: History, psychological and biological aspects. *Journal of the American Academy of Child* and Adolescent Psychiatry 1989, vol. 28, pp. 813–828.
7. Stevens, J., Story, M., Becenti, A., French, S.A., Gittelsohn, J., Going, S.B., Juhaeri, L. S., & Murray, D.M. Weight-related attitudes and behaviors in 2 fourth grade American Indian children. *Obesity Research* 1999, vol. 7, no.1, pp. 34–42.
8. Crago et al., 1996.
9. Welty, T. Health implications of obesity in American Indians and Alaska Natives. *American Journal of Clinical Nutrition* 1991, vol. 53, pp. 16165–16205.
10. Crago et al., 1996.
11. Story, M., French, S.A., Resnick, M., & Blum, R.W., Ethnic/racial differences in dieting behaviors and body image perceptions in adolescents. *International Journal of Eating Disorders* 1995, vol. 18, no. 2, pp. 173–179.
12. Story et al., 1995; and Story et al, 1997.

Section 16.4

Asian and Pacific Islander Girls

Office on Women's Health, updated October 2005.

Many people believe that only White girls are affected by eating disorders. In reality, no ethnic or socioeconomic group is immune to the dangers of this disease. Studies typically do not include ethnically diverse populations; therefore, cases of eating disorders among diverse racial ethnic groups, including Asian Americans, are often underreported. In addition, many Asian Americans equate psychological problems with weakness and shame; therefore, women and girls may avoid seeking treatment.[1]

The term Asian American/Pacific Islander refers to the more than seven million people from 28 Asian countries and 25 Pacific Island cultures in the U.S. The largest subgroups are Chinese, Filipino, Japanese, Asian Indians, Koreans, and Vietnamese. Hawaiians comprise the largest subgroups of Pacific Islanders (58%), followed by residents of Samoa, Guam, and Tonga. Each subgroup has its own history, language, and culture.[6]

Asian American Girls Express High Levels of Body Dissatisfaction

Many Asian American girls struggle with self-esteem and identity based largely on issues of attractiveness.[2] Research that included Asian American girls reported that often they are as concerned or more concerned than White girls about their weight and shape.[3]

In a study of more than 900 middle school girls in northern California, Asian American girls reported greater body dissatisfaction than White girls. Among the leanest 25% of girls, Asian girls reported significantly more dissatisfaction than White girls.[4]

Recent research on Asian Americans suggests that body dissatisfaction is increasing due to the promotion of the Western beauty ideal.[5] One study, for example, reported that Japanese Americans desired to be taller, weigh less, and have larger busts and smaller waists and hips.[7] Some researchers believe that racism and sexism may contribute to negative feelings among Asian American women regarding their physical features, such as eye and nose shape, skin color, straight hair, and short stature.[8] Eyelid and nose reconstruction are the most popular types of surgery requested by Asian American women.[9]

Perfectionism and Need for Control Can Also Contribute to Eating Disorders

Asian Americans are often perceived as the model minorities and are expected to be successful and high achieving. Asian American girls may try to seek power and identity through the pursuit of a physically ideal body. The drive to become the perfect Asian woman can lead to perfectionism, which is linked to eating disorders, particularly anorexia.[10] In addition, the cultural value of saving face, which promotes a façade of control, may also contribute to disordered eating or eating disorders.[11]

Acculturation May Increase Vulnerability

Adapting to a new culture creates a set of stressors that for Asian American and immigrant girls may cause confusion about identity, including gender roles. For example, an adolescent girl raised by her family to be obedient and demure may experience emotional turmoil in a Western culture that prizes independence and individualism.[12] For Asian American girls, acculturation can lead to feelings of isolation, low self-esteem, and the devaluation of native cultural identity, which can increase their vulnerability to eating disorders.[13]

Highly acculturated Chinese females are more likely to report bulimic behaviors and a drive for thinness than those who stay closer to their family values. One report found that the more acculturated Asian American girls were at greatest risk for adopting the dysfunctional behaviors of White American society, including poor eating habits and accepting media messages regarding standards of beauty.[14]

Obesity Is a Risk Factor

Rates of obesity are very high for some Asian/Pacific Islanders, such as Hawaiians and Samoans.[15] Overweight and obesity are risk factors for disordered eating behaviors, such as bingeing and purging. Dieting for weight loss is also associated with the development of eating disorders and other unhealthy behaviors, including skipping meals and diet-binge cycles.[16] One study, in fact, revealed that binge eating was more prevalent in Asian American than White females.[17]

End Notes

1. Hall, C.C. Asian eyes: Body image and eating disorders of Asian and Asian American Women. *Eating Disorders: The Journal of Treatment and Prevention* 1995, vol. 3, no. 1, pp. 8–18.
2. Root, M.P.P. Disordered eating in women of color. *Sex Roles* 1990, vol. 22, pp. 525–536.
3. Field, A.E., Colditz, G.A., & Peterson, K.E. Racial/ethnic and gender differences in concern with weight and bulimic behavior among adolescents. *Obesity Research* 1997, vol. 5, pp. 447–454; French, S.A., Story, M., Neumark-Sztainer, D., Downes, B., Resnick, M., & Blum, R. Ethnic differences in psychosocial and health behavior correlates of dieting, purging, and binge eating in a population-based sample of adolescent females. *International Journal of Eating Disorders* 1997, vol. 22, pp. 315–322; and Story, M., French, S.A., Resnick, M., & Blum, R.W., Ethnic/racial differences in dieting behaviors and body image perceptions in adolescents. *International Journal of Eating Disorders* 1995, vol. 18, no. 2, pp. 173–179.
4. Robinson, T.N., Killen, J.D., Litt, I.F., Hammer, L.D., Wilson, D.M., Haydel, K.F., Hayward, C., & Taylor, C.B. Ethnicity and body dissatisfaction: Are Hispanics and Asian girls at increased risk for eating disorders? *Journal of Adolescent Health*, Dec. 1996, vol. 19, no. 6, pp. 384–93.
5. Hall, 1995.
6. U.S. Census Bureau. *Resident population estimates of the United States by sex, race, and Hispanic origin*. Washington, DC: Author, 1990.
7. Hall, 1995.
8. Root, 1995.
9. Hall, 1995.
10. Hall, 1995.
11. Hall, 1995.
12. Hall, 1995.
13. Hall, 1995.
14. Hall, 1995.

15. World Health Organization. *Obesity: prevention and managing the global epidemic: Report of a WHO consultation on obesity*. WHO/NUT/NCD/98.1. Geneva, Switzerland: Author, 1998.

16. Patton, G.C. Eating disorders: Antecedents, evolution and course. *Annals of Medicine* 1992, vol. 24, pp. 281–285.

17. Story et al., 1995.

18. Wax, E. Immigrant girls are starving to be American, studies find. *Washington Post*, March 6, 2000, B01.

Section 16.5

Latina Girls

Office on Women's Health, updated October 2005.

Many people believe that only White girls are affected by eating disorders. In reality, no ethnic or socioeconomic group is immune to the dangers of this disease. Studies typically do not include ethnically diverse populations; therefore, cases of eating disorders among Hispanics are often underreported. Research on eating disorders among Latina girls is limited. However, recent studies indicate that Latina girls are expressing the same concerns about body weight as White girls and that many are engaging in disordered eating behaviors, including dieting and purging, to lose weight.

The terms Hispanic or Latino encompass diverse groups who immigrated to the U.S. Among the largest Hispanic populations in this country are Mexican Americans, Puerto Ricans, and Cuban Americans. The Hispanic population is growing faster than any other ethnic group in this country; it has more than doubled in the past 20 years. By the year 2020, it is estimated that Hispanics will be the single largest minority group in the U.S. Hispanics are predominantly young, with more than one in three being under the age of 18.

The myth that Latinas do not experience eating disorders contributes to the lack of identification of the disease among this population. Since the early detection of an eating disorder is very important for its successful treatment, this misperception can result in serious health problems for Latina girls.

Although this section addresses eating disorders among Latinas in general, these disorders will affect each subgroup of Latinas in a different way. There is no single Latino standard regarding body size and eating patterns. In addition, within each cultural group, socioeconomic status may also affect the risks for developing eating disorders. For example, Latinas from families with low incomes may face a greater risk for obesity, while those from higher income families may be at a higher risk for dieting to try to fit in with their middle or upper middle class peers.

Hispanic Girls Express High Levels of Body Dissatisfaction

Studies show that Latina girls express the same or greater concerns about their body shape and weight as White females.[1] In a study of more than 900 middle school girls in northern California, Hispanic girls reported higher levels of body dissatisfaction than any other group. Among the leanest 25% of girls, both Hispanic and Asian girls reported significantly more dissatisfaction than White girls.[2]

Media targeting Latinas, including Hispanic television and magazines, are increasingly reinforcing the ideal of thinness as beauty. For example, although Mexicans have traditionally preferred a larger body size for women, many Mexican American women are idealizing and desiring a thinner figure than the one they currently have.[3] For all racial and ethnic groups, body dissatisfaction is strongly linked with eating disorders.[4]

Low Self-Esteem and Depression Can Contribute to Eating Disorders

Research suggests that Latina girls are at a high risk for mental health problems such as depression.[6] Latina girls also report lower self-esteem and less body satisfaction than girls from other racial and ethnic backgrounds. Studies indicate that as Latinas move from elementary to middle school and on to high school, they may suffer a greater loss of self-esteem than White or Black girls.[7]

Hispanic girls may lack not only the high sense of self-worth demonstrated by many African American girls, but also the academic opportunities available to some White girls.[8] In addition, some Latinas may experience prejudice and discrimination based on ethnicity, language, and social status, which can contribute to low self-esteem and depression.

Obesity a Risk Factor for Eating Disorders

Hispanics, like African Americans, experience high rates of obesity. Among girls ages 5–17, Black and Hispanic girls have been found to have the highest measures of body mass index (BMI), exceeding those of White and Asian girls.[9] They are also less likely to exercise than their White counterparts.[10] Hispanic children consume the most fast food of all ethnic groups. Research has shown that high fat diets greatly contribute to the high rates of obesity among low-income Hispanic families.[11]

For Latinas, as well as women from other ethnic and cultural groups, obesity is linked with weight dissatisfaction and with a desire to be thinner. Overweight women are more likely than women of normal weight to experience teasing, criticism, or discrimination.[12] Obesity is also a risk factor for binge eating. In a recent study of 31 middle schools and high schools in Minnesota, binge eating was more prevalent among Hispanic girls than among those of other cultural backgrounds.[13]

Dieting and Purging Are Widely Prevalent among Hispanic Girls

Studies indicate that Latinas and White girls have similar rates of disordered eating behaviors.[14] In fact, Latina girls seem to be particularly at risk for two types of disordered eating behaviors: dieting and purging. Hispanic high school students have been found to have rates of bulimia comparable to those of Whites. Along with Black girls, Latinas have been found to use laxatives more frequently than girls from other racial groups.[15]

Acculturation May Increase Vulnerability

For Latinas and other groups, acculturation can have an impact on body size preference and body image. Heaviness is seen as a sign of affluence and success in some traditional Hispanic cultures; but as Hispanics acculturate to the standards of beauty in this country, they may seek to achieve thinner bodies.[16] Hispanic women born in the U.S. are more likely to prefer a smaller body size. Those who immigrate after age 17 are less likely to desire a thin body.[17]

High levels of acculturation are associated not only with a drive for thinness but also with less healthy eating behaviors. As a result, second and third generation Hispanic adolescents are more likely to be obese than their first generation peers.[18] Girls who are influenced by more than one race or culture may experience anxiety and confusion about their identity that may also contribute to disturbed eating behaviors.

End Notes

1. Striegel-Moore, R.H., & Smolak, L. The influence of ethnicity on eating disorders in women. In Eisler, R.M., & Hersen, M. (eds.). *Handbook of gender, culture, and health*. Mahway, NJ: Lawrence Erlbaum Associates, 2000, pp. 227–253.
2. Robinson, T.N., Killen, J.D., Litt, I.F., Hammer, L.D., Wilson, D.M., Haydel, K.F., Hayward, C., & Taylor, C.B. Ethnicity and body dissatisfaction: Are Hispanics and Asian girls at increased risk for eating disorders? *Journal of Adolescent Health*, Dec. 1996, vol. 19, no. 6, pp. 384–93.
3. Dounchis, J.Z., Hayden, H.A., & Wilfley, D.E. Obesity, eating disorders, and body image in ethnically diverse children and adolescents. In Thompson, J.K., & Smolak, L. (eds.). *Body image, eating disorders, and obesity in children and adolescents: Theory, assessment, treatment, and prevention.* Washington, DC: American Psychological Association, 2001, pp. 67–98.
4. Striegel-Moore & Smolak, 2000.
5. In Thompson, B.W. *A hunger so wide and so deep: A multiracial view of women's eating problems*. Minneapolis, MN: University of Minnesota Press, 1994.
6. Nichter, M., Vuckovic, N., & Parker, S. The looking good, feeling good program: A multi-ethnic intervention for healthy body image, nutrition, and physical activity. In Piran, N., Levine, M.P., & Steiner-Adair, C. (eds.). *Preventing eating disorders: A handbook of interventions and special challenges*, 1999, pp. 175–193.
7. Striegel-Moore & Smolak, 2000.
8. Orenstein, P. Schoolgirls: Young women, self-esteem, and the confidence gap. New York: Doubleday, 1994.
9. Dounchis et al., 2001.

10. Ibid.

11. Ibid.

12. Striegel-Moore, R., & Smolak, L. The role of race in the development of eating disorders. In Smolak, L., Levine, M.P., & Striegel-Moore. *The developmental psychopathology of eating disorders: Implications for research, treatment, and prevention.* Mahwah, NJ: Lawrence Erlbaum, 1996.

13. Neumark-Sztainer, D., Croll, J., Story, M., Hannan, P. J., French, S. A., & Perry, C. Ethnic/racial differences in weight-related concerns and behaviors among adolescent girls and boys. Findings from Project EAT. *Journal of Psychosomatic Research*, 2002, 53, pp. 963–974.

14. Smith, J.E., & Krejci, J. Minorities join the majority: Eating disturbances among Hispanic and Native American youth. *International Journal of Eating Disorders*, 1991, vol. 9, pp. 179–186.

15. Dounchis et al., 2001.

16. Kempa, M.L., & Thomas, A.J. Culturally sensitive assessment and treatment of eating disorders. *Eating Disorders*, 2000, vol. 8, pp. 17–30.

17. Lopez, E., Blix, G. G., & Blix, A. G. (1995). Body image of Latinas compared to body image of non-Latina White women. Health Values: *The Journal of Health Behavior, Education & Promotion*, 1995, vol. 19, no. 6, pp. 3–10.

18. Dounchis et al., 2001.

Chapter 17

Eating Disorder Risk Throughout the Life Cycle

During a plenary session at the 2004 International Conference on Eating Disorders, in Orlando, four eating disorders experts explored risk factors for development of eating disorders throughout the lifespan.

Dr. Leann Birch, Distinguished Professor at The Pennsylvania State University, University Park, Pennsylvania, described individual and familial risk factors identified in an ongoing longitudinal study. The study has followed 197 two-parent families and their 5-year-old daughters; the girls are now 13 and will be followed until they are 15 years old.

The family environment is particularly important for kids, Dr. Birch said, noting that parents often determine control of the eating environment by controlling portion sizes and second helpings. After this, media exposure may lead children to seek out certain foods. Parents' attempts to restrict certain foods usually backfire.

"Restricting access to snack foods high in fat and sugar leads to enhanced preferences for those foods, increased attention to those foods, and when the foods are present, increased intake of those foods," said Dr. Birch. Negative self-evaluation about eating those restricted foods has been reported among preschoolers as young as three to five years of age.

"2004 International Conference on Eating Disorders Panel Examines Risk for Eating Disorders Throughout the Life Cycle." Reprinted with permission from *Eating Disorders Review*, July/August 2004.

Feeding practices also play a role in the development of unhealthy eating habits—for example, a child's weight might be interpreted by parents in ways that influence their regular feeding practices, particularly restricting foods, and this could have an impact on a child's eating pattern. The parents' own eating patterns and weight play a role both in terms of the environment they are providing for kids and in terms of the genetics they bring to the situation, she added. According to Dr. Birch, development of dieting, overeating, and girls' self-evaluations are influenced by early weight status because, at least in middle-class America, weight tends to trigger certain kinds of parenting behavior, particularly restricted feeding practices.

Eating in the Absence of Hunger

Dr. Birch stated that one behavioral measure of disordered eating among young girls is eating in the absence of hunger. This is really a response to the presence of palatable food, she said; in addition, it captures some characteristics of binge eating. Some kids consume relatively large amounts of food in a short period, and during debriefing sessions they report feeling that their eating is somewhat out of control, similar to binge eating. This is promoted by restrictions imposed by others, not self-imposed restriction.

Girls who are overweight and have mothers who use a lot of restriction show the greatest increases in eating in the absence of hunger, said Dr. Birch. She added that even at age five, overweight status increases the risk for maladaptive eating attitudes, including eating in the absence of hunger, which the researchers view as a possible precursor of binge eating.

Maternal Weight

Among normal-weight mothers, maternal restriction is not related to daughters' eating in the absence of hunger and is not related to change in body mass index (BMI). Dr. Birch noted that about 65% of the mothers in her study are overweight, and the researchers have seen that maternal restriction in this group is quite strongly related to eating in the absence of hunger over time and to daughters' increases in body mass index (BMI).

Dr. Birch said that among middle class white girls, early overweight increases risk for at least some sorts of maladaptive eating. In her study, there was greater eating in the absence of hunger, negative self-evaluations of overeating, elevated weight concerns, elevated body dissatisfaction, early dietary restraint, and greater weight gain across middle childhood among those who were overweight at an early age.

One area that needs more study, according to Dr. Birch, is determining which factors are mediating risks conferred by early overweight. Dr. Birch concluded, "Overweight parents create eating and activity environments that are quite different from those of normal-weight parents. If we understood this better we'd have some good ideas about prevention."

Risk Factors for Eating Disorders

Studying risk factors for eating disorders helps clarify diagnoses and classifications, and also helps direct treatment, according to Ruth Striegel-Moore, Ph.D., Professor and Chair of Psychology at Wesleyan University, Middletown, Connecticut. She reported initial findings from the *National Growth and Health Study, Wave II*, sponsored by the National Institute of Mental Health and the National Institute of Diabetes, Digestive and Kidney Diseases. The goal of the one-year study is to identify eating disorders early by identifying high-risk populations.

One important question was whether ethnicity was a marker for an eating disorder. In the study, white women were significantly more likely than black women to meet diagnostic criteria for an eating disorder. There was also a significant difference in the number of women who met criteria for bulimia nervosa—four black women and twenty-three white women. Less marked ethnic differences were reported for binge eating disorder (BED). However, there were twice as many white women as black women who met diagnostic criteria for BED. Vomiting was much more common among white women, and very uncommon among black women, but no difference was seen in laxative abuse between white and black women. Dr. Striegel-Moore also reported that white women have an earlier onset compared to black women.

Three High-Risk Groups Identified

The researchers identified three high-risk groups: (1) those who had high weight concerns before age 14; (2) those who were less concerned about weight than the first group but who reported high perceived stress; and (3) a subgroup whose weight concerns and perceived stress were lower than those among group one or two, but who reported behavior conduct problems before age 14.

Research on risk factors so far has focused primarily on the question of whether a given variable is a risk factor for an eating disorder. Dr. Striegel-Moore emphasized that her group has attempted to show that for different subgroups different variables or different combinations of variables may increase risk. She also added a word of caution about matching treatment based on a risk profile, pointing out that treatment matching, particularly in substance abuse and alcoholism, has been spectacularly unsuccessful.

Finally, she said, "Our results underscore that we need to be very careful regarding our messages on what factors contribute to risk. When we design prevention programs or public education campaigns, simple messages may make for compelling sound bytes but they don't necessarily make for compelling truths. Our ultimate goal is to reduce suffering due to an eating disorder. We will succeed if we resist the urge to provide single-factor answers and pursue treatment interventions that keep in mind the complexity of the etiology of eating disorders."

Psychosocial and Genetic Risk Factors

Andreas Karwautz, M.D., Professor at the University Clinic of Neuropsychiatry, Vienna, Austria, described the value of the concept of non-shared environment for development of anorexia nervosa (AN) and the opportunities to use a discordant sister-pair design for clarifying risk for developing anorexia nervosa.

Discordant sister-pairs have several advantages for study over non-related case-control studies. These include similar socioeconomic status, living region, family structure, parental socio-academic status, and religious orientation of parents, for example. He added that this structure allows researchers to replicate and investigate found associations in between family studies using a within-family design. Genetic markers can also be included in the same samples and then researchers can focus at the end on gene environment interaction to help clarify the etiology and pathogenesis of these disorders.

Dr. Karwautz shared recent unpublished data on 120 sister-pairs discordant for anorexia nervosa studied in Vienna, London, and Barcelona. Fifty-five of the pairs had restricting type AN and 70 had binge-purge type AN. The two groups were similar in age and the age of onset of AN was around 16 years of age.

Among the 58 sister-pairs with restricting AN, researchers found that personal environment was significant and enhances the risk of developing AN. Some common features in this group included negative self-evaluation, perfectionism, no male friends, parental control, rivalry with the unaffected sister, and a need to compete with the sister's appearance and shape. Minor but still significant factors included shyness and premorbid anxiety disorders.

Among the 62 sister-pairs with binge-purge type AN, personal environment and dieting contributed to the development of their disorder. Girls with this subtype of AN had a number of the same characteristics as those with the restricting type of AN, but were also distressed by parental arguments, and life events the year before their illness developed. Two main items emerged in the dieting domain: repeated critical comments by family members about weight, shape, and eating, and teasing about shape and weight and appearance,

Vulnerability factors have a significant influence on the development of AN of both subtypes, while dieting vulnerability factors contributed to the development of binge-purge type AN. Data from the multicenter study adds new information about personal vulnerability in the two AN subtypes. Dr. Karwautz reported that personal vulnerability (for example, negative self-evaluation and perfectionism) is highly relevant to restricting AN. Internalizing behavior problems in childhood influence the development of restricting AN, and internalizing and externalizing problems contribute to the development of binge-purge AN.

The next step, said Dr. Karwautz, will be handling candidate gene data together with psychological and psychosocial risk factors in order to develop a gene environment interaction model of development of AN.

Older Adults with Eating Disorders

"We don't think much about eating disorders in older women, as illustrated by the fact that prevalence rates are often calculated and presented only for young women," Marika Tiggemann, Ph.D., Professor of Psychology at Flinders University, Adelaide, Australia, told the plenary session audience. Eating disorders can be a chronic condition throughout life, she said.

Dr. Tiggemann added that body dissatisfaction is one of the few robust and consistent risk factors that have been identified among adult women with eating disorders. She noted that it is reasonable to expect that body image would become more negative as women age—every year moves women further from the thin and youthful ideal.

Lifelong Dissatisfaction

Women seem to be more dissatisfied or negative about their bodies at all ages, according to Dr. Tiggemann. In fact, she said, body dissatisfaction seems to be remarkably stable across the entire female lifespan. Women aged 30 to 75 years show substantial levels of body dissatisfaction, just like younger women. Between 55% and 95% of women express dissatisfaction with their bodies, and chronic dieting may pose a particular health risk for women as they age.

Risk factors may have differing degrees of influence across the life span. An area that receives too little attention, according to Dr. Tiggemann, includes the biological developmental milestones in a woman's life. All women have the potential to increase fat deposition through the operation of sex hormones, and this physiological factor moves a women further from the thin and youthful ideal. The effects of menopause on body image haven't been studied very much, she said. At menopause, weight typically becomes redistributed and women's shapes change, so they have larger waists, becoming rounder in shape. Pregnancy also brings body dissatisfaction during the postpartum period.

Need for a Better Definition of Body Image

Dr. Tiggemann states that there is a need for a broader definition of body image. When talking about younger women and the predictors of disordered eating, it makes sense to focus on body size and weight; but for older women other aspects might come into play. She mentioned a study in 1996 when older women were asked to select the most attractive physical feature of an older person. Their answer was posture. This demonstrates that there may be many other aspects of body image among older women that are missed because of concentrating on young women and generalizing from what we know about younger women, she added.

Chapter 18

Kids and Eating Disorders

Eating is a fact of life. We need to eat to live. And, if you're a kid, you need to eat healthy food—and enough of it—so that you grow and develop the way you should. But for some people, food becomes the enemy. Because they're worried about being fat, they severely limit what they eat or make themselves vomit right after eating.

Doing this can make someone very sick. People have even died due to eating disorders and the harm it did to their bodies. Why, then, would anyone do it? There isn't just one answer.

Some people point to the perfect-looking bodies of models, movie stars, and sports stars. We all see these images on magazine covers and on television. That may be a piece of the puzzle, but it's more than that. Many people admire the way these people look, but don't change their eating habits so severely. Anyone can have an eating disorder, though they most often affect girls and women. Let's find out more about eating disorders.

What Is Anorexia?

You've probably heard about anorexia, which is also called anorexia nervosa (say: ah-nuh-rek-see-uh nur-voh-suh). With this eating

---

This chapter begins with "Kids and Eating Disorders," provided by KidsHealth, one of the largest resources online for medically reviewed health information written for parents, kids, and teens. For more articles like this one, visit www.KidsHealth.org, or www.TeensHealth.org. © 2004 The Nemours Foundation. "Boys and Eating Disorders," is from the Office on Women's Health, 2004.

disorder, the person is so afraid of being fat, he or she almost stops eating. People who have anorexia nervosa are obsessed with food, sometimes measuring it and weighing it or counting calories. They eat only very small amounts and may exercise for hours every day to burn off the calories.

A person who has anorexia might lose weight or maintain a weight that's too low for his or her height. Someone who normally weighs 100 pounds might drop to 80 pounds or even lower. But no matter how thin people with anorexia get, they think they are fat.

People with anorexia often have depression or anxiety. Anorexia is a difficult illness because it's not easily understood—no one really knows what causes it, it's difficult to treat, and it tends to be a long-term condition. To help someone with anorexia, evaluation and treatment are usually necessary. Some of the symptoms include:

- dropping lots of weight;
- denying feeling hungry;
- exercising excessively;
- feeling fat;
- withdrawing from social activities.

What Is Bulimia?

Instead of starving themselves, people who have bulimia nervosa (say: boo-lee-mee-uh nur-voh-suh) will binge and purge. That means they eat a huge amount of food in two hours or so (like a tub of ice cream, then a big bag of chips, then a box of cookies), then secretly try to get rid of it by vomiting or taking laxatives.

Girls who have bulimia often feel depressed and helpless. Bingeing and purging is a way for them to have some control. Kids sometimes develop bulimia when something new or stressful enters their life, like a move to a new town or a parent's divorce. Kids with bulimia can sometimes be harder to spot than kids with anorexia because their weight is often in the range of what's normal. Some of the symptoms that kids with bulimia might have include:

- making excuses to go to the bathroom immediately after meals;
- eating huge amounts of food without weight gain;
- using laxatives or diuretics;
- withdrawing from social activities.

What Causes Eating Disorders?

There really is no single cause for an eating disorder. Most girls who develop anorexia do so between the ages of 11 and 14 (although it can start as early as age 7), and there are many reasons why. Some kids just don't feel good about themselves on the inside and this makes them try to change the outside. They might be depressed or stressed about things and feel as though they have no control over their lives. They see what they eat (or don't eat) as something that they can control.

Sometimes girls involved in certain sports, like ballet, gymnastics, and ice-skating, might feel they need to be thin to compete. Girls who model also might be more likely to develop an eating disorder. All of these girls know their bodies are being watched closely, and they may develop an eating disorder in an attempt to make their bodies more "perfect."

When boys develop eating disorders, it's usually because they're in a sport that emphasizes weight, such as wrestling. Wrestlers compete based on weight classes. For instance, there's one class for 75-pound boys and another for 80-pound boys. Wrestlers feel pressure to stay in their weight class, which is called "making weight." Eating disorders also may run in families, which means if someone in your family has one, you might be at risk for developing one, too. A kid may be more likely to develop an eating disorder if a parent is overly concerned with the kid's appearance or if the parent isn't comfortable with his or her own body.

Can Somebody Catch an Eating Disorder?

You can't catch an eating disorder from someone the way you can catch a cold. But the friends who you spend time with can influence you and how you see yourself. If your friends think the most important thing is to be thin, you may start to feel that way, too. And if they are doing unhealthy things to be thin, you might feel pressure to do so, too.

Eating Disorders Do Damage

No one wants to be overweight, but your body needs some fat to work properly. If a person's weight gets too low, he or she will start having health problems. If this goes on too long, those problems may be severe and can cause death.

Someone who has anorexia may do damage to the heart, liver, and kidneys. A girl with anorexia may be delayed in getting her period or stop getting her period. Breathing, blood pressure, and pulse also may drop—this is the body's way of shifting into low gear to protect itself. Fingernails may break and hair may fall out, too.

Kids with anorexia often do not feel well—they suffer from headaches, dizziness, and concentration difficulties. They also may become withdrawn and moody. And people with anorexia will feel chilly even in warm weather because they don't have enough body fat to keep them warm.

For kids with bulimia, the most serious problem is that their purging means a loss of potassium, an important nutrient. Potassium is found in foods such as bananas, tomatoes, beans, and melons. Too little potassium can lead to dangerous heart problems.

Someone who has bulimia might have problems with tooth decay because puke is acidic. Too much throwing up also can cause "chipmunk cheeks," when glands in the cheeks actually expand. People with bulimia also may damage their stomachs and kidneys and have constant stomach pain. Like girls with anorexia, girls with bulimia may also stop menstruating.

In addition to the health problems, a person who has an eating disorder is probably not having much fun. Typically, these kids miss out on good times because they pull away from friends and keep to themselves. They don't want to have pizza with their friends or enjoy a birthday party.

Signs of Eating Disorders

Weight loss is not normal, or healthy, for kids. If you or someone you know is losing weight, you should talk with a parent or trusted adult. If a friend is skipping meals, becomes obsessed with how many calories are in food, or starts exercising all the time, these may be additional signs something is wrong. With bulimia, the signs would be someone who's spending a lot of money on food, then hiding out to binge and purge. Because kids with eating disorders feel guilty and depressed, they may start abusing alcohol and drugs, too.

Getting Well

Admitting there's a problem and getting help is the first step to getting back to being healthy again. It's important to take action as soon as possible. The person may see a doctor, a dietitian, and a counselor or therapist. Together, the team can help the person achieve the goals of reaching a healthy weight, following a nutritious diet, and feeling good about himself or herself again.

Boys and Eating Disorders

Boys Can and Do Develop Eating Disorders

Eating disorders often are seen as problems affecting only girls. However, studies suggest that hundreds of thousands of boys are experiencing these disorders. Although bulimia is not common among males, one in four preadolescent cases of anorexia have been found to occur in boys.[1] Studies also suggest that boys may be as likely as girls to develop binge eating disorder.[2]

Males make up the majority of people identified as having muscle dysmorphia, a type of body image disorder characterized by extreme concern with becoming more muscular.[3] People with this disorder, which has been found to occur among bodybuilders, see themselves as puny despite being very muscular, and are likely to use steroids and other drugs to gain muscle mass.

Factors Associated with Eating Disorders Are Similar for Males and Females

The characteristics of males with eating disorders are similar to those seen in females with eating disorders.[4] These factors include low self-esteem, the need to be accepted, an inability to cope with emotional pressures, and family and relationship problems. Homosexuality also appears to be a risk factor for males because it may include them in a subculture that places a premium on appearance.[5]

Both males and females with eating disorders are likely to experience depression, substance abuse, anxiety disorders, and personality disorders. However, substance abuse is more common among males than females with eating disorders.[6] Male patients with eating disorders have been found to be more severely affected by osteoporosis than female patients.[7]

The signs and symptoms of eating disorders are similar for boys and girls. It is important to look for these signs and symptoms in your interactions with boys.

Students of all ethnic and cultural groups are vulnerable to developing eating disorders. For example, Black and Hispanic boys have been found to be more likely to binge eat than Caucasian boys.[8]

Boys and Body Image

> "If there was one thing I'd change about my looks, I'd change my weight. I get poked at and yelled at all the time. I'd like to be mostly skinny instead of fat. Then I wouldn't be teased any

more, and I'd be able to do things I can't do now. I could run faster and be more active. I could swim, knowing I don't have all that weight on me."[9]—Mike, age 10.

Boys may try to lose fat and gain muscle to improve body image and/or athletic performance. While the female body ideal is thin, the male ideal is lean, V-shaped, and muscular. Unlike girls, who generally want to lose weight, boys are equally divided between those who want to lose weight and those who want to gain weight. Boys who consider themselves overweight want to lose weight, while those who think they are too thin want to gain weight. All want to be more muscular.[11]

Boys may try to lose fat and/or gain muscle for many reasons. Some of these are: to avoid being teased about being fat; to improve body image; to increase strength and/or to improve athletic performance in wrestling, track, swimming, or other sports. Overweight boys are at a higher risk for dieting than those who are not overweight.[12] Boys who think they are too small, on the other hand, may be at a greater risk than other boys for using steroids or taking untested nutritional supplements such as protein and creatine to increase muscle mass.

Diagnosing Eating Disorders in Boys

Boys are less likely to be diagnosed early with an eating disorder. Doctors reportedly are less likely to make a diagnosis of eating disorders in males than females.[13] Other adults who work with young people and parents also may be less likely to suspect an eating disorder in boys, thereby delaying detection and treatment. A study of 135 males hospitalized with an eating disorder noted that the males with bulimia felt ashamed of having a stereotypically female disorder, which might explain their delay in seeking treatment.[14] Binge eating disorder may go unrecognized in males because a male who overeats is less likely to provoke attention than a female who overeats.[15]

What Can Adults Do?

- Communicate openly about body image issues using messages that support acceptance of body diversity, discourage disordered eating, and promote self-esteem.
- Do not tolerate teasing and bullying in school, particularly when focused on a boy's body size or masculinity.

- Conduct media literacy activities that explore the extremely lean and muscular body shape as the cultural ideal and that build skills to resist such messages.
- Develop policies that prohibit student athletes from engaging in harmful weight control or bodybuilding measures.
- Connect young men with positive role models who will encourage personal growth and development.

Action Figures Are Bulking Up

A recent study noted that some of the most popular male action figures have grown extremely muscular over time.[10] Researchers compared action toys today—including GI Joe and Star Wars' Luke Skywalker and Hans Solo—with their original counterparts. They found that many action figures have acquired the physiques of bodybuilders, with particularly impressive gains in the shoulder and chest areas. Some of the action toys have not only grown more muscular but have also developed increasingly sharp muscle definition, such as rippled abdominals. As noted in the study, if the GI Joe Extreme were 70 inches in size, he would sport larger biceps than any bodybuilder in history.

End Notes

1. Bryant-Waugh R, Lask B. Childhood-onset eating disorders. In CG Fairburn, KD Brownell (eds.), *Eating disorders and obesity: A comprehensive handbook*, 2nd ed. New York: Guilford Press, 2002, pp. 210–214.
2. Andersen AE. Eating disorders in males. In CG Fairburn, KD Brownell (eds.), *Eating disorders and obesity: A comprehensive handbook*, 2nd ed. New York: Guilford Press, 2002, pp. 188–192.
3. Pope HG, Gruber AJ, Choi P, Olivardia R, Phillips KA. Muscle dysmorphia: an under-recognized form of body dysmorphic disorder. *Psychosomatics*, 38, 548–557, 1997.
4. Carlat DJ, Camargo CA, Herzog DB. Eating disorders in males: A report on 135 patients. *American Journal of Psychiatry*, 154(9), 1127-1132, 1997.
5. Andersen, Eating disorders in males, 2002.
6. Ibid.

7. Ibid.

8. Field AE, Colditz GA, Peterson KE, Racial/ethnic and gender differences in concern with weight and in bulimia behaviors among adolescents. *Obesity Research*, 5, 1997, pp. 447–454; Marcus MD, Kalarchian MA. Binge eating in children and adolescents. *International Journal of Eating Disorders*, 34, S47–57, 2003.

9. Bode J. Food Fight: *A Guide to Eating Disorders for Preteens and Their Parents*. New York: Aladdin, 1998, p. 35.

10. Pope HG, Olivardia, R. Gruber A, Borowiecki J. Evolving ideals of male body image as seen through action toys. *International Journal of Eating Disorders*, 26, 65–72, 1999.

11. Andersen, 2002.

12. Andersen, AE. Eating disorders in males: Critical questions. In R Lemberg (ed.), *Controlling Eating Disorders with Facts, Advice, and Resources*. Phoenix, AZ: Oryx Press, 1992, pp. 20–28.

13. Andersen, 1992.

14. Carlat et al., 1997.

15. Andersen, 2002.

Chapter 19

Young Adults and Eating Disorders

Chapter Contents

Section 19.1

Eating Disorders in Adolescents

Excerpts reprinted from *Journal of Adolescent Health*, Vol. 33, Issue 6, Eating Disorders in Adolescents: Position Paper of the Society for Adolescent Medicine by Golden, N.H., Katzman, D.K., Kreipe, R.E., Stevens, S.L., Sawyer, S.M., Rees, J., Nicholls, D., and Rome, E.S., pages 496–503.

Eating disorders are complex illnesses that are affecting adolescents with increasing frequency. They rank as the third most common chronic illness in adolescent females, with an incidence of up to 5%. Three major subgroups are recognized: a restrictive form in which food intake is severely limited (anorexia nervosa); a bulimic form in which binge eating episodes are followed by attempts to minimize the effects of overeating via vomiting, catharsis, exercise, or fasting (bulimia nervosa); and a third group in which all the criteria for anorexia nervosa or bulimia nervosa are not met. The latter group, often called "eating disorder not otherwise specified" or EDNOS, constitutes the majority of patients seen in referral centers treating adolescents. Eating disorders are associated with serious biological, psychological, and sociological morbidity and significant mortality. Unique features of adolescents and the developmental process of adolescence are critical considerations in determining the diagnosis, treatment, and outcome of eating disorders in this age group. This position statement represents a consensus from Adolescent Medicine specialists from the United States, Canada, United Kingdom, and Australia regarding the diagnosis and management of eating disorders in adolescents. In keeping with the practice guidelines of the American Psychiatric Association and the American Academy of Pediatrics, this statement integrates evidence-based medicine, where available.

Diagnosis

Diagnostic criteria for eating disorders such as those found in the *Diagnostic and Statistical Manual of Mental Disorders, Fourth Edition (DSM-IV)* are not entirely applicable to adolescents. The wide variability in the rate, timing, and magnitude of both height and weight gain during normal puberty, the absence of menstrual periods in early puberty along with the unpredictability of menses soon after menarche, limit the application of those formal diagnostic criteria to adolescents. Many adolescents, because of their stage of cognitive development, lack the psychological capacity to express abstract concepts such as self-awareness, motivation to lose weight, or feelings of depression. In addition, clinical features such as pubertal delay, growth retardation, or the impairment of bone mineral acquisition may occur at subclinical levels of eating disorders. Younger patients may present with significant difficulties related to eating, body image, and weight control habits without necessarily meeting formal criteria for an eating disorder. The American Academy of Pediatrics has identified conditions along the spectrum of disordered eating that still deserve attention in children and adolescents. It is essential to diagnose eating disorders in the context of the multiple and varied aspects of normal pubertal growth, adolescent development, and the eventual attainment of a healthy adulthood, rather than merely applying formalized criteria.

Medical Complications

No organ system is spared the effects of eating disorders. The physical signs and symptoms occurring in adolescents with an eating disorder are primarily related to weight-control behaviors and the effects of malnutrition. Most of the medical complications in adolescents with an eating disorder improve with nutritional rehabilitation and recovery from the eating disorder, but some are potentially irreversible. Potentially irreversible medical complications in adolescents include: growth retardation if the disorder occurs before closure of the epiphyses; loss of dental enamel with chronic vomiting; structural brain changes noted on cerebral tomography, magnetic resonance imaging and single-photon computerized tomography studies; pubertal delay or arrest; and impaired acquisition of peak bone mass, predisposing to osteoporosis and increased fracture risk. These features underscore the importance of immediate medical management, ongoing monitoring, and aggressive treatment by physicians who understand adolescent growth and development.

Nutritional Disturbances

Nutritional disturbances are a hallmark of eating disorders and are related to the severity, duration, and timing of dysfunctional dietary habits. Significant dietary deficiencies of calcium, vitamin D, folate, vitamin B_{12}, and other minerals are found. Inadequate intake of energy (calories), protein, calcium, and vitamin D are especially important to identify since these elements are crucial to growth and attainment of peak bone mass. Moreover, there is evidence that adolescents with eating disorders may be losing critical tissue components (such as muscle mass, body fat, and bone minerals) during a phase of growth when dramatic increases in these elements should be occurring. Detailed assessment of the young person's nutritional status forms the basis of ongoing management of nutritional disturbances.

Psychosocial and Mental Health Disturbances

Eating disorders that occur during adolescence interfere with adjustment to pubertal development and mastery of developmental tasks necessary to becoming a healthy, functioning adult. Social isolation and family conflicts arise at a time when families and peers are needed to support development. Issues related to self-concept, self-esteem, autonomy, and capacity for intimacy should be addressed in a developmentally appropriate and sensitive way. Given that adolescents with eating disorders usually live at home and interact with their families on a daily basis, the role of the family should be explored during both evaluation and treatment with particular attention given to the issues of control and responsibility for the adolescent within the family context.

Studies emphasize a frequent association between eating disorders and other psychiatric conditions. Important findings include a lifetime incidence of affective disorders (especially depression) of 50%–80% for both anorexia nervosa and bulimia nervosa; a 30%–65% lifetime incidence of anxiety disorders (especially obsessive-compulsive disorder and social phobia) for anorexia nervosa and bulimia nervosa; a 12%–21% rate of substance abuse for anorexia nervosa and a 9%–55% rate for bulimia nervosa. Estimates of comorbid personality disorders among patients with eating disorders range from 20% to 80%. All patients should therefore be carefully evaluated for comorbid psychiatric conditions.

Indications for Hospitalization in an Adolescent with an Eating Disorder

One or more of the following justify hospitalization:

- severe malnutrition (weight less than or equal to 75% average body weight for age, sex, and height)

- dehydration
- electrolyte disturbances (hypokalemia, hyponatremia, hypophosphatemia)
- cardiac dysrhythmia
- physiological instability
  - severe bradycardia (heart rate less than 50 beats/minute daytime; less than 45 beats/minute at night)
  - hypotension (less than 80/50 mm Hg)
  - hypothermia (body temperature less than 96° F)
  - orthostatic changes in pulse or blood pressure
- arrested growth and development
- failure of outpatient treatment
- acute food refusal
- uncontrollable binging and purging
- acute medical complications of malnutrition (for example, syncope, seizures, cardiac failure, pancreatitis)
- acute psychiatric emergencies (such as suicidal ideation, acute psychosis)
- comorbid diagnosis that interferes with the treatment of the eating disorder (for example, severe depression, obsessive-compulsive disorder, severe family dysfunction)

Treatment Guidelines

Eating disorders are associated with complex biopsychosocial issues that under ideal circumstances are best addressed by an interdisciplinary team of medical, nutritional, mental health, and nursing professionals who are experienced in the evaluation and treatment of eating disorders and who have expertise in adolescent health.

Various levels of care should be available to adolescents with eating disorders (outpatient, intensive outpatient, partial hospitalization, inpatient hospitalization, or residential treatment centers). Criteria, that justify inpatient treatment were initially published by the Society for Adolescent Medicine in 1995 and are in agreement with the recent revision of the American Psychiatric Association practice guidelines for the treatment of patients with eating disorders, the recently published American Academy of Pediatrics policy statement on identifying and treating eating disorders, and the American Dietetic Association position on nutrition intervention in the treatment of eating disorders. In children and adolescents, physiologic or physical evidence of medical compromise can be found even in the absence of significant weight loss. Not infrequently, inpatient treatment becomes necessary because of failure of outpatient treatment. In severely malnourished patients, the risk of the "refeeding syndrome" should be avoided through gradual increase of caloric intake and close monitoring of weight, vital signs, fluid shifts, and serum electrolytes (including phosphorus, potassium, magnesium, and glucose). Parenteral feeding is very rarely necessary. Short-term nasogastric feeding may be necessary in those hospitalized with severe malnutrition. There is no evidence to support the long-term role of nasogastric tube feeding.

Optimal duration of hospitalization has not been established, although there are studies that have shown a decreased risk of relapse in patients who are discharged closer to ideal body weight compared to patients discharged at very low body weight. The overall goals of treatment are the same in a medical or psychiatric inpatient unit, a day program, or outpatient setting: to help the adolescent achieve and maintain both physical and psychological health.

The expertise of the treatment team who work specifically with adolescents and their families is as important as the setting in which they work. Traditional settings, such as a general psychiatric ward, may be less appropriate than an adolescent medical unit, if the latter is available. Some evidence suggests a good outcome for patients treated on adolescent medicine units. On a specialized psychiatric inpatient eating disorders unit for adolescents, Strober et al. showed that 76% of patients met criteria for full recovery. This prospective study had a 10–15 year follow-up period and also showed that time to recovery was protracted, ranging from 57–79 months. Smooth transition from inpatient to outpatient care can be facilitated by an interdisciplinary team that provides continuity of care in a comprehensive, coordinated, developmentally-oriented manner. Given the rate of relapse, recurrence, crossover (change from anorexia nervosa to bulimia nervosa or vice versa) and comorbidity, treatment should be of sufficient frequency, intensity, and duration to provide effective intervention.

Mental health evaluation and treatment is crucial for all adolescents with eating disorders. The treatment may need to continue for several years. To date, there is a paucity of research on the treatment of adolescents with anorexia nervosa. Evidence-based research supports family-based treatment for adolescents and a manual has been published describing one of the treatment methods. Cognitive behavioral therapy is used in adults with anorexia nervosa but has not been evaluated in adolescents. There is some recent evidence to suggest that although antidepressants are of no clinical value in promoting weight gain, fluoxetine may be helpful in reducing the risk of relapse of symptoms in older adolescents with anorexia nervosa whose weight has been restored. The most effective treatment for older adolescents with bulimia nervosa is cognitive behavioral therapy that focuses on changing the specific eating attitudes and behaviors that maintain the eating disorder. Antidepressants have been shown to reduce binge eating and purging by 50% to 75%. In addition, interpersonal psychotherapy and dialectical behavior therapy have also demonstrated some beneficial effect in older adolescents with bulimia nervosa. Medications may also be helpful in older adolescents with a co-morbid depression or obsessive or compulsive symptoms.

The optimum treatment of the osteopenia associated with anorexia nervosa remains unresolved. Current treatment recommendations include weight restoration with the initiation or resumption of menses, calcium (1300–1500 milligrams (mg)/day) and vitamin D (400 international units (IU)/day) supplementation, and carefully monitored weight-bearing exercise. While hormone replacement therapy is frequently prescribed to treat osteopenia in anorexia nervosa, there are no documented prospective studies that have demonstrated the efficacy of hormone replacement therapy beyond standard treatment. Hormone replacement therapy can cause growth arrest in the adolescent who has not yet completed growth. The monthly hormone-induced withdrawal bleeding can also be misinterpreted by the adolescent as return of normal menstrual function and adequate weight restoration, and therefore interfere with the treatment process.

Barriers to Care

Interdisciplinary treatment of established eating disorders can be time-consuming, relatively prolonged, and extremely costly. Lack of care or insufficient treatment can result in chronicity with major medical complications, social or psychiatric morbidity, and even death. Barriers to care include lack of insurance, coverage with inadequate scope of benefits, low reimbursement rates, and limited access to health care specialists and appropriate interdisciplinary teams with expertise in eating disorders, which may be due either to geography or insurance limitations. In addition to these extrinsic barriers, patients and families often demonstrate ambivalence or resistance to the diagnosis or treatment, which threatens active engagement in the recovery process.

In most insurance plans, the scope of benefits for treatment of eating disorders is currently insufficient. The labeling of the disorder as a purely psychiatric illness by some insurance companies usually limits the ability of health care providers to meet the medical, nutritional, and psychological needs of patients in either the medical or psychiatric setting. In addition, some insurance companies limit the number of hospitalizations permitted per year, restrict the number of outpatient visits per year, establish lifetime caps on coverage, and preclude payment of some medical practitioners. Many plans limit the number of nutrition visits to one per year and the number of mental health visits to six or fewer per year. In addition, some treatment institutions have age limit policies that negatively affect treatment and limit access to care for older adolescents who may not satisfy the age limits at the institution able to provide the most appropriate care. The low reimbursement rates for psychosocial services that are common among insurers result in fewer qualified professionals being available who are willing to care for teenagers and young adults with eating disorders. Lack of compensation for care that is provided by hospitals, physicians, and other professionals threatens the survival of existing programs. Insurance reimbursement for care provided by multiple disciplines is an essential element of appropriate treatment but is far from the norm. Comprehensive insurance coverage is important for adolescents suffering from the full spectrum of disorders, ranging from disordered eating to those with severe and chronic eating disorders. Treatment should be dictated by generally accepted guidelines and should be based on clinical severity of the condition.

Many older adolescents who have had health insurance, no longer have it as young adults and withdraw from treatment owing to loss of coverage. Some insurers have limited or even reduced the age up to which students can continue to be covered as dependents under their parents' insurance. Some older adolescents who have lost insurance are unable to obtain new coverage because of limited eligibility based on the preexisting condition exclusions that are imposed by some insurance companies. The withdrawal of treatment owing to loss of insurance often occurs at an age when unemployment or temporary employment, without benefits, is the norm; and individuals who are ages 18 through 24 years lack insurance at a higher rate than any other age group.

Section 19.2

Eating Behaviors Impact Students' Ability to Learn

Excerpted from "Eating Disorders Information for Middle School Personnel," from *BodyWise Handbook*, Office on Women's Health, October 2005.

Students' Ability to Learn Is Affected by Disordered Eating and Eating Disorders

A review of research compiled by the Tufts University School of Nutrition Science and Policy concludes that undernutrition—even in its milder forms—during any period of childhood can have detrimental effects on the cognitive development of children.[1] Undernutrition has an impact on students' behavior, school performance, and overall cognitive development. Undernourished students are hungry. Being hungry—experienced by everyone on occasion—causes irritability, decreased ability to concentrate, nausea, headache, and lack of energy. Students with disordered eating behaviors may experience these sensations every day. Those who attend school hungry have diminished attention spans and may be less able to perform tasks as well as their nourished peers.

Deficiencies in specific nutrients, such as iron, have an immediate effect on students' memory and ability to concentrate. The effects of short-term fasting on academic performance are well documented. Numerous studies have reported significant improvements in students' academic achievement just from eating breakfast.

When students are not eating well, they can become less active and more apathetic, and interact less with their surrounding environment.[2] This in turn affects their social interactions, inquisitiveness, and overall cognitive functioning. In addition, undernourished students are tired and more vulnerable to illness. They are also more likely to be absent from school.

Preoccupation with Food and Weight

Undernourished students may be preoccupied with thoughts of food and weight. Students with eating disorders share some of the same physical and psychological symptoms as people who have experienced starvation. For example, preoccupation with food was documented in the Minnesota Human Starvation study,[3] and more recently has been observed in clinical practices with regard to eating disorders.[4] One of the major effects of starvation and semistarvation appears to be an obsession with food.[5]

> "In our clinical practice, we surveyed over 1,000 people with clinically diagnosed eating disorders. We found that people with anorexia nervosa report 90 to 100 percent of their waking time is spent thinking about food, weight, and hunger—an additional amount of time is spent dreaming of food or having sleep disturbed by hunger. People with bulimia nervosa report spending about 70 to 90 percent of their total conscious time thinking about food and weight-related issues. In addition, people with disordered eating may spend about 20 to 65 percent of their waking hours thinking about food. By comparison, women with normal eating habits will probably spend about 10 to 15 percent of waking time thinking about food, weight, and hunger."[6] Dan W. Reiff, M.P.H., Therapist and Author

> "Girls or boys who are self-conscious about their weight and shape, engage in restrictive dieting or excessive exercise, or think of their goals in terms of pounds or fashion models are less interested in and less able to participate in learning."[7] Michael Levine, Ph.D., Professor, Department of Psychology, Kenyon College, Therapist and Author

> "Although students with eating disorders may display deteriorating school performance, anorexic young women often have perfectionist attitudes which enable them to maintain high levels of academic achievement despite their being seriously malnourished." Harold Goldstein, Ph.D., Former Clinical Director, Eating Disorders Program, National Institutes of Mental Health

End Notes

1. Tufts University School of Nutrition Science and Policy. Statement on the link between nutrition and cognitive development in children. Boston: Center on Hunger, Poverty, and Nutrition Policy, 1998.

2. Ibid.

3. Keys A, et al. *The biology of human starvation*, vols. 1 and 2. Minneapolis: University of Minnesota Press, 1950 (cited in Reiff and Lampson-Reiff, 1999).

4. Reiff D, Lampson-Reiff KK. *Eating disorders: Nutrition therapy in the recovery process*. Mercer Island, WA: Life Enterprises, 1999.

5. Ibid.

6. Reiff D, Lampson-Reiff KK. *Eating disorders: nutrition therapy in the recovery process*, p. 285.

7. Personal conversation with Michael Levine, Ph.D., member of the Office on Women's Health Eating Disorders Steering Committee, June 1999.

Section 19.3

Avoid the Dangerous Online World of Anorexia and Bulimia

Imagine this: A 12 year old girl struggling with her weight, feeling insecure and alone goes online to find a better diet—something to help her lose weight faster before entering Grade 7. She often wonders if she has an eating disorder—not fully comprehending what that means. She goes to a search engine and types in "eating disorders"—up come 650,000 entries. Confused, she narrows her search to "anorexia"—417,000 entries. She clicks haphazardly on one entry and is taken to a page where she sees a photograph of an emaciated model and beside it the "10 Thin Commandments" which include:

1. If you aren't thin, then you aren't attractive.

2. Being thin is more important than being healthy.
3. You must buy clothes, cut your hair, take laxatives, starve yourself, and do anything to make yourself look thinner.
4. Thou shall not eat without feeling guilty.
5. Thou shall not eat fattening food without punishing oneself afterward.
6. Thou shall count calories and restrict intake accordingly.
7. What the scale says is the most important thing.
8. Losing weight is good; gaining weight is bad.
9. You can never be too thin.
10. Being thin and not eating are signs of true willpower and success.

She has stumbled upon a pro-anorexia website.

It seems unfathomable; a movement that encourages anorexia nervosa—a devastating eating disorder that claims the lives of thousands of women each year. Yet, through the unleashed power of the Internet, this is exactly what health professionals faced when the issue first came to light—hundreds of websites that describe anorexia as a chosen lifestyle, and refer to these potentially deadly disorders by affectionate pet names "Ana" (anorexia) and "Mia" (bulimia). With names like "Dying to be Thin," "Anorexic Nation," and "Stick Figures," these websites are fully developed web-based communities.

Background

It is not clear how or when this movement began. Some claim that they've known of sites like these for over four years. Yet, it was only during the summer of 2001 that the media found and exposed this underground world. There were articles in major newspapers and clips on the news; it shocked the health professional world and sent chills through the public. Organizations and associations struggled to figure out how to respond. One response was to petition the servers hosting these websites to shut them down. Yahoo decided to pull the plug on some of the websites citing that they violated their user agreement to not post "harmful, threatening, or abusive" material. Several other servers followed suit. Many of the websites are no longer in operation, others have simply changed servers and Internet addresses, added password protection, and gone further underground. Several months later the issue is still hot and widely debated, but the hype in the mainstream media has died down. Now the health profession must thoroughly contemplate the issues and work towards a long-term, strategic response.

What is on a pro-anorexia website?

The pro-anorexia movement is comprised of websites, chat rooms, and electronic message and discussion boards. The websites are largely created and hosted by girls and women struggling with eating disorders. Some websites are being run by girls as young as 14, and in one reported case, a young girl's site remained static but online after friends and family were unable to access the site following her death from her eating disorder.

These websites contain dangerous and incorrect information about restrictive eating, metabolism, bingeing, and laxatives. Common inclusions on pro-eating disorder websites are:

Journals filled with gory details of the lives of girls and women struggling to deal with very serious eating disorders, some of whom are also plagued by depression, anxiety, self-injury, abuse, and a host of other issues.

Triggers. Pictures intended to inspire visitors to stay thin or become thinner (they are called thinspiration); pictures of thin and often emaciated superstars like Kate Moss, Ally McBeal, and Lara Flynn Boyle. Sometimes these are modified to make the woman look thinner and sicklier; but, often there is no need to distort the pictures. Some sites also display pictures of individuals with anorexia who are extremely ill.

Reverse triggers. Pictures of fat women are intended to remind visitors that they "never want to end up looking like that."

Quotes are intended to inspire visitors to restrict their eating and maintain dangerously low weights—"If you eat over 500 calories, vomit, use laxatives, or fast the next day." "A good anorexic is one who does not die."

Tips and tricks on how to purge more effectively, binge secretly, trick doctors, restrict eating, burn extra calories, or use vegetarianism as an excuse.

Message boards and chat rooms where girls and women with eating disorders gather to share their struggles, their stories, their beliefs, their reluctance to consider treatment as an option, and to share tips on being a "good anorexic."

Why do these websites exist?

It's an obvious question to ask—why would anyone create such a disturbing website environment or torment themselves by viewing the contents? It's actually quite understandable when you consider the psychological and physiological affects of the disorder with which they are struggling. When the brain is starved for nourishment, judgment is impaired. The movement seems to make sense to these girls and women; they feel isolated and scared and most would acknowledge that they are ill; yet, they can't imagine their life without the eating disorder. To them, recovery means becoming fat and that simply is not an option. These sites provide them with a sense of community that is supportive, understanding, and non-judgmental. They look to each other to validate their behaviors and feelings because despite knowing that they are sick, they are too scared to give up "Ana." These women do not want to die; they want to be in control, and they use thinness as the visible means of this will power. Many of the women admit that they wouldn't wish anorexia on their worst enemy and don't wish to recruit new members, yet the eating disorder has become their identity and creates structure for their lives.

What are the risks?

Despite the support and understanding that these women get from each other, they also encourage each other to remain sick. Ironically, they encourage each other to "stay strong" and not to let "them" (parents or professionals) take "Ana" away from them. The messages on these websites are ambivalent, which coincides with how the women feel about their own eating disorder. On one hand you have a statement indicating that it is not their intention to recruit new "members," and on the other hand you will see tips on "how to become anorexic."

Many of these sites have disclaimers. They post warnings such as: some viewers may consider the materials offensive, if you don't want to be triggered—do not enter, and that their intentions are not to lure anyone into the world of anorexia. However, these disclaimers will not help a young girl who wants to know the fastest way to lose weight.

Dissension and Controversy

The issues around this movement are complex and controversy is brewing. Even among advocates of the pro-eating disorder movement, there is some discord around the meaning of pro-anorexia. Some women refer to themselves as pro-anorexic because they support the web environments that provide them with a venue to express themselves, but denounce sites that glamorize and celebrate the disorder. Others more openly advocate anorexia as an acceptable and even admirable lifestyle.

Professionals also face a quandary and have varying opinions on how to deal with the proliferation of these sites. Some professionals believe that these sites must be shut down in order to protect the vulnerable, and continue to encourage the companies hosting these sites to remove them. Others question the effectiveness of this, wondering if it alienates and discourages these women from seeking treatment. The fear is that such a strong reaction may push the movement further underground and make it more dangerous and defiant. This seems a valid concern given that the pro-anorexia community is very angry at the media which has labeled them as uncaring, insensitive, and evil, and is angry at the professional world which is trying to shut them down—they see it as a personal attack and feel as if they are being silenced.

Next Steps

It would be a superficial solution to blame the women who have created these sites and simply force them all to shut down. These women are not uncaring, insensitive, or evil—they suffer from a debilitating disorder, which affects their logic and their emotions. And sites forced to shut down pop up somewhere else while new ones are constantly being created. At the same time, we are forced to acknowledge the potentially dangerous consequences of vulnerable individuals coming across these sites. Young girls and women are learning how to slowly kill themselves. We need to focus on the big picture and figure out how to deal with this issue over the long-term—the Internet is here to stay, and it is likely that the movement will continue to grow as long as it continues to serve a purpose to its members. Focus needs to be on the bigger evils that exist by challenging the diet industry and the cultural messages that dictate thinness as the only acceptable size and the only means to self-efficacy and self-esteem. Health professionals must band together and find answers to the following questions:

- How do we protect vulnerable individuals from the dangerous effects of these websites without alienating a whole community in need?
- Does shutting the sites down create a greater divide between professionals and sufferers?
- Who is morally and legally responsible if a child were to die as a result of following the directions on one or more of these sites?
- Do these websites actually scare some women into treatment and recovery?
- Is the moral support these women seek outweighing the constant messages to stay sick?
- How do we effectively counteract these negative, unhealthy environments—what kind of positive online and off-line environments can we create to provide individuals with more options for support and sharing and opportunities to build resilience?

Section 19.4

Association between Childhood Abuse and Disordered Eating Behavior in Female Undergraduates

Excerpted from Suzanne E. Mazzeo and Dorothy L. Espelage, "Association Between Childhood Physical and Emotional Abuse and Disordered Eating Behaviors in Female Undergraduates," *Journal of Counseling Psychology*, 2002, Volume 49, Number 1, pp. 86–100, copyright © 2002 by the American Psychological Association. Reprinted with permission.

Over the past two decades, research on the correlates of disordered eating behaviors has increased exponentially. However, in spite of the quantity of literature addressing disordered eating, many questions about its etiology remain. In particular, several variables have been found to be significantly related to disordered eating behaviors. Yet the specific processes through which these variables potentially influence disordered eating have not been fully articulated, in part because researchers in this area have tended to rely heavily on univariate statistical approaches. In the present study, we used standard error of the mean (SEM) to address some of the potential indirect relationships among variables previously found to be associated with disordered eating. The major finding of this study is that the associations among family conflict, family cohesion, childhood physical and emotional abuse and neglect, and college women's disordered eating behaviors were mediated by depression and alexithymia. These results both integrate and expand the results of previous studies. In particular, they contribute to researchers' understanding of the continuum of disordered eating behaviors as they occur in nonclinical college women.

Previous research on the relevance of family cohesion and conflict to disordered eating behavior has found that these variables are related to disordered eating behaviors in some nonclinical samples (for example, Leung et al., 1996; Scalf-McIver and Thompson, 1989) and not in others (for example, Kent and Clopton, 1992). The present results suggest that low levels of family cohesion and high levels of family conflict were indirectly associated with disordered eating behaviors. Low levels of family cohesion and high levels of family conflict were directly related to higher levels of childhood physical and emotional abuse and neglect. It should be noted, however, that (in both the validation and cross-validation samples), the influence of family cohesion on childhood abuse was much stronger than that of family conflict. This suggests that family cohesion may be a particularly important aspect of family functioning to investigate further in future studies of the development of disordered eating. In addition, future research should evaluate the potential influence of other familial characteristics on disordered eating behaviors, including parental attachment and family constellation.

The present results differ from those of Kent and Clopton (1992), who found that family cohesion and conflict were not significantly associated with disordered eating. One reason for this difference may be because the present study included a much larger number of participants (406 participants per group vs. 72 participants divided into three groups); thus, there was much more power to detect differences in the present investigation. In contrast, in the present study we examined disordered eating behaviors on a continuum and assessed a wider range of disordered eating behaviors, including dieting and restricting.

Present results regarding the association between childhood physical and emotional abuse and neglect and disordered eating also add to the literature, as few previous studies have examined the association between nonsexual forms of childhood abuse and disordered eating severity. Moreover, to our knowledge, no studies have evaluated the impact of these forms of childhood trauma in combination with the other variables included in this model. Results suggest that childhood physical and emotional abuse and neglect were not directly associated with disordered eating. Rather, these childhood experiences were indirectly related to disordered eating by means of alexithymia and depression.

These results complement those found in previous studies. For example, Ray et al. (1991) found that low levels of family cohesion were associated with increased risk of childhood sexual abuse both within and outside of the family environment. Present results suggest that low levels of cohesion were also associated with high rates of physical and emotional abuse and neglect. One potential explanation for this association may be that, if an individual from an incohesive family environment becomes a victim of abuse (whether inside or outside the home), she may be less likely to receive the support she needs from family members to prevent negative psychological outcomes. Future research could examine this hypothesis by expanding the present model to include social support as a moderator of the association between family cohesion and abuse.

Present results also extend researchers' knowledge of the role of alexithymia in disordered eating. Previous research has investigated the association between alexithymia and disordered eating (for example, Laquatra and Clopton, 1994) and alexithymia and childhood abuse (for example, Camras et al., 1988). This study's results suggest that alexithymia mediates the association between abuse and disordered eating, implying that individuals who have difficulty identifying and describing their emotions may be more likely to engage in disordered eating behaviors.

Further, these results may indicate that the intense focus on appearance (turning outside) evident among women who engage in disordered eating behavior could be an attempt to cope with the difficulties they tend to have identifying and describing their emotions (turning inside). This result provides support for Heatherton and Baumeister's (1991) escape theory of disordered eating and suggests that emotion skills training may be an important addition to eating disorder prevention and treatment programs. Future research (particularly longitudinal research) is needed to further clarify the role of alexithymia in the development of disordered eating. Present results regarding the mediating role of alexithymia should not be overstated, given that, although this path contributed to the overall model, its coefficient was not particularly large in either subsample or in the invariant model. Nonetheless, a test of mediation as outlined by Holmbeck (1997) suggested that alexithymia fully mediated the association between childhood abuse and disordered eating.

The present results also expand the understanding of the role of depression as a mediator of the association between childhood physical and emotional abuse and neglect and disordered eating behaviors. These results differ from those of Kent et al., 1999, who found that depression did not mediate the relationship between emotional abuse and disordered eating behaviors. However, these authors used multiple regression analyses to test for mediation. Unlike SEM, multiple regression does not identify measurement problems that may influence results. The use of the more powerful SEM approach in the present study provided a more rigorous test of the role of depression in disordered eating behaviors.

An alternative explanation for why the present results differ from those of Kent et al. (1999) is that these authors also used measures of anxiety and dissociation in their study and found that depression was not a significant mediator of the association between childhood emotional abuse and disordered eating when anxiety and dissociation were taken into account. Unfortunately, we did not include measures of anxiety and dissociation in the present study; it is important to combine them with the variables used in the present model in future research.

Nonetheless, present results suggest that individuals who engage in disordered eating behaviors, as well as individuals at risk for developing these behaviors, may benefit from interventions that address adaptive ways to cope with depression. Taken together, results regarding the associations among alexithymia, depression, and disordered eating suggest that it is not the mere presence or absence of childhood emotional and physical abuse and neglect that is associated with disordered eating. Rather, the development of alexithymia and depressive symptomatology in response to these childhood experiences seems to be most strongly associated with disordered eating severity.

Overall, these results indicate that several factors simultaneously influence the severity of disordered eating. This suggests that there is a need for a holistic approach to the assessment of disordered eating behaviors. For example, these data indicate that low levels of family cohesiveness and, to a lesser degree, high levels of family conflict are associated with a greater incidence of emotional and physical abuse and neglect. Thus, practitioners working with college women with disordered eating behaviors should evaluate not only the presence or absence of cohesiveness and conflict in the student's family of origin but also the consequences of an incohesive or conflictual family environment (for example, did this student's family environment include abuse or increase her vulnerability to abuse outside the home?). Furthermore, when asking women about their experiences of abuse and neglect, practitioners should attempt to determine whether these individuals may have developed alexithymic or depressive symptomatology in response to experiences of abuse or neglect, as the present results highlight the influence of these factors on disordered eating.

Chapter 20

What Parents Can Do to Prevent Eating Disorders

Chapter Contents

Section 20.1

Creating a Healthy Environment

"Eating Disorders Prevention: Parents Are Key Players," used with permission of ANRED: Anorexia Nervosa and Related Eating Disorders, Inc. For additional information, visit http://www.anred.com.

Eating Disorders Prevention: Parents Are Key Players

Eating disorders are much easier to prevent than cure, and parents are in the best position to do that work. Almost all effective prevention strategies will be carried out in the context of the family, not in organized programs. If you are a parent, keep in mind that what you do is a much more powerful message than what you say.

Avoid Guilt and Denial

Most parents of eating disordered children are good people who have done the best they could as they raised their kids. In spite of their efforts, however, their children fell into anorexia, bulimia, or another eating disorder. Science is telling us that genetic factors that help determine personality characteristics are much more important than previously suspected in the development of eating disorders. Those factors seem to be activated when a vulnerable person begins to diet, buying into the belief that losing weight will somehow make life happier.

At that point parents tend to fall into guilt and denial. Neither is helpful. Instead of bemoaning what you did or didn't do (which may or may not have contributed to the current problem), take action and arrange an evaluation with your child's physician and a mental health specialist. The sooner treatment is begun, the easier it will be to turn matters around. The longer the symptoms are ignored, and the longer parents hope the behaviors are "just a phase," the longer and harder the road to recovery will be. Use the following suggestions to create a healthy environment for growth of your child's self-esteem and to counter some of the destructive media messages about body image flooding today's young people.

Suggestions for Prevention

Model Healthy Thoughts and Behaviors

Give your family and friends the gift of a healthy role model. If you are a mother, aunt, or sister, get comfortable with your own body and enjoy it, no matter what its size and shape. Never criticize your own appearance. If you do, you teach others to be overly concerned about externals and critical of their own bodies.

Fathers Must Behave Thoughtfully

If you are a man, never criticize anyone's appearance, especially a woman or child's. Phrases like "thunder thighs" and "bubble butt," even if they are meant in jest, can wound deeply and puncture self-esteem. Remember that people are more than just bodies. They all have talents, abilities, hopes, dreams, values, and goals—just like you do. Treat them as you would like to be treated, not as an object put on the planet for your visual enjoyment.

Prohibit Teasing about Body Shape and Size

Don't allow anyone in the family to tease others about appearance. Even so-called playful teasing can produce powerful, negative consequences.

Emphasize Fitness

Talk about the importance of fit and healthy bodies, not thin bodies. The goals should be health and fitness, not thinness. They don't always go together. Sometimes it is impossible to be fit if one is too thin.

Praise Children for Who They Are

Praise their positive personal qualities and what they accomplish—not how they look. A child who feels unattractive but is told that s/he is good looking will feel only anxiety, not improved self-esteem, and you will lose credibility in her/his eyes.

Don't Diet

It is especially important that you don't diet—ever. In the first place, diets don't work. They also send a dangerous and unrealistic message to kids about quick-fix solutions. Rather than diet, stick to a healthy routine of nutritious eating and fitness-promoting exercise.

Important fact: Three of the most powerful risk factors for the development of an eating disorder are (1) a mother who diets, (2) a sister who diets, and (3) friends who diet. In addition, girls and women who diet severely are eighteen times more likely to develop an eating disorder than non-dieters. (ANAD Newsletter, summer 2001)

Encourage Healthy Eating, Not Dieting

There is a difference. Also, make eating tasty food okay. Demonizing french fries and ice cream only makes them forbidden fruit (to mangle the metaphor).

Don't Forbid Certain Foods

Don't define some foods as bad. Healthy eating has room for just about all foods in moderation. In addition, learn what normal development and childhood and adolescent weight gain look like. It's not what you see in magazines or on television. Encourage normal, healthy development in your children.

Make Mealtime Pleasant

Enjoy eating with family and good friends. Treat your family to a special meal once a week, at home or in a restaurant. Watching what you eat in the service of health is fine, but obsessive attention to calories, fat grams, and weight can set up a vulnerable person to fear food and the consequences of eating. For too many folks, these preoccupations and expectations lead to anorexia and bulimia.

Get Help When Appropriate

If a child is bound and determined to diet, get a physician or registered dietitian involved to supervise the effort. Doctors and dietitians can provide information about healthy eating and weight levels that can counteract myths about "good" and "bad" foods and realistic weight goals. In addition, if the diet gets out of control, the resource person will already be available to intervene.

Promote Physical Activity

Help your children build and commit to an active lifestyle. You don't have to spend major money on athletic club memberships or participation in organized sports, but encourage activities such as biking, walking, and swimming that are pleasurable and can be done every day. Physical fitness promotes healthy self-image.

Explain What Normal Means

Talk to your children about the normal body changes expected at puberty. Sometimes kids interpret developing female curves as getting fat. Girls certainly need to know that normal development is necessary for health in general and healthy childbearing in particular. Boys need to hear the message too so they can rise above the "no fat chicks" mentality so prevalent in adolescent male culture.

Inoculate Kids Against Media Manipulation

Talk to your children about the unrealistic images they see in magazines, on television, and in the movies. Tell them that some models and actresses achieve their look by resorting to plastic surgery and eating disorders. It's the truth. Point out how advertisers prey on body image insecurities by sending vulnerable people messages about the benefits of being thin—and spending their money on the advertisers' products. Sit with your children and explore material online that helps them identify that kind of manipulation. Remind them that being thin doesn't make one popular and self-confident any more than smoking does, but the advertising techniques for cigarettes and diet products are almost identical.

What You Do Speaks Louder Than What You Say

Most important of all, show people—don't waste your time telling them—how you take care of yourself in healthy, responsible ways. Demonstrate how a competent person takes charge, solves problems, negotiates relationships, and builds a satisfying life without resorting to self-destructive behaviors. A healthy role-model parent is a child's best protection against a whole host of problems, including life-ruining eating disorders.

Conclusion

Recent research (University of California–Los Angeles (UCLA) and University of Pittsburgh) finds a strong genetic predisposition toward mood, personality, and behaviors that if not recognized and handled effectively, can lead to an eating disorder. Specifically, people with eating disorders tend to have family members who struggle with depression, alcohol dependency, drug abuse, anxiety, perfectionism, obsessive thoughts, and compulsive behaviors. Children in these families can become competitive and goal oriented, able to stay focused on achieving a single outcome to the exclusion of all else. If this pattern fits you or your family, be very careful. Don't even think of allowing a diet unless it is done under doctor's supervision. Be especially wary of thoughts that seductively promise you and your children that weight loss will lead to improved self-esteem and self-confidence. It won't, and whatever weight is lost will never be enough.

If you have a child for whom this pattern fits, consider the following guidelines:

- Don't let him or her diet. Provide opportunities for healthy eating instead.
- Don't nag your child about losing weight to make his weight class or fit into her prom dress. God and Mother Nature intended our bodies to be a certain healthy weight. Trying to override that weight can lead to tragic consequences.
- Never forget that dieting is the strongest eating disorders trigger there is.

Prevention, especially if your family carries some degree of genetic predisposition to the thoughts, moods, and behaviors that can combine to produce an eating disorder, demands a great deal of consciousness and vigilance on your part. Don't make the mistake of thinking, "We are good people and a good family. My child could never become eating disordered." Given sufficient peer pressure to diet, societal demands for thinness, and parental expectations of excellence, a vulnerable child can collapse into an obsessive pursuit of thinness and compulsive, unhealthy behaviors to reach that goal.

If you have trouble implementing these suggestions, or even believing that they are worthwhile, you might want to talk them over with a mental health therapist who is experienced in treating people with eating disorders. Please do so especially if your child begins to sound like a broken record about the need to lose weight and how fat s/he is (when that is clearly not the case).

Section 20.2

How to Feed a Child Athlete

Do You Know How to Feed Your Child Athlete?

All kids need to eat balanced meals and have a healthy diet. But should that balance change if your child is on a sports team or working out? Maybe. Your child needs to eat the right mix of foods to support that higher level of activity, but that mix might not be too different than what is considered a healthy diet. Eating for sports should be an extension of healthy eating for life.

There are many "sports" foods and drinks marketed to athletes, like energy bars and gels. In general, most young athletes do not need these products to meet their energy needs. These products don't have magic ingredients that will improve a child's sports performance, but they can come in handy if your child doesn't have time to prepare a healthy meal or snack.

Because athletic kids are particularly reliant on the nutrients that a balanced diet can provide, it's usually not a good idea for them to diet. In sports where weight is emphasized, such as wrestling, swimming, dance, or gymnastics, your child may feel pressure to lose weight. If a coach, gym teacher, or another teammate says that your child needs to go on a diet, talk to your doctor first. If your doctor thinks your child should diet, the doctor can work with your child or refer you to a nutritionist to develop a plan that allows your child to work on the weight in a safe and healthy way.

What Are the Nutritional Needs of Young Athletes?

If your child is eating healthy, well-balanced meals and snacks, your child is probably getting the nutrients that he or she needs to perform well in sports. The new food guide pyramid, called *MyPyramid*, can provide guidance on what kinds of foods and drinks should be included in your child's well-balanced meals and snacks.

But kids who are involved in strenuous endurance sports like cross-country running or competitive swimming, which involve 1½ to 2 hours of activity at a time, may need to consume more food to keep up with their increased energy demands. Most athletic young people will naturally crave the amount of food their bodies need, but if you are concerned that your child is getting too much or too little food, you may want to check in with your child's doctor.

Because different foods have different combinations of these nutrients, it's important to vary your child's meals and snacks as much as possible. It's a good idea to make sure that your child is getting the following nutrients:

- **Vitamins and minerals:** Your child needs a variety of vitamins and minerals. Brightly colored foods such as spinach, carrots, squash, and peppers tend to be packed with them. It's especially important your child get plenty of calcium and iron. Calcium helps your child build healthy bones, which are important especially if your child breaks a bone or gets a stress fracture. Calcium-rich foods include dairy products like milk, yogurt, and cheese, as well as leafy green vegetables such as broccoli. Iron helps carry oxygen to all the different body parts that need it. Iron-rich foods include red meat, chicken, tuna, salmon, eggs, dried fruits, leafy green vegetables, and whole grains.

- **Protein:** Protein can help build your child's muscles, along with regular training and exercise. But there's no need to overload on protein because too much of it can lead to dehydration and calcium loss. Protein-rich foods include fish, lean red meat and poultry, dairy products, nuts, soy products, and peanut butter.

- **Carbohydrates:** Carbohydrates provide energy for the body. Some diet plans have urged weight-conscious adults to steer clear of carbohydrates or "carbs" as they're often called. But for a young athlete, carbohydrates are an important source of fuel. There's not any need for your child to do any "carb loading" or eat a lot of carbs in advance of a big game, but without some of these foods in your child's diet, he or she will be running on empty. When you're choosing carbohydrates, look for whole grain foods that are less processed and high in fiber, like pasta, brown rice, whole grain bread, and cereal. Fiber helps lower cholesterol and may help prevent diabetes and heart disease.

It's a good idea to pack your child's meals with natural foods as much as possible. Natural foods such as whole wheat breads and baked potatoes are more wholesome choices than heavily processed foods, like white breads and potato chips. Usually the less processed the food, the more nutritious it is. Choose products with ingredients such as whole wheat or oats rather than white flour. Encourage your child to pick up a piece of fruit, rather than a fruit drink, which may have added sugar. Remember that sugar may be listed by another name such as sucrose or fructose.

Drink Up

It's important for young athletes to drink plenty of fluid to avoid any heat illness and dehydration, which can zap a child's strength, energy, and coordination, and lead to other health problems.

It's a good idea for your child to drink water or other fluids throughout the day, but especially before, during, and after periods of extended physical activity. Experts recommend that kids drink approximately one cup (240 milliliters) of water or fluid every 20 to 30 minutes of physical activity, depending on the child. Shorter competitions may not require drinking during the activity, but it's important to drink water after the game or event to restore whatever fluid your child lost through sweat during the event.

Children often don't recognize or respond to feelings of thirst. So it's a good idea to encourage your child to drink before thirst sets in.

Although many sports drinks are available, usually plain water is sufficient to keep kids hydrated. Sports drinks are designed to provide energy and replace electrolytes—such as sodium and potassium—that athletes lose in sweat. But your child's body typically has enough carbohydrates to serve as energy for up to 90 minutes of exercise. And in most cases, any lost electrolytes can be replenished by a good meal after the activity.

If your child participates in endurance sports such as long-distance running and biking or high-intensity exercise such as soccer, basketball, or hockey, it's a good idea for your child to replenish his or her body throughout the event. This is because the body can use the sugar immediately as energy to make up for the depleted energy stores in the body. Soda and juice may not quench your child's fluid needs as well because many of them have too much sugar and can upset the stomach. If your child wants juice, it's a good idea to mix it with water to reduce the concentration of sugar.

Pressures Facing Athletes

Some school-age athletes face unique pressures involving nutrition and body weight. In some sports, it's common for kids to feel they need to radically increase or reduce their weight to reach peak performance.

Unhealthy eating habits, like crash dieting, can also leave your child with less strength, endurance, and poorer mental concentration. Similar performance issues can come up when kids try to increase their weight too fast. When a person overeats, the food the body can't immediately use gets stored as fat. As a result, kids who overeat may gain weight, but their physical fitness will be diminished. If you are concerned about your child's eating habits, it's a good idea to talk to your child's doctor.

Game Day

It's important for your child to eat well on game days, but make sure your child eats at least two hours before the event—early enough to digest the food before game time. The meal itself should not be very different from what your child has been eating throughout training. It should have plenty of carbohydrates and protein and be low in fat because fat is harder to digest and can cause an upset stomach.

After the game or event, it's a good idea to make sure your child gets a well-balanced meal. Your child's body will be rebuilding muscle tissue and restoring carbohydrates and fluids for up to 24 hours after the competition. So it's important that your child get plenty of protein, fat, and carbohydrates in the postgame hours. And remember, when packing your child's bag for the big day, don't forget the water bottle or the sports drink.

Meal and Snack Suggestions

You can't make up for a poor diet on game day, so it's important to feed your child healthy meals and snacks on a consistent basis, even during the off-season. That will provide a solid foundation whenever your child heads out for a competition.

Breakfast might include low-fat yogurt with some granola or a banana. Lunch might include bean burritos with low-fat cheese, lettuce, and tomatoes. A turkey sandwich and fruit may also be a hit. Dinner might be grilled chicken breasts with steamed rice and vegetables or pasta with red sauce and lean ground beef, along with a salad. Snacks might be pretzels, raisins, and fruit.

Chapter 21

Information for School Personnel about Eating Disorders Prevention

Eating Disorders May Begin as Disordered Eating Behaviors at Very Young Ages

Many studies show that disordered eating behaviors begin as early as eight years of age, with complaints about body size or shape. The Harvard Eating Disorders Center (HEDC) reports that in a study of children ages eight to ten, approximately half of the girls and one-third of the boys were dissatisfied with their size. Most dissatisfied girls wanted to be thinner, while about half of dissatisfied boys wanted to be heavier and/or more muscular.

Many individuals with clinically diagnosed anorexia nervosa and bulimia nervosa remember being teased or recall that their problems first began when they started dieting. Similarly, they recall experiencing body dissatisfaction and/or fear of fat, even though they were within the natural weight range for their age. While only a small percentage of people who diet or express body dissatisfaction develop eating disorders, the beginning of an eating disorder typically follows a period of restrictive dieting, a form of disordered eating for youth.

Binge eating disorder is a newly recognized condition that affects millions of people. People with binge eating disorder have varying degrees of obesity. Most have a long history of repeated efforts to diet

---

Excerpted from "Eating Disorders Information for Middle School Personnel," *BodyWise Handbook*, Office on Women's Health, October 2005.

and feel desperate about their difficulty in controlling food intake. Binge eating behaviors can begin during childhood.

The middle-school years—grades six, seven, and eight—are opportune times to recognize and discourage disordered eating behaviors. Although these behaviors may not constitute a serious illness, they are still unhealthy practices that can affect students' ability to learn. They can also trigger a full-blown eating disorder in a susceptible individual that requires intensive treatment.

All School Personnel Are Important in Preventing Eating Disorders

Each member of a school community can help create an environment that discourages disordered eating and promotes the early detection of eating disorders. A study reported in the *Journal of the American Medical Association* found that of all the forces that influence adolescent health-risk behavior, the most critical are the family and school contexts. Both a high expectation for student performance and showing concern for a student's welfare communicate a sense of caring that is one of the major protective factors against a variety of risky behaviors.

The protective factors that are considered most amenable for classroom intervention are coping and life skills, such as problem solving, decision making, assertiveness, communication, and stress management. "Providing students with positive coping and life skills education may help in discouraging eating disorders as well as drug, alcohol, pregnancy, and delinquency problems. Changes in parental and teacher attitudes are important, as are changes in school policies concerning harassment, teasing, and being weighed in public." (Source: Linda Smolak, Ph.D., Professor, Department of Psychology, Kenyon College)

Media messages that equate thinness with beauty can contribute to development of negative body images among girls. A school-based study found that discontent with body weight and shape was directly related to the frequency of reading fashion magazines. Pictures in magazines had a strong impact on girls' perceptions of their weight and shape. Of the 548 5th- through 12th-grade girls, 69 percent reported that magazine images influenced their idea of the perfect body shape, and 47 percent reported wanting to lose weight because of magazine images. Training in media literacy can help students analyze media messages and resist those that feature thin and unrealistic body shapes.

Other effective strategies include conducting mentoring programs, changing school policies on harassment, and integrating into existing health and science curricula information on growth patterns in puberty and the negative consequences of dieting.

All teachers and staff can serve as personal agents of change, both inside and outside the classroom, to help students avoid disordered eating and other associated risk behaviors. They can accomplish this by providing appropriate information and skills as well as by creating an environment which students perceive to be caring and responsive to their needs.

School Culture

Answering the following questions will give you a snapshot of your school's culture and help you think about how you can integrate ways to discourage disordered eating and promote early detection of eating disorders into your school's ongoing activities.

Do we teach:

- the nature and dangers of dieting
- weight and size changes that occur during puberty
- genetic effects and diversity of weight and shape
- media literacy skills
- problem-oriented coping skills
- assertive communication skills
- listening skills

Do we discourage:

- calorie-restrictive dieting
- weight- and shape-related teasing
- gender stereotyping
- sexual harassment

Are we attentive to students who:

- express low self-esteem, anxiety, obsessive-compulsiveness, or perfectionism
- say they are too fat

- are teased about their weight or shape
- have a family history of eating disorders, drug abuse, or mental health problems
- experience adverse or stressful life events

Do we promote:

- role models of all sizes and shapes who are praised for accomplishments, not appearance
- definitions of beauty that focus on self-respect, assertiveness, and generosity of spirit
- pathways to success unrelated to external appearance

Do we offer:

- peer support groups
- adult mentoring programs
- opportunities for teachers, students, parents, and others to discuss school policies regarding teasing, bullying, sexual harassment, and gender role constraints
- speakers or in-service programs on eating disorders
- parent education on eating disorders and on how nutrition and positive body image affect learning
- partnerships in which school personnel work with community organizations
- opportunities for students to think critically about mass media and other sociocultural influences on body image and eating

Does our school:

- provide teachers with information about the signs and symptoms of eating disorders
- have a protocol that provides guidelines on the referral of students to health care providers knowledgeable about eating disorders
- have an eating disorders resource person who is acquainted with local and national resources for referral
- have a list of resources for school personnel who may want additional information on eating disorders

Chapter 22

Physical Education Teachers, Coaches, and Dance Instructors' Role in Preventing Eating Disorders

Physical Education Teachers, Coaches, and Dance Instructors

Physical education teachers, coaches, and dance instructors are in a unique position to enhance the self-esteem of their students, increase their physical activity levels, and help create an environment that discourages disordered eating and promotes the early detection of eating disorders. Eating disorders and serious health problems among athletes may begin as disordered eating behaviors at very young ages.

The National Collegiate Athletic Association (NCAA) has identified eating disorders as an important health problem. Participation in sports and other physical activities can help protect young people from eating disorders by enhancing self-esteem and body image. However, studies suggest that some young people who participate in athletic activities may be particularly vulnerable to developing eating disorders.[1] They include:

- elite athletes, especially those competing in lean sports such as dance and cheer leading;
- other dancers;

This chapter includes: "Physical Education Teachers, Coaches, and Dance Instructors," *BodyWise Handbook*, Office on Women's Health, October 2005; and "ATHENA Program Reduces Substance Abuse by Girls on High School Sports Teams," by Patrick Zickler, *NIDA Notes*, Vol. 20, No. 1, National Institute on Drug Abuse (NIDA), August 2005.

- athletes in sports in which low weight is believed to enhance performance, such as track and cross country;
- athletes in sports that have weight classifications such as wrestling, football, and weightlifting.

It is not psychologically or physically healthy for middle school students to attempt to achieve or maintain unnaturally low weights. Adolescence is a time of rapid growth and development. Restricting calories during this time can result in physical and emotional problems such as:

- stunted growth, loss of bone mass, and nutritional deficiencies;
- poor athletic or dance performance;
- irritability, moodiness, and poor concentration;
- feelings of not being good enough.

Furthermore, there is no evidence to support the belief that lower body weight will enhance performance in middle-school age students.[2]

The problem of eating disorders is a mental health as well as a physical health issue. Anorexia, bulimia, and binge eating disorder are associated with emotional problems and poor eating behaviors, within a culture that puts great emphasis on thinness and appearance. Students susceptible to developing an eating disorder may have a history of low self-esteem, difficulty handling stress, and/or a perfectionist attitude.

Vulnerable students are extremely sensitive to comments made by individuals who are important to them. An off-handed remark referring to an athlete or student as chubby or thunder thighs can become deeply embedded in the mind of a person at risk for eating disorders who desperately wants to please the coach.

You may be the first to notice that a student is developing an eating disorder. In middle school you are unlikely to see students with a full-blown case; rather, you may notice one or more of the following early signs:

- repeated comments about being fat or dissatisfaction with their bodies
- weight loss or lack of weight gain with increased height
- over-exercising or exercising when injured
- pretending to eat or not eating in social gatherings such as road trips, pre-game meals, postgame celebrations, and athletic banquets

- frequent trips to the bathroom
- evidence of interest in or use of diet pills, energy pills, steroids, or other unhealthy substances designed to alter body weight or shape, or to increase strength

Early detection of an eating disorder is important to increase the likelihood of successful treatment and recovery. Eating disorders occur in all socioeconomic and cultural groups, as well as in boys.

A student may tell you about a friend before you notice any signs yourself. Here are some suggestions for talking to students who are concerned about a friend:

- Ask students to describe what they have seen or heard their friend say.
- Tell them that you will follow through and talk with their friend.
- Discuss whether they want the conversation to be confidential or whether you may use their names when you talk with their friend. Ask if they would like to be present when you talk to their friend.
- Reassure them that talking with you was the right thing to do.
- Ask students who approach you if they are worried about having an eating disorder themselves.
- Consider whether they need to talk with a counselor about their concern for their friend.

Take Action

Take immediate action when you are concerned about a student.

Recognize that you do not have the skills to deal with the underlying emotional turmoil that often accompanies eating and exercise problems.

Share information with your school's eating disorders resource person, school nurse, and other teachers or staff members who know the student.

Decide together the best course of action and who should talk to the student and family members. Your goal is to communicate to the student that you care and to refer her or him to a health care provider who is knowledgeable about eating disorders.

Build Self-Esteem and Positive Body Image

Remind your students that their body shape and size or physical ability does not determine their self-worth or identity. Focus on areas over which they have more control—such as strength, physical conditioning, and the mental and emotional components of performance.

Other suggestions for building positive body image and self-esteem include the following:

- Do not require weigh-ins or tape-measure checks, or discuss weight in an evaluation of a student's ability and performance.
- Encourage students to express their concerns if they feel harassed about their appearance.
- Show dance videos by successful choreographers who incorporate diversity of age, size, ethnicity, and weight into their artistic expression (for example, Bill T. Jones, Mark Morris, and African Bush Women).
- Compliment students on issues not related to physical appearance, such as having creative ideas, displaying acts of kindness, or engaging in community service.

Educate Students

Engage in frequent and open discussions about positive body image and how good nutrition improves performance. Explain how some weight control behaviors, such as fasting; severe restriction of certain foods; self-induced vomiting; and use of laxatives, diuretics (water pills), or diet pills are dangerous and can hurt their performance.

Emphasize that student athletes are at risk for undernourishment and dehydration, which cause loss of muscular strength and endurance, decreased speed, loss of coordination, and poor judgment. Continued poor nutrition and dehydration can result in impaired brain function, irritability and inability to concentrate, depression, and social withdrawal.

Other suggestions for educating your students include the following:

- Educate serious athletes and performers on how to train safely during formative years.

- Explain the female athlete triad—disordered eating, absence of menstruation, and loss of bone mass—which can begin in the middle school years.
- Encourage students to speak with you or another adult if they think they or a friend of theirs may have an eating disorder.

Encourage the Love of Sports and Dance

Some students' body size and shape may not fit the ideal for a specific type of dance or sport. If so, refocus their attention without mentioning body size, shape, or weight. Tell them about other ways to be involved with dance and sports, such as:

- choreography, costuming, or staging;
- athletic training or coaching;
- refereeing or judging;
- sports or dance research or management.

National Ballet School Program: A Case Study

A program conducted at the National Ballet School in Toronto demonstrates how early intervention, nutrition education, and counseling can greatly reduce the chances of dancers developing eating disorders.[3] In small group meetings several times a year, students were encouraged to discuss their experiences regarding unrealistic demands on their behavior or appearance, and their feelings of powerlessness, shame, and fear. Students who became preoccupied with shape, weight, or food were encouraged to request help promptly.

Before the program was started, the incidence of new cases of anorexia or bulimia was about 1.6 per year for 100 girls ages 12 to 18. For the past eight years, there has been only one case of anorexia and one of bulimia.[4]

ATHENA Program Reduces Substance Abuse by Girls on High School Sports Teams

High school girl athletes who participated in a recently evaluated National Institute on Drug Abuse (NIDA)-supported nutritional and behavioral guidance program were less likely than nonparticipating peers to engage in substance abuse and other high-risk behaviors. Girls on teams that used ATHENA (Athletes Targeting Healthy Exercise and Nutrition Alternatives) were less likely than girls on teams that received only printed information to use diet pills or so-called performance-enhancing substances such as steroids, amphetamines, and muscle-building supplements. The ATHENA team members also were less likely to be sexually active and more likely to wear seat belts, and they experienced fewer injuries during the sports season.

In the ATHENA program, developed at the Oregon Health & Science University in Portland by Drs. Diane Elliot and Linn Goldberg, selected team leaders receive a 90-minute orientation and then conduct discussion and activity sessions during scheduled team practices. Each team leader works with a squad of approximately six teammates, following a manual that is much like a playbook, with scripts for eight 45-minute sessions dealing with the harmful consequences of substance abuse and other unhealthy behaviors and the beneficial effects of good diet and exercise. Along with providing information, the workbook engages the girls in activities such as critiquing magazine advertising and other media influences on self-image; classifying various foods according to carbohydrate, fat, and protein content; and determining the best balance of dietary fuels for athletic training and competition. Each ATHENA athlete uses a pocket-sized nutrition and training guide to monitor diet and exercise. Coaches and other staff members receive an orientation to assist the team leaders as timekeepers and facilitators for the sessions.

To evaluate ATHENA, the researchers recruited 40 girls' sports teams in 18 public high schools in northwest Oregon and southwest Washington. Teams from half the schools followed the ATHENA program. The other teams received printed information about eating disorders, substance abuse, and sports nutrition, but did not take part in discussion or group activities. Before the first practice of their sports season and again within two weeks after the season ended, each girl filled out a questionnaire about her eating patterns; nutritional awareness; use of diet pills, amphetamines, anabolic steroids, and muscle-building supplements; and other health-related behaviors.

Preseason survey results were essentially the same for girls on ATHENA teams and those in the control group, but in postseason surveys the ATHENA participants reported significant decreases in risky behaviors. According to Dr. Elliot, the control athletes were three times more likely to begin using diet pills and almost twice as likely to begin using other body-shaping substances, including amphetamines, anabolic steroids, and muscle-building supplements, during the season. The use of diet pills went up among control girls, while it fell to approximately half its preseason level among ATHENA girls. ATHENA athletes also were more likely to use seat belts and less

Table 22.1. ATHENA's Impact on Behavior and Nutrition

	Control Group		Experimental Group	
	Before Intervention	After Intervention	Before Intervention	After Intervention
Nutrition, Exercise Abilities, and Beliefs*				
Tracking protein intake	2.11	2.03	2.16	2.54
Eating more protein in the last 2 months	3.95	3.92	4.19	5.10
Knowing how to lift weights to improve strength	5.48	5.61	5.15	5.92
Self-rating of skill in strength training	5.48	5.61	5.15	5.92
Believing that nutrition affects sport performance	5.75	5.64	6.06	6.01
Additional Health-Influencing Behaviors				
Rode in a car with an alcohol-consuming driver**	0.44	0.42	0.41	0.26
Knowing how to turn down down unhealthy weight-loss behaviors*	5.80	5.77	5.91	6.14
No. of sport injuries so could not train in the last 3 months	0.32	0.36	0.32	0.26
Intentions Toward Future Disordered Eating Behaviors and Drug Use*				
Diet pill use	1.74	1.79	1.87	1.62
Vomiting to lose weight	1.66	1.76	1.62	1.57
Tobacco use	1.56	1.79	1.55	1.58
Creatine (muscle-building supplement) use	1.87	1.77	1.72	1.51

Data are significant differences expressed as the mean.

*Scored using a seven-item agreement scale ranging from 1 (strongly disagree) to 7 (strongly agree).

**Scored 0 to 4 for times occurred with 0 indicating none; 1, once; 2, two or three times; 3, four or five times; or 4, six or more times.

likely to ride in a car with a driver who had been drinking, to believe claims in advertising, or to agree with the statement that men find thin women most attractive.

Research has shown that adolescent girls experience social and cultural pressure about body image, and they look to each other for role models more than they follow the guidance offered in classrooms. The competitive environment of athletic programs may compound the pressure, leading to disordered eating and the use of body-shaping substances such as steroids, diuretics, laxatives, and even tobacco, Dr. Elliot says. However, the athletic environment can exert positive peer pressure also. The researchers modeled ATHENA's use of sports teams as a forum to promote healthy lifestyles on a similar program they developed for male high school athletes titled ATLAS (Athletes Training and Learning To Avoid Steroids). "We found that the team-based approach used in ATLAS produced greater positive change than did a more conventional classroom-style approach," Dr. Elliot says.

"Two features of the ATHENA program are striking," says Dr. Larry Seitz of NIDA's Division of Epidemiology, Services and Prevention Research. "One is the peer-based rather than classroom-based approach, and the other is the effect on a wide spectrum of linked behaviors, from vomiting to induce weight loss to believing nutritional claims in advertising. Improvements like these can help young female athletes make healthier choices throughout life, not just during the sport season."

Source: Elliot, D.L., et al. Preventing substance use and disordered eating: Initial outcomes of the ATHENA program. *Archives of Pediatric and Adolescent Medicine* 158(11):1043–1049, 2004. [Abstract]

Like ATHENA, ATLAS Targets High School Athletes

ATLAS (Athletes Training and Learning To Avoid Steroids), the result of five years of NIDA-supported development, is a program for male high school athletes to help reduce use of anabolic steroids and other sport supplements, alcohol, and other drugs. ATLAS emphasizes the immediate impact of alcohol and other drugs on athletic performance and conditioning rather than potential and abstract long-term effects. An evaluation of the program in 15 high schools showed that, compared with a control group, one year after completion of the program, ATLAS-trained students had:

- half the incidence of new use of anabolic steroids and less intention to use the drugs in the future;

- less use of alcohol, marijuana, amphetamines, and narcotics;
- less use of "athletic enhancing" supplements;
- less likelihood of engaging in hazardous substance abuse behaviors such as drinking and driving;
- reduced substance abuse risk factors;
- improved substance abuse protective factors.

References

1. Smolak, L., Murnen, S. K., and Ruble, A. E. Female athletes and eating problems: A meta-analysis. *International Journal of Eating Disorders*, 27, 371–380, 2000.
2. U.S. Olympic Committee Sports Medicine Council. Eating Disorders. International Center for Sports Nutrition and the University of Nebraska Medical Center Eating Disorders Program, 1993.
3. Piran, N. et al. (eds.). *Preventing Eating Disorders: A Handbook of Interventions and Special Challenges*. Philadelphia: Brunner/Mazel, 1999.
4. Piran, N. *On Prevention and Transformation*. Toronto Department of Applied Psychology, Ontario Institute for Studies in Education.

Additional Resources

Karol Media
Hanover Industrial Estates
375 Stewart Road
P.O. Box 7600
Wilkes-Barre, PA 18773-7600
Toll-Free: 800-526-4773
Phone: 570-822-8899
Fax: 570-822-8226
Website: http://www.karolmedia.com

Offers videos developed by the National Collegiate Athletic Association including:

- Afraid to Eat: Eating Disorders and the Student Athlete

- Eating Disorders: What You Can Do
- Out of Balance: Nutrition and Eating Disorders

National Association for Girls and Women in Sports
1900 Association Drive
Reston, VA 20191-1599
Toll-Free: 800-213-7193
Phone: 703-476-3400
Website: http://www.aahperd.org/nagws

Oregon Health & Science University
3181 S.W. Sam Jackson Park Rd.
Portland, OR 97239-3098
Phone: 503-494-8311
Website: http://www.ohsu.edu/hpsm/index.html

Offers additional information about the ATHENA and ATLAS programs.

Chapter 23

Eating Disorders at Middle Age

Until recently, the problem of eating disorders among middle-aged women was largely overlooked in psychiatry and medicine. The definition of middle life is somewhat arbitrary and in current flux, due in part to the increased longevity of people in the U.S. and Western Europe. This chapter focuses on increasing the knowledge of eating disorders in this population, which is defined here as the period of life between 35 and 65 years of age.

Individuals may develop an eating disorder for the first time at middle life, but to date most patients described in the literature have had the problem for at least ten years. While the manifest problem may be understood as a pathologic means of coping with changes in body image due to aging, the clinical course and motivation behind this maladaptive mechanism lead to different clinical presentations.

This chapter's purpose is to increase awareness of this neglected clinical problem, to offer some recommendations for treatment, and to encourage others to augment the knowledge base by describing how eating disorders in middle life are both similar to and different from eating problems at other periods in the life cycle.

This chapter contains "Eating Disorders at Middle Age, Part 1," By Katherine Zerbe, M.D., and Diana Domnitei, BS. Reprinted with permission from *Eating Disorders Review,* March/April 2004. © 2004 Gurze Books. And "Eating Disorders at Middle Age, Part 2," By Katherine Zerbe, M.D., and Diana Domnitei, BS. Reprinted with permission from *Eating Disorders Review,* May/June 2004. © 2004 Gurze Books.

Introduction

Despite the overall increased awareness of the negative effects of being overweight, as well as a greater than $15 billion diet industry, Americans are getting larger more quickly than the rest of the world. Nations like France, where people consume a diet rich in fatty foods such as cheese, cream, and whole milk, manage to maintain an obesity rate of slightly over 6%. Americans, despite many low-fat and no-fat foods, maintain an average national obesity rate of over 40%. Current data argue that this disparity is related to larger portion sizes, higher stress levels, and lower levels of regular exercise, not to food itself. Our attitudes towards food govern the way in which we consume food and help explain why we eat so much. Likewise, a combination of physical, interpersonal, and cultural factors determine our body image at any given point in the life cycle. Americans measure self-worth by appearance and make pejorative comments about their bodies despite objective measures to the contrary. How we will use or abuse food as we age is only one factor in how we alter that image to sustain a sense of self or of self-esteem.

According to a 1997 *Psychology Today* poll, which is the largest study on body image and eating disorders to date (involving more than 3,400 women and 500 men between 13–90 years of age), gaining weight is at the top of the list for negative influences on body image in both men and women.[1] This was true even though most were of normal weight. Two-thirds of the women and a third of the men said that gaining weight produced the greatest detriment to their self-image. Nearly half of the women polled reported being preoccupied with weight and finding displeasure with their weight regardless of age. In contrast, the poll found that men of all ages were much less dissatisfied with their appearance. Those from 30–39 and 50–59 years old were most dissatisfied. Another large-scale survey, which included women up to age 75, found that more than 70% of women aged 30–74 were dissatisfied with their weight even though they were of normal weight.[2] As women age, body dissatisfaction increases.

Biological Bedrocks

Physiologic aging has various effects on the human body that also alter body image, particularly in women. Until age 60, women tend to gain 5–10 pounds per decade of life. Body shape changes, skin loses its elasticity (crows' feet), and hair turns gray and thins. These normal life cycle changes are likely to be particularly problematic for women because body fat deposition tends to increase with each developmental milestone, for example, puberty, pregnancy, and menopause.[3]

Body image can also be threatened by any medical problem, chronic illness, restriction in social activity, and change in relationships with family and friends (for example; divorce or becoming a grandparent). This gender-based finding likely contributes to the normative discontent women feel about their bodies, and may contribute to the initiation and/or maintenance of eating disorders and exercise addiction in middle life.

In clinical practice, we educate women that these biological facts about midlife transition are likely genetically based because females are: (1) born with more fat cells than males; (2) have slower metabolic rates than males; and (3) have different hormonal influences than males (estrogen and progesterone), which increase the likelihood of weight gain throughout the life cycle. Women may also feel worse about their bodies with age because of lowered energy levels and other sensory and motor changes.

While all body systems change with age, it appears that women worry most about their weight and skin. For example, skin changes can be the most devastating for women because they are the most visible and also are the target of increasing media pressure for change. Women are bombarded with suggestions about defying their age and urged to "lie about [their] age," leaving them with the impression that aging is bad and that they should not be satisfied with themselves when they see crows' feet or other signs of aging developing. The overall message is that aging is bad and wrinkles are worse, and that the only solution is to use products, reconstructive surgery, or virtually anything in order to achieve a younger, more ideal look.

Herein lies the difficult assessment that women must make about themselves in order to age successfully: Do they accept society's message that younger is better and strive for unattainable or unnatural ideals, or allow themselves to become internally self-worthy and maintain a positive body image despite some noticeable and possibly inevitable physiological shifts?

Scope of the Problem

Body image derives from conscious and unconscious processes, a manifestation of internal and external prompting that has been shaped over the years by life experience, media images, and feedback from other people. Separating out the potential developmental antecedents of the body image disturbance that has led to and helped nurture the eating disorder allows the patient to better understand herself, her life, and the struggles that have shaped her into who she is today.

As a whole, 89% of the women polled by *Psychology Today* wanted to lose weight. The average woman is 5'5" tall and weighs 140 pounds, but would like to weigh 125 pounds, a desire that 15% of women said would be worth sacrificing more than five years of their lives to achieve. Another 24% of the women surveyed would sacrifice three years of their lives to achieve their desired weight.[1]

It is no surprise that preoccupation with body image affects a woman's sense of herself. For over 56% of women in our society, being a woman entails preoccupation and dissatisfaction with her overall appearance and body size. This desire to diet runs deeper than just a willingness to restrict calories and to exercise. Instead, it goes far beyond, to a pathological "I'll do anything" mindset to lose weight. This mentality is most commonly associated with women in their adolescent or young adult years. Thus, it is not surprising that 62% of females 13–19 years old are dissatisfied with their weight. What has been neglected and unrecognized is the larger percentage of older women who are dissatisfied with their body weight. This dissatisfaction with body weight rises to 67% in females over the age of 30.[1] Today's young women are being initiated to feelings of body dissatisfaction at a young age; these attitudes about their bodies stay with them and later prevent a normal transition into middle life.

Because middle life is usually viewed as that time when men and women have achieved identity and a personal sense of power, one begins to wonder why a focus on body image is so pervasive in this age group. Body dissatisfaction is not only higher than in past years, it has been accelerating—from 25% in 1972 to 38% in 1985 to 56% in 1997.[1]

Diets leave women unsatisfied with the results. In 2001, over 93% of liposuction patients were women between the ages of 17 and 74 years old, but 98.7% were within 50 pounds of their ideal chart weight. While the procedures have been improved and significant medical complications (such as bleeding or pulmonary emboli) have decreased, the success of liposuction does not address the increasingly negative body image of millions of women who believe that weight reduction or body fat removal will make them happier and healthier human beings. It seems as though the alternative of liposuction only addresses part of the problem, namely the female desire to come closer to the slender ideal, while it fails to resolve the negative body image that fuels the self-defeating dieting that often precedes and follows such procedures. Consideration of these facts makes clinicians wonder if women who seek plastic surgery at middle life should be screened for an eating disorder.

Clinical Presentation

Eating disorders at middle life are often accompanied by addiction to stimulants or cocaine to reduce weight. Herbal remedies, over-the-counter medications, or prescribed medications are also ubiquitously used to counter the normal 5 to 10 pound weight gain of middle life. Some individuals literally exercise themselves to death, spending hours in the gym or fanatically racing from one activity to the next. These addictions may be a final common pathway to cause morbidity and mortality at middle life, an under-recognized issue in women's health care.

Just as the adolescent or young adult with body image disturbances, the individual at middle age may be unhappy with her appearance. However, because time and money are more available to them, affluent individuals may seek out plastic surgery to obliterate the signs of aging. Individuals may struggle with a psychological concern that gets channeled into an eating disorder; that is, the eating disturbance becomes a focus so that the individual avoids facing conflicts, losses, normative life-transition concerns (such as children going to college or aging parents) and even one's mortality.

Middle age is the time of life when one begins to take stock and to shift the focus from one's own life to encouraging and helping shape the lives of the younger generation. Psychologist Eric Erickson described the core issue of middle life as generating vs. stagnating. Any emotional or physical problem can prevent an individual from taking his or her place in the cycle of the generations. Eating disorders at middle life have both emotional and physical components that derail adaptive choices at this point in the life cycle. A focus on spirituality may enable some individuals to place greater emphasis on fundamental values, and personal transcendence, rather than on appearance, as a symbol of what constitutes a life lived well.

Treatment Recommendations

Part of the challenge in treating women with eating disorders at midlife is effectively educating them about the normal process of aging. They must come to terms with the fact that the thinness they enjoyed as younger women is probably an unrealistic goal in middle age. We recommend that clinicians tell the patient that female weight gain in midlife is a result of normal hormonal and metabolic shifts, which are likely the result of aging and menopause. Large weight gains should be avoided by exercise and an individualized nutrition plan, because fewer calories are needed than when one is young; however, for most patients some weight gain is inevitable. One of the few boosters of body image is regular exercise, which plays an even larger positive role on the body image of overweight women compared to normal-weight women. As noted before, excess exercise must be avoided.

The journey of psychological discovery into the very source of the eating disorder is usually the keystone of the treatment process. Grappling with unresolved adolescent or adult conflicts or trauma, and addressing maladaptive behaviors such as smoking, food restriction, or drug abuse, or mourning personal issues and/or idealized body image can be costly in terms of time and money but hold the most hope for improvement.

In order for patients to gain a sense of mastery over their feelings about aging, encourage them to focus on why staying youthful takes on inordinate importance to them and try to help them to understand that nothing can stop the body from slowing down. In essence, existential issues must be dealt with by gently, but persistently, confronting denial.

Teasing apart the potential developmental antecedents of the body image disturbance that have led to and nurtured the eating disorder into existence includes helping patients to better understand themselves and their lives and the struggles that have shaped them into who they are today. This is vital not only for discovering and understanding the life events that have shaped the patients' eating disorders, but also for fully recognizing and appreciating their own personal growth. Doing so will allow them to gain the pride and sense of internal beauty that comes from the realization that they have lived a worthwhile life. Finding meaning in one's personal history provides a unique pathway to understanding the illness and ways to begin accepting the changes that accompany aging.[5, 6]

Some patients ask for more specifics. Summarize these extant theories on aging and provide references for them to explore further. In particular, direct them to the growing biographical and mental-awareness literature that describe positive modes for aging.

Conclusion

As women enter middle age, it becomes increasingly important that they accept the normal physical changes that accompany aging and maintain a positive body image. Because the average woman gains 5–10 pounds per decade of life, the focus must shift from deriving excessive self worth from the external to personal development. These achievements include positive relationships with others and self-growth and are vital to making a successful transition into middle life. Greater awareness of the widespread body dissatisfaction among women in middle life, and particularly of those who have the additional symptoms of disordered eating and excessive exercise, will promote women's health at this crucial point in the adult life cycle.

References

1. Garner DM. *Psychology Today*, February 1997.
2. Allaz AF, Bernstein M, Rouget P, et al. Body weight preoccupation in middle age and ageing women: A general population survey. *Int J Eat Disord* 1998; 23: 287.
3. Tiggemann M. Body Image Research Summary: Body Image and Aging. Body Image & Health Inc. *Research Summaries* 1999.
4. Rodin J, Silberstein L, Streigel-Moore R. *Women and weight: A normative discontent*. Nebraska Symposium on Motivation 1985; 266.
5. Zerbe K. The crucial role of psychodynamic understanding in the treatment of eating disorders. *Psychiatr Clin N Am* 2001; 2:24.
6. Zerbe K. Eating Disorders Over the Lifecycle: Diagnosis and Treatment. *Primary Psychiatry* 2003; 10: 6.

Chapter 24

Males with Eating Disorders

The stereotypical anorexic, bulimic, and binge eater is female. The stereotype is misleading. Just like girls and women, boys and men get anorexia nervosa and bulimia nervosa. Many males describe themselves as compulsive eaters, and some may have binge eating disorder. There is no evidence to suggest that eating disorders in males are atypical or somehow different from the eating disorders experienced by females.

How many males have eating disorders?

The numbers seem to be increasing. Twenty years ago it was thought that for every 10–15 women with anorexia or bulimia, there was one man. Today researchers find that for every four females with anorexia, there is one male, and for every 8–11 females with bulimia, there is one male (*American Journal of Psychiatry*, 2001: 158: 570–574).

Binge eating disorder seems to occur almost equally in males and females, although males are not as likely to feel guilty or anxious after a binge as women are sure to do.

Clinics and counselors see many more females than males, but that may be because males are reluctant to confess having what has become known as a "women's problem." Also, health professionals do not

---

Information used with permission of ANRED: Anorexia Nervosa and Related Eating Disorders, Inc. © 2006 ANRED. For additional information, visit http://www.anred.com.

expect to see eating disorders in males and may therefore underdiagnose them.

Are the risk factors for males any different than the ones for females?

Eating disorder risk factors for males include the following:

- They were fat or overweight as children.
- They have been dieting. Dieting is one of the most powerful eating disorder triggers for both males and females, and one study indicates that up to seventy percent of high school students diet at one time or another to improve their appearance. (Theodore Weltzin, M.D.; Rogers Memorial Hospital)
- They participate in a sport that demands thinness. Runners and jockeys are at higher risk than football players and weight lifters. Wrestlers who try to shed pounds quickly before a match so they can compete in a lower weight category seem to be at special risk. Body builders are at risk if they deplete body fat and fluid reserves to achieve high definition.
- They have a job or profession that demands thinness. Male models, actors, and entertainers seem to be at higher risk than the general population.
- Some, but not all, males with eating disorders are members of the gay community where men are judged on their physical attractiveness in much the same way that women are judged in the heterosexual community.
- Living in a culture fixated on diets and physical appearance is also a risk factor. Male underwear models and men participating in reality show make-overs lead other males to compare themselves with these so-called ideal body types. So do ads for male skin and hair care products. Weight loss and workout programs, as well as cosmetic surgery procedures, whose goal is chiseled muscularity can lead to the same sort of body dissatisfaction that afflicts women who read fashion magazines and watch movies and television shows featuring "perfect" people.

In May 2004, researchers at the University of Central Florida released a study saying men who watched television commercials with muscular actors felt unhappy about their own physiques. This culture of muscularity can be linked to eating disorders and steroid abuse, the researchers said.

Much has been made of the effect the Barbie doll has on the body image of a young girl. Now we have the Wolverine action figure (and others) marketed to boys. If Wolverine were life size, his biceps would be 32 inches around. Advertisers are marketing to males the same way they have pitched goods to females, with apparently many of the same related problems.

Males and Females with Eating Disorders: Similarities and Differences

Males often begin an eating disorder at older ages than females do, and they more often have a history of obesity or overweight.

Heterosexual males are not exposed to the same intense cultural pressures to be thin that women and girls endure. A casual review of popular magazines and television shows reveals that women are encouraged to diet and be thin so they can feel good about themselves, be successful at school and at work, and attract friends and romantic partners. Men, on the other hand, are exhorted to be strong and powerful, to build their bodies and make them large and strong so they can compete successfully, amass power and wealth, and defend and protect their frail, skinny female companions.

It's interesting to note that when women are asked what they would do with one magic wish, they almost always want to lose weight. Men asked the same question want money, power, sex, and the accessories of a rich and successful lifestyle. They often think their bodies are fine the way they are. If they do have body concerns, they usually want to bulk up and become larger and more muscular, not tiny like women do. Males usually equate thinness with weakness and frailty, things they desperately want to avoid.

Treatment of Males with Eating Disorders

Because eating disorders have been described as female problems, males are often exceedingly reluctant to admit that they are in trouble and need help. In addition, most treatment programs and support groups have been designed for females and are populated exclusively by females. Males report feeling uncomfortable and out of place in discussions of lost menstrual periods, women's sociocultural issues, female-oriented advertising, and similar topics.

Nevertheless, like females, males almost always need professional help to recover. The research is clear that males who complete treatment given by competent professionals have good outcomes. Being male has no adverse affect on recovery once the person commits to an effective, well-run program.

The wisest first step is a two-part evaluation: one component done by a physician to identify any physical problems contributing to, or resulting from, the eating disorder; and a second part done by a mental health therapist to identify psychological issues underlying problematic food behaviors. When the two parts of the evaluation are complete, treatment recommendations can be made that address the individual's specific circumstances.

It is important to remember that eating disorders in males, as well as in females, can be treated, and people of both genders do recover. Almost always, however, professional help is required.

If you are concerned about yourself or your child, find a physician and mental health therapist who will be sympathetic to the male perspective. The sooner treatment is begun, the sooner the person can turn the problem around and begin building a happy, satisfying life. The longer symptoms are ignored or denied, the harder that work will be when it is finally undertaken.

Chapter 25

Eating Disorders in Older People

Eating disorders are usually thought of as problems afflicting teenagers and people in their twenties. However, there are significant numbers of middle aged people, especially women, who never recovered from adolescent eating problems or who develop these disorders for the first time in middle age. Defying our belief that age brings wisdom, a recent study at the University Medical Clinic at Innsbruck, Austria, shows that women between 60 and 70 years of age have eating behaviors and body image attitudes similar to those of much younger women (*Eating Disorders Review*, Nov/Dec 2004). In addition, there are people in mid to late old age whose behavior suggests anorexia nervosa or bulimia, disorders that are still relatively rare in a senior population.

Eating Disorders and Middle-Aged Women

Risk factors for eating disorders in middle-aged women include:

- Body dissatisfaction and despair. As women (men too) age, they move further and further away from the cultural ideal of young, thin, firm, and unblemished. Women and many men in developed countries measure their self-worth in terms of appearance. Other people measure them that way as well.

This chapter includes: "Eating Disorders and Older People," used with permission of ANRED: Anorexia Nervosa and Related Eating Disorders, Inc. © 2006 ANRED. For additional information, visit http://www.anred.com. Also, "Growing Older, Eating Better," *FDA Consumer*, Pub. No. FDA 04–1301C, March 2004.

- Improved access to rich food as careers move into high gear or increased leisure time allows more restaurant meals and indulgent home cooking.
- Higher stress levels might be caused by the need to care for parents as well as fledging children and perhaps grandchildren, and some experience divorce. Economic worries and health concerns may increase stress as retirement approaches.
- Loneliness, marriage problems, and lack of romance and intimacy increase concerns that one is no longer desirable.
- Exercise is less regular and less strenuous.
- An empty nest may be a risk if people define their worth in terms of their roles as parents, mothers in particular, they may wonder if they have any value at all when their children leave home for school, work, or relationships of their own.

Related problems include the following:

- use of, or addiction to, cocaine and other stimulants in the service of weight management
- misuse of alcohol and prescription drugs to numb emotional pain
- excessive, compulsive exercise
- unnecessary plastic surgery
- loss of sexual desire, probably related to negative body image rather than the hormonal changes that accompany menopause. According to researchers at Penn State University, the more a woman sees herself as unattractive, the more likely she will experience a decline in sexual desire and activity.
- depression, anxiety, cynicism, and disillusionment as one acknowledges that youth and physical beauty are important measures of desirability in affluent cultures and wannabe affluent cultures
- despair and perhaps anger as one acknowledges that, as time passes, the chances of recapturing youthful beauty and thinness are increasingly unrealistic and unachievable goals

Treatment and Recovery

Although it must be tailored to the needs of older people, treatment should include discussion of the normal, natural physiological changes experienced by the aging body. Waists thicken. Hips enlarge, so do thighs. Buttocks and bellies sag, as do breasts. Skin wrinkles. Hair grays and may thin. Some cultures see these changes as proof of wisdom and experience. Older people are treasured as civic and family resources. Good treatment should provide women everywhere with opportunities to create similar identities for themselves.

As with younger people, some older patients and clients will recover, some will improve, and some will remain chronically eating disordered. Because older bodies cannot tolerate the same degree of abuse as younger bodies can, or as prolonged deprivation, treatment should begin as soon as possible to prevent permanent damage or even death.

Eating Disorders and Seniors

"An elderly relative of mine has suddenly lost his appetite. He is losing quite a bit of weight, and I am concerned. Do older people get anorexia nervosa?" Yes, but it is rare in that age group. There are other, more common, reasons why seniors stop eating. They include:

- An undiscovered illness or infection can cause loss of appetite.
- Some medications cause loss of appetite.
- Other medications cause stomach upset or pain that discourages eating.
- Missing or decaying teeth make it difficult to eat.
- Poorly fitted dentures may cause pain so the person avoids eating.
- Alcohol is an appetite depressant.
- Memory lapses may be a factor as the person may not remember if she or he ate.
- Lack of enthusiasm for grocery shopping and food preparation can discourage eating.
- Poverty is a problem for many seniors as they have little money to buy food.
- Depression is a major appetite depressant as are loneliness and lack of meaningful connections with other people. Some older folks have given up on life and resigned themselves to approaching death. All of these psychological states are treatable.

Arrange to have your relative evaluated by a physician. If you suspect depression, include a psychiatrist or other mental health counselor in the process. Go with your relative to the appointments and tell the doctor and counselor what you have observed.

Growing Older, Eating Better

Nutrition remains important throughout life. Many chronic diseases that develop late in life, such as osteoporosis, can be influenced by earlier poor habits. Insufficient exercise and calcium intake, especially during adolescence and early adulthood, can significantly increase the risk of osteoporosis, a disease that causes bones to become brittle and crack or break easily. But good nutrition in the later years still can help lessen the effects of diseases prevalent among older Americans or improve the quality of life in people who have such diseases. They include osteoporosis, obesity, high blood pressure, diabetes, heart disease, certain cancers, gastrointestinal problems, and chronic undernutrition.

Studies show that a good diet in later years helps both in reducing the risk of these diseases and in managing the diseases' signs and symptoms. This contributes to a higher quality of life, enabling older people to maintain their independence by continuing to perform basic daily activities, such as bathing, dressing, and eating. Poor nutrition, on the other hand, can prolong recovery from illnesses, increase the costs and incidence of institutionalization, and lead to a poorer quality of life.

The Single Life

Whether it happens at age 65 or 85, older people eventually face one or more problems that interfere with their ability to eat well. Social isolation is a common one. Older people who find themselves single after many years of living with another person may find it difficult to be alone, especially at mealtimes. They may become depressed and lose interest in preparing or eating regular meals, or they may eat only sparingly.

In a study published in the July 1993 *Journals of Gerontology*, researchers found that newly widowed people, most of whom were women, were less likely to say they enjoy mealtimes, less likely to report good appetites, and less likely to report good eating behaviors than their married counterparts. Nearly 85 percent of widowed subjects reported a weight change during the two years following a spouse's death, as compared with 30 percent of married subjects. The widowed group was more likely to report an average weight loss of 7.6 pounds (3.4 kilograms). According to the study, most of the women said they had enjoyed cooking and eating when they were married, but as widows, they found those activities a chore, especially since there was no one to appreciate their cooking efforts.

For many widowed men who may have left the cooking to their wives, the problem may extend even further—they may not know how to cook and prepare foods. Instead, they may snack or eat out a lot, both of which may lead people to eat too much fat and cholesterol and not get enough vitamins and minerals.

Special Diets

At the same time, many older people, because of chronic medical problems, may require special diets: for example, a low-fat, low-cholesterol diet for heart disease, a low-sodium diet for high blood pressure, or a low-calorie diet for weight reduction. Special diets often require extra effort, but older people may instead settle for foods that are quick and easy to prepare, such as frozen dinners, canned foods, lunch meats, and others that may provide too many calories, or contain too much fat and sodium for their needs.

On the other hand, Mona Sutnick, Ed.D., a registered dietitian in private practice in Philadelphia, points out that some people may go overboard on their special diets, overly restricting foods that may be more beneficial than detrimental to their health. “My advice for a 60-year-old person might be ‘watch your fat’ but for an 80-year-old who’s underweight, I’d say, ‘eat the fat, get the calories,’” Sutnick says.

Physical Problems

Some older people may overly restrict foods important to good health because of chewing difficulties and gastrointestinal disturbances such as constipation, diarrhea, and heartburn. Because missing teeth and poorly fitting dentures make it hard to chew, older people may forego fresh fruits and vegetables which are important sources of vitamins, minerals, and fiber. Or they may avoid dairy products, believing they cause gas or constipation. By doing so, they miss out on important sources of calcium, protein, and some vitamins.

Adverse reactions from medications can cause older people to avoid certain foods. Some medications alter the sense of taste which can adversely affect appetite. This adds to the problem of naturally diminishing senses of taste and smell, common as people age.

Other medical problems, such as arthritis, stroke, or Alzheimer disease, can interfere with good nutrition. It may be difficult, if not impossible, for people with arthritis or who have had a stroke to cook, shop, or even lift a fork to eat. Dementia associated with Alzheimer disease and other diseases may cause them to eat poorly or forget to eat altogether.

Money Matters

Lack of money is a particular problem among older Americans, who may have no income other than Social Security. Lack of money may lead older people to scrimp on important food purchases—for example, perishable items like fresh fruits, vegetables, and meat—because of higher costs and fear of waste. They may avoid cooking or baking foods like meats, stews, and casseroles because recipes for these foods usually yield large quantities. Financial problems also may cause older people to delay medical and dental treatments that could correct problems that interfere with good nutrition.

Food Programs

Many older people may find help under the Older Americans Act, which provides nutrition and other services that target older people who are in greatest social and economic need. The program focuses particular attention on low-income minorities and rural populations. According to the U.S. Administration on Aging, which administers the Older Americans Act, the nutrition programs were set up to address the dietary inadequacy and social isolation among older people.

Home-delivered meals and congregate nutrition services are the primary nutrition programs. The congregate meal program allows seniors to gather at a local site, often the local senior citizen center, school or other public building, or a restaurant, for a meal. Sometimes health screenings, exercise, or recreational activities are also offered.

Available since 1972, these programs, funded by the federal, state, and local governments, ensure that older people get at least one nutritious meal five to seven days a week. Under current standards, that meal must comply with the *Dietary Guidelines for Americans 2005* and provide at least one-third of the recommended dietary allowances (RDA) for an older person. Often, people receive foods that correspond with their special dietary needs, such as no-added-salt foods for those who need to restrict their sodium intake or ground meat for those who have trouble chewing. Other nutrition services provided under the Older Americans Act are nutrition education, screening, and counseling.

While these nutrition programs target poor people, they are available to other older people regardless of income, according to Jean Lloyd, a registered dietitian and the national nutritionist with the Administration on Aging. Although no one is charged for the meals, older people can voluntarily and confidentially donate money, she says. The meals provide not only good nutrition, but they also give older people a chance to socialize—a key factor in preventing the adverse nutritional effects of social isolation and a way of keeping people actively and socially engaged.

For those who qualify, food stamps are another aid for improving nutrition. For the homebound, grocery-shopping assistance is available in many areas. Usually provided by non-government organizations, this service shops for and delivers groceries to people at their request. The recipient pays for the groceries and sometimes a service fee. In some communities, private organizations also sell home-delivered meals.

Other Assistance

Family members and friends can help ensure that older people take advantage of food programs by putting them in touch with the appropriate agencies or organizations and helping them fill out the necessary forms. Some other steps they can take include the following:

- looking in occasionally to ensure that the older person is eating adequately
- preparing foods and making them available to the older person
- joining the older person for meals

In some cases, they may help see that the older person is moved to an environment, such as their home, an assisted-living facility, or a nursing home, that can help ensure that the older person gets proper nutrition. A review of basic diet principles may help improve nutrition. Explaining to older people the importance of good nutrition in the later years may motivate them to make a greater effort to select nutritious foods.

Whatever an older person's living situation, proper medical and dental treatment is important for treating medical problems, such as gastrointestinal distress and chewing difficulties that interfere with good nutrition. If a medication seems to ruin an older person's taste and appetite, a switch to another drug may help.

Look to the Label

The food label can help older people select a good diet. The label gives the nutritional content of most foods and enables consumers to see how a food fits in with daily dietary recommendations. Some of the information appears as claims describing the food's nutritional benefits: for example, "low in cholesterol" or "high in vitamin C." Under strict government rules, these claims can be used only if the food meets certain criteria. This means that claims can be trusted. For example, a "low-cholesterol" food can provide no more than 20 milligrams of cholesterol and no more than two grams of saturated fat per serving.

Less common, but also helpful, are label claims linking a nutrient or food to the risk of a disease or health-related condition. These claims are supported by scientific evidence. One claim links whole grain foods to risk of heart disease and cancer. On the food label, this claim would read like this: "Diets rich in whole grain foods and low in total fat, saturated fat, and cholesterol may reduce the risk of heart disease and some cancers."

More in-depth information is found on the "Nutrition Facts" panel on the side or back of the food label. This information is required on almost all food packages. This nutrition information is easy to read and is usually on a white or other neutral contrasting background. Some nutrition information also may be available for many raw meats, poultry, fish, fresh fruits, and vegetables at the place of purchase. The information may appear in brochures or on posters or placards.

Physical Activity

Besides diet, physical activity is part of a healthy lifestyle at any age. It can help reduce and control weight by burning calories. Moderate exercise that places weight on bones, such as walking, helps maintain and possibly even increases bone strength in older people. A study published in the Dec. 28, 1994, *Journal of the American Medical Association* found that intensive strength training can help preserve bone density and improve muscle mass, strength, and balance in postmenopausal women. In the study, subjects used weight machines for strength training.

Scientists looking into the benefits of exercise for older people agree that regular exercise can improve the functioning of the heart and lungs, increase strength and flexibility, and contribute to a feeling of well-being. Any regular physical activity is good, from brisk walking to light gardening. Common sense is the key. However, before a vigorous exercise program is started or resumed after a long period of inactivity, a doctor should be consulted.

Taking time out for exercise, using the food label to help pick nutritious foods, taking advantage of the several assistance programs available, and getting needed medical attention can go a long way toward helping older people avoid the nutritional pitfalls of aging and more fully enjoy their senior years.

Chapter 26

Responsible Media Coverage of Eating Disorder Issues

Tips for Responsible Media Coverage

The media is one of the most important allies in the effort to raise awareness about the dangers of eating disorders. One challenge of explaining the causes and effects of eating disorders is the complex interplay of biological, psychological, and social forces that combine to ignite the onset of an eating disorder. Eating disorders, like suicide or terrorism, are issues that must be covered in a careful and responsible way in order to inadvertently glamorize or promote copycats to experiment with these life-threatening behaviors.

Several common coverage mistakes can cause serious harm. When covering eating disorders, please:

- Do not focus on graphic images or descriptions of the bodies of eating disorder sufferers. Research proves that coverage dramatizing dangerous thinness can provoke a "race to the bottom" among other sufferers for example, "She is thinner than I am and she's still alive. I should lose more weight."
- Do not play the numbers game. "She ate only 400 calories a day" or "He took as many as 10 laxatives at a time," can turn a well-intentioned article into a recipe for disaster.

Reprinted with permission from "Tips for Responsible Media Coverage," For additional information visit, http://www.NationalEatingDisorders.org.

- Watch out for "anorexia chic." Eating disorders and their sufferers should not be glamorized or, worse yet, presented as people with astounding will-power or incredible self-control.
- Be careful with narratives of those who "bravely fought their illness alone." Perhaps your subject did, but most do not. The vast majority of those who beat eating disorders do it only with the ongoing help of trained medical professionals. Consider how a person would write about someone bravely fighting alcohol or drug addiction without proper intervention and professional care.

Tips for Covering Eating Disorders Issues with Sensitivity and Fairness

- Try to strike a balance between serious and hopeless, and always encourage people to seek help for themselves or loved ones who are suffering. Recovery is long and often expensive, but it is achievable and there are many options available.
- Include contact numbers, addresses, or web links to information and treatment resources wherever possible. Otherwise fears and concerns may be raised without providing an outlet, which is a lot like leaving the FBI's phone number off a story about a dangerous criminal.
- Seek expert information. The National Eating Disorders Association in many cases may be able to provide contact information of treatment professionals or prevention volunteers in your coverage area. (For ethical and legal reasons, names of sufferers cannot be provided.)

Additional Information

National Eating Disorders Association
603 Stewart St., Suite 803
Seattle, WA 98101
Toll-Free: 800-931-2237
Phone: 206-382-3587
Website: http://www.NationalEatingDisorders.org
E-mail: info@NationalEatingDisorders.org

Chapter 27

Federal Legislation about Eating Disorders

There has been very little legislative activity on eating disorders in the history of Congress. The first bill addressing eating disorders was introduced in 1987 in both the House and Senate, and was a resolution designating a week as the National Eating Disorders Awareness Week for that year. Only one bill was ever passed into public law. In total there have been 17 freestanding bills that have dealt with eating disorders. Of those, twelve bills are specifically about eating disorders and the remaining five bills are more omnibus women's health or education bills which include the language of an eating disorders bill in it. Although there are 17 bills that have addressed eating disorders, until this Congress (the 106th), all the bills have simply been a recycling of the following two bills:

- **Awareness Week/Day:** A popular idea for a legislative initiative to address eating disorders is to establish an eating disorders awareness week or day. This idea was the first eating disorder initiative ever introduced in 1987 and a version of this idea was introduced as a resolution in the 100th, 101st, 102nd and 105th Congress. It was only passed into Public Law once in 1989, which designated October 23 through October 29, 1989 as Eating Disorders Awareness Week.

- **Information and Education:** The second popular idea first introduced by Representative Schroeder in the 103rd Congress (1993) was to require the Secretary to carry out a program to provide information and education to the public on the prevention and treatment of eating disorders, including the operation of toll-free 24-hour telephone communications. A version of this bill was introduced every year until the language was partly included in the 1998 *Committee Report of Departments of Labor, Health and Human Services and Education, and Related Agencies Appropriation Bill*. Once the goals of this bill were included in the report language the Office of Women's Health, the Secretary's Office responded by creating the *BodyWise* project and including eating disorders in their women's health hotline.

New Ideas

In the 106th Congress, two new eating disorders initiatives were introduced.

- **Effect of eating disorders on learning:** This bill was introduced in the House to work within the school system (by amending title VI of the *Elementary and Secondary Education Act of 1965*) to raise awareness of eating disorders and to create educational programs concerning the same.
- **Relationship between eating disorders and the media:** The second bill is a congressional resolution expressing the sense of the Congress with respect to the relationship between eating disorders in adolescents and young adults and certain practices of the advertising industry. This bill was written in response to a constituent's concern. There are no cosponsors and it hasn't received any since it's introduction. This means that the member introduced it but is not creating any activity around it.

Congress Mandating Federal Agencies to Address Eating Disorders

Perhaps the most activity has come from Congress mandating agencies to address the problem of eating disorders through appropriations report language. Eating disorders were first addressed through appropriations language in 1997. The agencies targeted were National Institute of Mental Health (NIMH), National Institute of Child Health and Human Development (NICHD), and the Secretaries Office. This may be why we see very little activity from federal agencies on eating disorders until recently. In fact, one person contacted at NICHD stated explicitly that they now do have eating disorders activity because Congress mandated them to address this concern through report language.

The report language focused on the need for more research and education to better understand eating disorders. Examples include:

- In 1997—The Committee urges NICHD to further investigate behavioral, social, and cultural factors that affect adolescent girls' eating habits, with the goal of learning how to prevent and treat eating disorders.
- In 1997—The Committee encourages the Secretary to develop a national media campaign targeting, but not limited to, adolescent girls and women to educate them about healthy eating behaviors. The program should educate the public about the risks of restrictive dieting and the prevention of eating disorders. The Secretary may consult with other agencies as appropriate, including the Centers for Disease Control and Prevention and other public health agencies. Such program may include development of a toll-free number and information clearinghouse on eating disorders.

Report language typically inspires the named federal agency to respond to Congress's concerns. The response of the report language to NICHD is that they included research in their Endocrinology, Nutrition, and Growth Branch which addresses eating disorders. Again, as mentioned earlier, as a result of the report language quoted in the second example (which is language from the Eating Disorders Information and Education Act) the Office of Women's Health created the *BodyWise* project.

Activity in Federal Agencies

The activity of federal agencies on eating disorders can be summarized as follows:

1. Most of the activity on eating disorders has occurred in the last few years.
2. For the majority of agencies that address eating disorders they do so by offering a fact sheet or other information on their web site.

3. NIMH is the most active agency. They have hosted workshops, created educational materials, created task forces, and offered research funding.

4. Other agencies have investigated eating disorders as they relate to the diseases and populations that are of concern to that particular agency. For example the National Institute of Allergy and Infectious Diseases is conducting a study with patients who have human immunodeficiency virus (HIV)-wasting syndrome, which is characterized by severely debilitating anorexia and weight loss.

5. A number of federal agencies have not addressed eating disorders at all such as the Department of Defense, Center for Disease Control, Indian Health Services, and the Department of Education.

Conclusions and Recommendations

1. The time is ripe for promoting policies that address the range of concerns in the eating disorders field or arena. Congress and federal agencies have increased their activity in this area, yet there is clearly much more that needs to be done in order to better understand the dynamics of eating disorders and to prevent the incidence rate from increasing.

2. There is an interrelationship between the actions of Congress and the activity of federal agencies.

3. Now that a number of agencies are addressing eating disorders, it is recommended to work directly with the federal agency to promote further attention to eating disorders.

4. Report language on eating disorders first appeared in 1997 as a result of advocates working with members of Congress. This is clearly an important route toward promoting further eating disorders policies.

Part Three

Health Effects of Eating Disorders

Chapter 28

Diagnosing Eating Disorders

Unintentional Weight Loss

Weight loss will occur with decreased food intake, increased metabolism, or both. There are many causes of unintentional weight loss including endocrine, gastrointestinal, neurological, psychiatric, and eating disorders, as well as nutritional deficiencies, infections, and tumors.

Call your health care provider if:

- An adolescent daughter (or son) has an unrealistic self-image and seems to be dieting excessively.
- Weight loss is excessive (greater than 10% of normal body weight) and unexplained.
- Weight loss is accompanied by other unexplained symptoms.

What to Expect at Your Health Care Provider's Office

The health care provider will obtain your medical history and will perform a physical examination. Medical history questions documenting weight loss in detail may include the following:

This chapter includes: Excerpts from "Weight Loss—Unintentional," © 2006 A.D.A.M. Inc. Reprinted with permission; and an excerpt titled, "Screening and Diagnosis of Eating Disorders," from "Eating Disorders Information Sheet: Health Care Providers," Office on Women's Health, October 2005.

- When did the weight loss begin?
- Has it been sudden or gradual?
- How much weight has been lost?
- Has appetite decreased?
- Has amount or kinds of food eaten changed?
- Has physical activity level increased?
- Has there been an illness?
- Have there been dental problems or mouth sores?
- Have stress or anxiety levels increased?
- Is there vomiting? Is there self-induced vomiting?
- Is there an apparent increased energy level?
- Has there been excessive physical exercise?
- Is there fainting?
- Is there occasional uncontrollable hunger with palpitations, tremor, and sweating?
- Has there been a change in vision?
- Is there increased sensitivity to cold or heat?
- Is there constipation or diarrhea? Is there increased thirst or drinking?
- Is there increased urinary output?
- Has there been any hair loss?
- What medications/drugs are being taken?
    - diuretics
    - laxatives
    - alcohol
    - street drugs
- Has there been severe depression?
- How is the body image—are you aware of the weight loss? Are you pleased or concerned?

The physical examination may include a general physical examination and a measurement of the body weight. Diagnostic tests that may be performed include the following:

- nutritional assessment
- blood tests including a chemistry profile

Psychological counseling may be recommended in cases where anorexia nervosa or depression are the cause of the weight loss. In the early stages, anorexia nervosa may be best treated in a hospital with close supervision. Even after anorexia nervosa has apparently been cured, the individual should visit the doctor periodically. Relapse is not uncommon.

For weight loss caused by a chronic illness, tube feeding may be administered in order to maintain nutrition and to prevent edema, poor healing, and muscle wasting.

The patient may be referred to a dietitian for nutritional counseling.

Screening and Diagnosis of Eating Disorders

Eating disorders can pose serious health risks to young people. Approximately one out of every 100 adolescent girls develops anorexia nervosa, and another two to five develop bulimia nervosa.[1] Both can lead to serious health complications and even death. Binge eating disorder affects millions more and can result in complications associated with obesity. Anorexia, bulimia, and binge eating disorder are serious and chronic mental health problems associated with anxiety and depression.

Children and Adolescents Should Be Routinely Screened for Eating Disorders

Eating disorders are often preceded by troublesome eating behaviors known as disordered eating in children as young as eight years old. Primary care providers are in a unique position to detect eating disorders in the early or subclinical stages. Early detection through routine screening greatly increases the likelihood of successful treatment and recovery. The prevalence of eating disorders is increasing in boys as well as girls, and these disorders affect young people of most ethnic, cultural, and socioeconomic groups. Routine screening for eating disorders is an increasingly important aspect of young patients' care.

The American Medical Association's Guidelines for Adolescent Preventive Services (GAPS) describe the recommended content and delivery of comprehensive clinical preventive services for adolescents between 11 and 21 years of age. GAPS recommends that all adolescents be screened annually for eating disorders and obesity by determining weight and stature, and asking questions about body image and dieting patterns.[2]

Adolescence Is a Time of Change

Pre- and early adolescence is a time of dramatic physical and psychological change. Along with physical changes such as height and weight gains and sexual maturation, pre-adolescents often experience mood swings and wavering self-esteem. Influenced by the media and susceptible to peer pressure, young people may become increasingly concerned about body image during these years and base their feelings of self-esteem and self-worth on their appearance. They may be teased about their developing bodies by family or friends or may use food as a way of coping with the pressures in their lives. Body dissatisfaction, fear of fat, being teased, dieting, and using food to deal with stress are major risk factors associated with disordered eating.[3]

Definition of an Eating Disorder

Eating disorders are complex illnesses that rank as the third most common chronic illness in adolescent females, with an incidence rate of up to five percent.[4] The American Psychiatric Association's DSM-IV criteria for anorexia and bulimia follow. Binge eating disorder has been introduced provisionally in the DSM as a specific type of eating disorder not otherwise specified (EDNOS).

DSM-IV Diagnostic Criteria[5]

Anorexia Nervosa

- Refusal to maintain body weight at or above a minimally normal weight for height and age, or failure to make expected weight gain during period of growth, leading to body weight 15% below that expected.
- Intense fear of gaining weight or becoming fat, even though underweight.
- Disturbance in the way one's body weight or shape is experienced, undue influence of body shape and weight on self-evaluation, or denial of the seriousness of current low body weight.

- In post-menarcheal females, amenorrhea—the absence of at least three consecutive menstrual cycles.

Restricting type: The person does not regularly engage in binge eating or purging during the anorexia episode.

Binge eating/purging type: The person regularly engages in binge eating or purging during the anorexia episode.

Bulimia Nervosa

- Recurrent episodes of binge eating (eating an abnormally large amount of food in a discrete period of time, with a sense of lack of control over eating during the episode).
- Recurrent inappropriate compensatory behavior to prevent weight gain, such as self-induced vomiting; misuse of laxatives, diuretics, or other medications; fasting; or excessive exercise.
- Binge eating and inappropriate compensatory behaviors both occur, on average, at least twice a week for three months.
- Self-evaluation is unduly influenced by body shape and weight.
- The disturbance does not occur exclusively during episodes of anorexia nervosa.

Binge Eating Disorder

- Recurrent episodes of food consumption substantially larger than most people would eat in a similar period of time under similar circumstances.
- A feeling of being unable to control what or how much is being eaten.
- Associated with three (or more) of the following:
  - Eating very rapidly
  - Eating until feeling uncomfortably full
  - Eating large amounts of food when not feeling physically hungry
  - Eating alone because of being embarrassed by how much one is eating
  - Feeling disgust, guilt, or depression after overeating

- Marked distress or unpleasant feelings during and after the binge episode, as well as concerns about the long-term effect of binge eating on body weight and shape.
- Binge eating that occurs, on average, at least two days a week for six months.
- The binge eating is not associated with the regular use of inappropriate compensatory behaviors (for example; purging, fasting, excessive exercise) and does not occur exclusively during the course of anorexia nervosa or bulimia nervosa.

Other Types of Eating Disorders and Disordered Eating

- Eating disorder not otherwise specified (EDNOS) includes characteristics of one or more eating disorders but does not fit the diagnostic criteria for any one disorder.
- Disordered eating refers to troublesome eating behaviors that are less frequent or less severe than those that occur in an eating disorder.
- Over-exercising is exercising compulsively for long periods of time as a way to control weight. It is often viewed as a type of purging behavior, frequently associated with bulimia or anorexia.

Eating Disorders Can Cause Serious Complications

Anorexia has the highest rate of premature death of any psychiatric illness, with one in ten cases leading to death by cardiac arrest, starvation, other medical complications, or suicide.[6] Complications of anorexia may include heart failure due to malnutrition, hypometabolism, and increased risk of osteoporosis. Young women with anorexia have an increased risk of bone fractures.[7] In addition, anemia, reduced muscle mass, cessation of menstruation, and edema may accompany weight loss in anorexia.[8]

Most complications of bulimia result from electrolyte imbalance or trauma from repeated purging behaviors. Loss of potassium damages heart muscle, increasing the risk for cardiac arrest. Repeated vomiting can cause esophagitis, enlargement of salivary glands, and erosion of tooth enamel.[9]

Individuals with anorexia and bulimia have high rates of clinical depression, and often suffer from anxiety or personality disorders.

Eating disorders may be related to other health risk behaviors, such as substance abuse and unprotected sexual activity.[10]

Binge eating disorder affects up to four percent of the general population. Complications are similar to those found in obesity, including high blood pressure, diabetes, and increased risk of gallbladder disease, heart disease, and some types of cancer. Individuals with binge eating disorder also have high rates of depression.[11]

Although large numbers of teenagers who have disordered eating do not meet the strict DSM-IV criteria for either anorexia nervosa or bulimia nervosa, many have similar levels of emotional distress. Up to 60 percent of adolescent girls consider themselves overweight and have attempted to diet. In one study, more than half of the adolescents evaluated for eating disorders had subclinical disease but suffered a similar degree of emotional distress as those who met strict diagnostic criteria.[12]

Eating Disorders Should Be Diagnosed in the Context of Multiple Aspects of Normal Growth and Development

Applying strict diagnostic criteria for eating disorders such as DSM-IV may not be the best way to detect eating disorders in adolescents. For example, weight loss—one of the diagnostic criteria for anorexia—is not necessarily present in younger adolescents whose weight may remain stable as they grow in stature. Severe nutritional deficits can occur even in the absence of weight loss in early adolescence. The use of strict criteria may also make it more difficult to recognize eating disorders in their early stages and subclinical form. It is essential to diagnose eating disorders in adolescents in the context of the multiple and varied aspects of normal adolescent growth and development.[13] The rate of most rapid weight gain for girls is from age 9 to 14. By the time a girls reaches 18 years, it is likely she will nearly double her weight.[14] Families and health care providers may notice this rapid weight gain but fail to provide adequate reassurance to the girls that their body sizes and weights are in the normal range. Adolescent depression may camouflage an underlying eating disorder that may go undetected but which requires a separate treatment plan.

Communicate with Patients and Parents

Patients with eating disorders often feel shame, guilt, and fear that their illness will be discovered. Their eating disorder is not simply a physical problem; it is a way of coping with emotional distress. They may distrust health care providers and resist pressure to give up the disorder. In order to trust a health care provider, they must perceive that she or he has empathy, respect, and a genuine concern for them. It is important to be sensitive to and validate the patient's feelings; provide a nonjudgmental, caring environment; and ensure confidentiality.[15]

Team Approach Is Best

The primary care provider plays an essential role in the early diagnosis and treatment of an eating disorder; however, the complexity of the illness calls for a team approach. Assessment and ongoing management is best undertaken by a team of medical, nutritional, and mental health professionals to evaluate the severity and meaning of the symptoms and to both prescribe and provide care. It is essential that team members communicate regularly about the patient and clarify their roles in treatment on an ongoing basis, to the patient and the family, as well as to each other.[16]

End Notes

1. Office on Women's Health. *BodyWise handbook: Eating disorders information for middle school personnel.* Washington, DC.: Author, 1999.
2. American Medical Association. *Guidelines for adolescent preventive services (GAPS): Clinical Evaluation and Management Handbook,* 1995, pp. 78–83.
3. French S.A., Story M., Downes B., Resnick M.D., Blum R.W. Frequent dieting among adolescents: psychosocial and health behavior correlates. *American Journal of Public Health.* 1995; 85:695–701; Striegel-Moore R.H., Silberstein L.R., Rodin J. Toward an understanding of risk factors for bulimia. *American Psychologist.* 1986; 41:246–263.
4. Eating disorders in adolescents: A position paper of the Society for Adolescent Medicine. *Journal of Adolescent Health* 1995, vol. 16, pp. 478–480.
5. American Psychiatric Association. (1994). *Diagnostic and statistical manual of mental disorders (4th edition).*Washington, DC: APA Press, 1994.

6. National eating disorders screening program: National mental illness screening project, 1999. http://www.nmisp.org/eat/eat-fact.htm.

7. Mayo Clinic proceedings. *Medscape Wire*, October 14, 1999.

8. Office on Women's Health. *Information sheet: Eating disorders*, 1999.

9. Ibid.

10. Ibid.

11. Ibid.

12. Rome E.S., Ammerman S., Rosen D.S., et al. Children and Adolescents with Eating Disorders: The State of the Art. *Pediatrics.* 2003 Jan; 111(1):e98–108.

13. Ibid. And, Eating disorders in adolescents: A position paper of the Society for Adolescent Medicine. *Journal of Adolescent Health* 1995, vol. 16, pp. 478–480.

14. Centers for Disease Control and Prevention. *CDC growth charts: United States*. Developed by the National Center for Health Statistics in collaboration with the National Center for Chronic Disease Prevention and Health Promotion, 2000.

15. Pennsylvania Educational Network for Eating Disorders. (Spring 1999). *Food for thought,* spring 1999, vol. 15, no. 1; Something Fishy Web site on Eating Disorders, Tips for doctors, 1999, http://www.something-fishy.org/drtips.htm; and Muscari ME. Walking a thin line: Managing care for adolescents with anorexia and bulimia. *The American Journal of Maternal / Child Nursing,* vol. 23, no. 3, May/June 1998, pp. 130–141.

16. Rome E.S., Ammerman S., Rosen D.S., et al. Children and Adolescents with Eating Disorders: The State of the Art. *Pediatrics*. 2003 Jan; 111(1):e98–108. 4.

Chapter 29

Medical and Psychological Complications of Eating Disorders

Psychosocial

Eating disorders profoundly impact an individual's quality of life. Self-image, relationships, physical well-being, and day to day living are often adversely affected. Eating disorders are also often associated with mood disorders, anxiety disorders, and personality disorders. Bulimia nervosa may be particularly associated with substance abuse problems. Anorexia nervosa is often associated with obsessive-compulsive symptoms. The scope of related problems associated with eating disorders highlights the need for prompt treatment and intervention.

Medical

The process of starvation associated with anorexia nervosa can affect most organ systems. Physical signs and symptoms include but are not limited to constipation, abnormally low heart rate, abdominal distress, dryness of skin, hypotension, fine body hair, lack of menstrual periods. Anorexia nervosa causes anemia, cardiovascular problems, changes in brain structure, osteoporosis, and kidney dysfunction.

Self-induced vomiting can lead to swelling of salivary glands, electrolyte and mineral disturbances, and enamel erosion in teeth. Laxative abuse can lead to long lasting disruptions of normal bowel functioning. Complications such as tearing the esophagus, rupturing

---

the stomach, and developing life-threatening irregularities of the heart rhythm may also result.

Sometimes those suffering with anorexia and bulimia do not appear underweight—some may be of average weight, some may be slightly overweight, variations can be anywhere from extremely underweight to extremely overweight. The outward appearance of a person suffering with an eating disorder does not dictate the amount of physical danger they are in, nor does is determine the severity of emotional conflict they are enduring.

Some Symptoms and Complications of Eating Disorders

Amenorrhea is loss of menstrual cycle.

Barrett esophagus is associated with cancer of the esophagus and caused by esophageal reflux; this is a change in the cells within the esophagus.

Blood sugar level disruptions including:

- **Low blood sugar** can indicate problems with the liver or kidneys and can lead to neurological and mental deterioration.
- **Elevated blood sugar** can lead to diabetes, liver and kidney shut down, and circulatory and immune system problems.

Callused fingers are caused by repeated using the fingers to induce vomiting.

Chronic fatigue syndrome is a crippling fatigue related to a weakened immune system.

Cramps, bloating, constipation, diarrhea, or incontinence are caused by increased or decreased bowel activity.

Death may be caused by any of the following or any combination of the following:

- heart attack or heart failure
- lung collapse
- internal bleeding
- stroke
- kidney failure
- liver failure
- pancreatitis
- gastric rupture
- perforated ulcer
- depression and suicide

Dehydration is caused by lack of intake of fluids in the body.

Dental problems which include decalcification of teeth, erosion of tooth enamel, and severe decay.

Gum disease caused by stomach acids and enzymes from vomiting, lack of vitamin D and calcium, or hormonal imbalance.

Depression causes mood swings and depression caused by physiological factors such as electrolyte imbalances, hormone and vitamin deficiencies, malnutrition, and dehydration. Living with the eating disorder behaviors can cause depression. Depression can also lead the victim back into the cycle of the eating disorder (or may have initially been the problem before the onset of the ED). Stress within family, job, and relationships can all be causes. There are also a percentage of people born with a predisposition to depression based on family history.

Diabetes is high blood sugar as a result of low production of insulin. This can be caused by hormonal imbalances, hyperglycemia, or chronic pancreatitis.

Digestive difficulties result when a deficiency in digestive enzymes leads to the body's inability to properly digest food and absorb nutrients. This can lead to malabsorption problems, malnutrition, and electrolyte imbalances.

Dry skin and hair, brittle hair and nails, and hair loss caused by vitamin and mineral deficiencies, malnutrition, and dehydration.

Edema is swelling of the soft tissues as a result of excess water accumulation. Most common in the legs and feet of compulsive overeaters and in the abdominal area of anorexics and/or bulimics (can be caused by laxative and diuretic use).

Electrolyte imbalances. Electrolytes are essential to the production of the body's natural electricity that ensures healthy teeth, joints and bones, nerve and muscle impulses, kidneys and heart, blood sugar levels, and the delivery of oxygen to the cells. There are many factors associated with having an eating disorder that can lead to heart problems—bad circulation, slowed or irregular heartbeat, arrhythmias, angina—or a heart attack. Sudden cardiac arrest can cause permanent damage to the heart, or instant death. Electrolyte imbalances (especially potassium deficiency), dehydration, malnutrition, low blood pressure, extreme orthostatic hypotension, abnormally slow heart rate, electrolyte imbalances, and hormonal imbalances all cause serious problems with the heart.

Esophageal reflux—acid reflux disorders. Partially digested items in the stomach, mixed with acid and enzymes, regurgitate back into the esophagus. This can lead to damage to the esophagus, larynx, and lungs and increases the chances of developing cancer of the esophagus and voice box.

Gastric rupture is spontaneous stomach erosion, perforation, or rupture.

High blood pressure or hypertension is elevated blood pressure exceeding 140 over 90. High blood pressure can cause: blood vessel changes in the back of the eye creating vision impairment; abnormal thickening of the heart muscle; kidney failure; and brain damage.

Hyperactivity includes manic behavior; not being able to sit still.

Impaired neuromuscular function is due to vitamin and mineral deficiencies and malnutrition.

Infertility, the inability to have children, is caused by loss of menstrual cycle and hormonal imbalances. Malnutrition and vitamin deficiencies can also make it impossible to succeed with a full-term pregnancy, and can increase the chances significantly of a baby born with birth defects.

Insomnia is having problems falling and/or staying asleep.

Iron deficiency or anemia makes the oxygen transporting units within the blood useless and can lead to fatigue, shortness of breath, increased infections, and heart palpitations.

Kidney infection and failure. The kidneys cleanse the poisons from your body, regulate acid concentration, and maintain water balance. Vitamin deficiencies, dehydration, infection, and low blood pressure increase the risks of and associated with kidney infection thus making permanent kidney damage and kidney failure more likely.

Lanugo (soft downy hair on face, back and arms) is caused due to a protective mechanism built into the body to help keep a person warm during periods of starvation and malnutrition, and the hormonal imbalances that result.

Liver failure. The liver aids in removing waste from cells, and aids in digestion. Fasting and taking acetaminophen (drug found in over-the-counter painkillers) increases your risks for liver damage and failure. Loss of menstruation and dehydration (putting women at risk for too much iron in their system), and chronic heart failure can lead to liver damage or failure.

Low blood pressure, hypotension, is caused by lowered body temperature, malnutrition, and dehydration. It can cause heart arrhythmias, shock, or myocardial infarction.

Lowered body temperature is caused by loss of healthy insulating layer of fat and lowered blood pressure.

Malnutrition is caused by not eating enough or overeating. Malnutrition indicates deficiency for energy, protein, and micronutrients (such as vitamin A, iodine, and iron) either singularly or in combination. It can cause severe health risks including (but not limited to) respiratory infections, kidney failure, blindness, heart attack, and death.

Mallory-Weiss tear is associated with vomiting, a tear of the gastroesophageal junction.

Muscle atrophy is wasting away of muscle and decrease in muscle mass due to the body feeding off of itself.

Orthostatic hypotension is a sudden drop in blood pressure upon sitting up or standing. Symptoms include dizziness, blurred vision, passing out, heart pounding, and headaches.

Osteoporosis causes thinning of the bones with reduction in bone mass due to depletion of calcium and bone protein, predisposing to fractures.

Osteopenia is below normal bone mass indicating a calcium and/or vitamin D deficiency and leading to osteoporosis. Hormone imbalance or deficiencies associated with the loss of the menstrual cycle can also increase risks of osteoporosis and osteopenia.

Pancreatitis occurs when the digestive enzymes attack the pancreas. It is caused by repeated stomach trauma, alcohol consumption, or the excessive use of laxatives or diet pills.

Peptic ulcers are caused by increased stomach acids, cigarette smoking, and high consumption of caffeine or alcohol.

Pregnancy problems, including potential for high-risk pregnancies, miscarriage, still born babies, and death; or chronic illnesses from minor to severe in children born—all due to malnutrition, dehydration, and vitamin and hormone deficiencies.

Swelling may occur in the face and cheeks following self-induced vomiting.

Seizures. The increased risk of seizures in anorexic and bulimic individuals may be caused by dehydration. It is also possible that lesions on the brain caused by long-term malnutrition and lack of oxygen-carrying cells to the brain may play a role.

Tearing of esophagus is caused by self-induced vomiting.

Temporomandibular joint dysfunction (TMJ) syndrome is a degenerative arthritis within the temporomandibular joint in the jaw (where the lower jaw hinges to the skull) creating pain in the joint area, headaches, and problems chewing and opening and/or closing the mouth. Vitamin deficiencies and teeth grinding (often related to stress) can both be causes.

Weakness and fatigue may cause generalized poor eating habits, electrolyte imbalances, vitamin and mineral deficiencies, depression, malnutrition, or heart problems.

Sources

American Psychiatric Association (1998), Eating Disorders.

Dept. of Health and Human Services (1987, 1995). Anorexia Nervosa and Bulimia.

Also adapted from EDAP, Eating Disorder Awareness and Prevention, 1998, www.edap.org.

Chapter 30

Malnutrition

Malnutrition is a disparity between the amount of food and other nutrients that the body needs and the amount that it is receiving. This imbalance is most frequently associated with undernutrition, the primary focus of this chapter, but it may also be due to overnutrition.

Chronic overnutrition can lead to obesity and to metabolic syndrome, a set of risk factors characterized by abdominal obesity, a decreased ability to process glucose (insulin resistance), dyslipidemia (unhealthy lipid levels), and hypertension. Those with metabolic syndrome have been shown to be at a greater risk of developing type 2 diabetes and cardiovascular disease. Another relatively uncommon form of overnutrition is vitamin or mineral toxicity. This is usually due to excessive supplementation, for instance, high doses of fat-soluble vitamins such as vitamin A rather than the ingestion of food. Toxicity symptoms depend on the substance(s) ingested, the severity of the overdose, and whether it is acute or chronic.

Undernutrition occurs when one or more vital nutrients are not present in the quantity that is needed for the body to develop and function normally. This may be due to insufficient intake, increased loss, increased demand, or a condition or disease that decreases the body's ability to digest and absorb nutrients from available food. While the need for adequate nutrition is a constant, the demands of the body will vary, both on a daily and yearly basis.

- **During infancy, adolescence, and pregnancy** additional nutritional support is crucial for normal growth and development. A severe shortage of food will lead to a condition in children called marasmus that is characterized by a thin body and stunted growth. If enough calories are given, but the food is lacking in protein, a child may develop kwashiorkor—a condition characterized by edema (fluid retention), an enlarged liver, apathy, and delayed development. Deficiencies of specific vitamins can affect bone and tissue formation. A lack of vitamin D, for instance, can affect bone formation—causing rickets in children and osteomalacia in adults, while a deficiency in folic acid during pregnancy can cause birth defects.

- **Acute conditions** such as surgery, severe burns, infections, and trauma can drastically increase short-term nutritional requirements. Those patients who have been malnourished for some time may have compromised immune systems and a poorer prognosis. They frequently take longer to heal from surgical procedures and must spend more days in the hospital. For this reason, many doctors screen and then monitor the nutritional status of their hospitalized patients. Patients having surgery are frequently evaluated both prior to surgery and during their recovery process.

- **Chronic diseases** may be associated with nutrient loss, nutrient demand, and with malabsorption (the inability of the body to use one or more available nutrients). Malabsorption may occur with chronic diseases such as celiac disease, cystic fibrosis, pancreatic insufficiency, and pernicious anemia. An increased loss of nutrients may be seen with chronic kidney disease, diarrhea, and hemorrhaging. Sometimes conditions and their treatments can both cause malnutrition through decreased intake. Examples of this are the decreased appetite, difficulty swallowing, and nausea associated both with cancer (and chemotherapy), and with human immunodeficiency virus/acquired immune deficiency syndrome (HIV/AIDS) and its drug therapies. Increased loss, malabsorption, and decreased intake may also be seen in patients who chronically abuse drugs and/or alcohol.

- **Elderly patients** require fewer calories but continue to require adequate nutritional support. They are often less able to absorb nutrients due in part to decreased stomach acid production and are more likely to have one or more chronic ailments that may affect their nutritional status. At the same time, they may have more difficulty preparing meals and may have less access to a variety of nutritious foods. Older patients also frequently eat less due to a decreased appetite, decreased sense of smell, and/or mechanical difficulties with chewing or swallowing.

Signs and Symptoms

General malnutrition often develops slowly, over months or years. As the body's store of nutrients is depleted, changes begin to happen at the cellular level, affecting biochemical processes and decreasing the body's ability to fight infections. Over time, a variety of symptoms may begin to emerge, including the following:

- anemia
- weight loss, decreased muscle mass, and weakness
- dry scaly skin
- edema (swelling, due to lack of protein)
- hair that has lost its pigment
- brittle and malformed (spooned) nails
- chronic diarrhea
- slow wound healing
- bone and joint pain
- growth retardation (in children)
- mental changes such as confusion and irritability
- goiter (enlarged thyroid)

Specific nutrient deficiencies may cause characteristic symptoms. For instance, vitamin B_{12} deficiency can lead to tingling, numbness, and burning in the hands and feet (due to nerve damage), a lack of vitamin A may cause night blindness and increased sensitivity to light, and a lack of vitamin D can cause bone pain and malformation. The severity of symptoms depends on the intensity and duration of the deficiency. Some changes, such as to bone and nerves, may be irreversible.

Tests

Malnutrition will often be noticeable to the doctor's trained eye before it causes significant abnormalities in laboratory test results.

During physical examinations, doctors will evaluate patients' overall appearance: their skin and muscle tone, the amount of body fat they have, their height and weight, and their eating habits. In the case of infants and children, doctors will look for normal development and a normal rate of growth.

If there are signs of malnutrition, the doctor may order general laboratory screening tests to evaluate a patient's blood cells and organ function. Additional individual tests may be ordered to look for specific vitamin and mineral deficiencies. If general malnutrition and/or specific deficiencies are diagnosed, then laboratory testing may be used to monitor the response to therapy. A person who has malnutrition because of a chronic disease may need to have his or her nutritional status monitored on a regular basis.

Hospitalized patients are often assessed for nutritional status prior to or at the time of admission. This may include a history, an interview by a dietitian, and laboratory tests. If the results of these tests indicate possible nutritional deficits, patients may be provided nutritional support prior to a surgery or procedure and be monitored regularly during recovery.

Laboratory Tests

General screening and monitoring tests may include the following:

- lipids
- complete blood count (CBC)
- comprehensive metabolic panel (CMP)
- albumin
- total protein

Nutritional status and deficiencies lab tests may include the following:

- prealbumin (is decreased in malnutrition, rises and falls rapidly, and can be used to detect short-term response to treatment)
- iron tests (such as iron, total iron binding capacity (TIBC), and ferritin)
- vitamin and minerals (such as B_{12} and folate, vitamin D, vitamin K, calcium, and magnesium)

Non-Laboratory Tests

Imaging and radiographic scans may be ordered to help evaluate the health of internal organs and the normal growth and development of muscles and bones. These tests may include the following:

- x-rays
- computed tomography (CT)
- magnetic resonance imaging (MRI)

Treatments

Treatment of undernutrition includes the following:

- Restoring the nutrients that are missing, making nutrient-rich foods available, and providing supplements for specific deficiencies. In someone who is severely malnourished, this must be done slowly until the body has had time to adjust to the increased intake and then maintained at a higher than normal level until a normal or near normal weight has been achieved.
- Regular monitoring of those patients who have chronic malabsorption disorders or protein- or nutrient-losing conditions. Once the deficiencies have been addressed, putting a treatment plan into place is needed to prevent the malnutrition from recurring.
- Addressing any social, psychological, educational, and financial issues that may be causing or exacerbating the malnutrition, such as access to nutritious food.

Chapter 31

Osteoporosis and Eating Disorders

Anorexia Nervosa

Anorexia nervosa is an eating disorder characterized by an irrational fear of weight gain. People with anorexia nervosa believe that they are overweight even when they are extremely thin. According to the National Institute of Mental Health (NIMH), an estimated 0.5 to 3.7 percent of females have anorexia nervosa. While the majority of people with anorexia are female, an estimated five to fifteen percent of people with anorexia are male. Individuals with anorexia become obsessed with food and severely restrict their dietary intake. The disease is associated with several health problems and, in rare cases, even death. The disorder may begin as early as the onset of puberty. If a girl has anorexia when she reaches puberty, her first menstrual period is typically delayed. For girls who have already reached puberty, menstrual periods are often infrequent or absent.

Osteoporosis

Osteoporosis is a condition in which the bones become less dense and more likely to fracture. Fractures from osteoporosis can result in significant pain and disability. It is a major health threat for an estimated 44 million Americans, 68 percent of whom are women.

"What People with Anorexia Nervosa Need to Know about Osteoporosis," National Institutes of Health (NIH) Osteoporosis and Related Bone Diseases National Resource Center, June 2005.

Risk factors for developing osteoporosis include the following:

- being thin or having a small frame
- having a family history of the disease
- for women, being postmenopausal, having an early menopause, or not having menstrual periods (amenorrhea)
- using certain medications, such as glucocorticoids
- not getting enough calcium
- not getting enough physical activity
- smoking
- drinking too much alcohol

Osteoporosis is a silent disease that can often be prevented. However, if undetected, it can progress for many years without symptoms until a fracture occurs. It has been called a pediatric disease with geriatric consequences because building healthy bones in one's youth will help prevent osteoporosis and fractures later in life.

The Anorexia Nervosa and Osteoporosis Link

Anorexia nervosa has significant physical consequences. Affected individuals can experience nutritional and hormonal problems that negatively impact bone density. Low body weight in females causes the body to stop producing estrogen, resulting in a condition known as amenorrhea, or absent menstrual periods. Low estrogen levels contribute to significant losses in bone density.

In addition, individuals with anorexia often produce excessive amounts of the adrenal hormone cortisol, which is known to trigger bone loss. Other problems—such as a decrease in the production of growth hormone and other growth factors, low body weight (apart from the estrogen loss it causes), calcium deficiency, and malnutrition—contribute to bone loss in girls and women with anorexia. Weight loss, restricted dietary intake, and testosterone deficiency may be responsible for the low bone density found in males with the disorder.

Studies suggest that low bone mass (osteopenia) is common in people with anorexia and that it occurs early in the course of the disease. Girls with anorexia are less likely to reach their peak bone density and therefore may be at increased risk for osteoporosis and fracture throughout life.

Osteoporosis Management Strategies

Up to one-third of peak bone density is achieved during puberty. Anorexia is typically identified during mid to late adolescence, a critical period for bone development. The longer the duration of the disorder, the greater the bone loss and the less likely it is that bone mineral density will ever return to normal. The primary goal of medical therapy for individuals with anorexia is weight gain and, in females, the return of normal menstrual periods. However, attention to other aspects of bone health is also important.

Nutrition: A well-balanced diet rich in calcium and vitamin D is important for healthy bones. Good sources of calcium include low-fat dairy products; dark green, leafy vegetables; and calcium-fortified foods and beverages. Also, supplements can help ensure that the calcium requirement is met each day. Vitamin D plays an important role in calcium absorption and bone health. It is synthesized in the skin through exposure to sunlight. Individuals may require vitamin D supplements in order to ensure an adequate daily intake.

Exercise: Like muscle, bone is living tissue that responds to exercise by becoming stronger. The best exercise for bones is weight-bearing exercise that forces you to work against gravity. Some examples include walking, climbing stairs, weight lifting, and dancing. While walking and other types of regular exercise can help prevent bone loss and provide many other potential health benefits, these potential benefits need to be weighed against the risk of fractures, delayed weight gain, and exercise-induced amenorrhea in people with anorexia and those recovering from the disorder.

Healthy lifestyle: Smoking is bad for bones as well as the heart and lungs. In addition, smokers may absorb less calcium from their diets. Alcohol can also negatively affect bone health. Those who drink heavily are more prone to bone loss and fracture because of both poor nutrition as well as increased risk of falling.

Bone mineral density test: Specialized tests known as bone mineral density (BMD) tests measure bone density in various sites of the body. These tests can detect osteoporosis before a fracture occurs and predict the chances of future fractures.

Medication: There is no cure for osteoporosis. However, there are medications available to prevent and treat the disease in postmenopausal women, men, and both women and men taking glucocorticoid medication. Some studies suggest that there may be a role for estrogen preparations among girls and young women with anorexia. However, experts agree that estrogen should not be a substitute for nutritional support.

Additional Information

National Institute of Mental Health
6001 Executive Boulevard
Room 8184, MSC 9663
Bethesda, MD 20892-9663
Toll-Free: 866-615-6464
Toll-Free TTY: 866-415-8051
Phone: 301-443-4513
Fax: 301-443-4279
Website: http://www.nimh.nih.gov
E-mail: nimhinfo@nih.gov

Osteoporosis and Related Bone Diseases
National Resource Center
2 AMS Circle
Bethesda, MD 20892-3676
Toll-Free: 800-624-2663
Phone: 202-223-0344
TTY: 202-466-4315
Fax: 202-293-2356
Website: http://www.osteo.org
E-mail: NIAMSBONEINFO@mail.nih.gov

Chapter 32

Eating Disorders and Diabetes

The roots of eating disorders are complex, but eating disorders are a decidedly female phenomenon. Ninety to ninety-five percent of people with eating disorders are female. Some experts feel that role models on television and in magazines set impossible standards of thinness that girls feel they should measure up to. Health Canada's survey "The Health of Canada's Youth" found that 42% of 13 year-old girls and 48% of 15 year-old girls say they need to lose weight.

Diabetes and eating disorders can go hand in hand. Researchers from the Joslin Clinic in Boston surveyed 341 women with type 1 diabetes to determine how often eating disorders accompany diabetes. What they found is that a whopping 31% of the women had intentionally withheld insulin to produce sugar in their urine to promote weight loss. About 9% of the women withheld insulin to lose weight on a regular basis.

Teens with diabetes must eat at set times rather than eating in response to the body's natural hunger cues. Some experts believe this timetable eating may set the stage for disordered eating patterns.

The Boston researchers also reported that the weight gain following the diagnosis of diabetes and the start of treatment was particularly distressing. They identified women between the ages of 15 and 30 as those most likely to withhold insulin to lose weight.

This chapter begins with "Diabetes and Eating Disorders," © 2006 Roche Diagnostics. Reprinted with permission. It continues with additional information from "Diabetes and Eating Disorders," used with permission of ANRED: Anorexia Nervosa and Related Eating Disorders, Inc. © 2005 ANRED. For more information visit, http://www.anred.com.

Signs of an eating disorder specific to a teenage girl with diabetes include the following:

- wild swings in blood glucose levels
- an irregular menstrual cycle
- fear of being weighed
- avoiding healthcare providers

Are you unknowingly telling your daughter that there's something wrong with her weight? The following guidelines may help her to develop a healthy body image.

- Accept your own weight and shape. If you stand in front of the mirror poking at what you perceive as imperfections, your child will follow suit.
- Take the time to help your teen find a style that looks good on her. No one looks good in everything.
- Challenge stereotypes. Ask whether the female star must always be wafer thin.
- Encourage your teen to enjoy her body. After she's had a hard day at school, offer to massage her back or draw a soothing bath. Your own comfort with your daughter's body sends a strong message that her body is lovable.
- Boost her self-esteem. Make a point of praising your daughter. Your child can't have good self-esteem if she has a poor image of her body.

Information about Diabetes and Eating Disorders from ANRED

Because both diabetes and eating disorders involve attention to body states, weight management, and control of food, some people develop a pattern in which they use the disease to justify or camouflage the disorder. Because the complications of diabetes and eating disorders can be serious and even fatal—responsible, healthy behavior is essential.

How many people have both an eating disorder and diabetes?

We are not sure, but the combination is common. Some clinicians think that eating disorders are more common among folks with diabetes than they are in the general population. Research is currently underway to find out if this is so.

Does diabetes cause anorexia nervosa or bulimia?

No, diabetes does not cause eating disorders, but it can set the stage, physically and emotionally, for their development. Once people develop eating disorders, they can hide them in the overall diabetic constellation. This makes treatment and even diagnosis difficult. In some of these cases the eating disorder has gone undetected for years, sometimes coming to light only when life-altering complications appear.

What are some of those life-altering complications?

Complications include blindness, kidney disease, impaired circulation, nerve death, and amputation of limbs. Death, of course, is the ultimate life-altering complication.

People who have both diabetes and an eating disorder eat in ways that would make their doctors shudder. Many believe that being fat is far worse than the consequences mentioned, which, they rationalize, may never happen, or, if they do, will happen years down the road. Many of these people superstitiously believe they will escape complications. They are wrong.

What is the main mechanism that connects diabetes and eating disorders?

People who take insulin to control diabetes can misuse it to lose weight. If they reduce the required dosage, blood sugar will rise and spill over into the urine. These folks will lose weight, but the biochemical process is particularly dangerous. Reducing insulin causes body tissues to dissolve and be flushed out in urination.

Once diabetics discover that they can manipulate their weight this way, they are reluctant to stop, even if they know about potential consequences, because weight loss is rewarding in our fat-phobic culture. They decide to maintain the weight loss, and that decision can serve as the trigger for a full-blown eating disorder.

What are the similarities between diabetes and eating disorders?

Both demand that people pay close attention to body states, weight management, types and amounts of food consumed, and the timing and content of meals. Both encourage people to embrace some foods as safe and good and fear others as dangerous and bad.

Control is a central issue in both diabetes and eating disorders. Diabetics may feel guilty, anxious, or out of control if their blood sugar swings more than a few points. Anorexics and bulimics may feel the same way if their weight fluctuates. People with both problems may become consumed with strategies to rigidly control both weight and blood sugar.

Children with diabetes may have parents they perceive as overprotective and controlling. The parents of young people with eating disorders are often described in similar terms. In both kinds of families over involvement and enmeshment can lead children to rebellion and dramatic, potentially catastrophic, acts of independence.

People with eating disorders are preoccupied with weight, food, and diet. So are folks with diabetes. In fact, the latter can use their diabetes to hide anorexia or bulimia because, after all, they are supposed to be watching what they eat, and they can blame poorly controlled diabetes for alarming weight loss.

Are there any other problems related to a combination of diabetes and eating disorders?

Yes, when people misuse insulin to lose weight, sometimes that weight loss seems to improve diabetes, at least temporarily, by reducing or eliminating the need for insulin. It is interesting to note that starvation was a primary treatment for diabetes before commercial production of supplemental insulin. However, this weight loss method is not without problems. If continued, the person may experience life-threatening organ failure and possible death.

What kind of treatment is appropriate for people who have both diabetes and eating disorders?

Getting them into treatment is the first step. Many of these folks are embarrassed to admit that they have been doing something as unhealthy as an eating disorder. Often they defiantly hang onto starving and stuffing behaviors in spite of real threats to life and health. Families sometimes collude by denying that anything is wrong.

Nevertheless, it is important to begin treatment early. Eating disorders can be treated, and people do recover from them, but the longer symptoms are ignored, the harder it is to turn them around and deal with the harsher the effects on the body.

The best treatment is team treatment. That means that many professionals are involved with the patient and perhaps with the family as well: a physician to manage the diabetes and the effects of starving and stuffing, a mental health therapist to help define and deal with underlying emotional issues, a family therapist to help the family, and a dietitian to provide nutritional counseling and education.

The first priority is restoration of physical health. For diabetic anorexics that means weight gain back to healthy levels. For diabetic anorexics and bulimics the next step is implementation of balanced, varied, and healthy meal plans that provide adequate calories and nutrients. After physical health is stabilized, treatment can focus on the underlying psychological issues, plus of course ongoing attention to the diabetes.

Most treatment for eating disorders is outpatient, but if the patient is suicidal, severely depressed, or in any kind of medical danger, hospitalization is appropriate until the crisis has passed. Medication may be used to ease depression and anxiety, but it must be carefully monitored by a physician.

Summary

Diabetes and eating disorders are a nasty combination with very real potential for catastrophic complications, including death. The good news, however, is that in most cases diabetes can be controlled, and eating disorders can be treated. Many people recover from anorexia nervosa and bulimia, but almost always professional help is required.

If you are concerned about yourself, arrange right now to talk to your physician. Don't let shame or embarrassment stop you from telling the truth. Ask for a referral to a mental health professional who works with people with eating disorders. Contact that person and ask for an evaluation. Then follow up on any treatment recommendations that come from the evaluation.

Chapter 33

Dentists Often Find First Signs of Eating Disorders

The physical signs of an eating disorder may first show up in the mouth. That is why it is important for members of the dental team to be alert for the oral signs of eating disorders, so they can provide referrals to health care professionals trained in dealing with such disorders, says Barbara J. Steinberg, D.D.S., clinical professor of surgery at Drexel University College of Medicine in Philadelphia. Dr. Steinberg presented at the October 2003 American Dental Association's 144th Annual Session in San Francisco with her colleague Shirley Brown, D.M.D, Ph.D., a practicing dentist and clinical psychologist specializing in eating disorders.

Experts say more than five million people in the United States suffer from eating disorders. "The mouth reflects the rest of the body," Dr. Steinberg states. "A patient's oral status may be indicative of an eating disorder, particularly bulimia, when it involves chronic bingeing and vomiting."

The frequent vomiting and nutritional deficiencies often associated with eating disorders can severely affect oral health. According to the National Eating Disorders Association, studies find up to 89 percent of bulimic patients have signs of tooth erosion, due to the effects of powerful stomach acid. Over time, this loss of tooth enamel can be considerable, and the teeth change in color, shape and length. They can also become brittle, translucent, and sensitive to temperature. The

---

"News Release: Changes in Mouth often First Signs of Eating Disorders,"

salivary glands may swell, causing the jaw to widen and appear squarish. Lips may become reddened, dry, and cracked, and the patient may also experience chronic dry mouth. Drs. Steinberg and Brown tell members of the dental team to advise their patients who experience these behaviors to rinse with plain water immediately followed by an over-the-counter fluoride rinse to help the teeth re-mineralize. Left untreated, extreme cases of eating disorders may expose the innermost layer of the teeth, the pulp, which can result in infection, discoloration, or even pulp death. If pulp death occurs, the patient may need a root canal or to have the tooth extracted.

"Dentists can treat the oral effects of eating disorders, but they need to keep the patient's overall physical and mental health in mind, too," Dr. Brown says, "particularly since anorexia and bulimia are associated with a fairly high rate of suicide. By referring patients with suspected eating disorders to appropriate health care professionals, dentists, and the dental team may play a crucial role in helping to save their patients' lives."

Additional Information

American Dental Association
211 East Chicago Ave.
Chicago, IL 60611-2678
Phone: 312-440-2500
Website: http://www.ada.org

Chapter 34

Pregnancy and Eating Disorders

Perinatal Complications Linked to Eating Disorders

Certain complications during and immediately after birth are associated with the development of the eating disorders anorexia nervosa and bulimia nervosa, according to a study in the January 2006 issue of the *Archives of General Psychiatry*, one of the *JAMA/Archives* journals.

Eating disorders are believed to be caused by a complex interaction of genetic and environmental factors, according to background information in the article. Observational reports suggest that problems during neurodevelopment in the fetus might lead to anorexia nervosa or bulimia nervosa later in life, and some studies have found a correlation between obstetric complications and anorexia nervosa. "Obstetric complications might have more than one role in the etiopathogenesis of eating disorders; first, they may cause hypoxic-induced damage to the brain that impairs the neurodevelopment of the fetus, and second, the adequacy of nutrition during pregnancy and in the immediate postnatal period seems to influence the nutritional status

---

This chapter begins with "Press Release: Perinatal Complications Linked to Eating Disorders," January 2, 2006, reprinted with permission from the *JAMA/Archives* Office of Media Relations. Text under the heading "Eating Disorders and Pregnancy: Questions and Answers" is from "Eating Disorders and Pregnancy," used with permission of ANRED: Anorexia Nervosa and Related Eating Disorders, Inc. © 2006 ANRED. For additional information visit, http://www.anred.com.

of the adult and appetite programming throughout life," the authors write.

Angela Favaro, M.D., Ph.D., and colleagues at the University of Padua, Italy, completed an analysis of 114 females with anorexia nervosa, 73 with bulimia nervosa and a control group of 554 without either condition, all born at Padua Hospital between January 17, 1971, and December 30, 1979. Fifteen of the people with anorexia, 22 with bulimia, and all of the control subjects had participated in a previous study of the prevalence of eating disorders in Padua. The authors added in a sample of 99 people with anorexia and 51 with bulimia who had been referred to an outpatient clinic for their conditions. They then merged the samples and analyzed data about obstetric complications obtained from hospital archives.

Several specific complications in the mother—including maternal anemia (low levels of hemoglobin in the blood), diabetes mellitus, and placental infarction (death of part of the tissue of the placenta)—increased a child's risk of developing anorexia nervosa. Neonatal heart problems, hypothermia (low body temperature), tremors, and hyporeactivity (a less than normal response to stimuli) also were associated with later development of anorexia. Placental infarction, neonatal hyporeactivity, early difficulties with eating, shorter than average birth length, and low birth weight were associated with bulimia nervosa.

In addition, the number of complications affected the age at which the children developed anorexia nervosa. Those with more than five complications developed the disorder at an average age of 16.3, compared with 17.5 years for those with one to five complications and 18.8 years for those with no complications. "This type of relationship is considered evidence of a causal link and would indicate that an impairment in neurodevelopment could be implicated in the pathogenesis of anorexia nervosa," the authors write.

"These findings seem to show some resemblance to what has been found in schizophrenia and, with less evidence, in other severe psychiatric disorders," they report, observing that some obstetric complications may contribute to the development of psychiatric illnesses by robbing a fetus of the oxygen and nutrients needed for proper neurodevelopment or by causing neonatal brain damage. "However, this observation should lead to a search for other more specific risk factors that interact with perinatal factors and are able to predict the development of one particular psychiatric disorder rather than another."

In addition, they write, future research "should try to assess the prognostic impact of the presence of obstetric complications and whether this factor might help in the choice of appropriate and effective treatment." (*Arch Gen Psychiatry*. 2006;63:82–88)

Eating Disorders and Pregnancy: Questions and Answers

Eventually some women who have, or have had, an eating disorder decide that having a baby is more important than being bone thin. Then they worry that they might have done something that will hurt the baby, themselves, or both. Here is basic information. For specifics, each woman is encouraged to ask her own physician for specific suggestions to increase the chances of her having a healthy pregnancy and infant.

I have an eating disorder, but I want to have a family someday. Will I be able to have babies?

Because dieting, excessive exercise, stress, and low weight negatively impact a woman's endocrine (hormone) system, you may have trouble conceiving a baby and carrying it to term. The closer to normal your weight is, and the healthier your diet, the better your chances of a successful pregnancy. If you are underweight or overweight, and if you do not eat a wide variety of healthy foods, you and your baby may have problems.

A study in Denmark suggests that even eight years after successful eating disorder (ED) treatment, the chances of having a high-risk pregnancy are the same as those for women who receive treatment immediately before they conceive. (Secher, et al. *American Journal of Obstetrics and Gynecology*, January 2004). It appears that a history of disordered eating may predict reproductive trouble even years after treatment and progress in recovery. In the U.S., about 20 percent of women patients who ask for help at fertility clinics have had an eating disorder.

If I do manage to get pregnant before I'm recovered, could I hurt my baby by being eating disordered?

You might. Women with eating disorders have higher rates of miscarriage than do healthy, normal women. Also, your baby might be born prematurely, meaning that it would not weigh as much, or be as well-developed, as babies who are born full term. Low birth weight babies are at risk of many medical problems, some of them life-threatening.

An article in the January 2002 *New England Journal of Medicine* reports that premature babies have neurological and developmental problems well into early adulthood, and possibly longer. Some of the problems include lower intelligent quotients (IQs), learning disabilities, cerebral palsy, and psychiatric illnesses such as anxiety and attention deficit hyperactivity disorder. Additional problems include increased chances of infant death and failure to thrive in the first year following birth. Even if low birth weight babies seem to be healthy, they may not reach full expected adult stature, remaining small and short throughout their lives. The more premature the baby and the lower its weight, the more likely the disability.

Babies born to women with active eating disorders seem to be at higher risk of birth defects than those born to asymptomatic mothers. In particular, major handicaps such as blindness and mental retardation are common in those who survive.

I know this sounds selfish, but could I hurt myself by trying to have a baby before I am recovered?

You are wise to think ahead. If you become pregnant before recovering from an ED, you could seriously deplete your own body. The baby will take nourishment from you, and if you don't replenish your own reserves, you could find yourself struggling with the depression and exhaustion associated with malnutrition. You would also have to deal with the physical and emotional demands of pregnancy. You might find yourself overwhelmed and feeling out of control.

In addition, according to an article in the September 2001 *American Journal of Psychiatry*, pregnant women with active eating disorders or a history of eating disorders are at increased risk of delivery by caesarean section and postpartum depression, which makes taking care of themselves and their infants very difficult.

Are there any specific medical problems I might have trouble with?

Your teeth and bones might become weak and fragile because the baby's need for calcium takes priority over yours. If you don't replenish calcium with dairy products and other sources, you could find yourself with stress fractures and broken bones in later years. Once calcium is gone from your bones, it is difficult to replace it.

Pregnancy can exacerbate other problems related to the eating disorder such as potentially fatal liver, kidney, and cardiac damage.

A woman who is eating disordered, pregnant, and diabetic is at especially high risk for serious problems. All pregnant women should receive prenatal care. Those who have one or more of the mentioned complicating factors should consult with a physician as soon as they think they might be pregnant. To increase their own, and the baby's, chances of life and health, they should follow recommendations scrupulously.

That's pretty scary, but I'm more concerned about my baby than I am about myself. Assuming it was born healthy, would it be okay from then on?

There is evidence suggesting that babies born to eating disordered mothers may be retarded or slow to develop. Physically they may be smaller, weaker, and slower growing than other children their age. Intellectually they may lag behind peers and classmates. Emotionally they may remain infantile and dependent. They also may not develop effective social skills and successful relationships with other people.

The October 2006 issue of the medical journal *Pediatrics* cites a study done by Catherine Limperopoulos and colleagues at Children's Hospital in Boston. They found that up to half of premature babies develop language and learning disabilities. Previously the same research team showed that preemies, as they grow older, exhibit language and social delays.

At this point no one knows how many of a child's developmental difficulties are due to prematurity, per se, and the medical consequences of a maternal eating disorder and how many are the result of being parented by someone who is emotionally troubled and overconcerned about food and weight.

What else could go wrong if I try to have a baby?

You could become depressed and frantic because of weight gain during pregnancy. You might feel so out of control of your life and body that you would try to hurt yourself or the unborn baby. You might worry and feel guilty about the damage you could be causing the baby.

You might underfeed your child to make her thin, or, you might overfeed her to prove to the world (and yourself) that you are a nurturing parent. Power struggles over food and eating often plague families where someone has an eating disorder. You could continue that pattern with your child.

Research suggests that mom's dieting and low weight can create problems for the fetus, who may slow its metabolism to conserve energy. As with adults, this adjustment can lead to obesity, heart disease, and diabetes later in life. Mom's dieting can also shunt scarce nutrients to the fetal brain, short changing organs like the liver.

On the other hand, when a fetus is overnourished (mom eats too much and is overweight), it may be at risk for adult obesity and breast cancer. Elevated blood sugar can retard growth of the placenta as well. Our best advice: eat healthy, well balanced meals, and maintain a healthy normal weight for several months before you conceive and throughout the duration of your pregnancy.

I think I would be a good mother. Would the eating disorder be that important if I had a child?

Motherhood is stressful. If you are not strong in your recovery, you will be tempted to fall back on the starving and stuffing coping behaviors that are so familiar to you. Ideally, as you begin raising a family, you will already have learned, and will have had practice using, more healthy and effective behaviors when you feel overwhelmed.

Also, eating disordered women make poor role models. Your influence could lead your daughters to their own eating disorders and your sons to believe that the most important thing about women is their weight.

I really want a baby and think having one would give me the motivation to recover and handle the weight gain of pregnancy. What can I do to give myself and my child the best possible chance of success?

Some women with eating disorders welcome pregnancy as a vacation from weight worries. They believe they are doing something important by having a baby and are able to set aside their fear of fat in service to the health of the child. Others fall into black depression and intolerable anxiety when their bellies begin to swell. Most are somewhere between these two extremes.

If you think you are pregnant, or if you want to become pregnant, tell your physician as soon as possible. Cooperate with prenatal care to increase the chances that your baby will be born healthy. Also, this would be a good time to check with a counselor who can help you manage your doubts, fears, and worries as you proceed through pregnancy. A couple of classes on pregnancy, childbirth, and child development after birth can give you reassuring information about what to expect. You can learn parenting skills, but role modeling comes from your sense of yourself. Acquire the former and improve the latter.

Conclusion

We now have evidence that what, and how much, a mother eats during pregnancy can influence a child's physiology and metabolism after birth, perhaps setting the stage for metabolic and hormonal problems that can lead to medical and psychological problems in the child's later life. For example, undernourished pregnant moms often produce underweight, premature babies. Those infants experience a 35% higher rate of coronary death in later life and a six-fold increase in the risk of diabetes and impaired sugar metabolism than do children of mothers who received adequate nutrition while they were pregnant. Related problems include faulty insulin sensitivity, diabetes, high blood pressure, high triglyceride levels, and too little good cholesterol. Maternal malnutrition can also lead to impaired liver development in the child and problems with blood clotting that can lead to heart attack and stroke in adult life. (Reported by Jane Brody in the *New York Times*, October 1996.)

Studies also indicate that undernourished moms give birth to children at increased risk of major affective disorders (depression, manic-depression or bipolar disorder) when they reach adolescence and adulthood. Apparently healthy fetal development of brain and nervous system requires specific nutrients, and enough of them, that may not be provided by weight loss or weight management diets.

New research also indicates that pregnant women need extra energy intake (calories and nutrition) over and above their requirements when they are not pregnant. According to Nancy Butte, Ph.D., U.S. Department of Agriculture (USDA) Children's Nutrition Research Center, Baylor College of Medicine, "Extra dietary energy is required during pregnancy to make up for the energy deposited in maternal and fetal tissues and the rise in energy expenditure attributable to increased basal metabolism and to changes in the energy cost of physical activity." Women with eating disorders should consider this fact before they become pregnant and decide if they can handle the increased nutrition requirements of a healthy pregnancy. (Reported in the May 2004 issue of the *American Journal of Clinical Nutrition.*)

Chapter 35

Eating Disorders and Alcohol and Other Substance Use Disorders

Alcoholism and eating disorders frequently co-occur and often co-occur in the presence of other psychiatric and personality disorders. Although this co-occurrence suggests the possibility of common or shared factors in the etiology of these two problems, research to date has not established such links. Regardless of the precise meaning of the association, the reality that eating disorders and alcohol use disorders frequently co-occur has important implications for assessment, treatment, and future research.

Numerous studies suggest that eating disorders and alcohol and other drug use disorders (referred to throughout this chapter as substance use disorders) frequently co-occur and often co-occur in the presence of other psychiatric and personality disorders. This review will consider the extent and nature of such co-occurrences and whether research supports the possibility of common or shared factors in the etiology or maintenance of eating disorders and substance use disorders. The reality that eating disorders and substance use disorders frequently co-occur has important implications for assessment, treatment, and future research.

Excerpts from "Eating Disorders and Alcohol Use Disorders," by Carlos M. Grilo, Ph.D., Rajita Sinha, Ph.D., and Stephanie S. O'Malley, Ph.D., National Institute on Alcohol Abuse and Alcoholism (NIAAA), 2002. Complete citations for the studies mentioned in this chapter can be found online at http://pubs.niaaa.nih.gov/publications/arh26-2/151-160.htm.

Eating Disorders

The current classification system, the fourth edition of the *Diagnostic and Statistical Manual of Mental Disorders (DSM-IV)* (American Psychiatric Association [APA] 1994) specifies three eating disorder diagnoses. The formal diagnoses are anorexia nervosa (AN), bulimia nervosa (BN), and eating disorder not otherwise specified (EDNOS). In addition, the *DSM-IV* includes a new eating disorder category—binge eating disorder (BED)—as a research category. BED is a specific example of EDNOS.

Anorexia nervosa is characterized by a refusal to maintain normal body weight (defined as 15 percent below normal weight for age and height), an intense fear of becoming fat, and (in females) skipped menstrual periods (amenorrhea) for at least three months. People with AN have a severely distorted body image. They see themselves as overweight despite being overly thin, and they tend to deny the seriousness of their low body weight. The *DSM-IV* specifies two subtypes of AN—a restricting type, characterized by strict dieting or exercise without binge eating; and a binge eating/purging type, marked by episodes of binge eating and/or purging via self-induced vomiting or misusing laxatives, enemas, or diuretics. In severe cases, medical complications or death from starvation can occur. Roughly 50 percent of people with AN may eventually develop bulimia nervosa. Anorexia nervosa is a rare disorder; it occurs disproportionately in women, and is estimated to have a prevalence of roughly one percent in adolescent and young adult women.

Bulimia nervosa is characterized by recurrent episodes of binge eating (defined as consuming unusually large amounts of food in a discrete period of time plus a subjective sense of lack of control over eating). BN is further characterized by regular use of extreme weight control methods (such as vomiting; abuse of laxatives, diet pills, or diuretics; severe dieting or fasting; vigorous exercise) and by dysfunctional attitudes about weight or shape that unduly influence self-evaluation. For a diagnosis of bulimia nervosa, the *DSM-IV* requires both the binge eating and inappropriate weight control methods to have occurred, on average, at least twice per week during the past three months. The *DSM-IV* specifies two subtypes of BN—a purging type and a non–purging type which is limited to the severe dieting, fasting, or exercise forms of weight control behaviors. If either form of BN occurs during a current episode of AN, the assigned diagnosis is AN. BN, like AN, is more common in females and has an estimated prevalence rate of two percent to three percent in young females.

Eating disorder not otherwise specified (ENOS) is generally considered the most prevalent form or category of eating disorder and the least studied. Outside of research centers with specific recruitment requirements, the majority of patients who present for treatment for eating-related problems are partial syndrome or EDNOS cases. That is, they fail to meet all the diagnostic requirements for one of the formal eating disorders, but they have significant symptoms and associated problems. Indeed, researchers have questioned the significance of the failure to meet some of the specific criteria (such as the necessity that amenorrhea be present in female patients for a diagnosis of AN to be made). Investigators have also claimed that some of the diagnostic criteria for the formal eating disorder are too stringent. Many patients experience significant and clinically meaningful problems with eating and body image, but do not always fulfill the exact requirements for the diagnoses of AN or BN.

Binge eating disorder (BED), included as a provisional category in the *DSM-IV*, is a specific example of an EDNOS. BED is characterized by recurrent episodes of binge eating (an average of two days with binge episodes per week over a six month period is required; and marked distress exists because of the binge eating) without the compensatory weight control methods that are required for the diagnosis of BN. BED, unlike AN and BN, is common in males and in people of color. It is most frequently seen in adults, and has an estimated prevalence of three percent in adults and roughly eight percent in obese persons. BED is associated with increased risk for obesity and thus for the plethora of medical problems associated with obesity.

Age Ranges and Gender

Eating disorders most frequently develop during adolescence or early adulthood, but their onset can occur during childhood or much later in adulthood. The peak age range for onset of AN is 14 to 18 years, although some patients develop AN as late as their 40s. Similarly, the peak age range for BN is adolescence through early adulthood. BED most frequently occurs in young to middle adulthood. Although developmental challenges and severe dieting generally predate AN and BN, it appears that a significant proportion of people with BED report no dieting prior to the onset of binge eating. Although

AN and BN occur mostly in females and BED is more common in females than males, it is important to not overlook these eating disorders in men. Available research suggests that among eating disordered patients, few gender differences exist in the specific features of the eating disorder.

Co-Occurrence of Substance Use Disorders and Eating Disorders

Most studies have reported that eating disorders and substance use disorders frequently co-occur, with especially high rates observed among patients in treatment. Although research has generally reported high rates of co-occurrence between eating disorders and substance use disorders, perhaps most striking is the marked inconsistency or variability in the reported co-occurrence rates across studies. A previous review by Holderness et al. in 1994 noted that estimates of BN in patients with substance use disorders ranged from eight percent to 41 percent and estimates for AN ranged from two percent to ten percent.

Co-Occurrence Versus Comorbidity

Research with both people in treatment and in the general population that used systematic recruitment methods, standardized diagnostic interviews (rather than self-report), and relevant comparison groups has revealed that, although eating disorders and substance use disorders co-occur, the co-occurrence is either not significantly greater, or if so, is only marginally greater than the co-occurrence rate in relevant comparison groups (for example, patient groups of comparable severity chosen to provide a context as opposed to the frequently used normal control group). Grilo and colleagues (1995a, 1995b) found that, although eating disorders are frequently diagnosed among inpatients with substance use disorders, they are also frequently diagnosed in other psychiatric inpatients. In this controlled study, the frequency of AN and BN was not greater in patients with substance use disorders than without substance use disorders. Subthreshold manifestations of eating disorders (such as EDNOS—cases where insufficient criteria were present to warrant either BN or AN diagnoses) were diagnosed significantly more frequently in the patients with substance use disorders than without. Some research has also suggested that patients with nonpurging AN may be less likely than patients with other forms of eating disorders, including AN purging subtype, to have substance use disorders.

The three studies of comorbidity in BED that used relevant comparison groups found high rates of lifetime alcohol use and substance use disorders but not higher rates than observed in the comparison groups. Von Ranson and colleagues (2002) reported findings from a large community study of two groups (672 adolescent girls, 718 adult women) assessed using diagnostic interviews. The authors reported that eating disorders and substance use were positively related, but the association was not significant. They concluded that there is no strong overarching relationship between these problems. These findings suggest caution in interpreting comorbidity between different forms of eating disorders and substance use disorders.

Other Comorbid Psychiatric Disorders

Although this review focuses primarily on the co-occurrence of eating disorders and substance use disorders, both of these classes of disorders frequently co-occur with other forms of psychopathology. A large body of research has documented associations between eating disorders and other psychiatric and personality disorders as well as between substance use disorders and other psychiatric disorders.

Controlled studies have suggested that some of the apparent co-occurrence between eating disorders and substance use disorders may be related, in part, to other psychiatric comorbidities. Specifically, Dansky and colleagues (2000) reported that the relationship between BN and alcohol use disorders reported by the National Women's Study was likely indirect and the result of associations with other psychiatric disorders, most notably major depressive disorder and post-traumatic stress disorder. Grilo and colleagues (1995b) compared inpatients who had eating disorders with and without substance use disorders with a comparison group who had substance use disorders but not eating disorders. In this controlled comparison, personality disorders characterized as cluster B (erratic or unstable) were diagnosed more frequently in the patients with co-occurring eating disorders and substance use disorders, whereas cluster C personality disorders (anxious or fearful) were diagnosed more frequently in patients with eating disorders without co-occurring substance use disorders. This three-group comparison allowed for a finer distinction regarding potential comorbidity and raised the possibility of subgroups of patients (such as those with borderline personality disorder) who might be most likely to have problems with both eating and substance use disorders. Consistent with this, Bulik and colleagues (1997) found that, although women with alcoholism and BN had higher rates of a variety of psychiatric problems than women with BN without histories of alcohol use disorders, multivariate analyses revealed that borderline personality disorder was the sole distinguishing variable between the two groups. Wiseman and colleagues (1999) found that the order of onset of the two disorders might be important. Patients who developed eating disorders early and prior to substance use disorders had greater levels of psychiatric and personality disorder psychopathology compared with patients who developed the eating disorder after the substance use disorder and with patients who had an eating disorder but no substance use disorder.

These findings suggest that additional psychiatric disorders frequently co-occur with eating disorders and substance use disorders, and may play a role in their relationship to each other. In particular, these findings suggest that patients who suffer from both eating disorders and substance abuse disorders may have deficits in impulse control. Related to this line of investigation, recent years have witnessed increased attention to the potential role of childhood abuse, perhaps mediated by personality disorders, as a common factor in patients with both eating disorders and substance use disorders. Research, however, has not generally supported specific or strong associations between childhood abuse and specific disorders. Another issue to examine in the relationship between these disorders is the significant frequency with which eating disorder symptoms occur with substance use disorders.

Eating Disorder Symptoms among Women with Substance Use Disorders

Grilo and colleagues (1995a) have reported that EDNOS (but not AN or BN) was significantly more common in people with substance use disorders than without substance use disorders. This suggests that it is important for clinicians to consider and screen for subthreshold levels of eating disorders in addition to formal eating disorder diagnoses. Moreover, assessment of co-occurring subthreshold eating problems may facilitate earlier intervention to prevent later development of the full-blown disorder.

A few studies have examined the specific features of eating disorders present among patients with substance use disorders. Sinha and colleagues (1996) assessed eating behaviors and the attitudinal features of eating disorders in a community-based sample of 201 young women (ages 18 to 30) who comprised the following four groups: alcohol dependent, alcohol dependent with anxiety disorders, anxiety disorders only, and neither alcohol nor anxiety disorders. Women with alcohol dependence had significantly higher levels of the behavioral and attitudinal features of eating disorders and were more likely to meet the criteria for BN and EDNOS than women without alcohol dependence. Interestingly, these authors found that alcoholism was more closely related to the attitudinal features, whereas anxiety disorders were more closely associated with the behavioral features of eating disorders.

Eating Disorder Symptoms by Gender and Ethnicity

Jackson and Grilo examined the specific features of eating disorders and tested for gender and ethnic differences in a racially diverse group of outpatients with substance use disorders. Similar to previous studies with primarily Caucasian samples, eating-related problems were not uncommon in substance abusers. Roughly 20 percent of men and women reported binge eating, and 12 percent reported some form of inappropriate weight compensatory behaviors. Problematic attitudes about body shape were also common; 28 percent of the Jackson and Grilo sample reported overvalued ideas regarding shape at levels considered to be clinically significant—as compared with 28 percent in the study of young women reported by Sinha and colleagues (1996) and 26 percent in the study reported by Peveler and Fairburn (1990). Jackson and Grilo (2002) found no significant ethnic differences in obesity, in features of eating disorders, or in levels of body image dissatisfaction. Men and women were similar in terms of overweight and behavioral features, but women had significantly higher levels of attitudinal features of eating disorders. Thus, contrary to clinical lore, weight- and eating-related problems are not uncommon in males or in minority groups.

Research Investigating Whether Common Factors May Underlie the Co-Occurrence of Eating Disorders and Substance Use Disorders

The studies previously described demonstrate that eating disorders and substance use disorders often co-occur and that eating disorder symptoms are significantly more common in people with substance use disorders than without substance use disorders. Although research is ongoing, reasons for this co-occurrence have not been reported. One potential explanation is that these disorders are different manifestations of a common underlying factor. Three types of research provide support for this hypothesis: studies of dieting and substance use, studies of brain chemistry, and family and genetic studies.

Studies of Dieting Behavior and Substance Use

Research has documented significant associations between dieting and eating problems and substance use in younger populations. Krahn and colleagues (1992), for example, found that among college women, increasing severity of dieting and problems associated with eating disorders were associated with increased rates of alcohol, cigarette, and other drug use. Krahn and colleagues (1996) also found that dieting during pre-adolescence (among sixth grade students) predicted future alcohol use. Such findings, when considered with studies showing that food deprivation can increase self-administration of alcohol and other drugs in laboratory animals are consistent with models positing that common mechanisms may play a role in eating disorders and substance use disorders. For example, Krahn (1991) suggested that food deprivation might cause alterations in the central nervous system's reward pathways, thus increasing the consumption of reinforcing substances (such as alcohol). However, as previously emphasized, and by other reviews, the fact that these problems are associated does not demonstrate a specific or common cause.

Studies of Brain Chemistry

Animal studies of brain chemistry have provided some support for the view that eating disorders and alcohol use disorders may have some shared factors. Some research, for example, has suggested that both disorders may be related to atypical endogenous opioid peptide (EOP) activity. EOPs have been found to influence both alcohol and food consumption and may play roles in the control of eating behavior as well as the development of alcoholism. In addition, brain neurotransmitter systems, including the serotonin, gamma-aminobutyric acid (GABA), and dopamine systems, are the focus of active research across a wide range of psychiatric and behavioral problems, including food and alcohol consumption. Particularly active attention has been paid to the role of serotonin, which has been implicated in the control of eating, mood, and impulsivity. In addition, treatment studies have reported some support for the efficacy of selective serotonin reuptake inhibitors (SSRIs) across different eating disorders.

Family and Genetic Studies

Early research reported that people with eating disorders are more likely than those without eating disorders to have family histories of substance use disorders. However, several large, carefully conducted studies have found that eating disorders (especially BN) and substance use disorders segregate independently in families—that is, eating disorders and substance use disorders most likely do not have the same genetic, familial, and environmental risk factors. For example, Kaye and colleagues (1996) reported that alcohol or other drug dependence was increased only in first-degree relatives of women with BN who themselves also had alcohol or other drug dependence. Schuckit and colleagues (1996), in a large study of alcohol-dependent people and their relatives, also reported weak evidence at best for familial transmission between alcohol dependence and BN. Lilenfeld and colleagues (1997) reported that women with co-occurring BN and substance use disorder have higher rates of problems with anxiety, a variety of personality disturbances including antisocial behavior, and high rates of familial substance use disorder, anxiety, impulsivity, and affective instability. These authors hypothesized that a familial vulnerability for impulsivity and affective instability may contribute to the development of substance use disorder in a subgroup of BN patients. Using data from a large epidemiological sample of female twin pairs, Kendler and colleagues (1995) demonstrated that most of the genetic factors associated with vulnerability to alcoholism in women do not alter the risk for development of BN.

Treatment of Co-Occurring Alcoholism and Eating Disorders

Although alcoholism and other substance use disorders frequently occur with eating disorders, research has not established common or shared factors in the etiology or maintenance of this co-occurrence. Nonetheless, the frequent co-occurrence of problems with eating and alcohol may signal greater psychiatric disturbances and greater medical risk. These clinical realities represent considerable challenges to practitioners and researchers. The most common questions include how to identify the presence of possible problems, which problem to focus on first, or whether or how to address both concurrently. These are important questions and there is a pressing need for research on these treatment issues. Not only has little research been done on treating these co-occurring conditions, but many treatment studies with eating disordered patients either exclude patients with substance dependence or enroll few such patients.

Assessment and Screening for Eating Disorders

Good, comprehensive assessment of patients is necessary for good treatment. Assessment protocols should involve questionnaires (instruments) that are sensitive enough to flag patients with potential problems for further evaluation. Failure to identify all problems may contribute to poor retention and treatment outcomes even for the targeted problem. Although standardized interviews are generally thought to hold important advantages for accurate and thorough assessment of eating disorders, it may not be possible or practical for many types of clinical facilities to use them because of cost, time, and lack of training.

The authors of this article recommend two self-report instruments for the screening and preliminary assessment of eating disorders. The first is the *Questionnaire on Eating and Weight Patterns–Revised (QEWP-R)*, a well-established and easy-to-complete self-report instrument. The *QEWP-R*, widely used in research programs, screens for the presence of the specific eating disorder categories and provides useful information about the frequency of problem eating and dieting behaviors. The second instrument is the *Eating Disorder Examination–Questionnaire Version (EDEQ)*, the self-report version of the *Eating Disorder Examination* interview. The *EDEQ* offers a number of advantages over other self-report measures and provides detailed information about the behavioral and attitudinal features of eating disorders. The *EDEQ* has received some support for its utility and has been used with substance abusers. Briefly, such instruments are generally thought to underestimate the frequency of some of the behavioral features of eating disorders (such as binge eating) and overestimate some of the cognitive or attitudinal symptoms, compared with interviews. These limitations notwithstanding, such screens are useful for efficiently identifying people with possible problems. Of course, in addition, it is important for clinicians and researchers alike to consider comprehensive medical and psychiatric evaluations for these patient groups. In particular, patients with these co-occurring problems require careful medical evaluation and follow-up. In terms of follow-up, it may be particularly useful for repeated assessments to include the eating disorder screens. Some clinical experience suggests the possibility that successful cessation of substance or alcohol use may be followed by the re-emergence of eating disorder symptoms in some patients. Although this hypothesis awaits conclusive research, it highlights the usefulness of repeated assessments.

Pharmacological Treatments

Pharmacological treatments have generally been found to have little effect on AN either as the primary approach or as an augmentation approach, although the antidepressant fluoxetine was found to decrease frequency of relapse in one study. In contrast, pharmacological treatments, particularly antidepressant medications, have generally been found to be superior to placebo for the treatment of BN. It is worth stressing that these studies generally find, particularly for fluoxetine, that high doses are required to produce effects (as high as 60 milligrams per day in the case of fluoxetine). Unfortunately, surveys have revealed that most patients with BN treated with pharmacotherapy by community practitioners received inadequate dosing. Nevertheless, fluoxetine has also been shown to reduce depressive symptoms and alcohol consumption in depressed alcoholics. Controlled research testing the efficacy of this medication among women with both alcoholism and eating disorders is needed.

Medications designed to block the action of opioids (opioid antagonists) have demonstrated efficacy for reducing alcohol use and relapse, and increasing abstinence rates among alcoholic patients. The opioid antagonist naltrexone has also been studied as a treatment for eating disorders. One study that compared naltrexone, imipramine, and placebo among BED patients found that both medications produced reductions in binge eating, but neither was superior to placebo (high placebo response occurred in this study). One study found that naltrexone reduced the frequency of binge eating in patients with BN during the first few weeks of treatment, but the effects did not last.

Psychological Treatments of Eating Disorders

Cognitive behavioral therapy (CBT) has received the most consistent support of any psychological or pharmacologic treatment for eating disorders. Briefly, CBT is a focal and structured treatment that involves a collaborative effort between patients and clinicians. CBT for eating disorders can be delivered via individual or group approaches and generally follows three phases. The first phase involves education and presentation of the treatment model, including expectations for treatment and homework, teaching behavioral strategies such as self-monitoring to identify problems, and a graded approach to normalization of eating. The second phase involves the use of cognitive restructuring methods to identify, challenge, and modify maladaptive thinking. The final stage involves relapse prevention techniques and problem solving to generalize the skills to other areas and to consolidate improvements. CBT has been found to be superior to control conditions, to most other forms of psychological therapies, to behavioral therapies without the cognitive components, and to the pharmacological treatments. Moreover, self-help versions of standard CBT therapist manuals have demonstrated efficacy. This approach may provide general practitioners with expertise in CBT with the technology to help certain eating disordered patients.

Although CBT is generally regarded as the first-line treatment of choice for eating disorders, research is needed to determine its usefulness for patients with co-occurring alcoholism and eating disorders, and to develop integrated psychological treatment approaches for patients with alcoholism and eating disorders. Although the data are sparse, the treatment literature has not suggested that alcoholism or a history of alcoholism diminishes CBT treatment effectiveness for BN or BED. No available studies have examined whether eating disturbances influence the outcome of alcoholism treatment. Although clinical lore suggests that personality disorders, if present, are associated with negative treatment outcomes, this has not received empirical support in treatment studies of patients with eating disorders, and findings from treatment studies of patients with substance use disorder are mixed.

Based on clinical experience with both patient groups, the authors suggest that certain CBT-based treatments represent a good starting point for treating co-occurring alcohol use and eating disorders. Basic aspects of the cognitive behavioral approach (such as coping skills therapy) have been found effective for treating alcohol dependence and are useful for eating disordered patients. However, behavioral therapies without the specific cognitive components of CBT have inferior long-term outcomes compared with CBT. Nevertheless, specific forms of behavioral and coping skills treatments (without the specific cognitive components of the CBT approaches for eating disorders) have been used successfully with substance abusers and seem to be readily integrated with pharmacological approaches.

Thus, an approach that targets alcohol use and pathologic eating behaviors may be especially appropriate for treating patients with both disorders. Treatment designed to teach new coping skills to patients with alcoholism could also have a beneficial effect on eating disorders even if the eating disorder is not specifically targeted. Given the well-known ambivalence that characterizes many of these patients, another potentially relevant approach involves motivational enhancement interviewing, which has received some support for substance use disorders and eating disorders.

Another promising approach is dialectical behavior therapy (DBT), which initial research supports for both BN and BED. DBT, which focuses on awareness of problems and choices, mood regulation techniques, and coping skills, directly addresses many of the needs of both eating disorders and alcohol use disorder patients, including the frequently co-occurring borderline personality disorder. Indeed, the initial treatment outcome findings for DBT for both BN and BED suggest that addressing a potential vulnerability (for example, problems with mood regulation and coping) can lead to improvements in eating disorders even without a direct focus on the eating behaviors, a finding that parallels that reported for interpersonal psychotherapy. Telch and colleagues (2001) speculated that DBT may be particularly helpful for eating disordered patients characterized by high levels of negative affect. Studies with BN and BED revealed two subtypes of these eating disorders: dietary and a mixed dietary-negative affect. The dietary subgroup was characterized primarily by eating-specific psychopathology without associated problems with self-esteem and depression (negative affect). Patients with the mixed dietary-negative affect subtype also had high rates of alcohol and other drug problems. It is possible that such patients, particularly if they have problems with impulsivity or have co-occurring borderline personality disorder, might benefit from affect regulation and coping skills approaches such as DBT.

Conclusion

Alcoholism and eating disorders frequently co-occur and often co-occur in the presence of other psychiatric and personality disorders. Although such diagnostic co-occurrence suggests the possibility of shared factors in the etiology or maintenance of these problems, research has not established such links. The clinical reality that eating and alcohol use disorders frequently co-occur has important implications for assessment, treatment, and research. Comprehensive assessment is necessary for good treatment. Research on methods of treating people with co-occurring alcohol and eating problems represents a major need. Until further guidance is provided, the authors recommend concurrently addressing both disorders. CBT, coping skills, or DBT approaches seem to be reasonable starting points.

Additional Information

National Institute on Alcohol Abuse and Alcoholism (NIAAA)
5635 Fishers Lane, MSC 9304
Bethesda, MD 20892-9304
Website: http://www.niaaa.nih.gov

Chapter 36

Neuroimaging Studies Reveal Impact of Eating Disorders

Focus Points

- The most studies of anorexia nervosa show gray and white matter alterations that, at least in part, remit with recovery; functional imaging studies suggest limbic, frontal, and parietal cortex as areas of disturbance; serotonin receptor alterations exist when ill and after recovery.
- Bulimia nervosa also shows serotonin receptor alterations after recovery, but very few studies exist in this disorder.
- There may be common and distinct areas of disturbance when comparing those brain imaging findings with other psychiatric disorders (for example, obsessive-compulsive disorder), but this needs to be studied further.

Introduction

The conceptual framework of the pathophysiology and etiology of the eating disorders (ED) has undergone significant changes in

---

Excerpts from "Neuroimaging Studies in Eating Disorders" reprinted with permission from *CNS Spectrums*, Volume 9, Number 7, July 2004. © 2004 MBL Communications. The complete text of this document, including references, can be found online at http://www.wpic.pitt.edu/research/anbnbrainimaging/Frank%20CNS%20Spectr%202004%20Neuroimaging%20Studies%20in%20EDs.pdf

the past decades. The etiology of ED is still unknown. Several lines of research have raised the possibility that trait disturbances of brain neurotransmitters may contribute to the pathogenesis of ED. These neurotransmitter systems include serotonin (5-hydroxytryptamine [5-HT]) and dopamine pathways and a number of neuropeptides. A major reason for our lack of understanding of brain and behavior is that tools for measuring neurotransmitter activity have been limited. These include indirect measures, such as concentrations of neurotransmitters in cerebrospinal fluid (CSF) or hormonal responses to drug challenges. Brain imaging techniques now give us the opportunity to assess regional brain activity and neuroreceptor function in vivo in humans and, therefore, may help us understand how neuronal circuits are related to behavior and pathophysiology.

A range of neuroimaging tools are now available. Structural imaging techniques, such as computer tomography (CT), may provide information on gross structural abnormalities. Magnetic resonance spectroscopy (MRS) can detect brain chemicals that are involved in brain metabolism. Positron emission tomography (PET), single photon emission computed tomography (SPECT), or functional magnetic resonance imaging (fMRI) can be used to assess brain activity thought to be associated with changes in regional cerebral blood flow (rCBF) or glucose metabolism (rCGM). Neurotransmitter-receptor and transporter function can be assessed with PET and SPECT.

Studies in a number of psychiatric disorders suggest brain structures, such as the amygdala or frontal cortical areas, are involved in emotional processing. Patients with ED have comorbid mood disturbances and anxiety, and it has been hypothesized that similar biological markers, as in other disorders might be found. Moreover, people with ED have poorly understood symptoms, such as body image distortions and restrictive eating. Over the past decade, brain imaging studies have begun to help us understand the brain pathways that may contribute to such symptoms.

Anorexia Nervosa (AN)

Anorexia nervosa is a disorder that usually begins during adolescence in females, and is associated with an intense fear of gaining weight, feeling fat, emaciation, and amenorrhea. A restricting type (AN-R) has been distinguished from a binge eating/purging type (AN-B/P). Comorbid obsessive-compulsive disorder (OCD), depression, and anxiety are common.

Computed Tomography and Magnetic Resonance Imaging Studies

It is well known from CT and MRI studies that underweight AN patients tend to have enlarged sulci and ventricles and decreased brain mass. While these alterations shift towards normal with weight restoration, it is not certain whether they normalize. It is not clear whether these changes during the ill state are related to changes in gray or white matter, or the extracellular space. Moreover, it remains uncertain whether these are generalized brain changes or are specific to particular brain regions. The most extensive structural studies have been done by Katzman and colleagues. They found, in 13 adolescent AN women, reduced total gray matter and white matter as well as increased CSF volume during the ill state. By contrast, in a cohort of ill AN, BN [bulimia nervosa], and controls, Husain and colleagues assessed the midsagittal plane acquired by MRI, finding reduced midbrain and thalamic size in AN but no gray matter alterations. Lambe and colleagues studied recovered anorexics and found that they had reduced gray matter and increased CSF volume compared with controls, but greater gray matter and smaller CSF volume compared with subjects with AN. Furthermore, a longitudinal study of six women during the ill state and after weight recovery (mean: 16 months) showed that white matter volume was remitted after weight recovery, but a gray matter deficit and CSF volume persisted.

The reason for changes in brain volume is also unknown. Some data suggest that cortisol may contribute to brain alterations. Katzman and colleagues found that urinary free cortisol was positively correlated with CSF, but inversely with gray matter volume. AN patients have increased CSF cortisol. Therefore, it is possible that hypercortisolemia may play a role in reduced brain mass in AN. Recently, mesial temporal (amygdala-hippocampal complex) size was found to be reduced in AN, but there was no relationship with hormonal levels, including urinary free cortisol. It is unclear if this finding was confined to the mesial temporal cortex or ubiquitous, making its interpretation difficult.

The question of whether alterations in brain mass contribute to cognitive or mood changes in AN has not been well studied. Kingston and colleagues combined structural imaging with psychological assessments, including anxiety, depression, attention, and memory, in 46 AN inpatients before and after weight gain, compared with controls. No significant correlations were found, suggesting either no specificity of disturbance that can be related to specific behavior or simply inefficient analysis methods.

In summary, these studies tend to indicate that during the ill state a gray matter and probably white matter volume loss occurs that at least partially recovers with weight restoration. Those structural alterations are relatively non-specific, and behavioral correlates have not been discovered.

Magnetic Resonance Spectroscopy (MRS) Studies

MRS can give information on nerve cell damage by assessing brain metabolites such as choline, N-acetyl-aspartate (NAA), phosphorus, and myo-inositol. MRS studies in juvenile AN patients found higher choline containing compounds relative to total creatine and lower ratios of NAA relative to choline in white matter. Those changes were interpreted to be altered cell membrane turnover, as they were reversible with recovery. Two studies showed reduced brain phospholipids that positively correlated with body mass index, also suggesting a state dependent phenomenon. The latter study also found body mass index positively correlated with frontal cortex myo-inositol, which is a part of the 5-HT second messenger neurotransmission system and could be consistent with reduced 5-HT activity in AN.

Positron Emission Tomography and Single Photon Emission Computed Tomography Studies: Resting Condition

Most studies that have assessed resting brain activity in AN have used SPECT. Gordon and colleagues found that 13 of 15 individuals with AN had unilateral temporal lobe hypoperfusion that persisted in the subjects studied after weight restoration. Kuruoglu and colleagues studied two patients with AN with bilateral hypoperfusion in frontal, temporal, and parietal regions which normalized after three months of remission. Takano and colleagues found hypoperfusion in the medial prefrontal cortex and anterior cingulate and hyperperfusion in the thalamus and amygdala-hippocampal complex. In a study by Chowdhury and colleagues, adolescent subjects with AN had unilateral tempora-parietal and frontal lobe hypoperfusion, and Rastam and colleagues found tempora-parietal and orbitofrontal hypoperfusion in ill and recovered AN subjects. Fewer studies have assessed glucose metabolism using PET. Delvenne and colleagues studied individuals with AN with frontal and parietal hypometabolism compared with controls, who normalized with weight gain.

Taken together, studies in the resting condition most frequently suggest alterations of the temporal, parietal, or cingulate cortex during the ill state, and a few studies suggest persistent alterations in those areas after weight gain. This could be a potentially important finding given that the mesial temporal cortex is implicated in emotional processing and increased anxiety in AN could be related to altered amygdala function. However, studies have been generally small and need replication in AN subgroups, stratified by restricting and binge eating/purging type in order to clarify the results.

Positron Emission Tomography, Single Photon Emission Computed Tomography, and Functional Magnetic Resonance Imaging Task-Activation Studies

Functional imaging has been done in conjunction with paradigms and tasks that are meant to elicit areas of brain activation that might be specific for AN pathophysiology. Several different paradigms have been used. Eating custard cake showed increased brain activity in AN compared to controls using SPECT in frontal, occipital, parietal, and temporal areas. Food imagination on SPECT showed that AN-B/P had greater right-sided parietal and prefrontal activation compared with controls and AN-R, and Gordon and colleagues found in AN that high calorie foods provoked anxiety and led to greater temporo-occipital activation when compared with low-calorie foods using PET. Ellison and colleagues, using fMRI, also found that visual high calorie presentation elicited high anxiety in AN together with left mesial temporal as well as left insular and bilateral anterior cingulate cortex (ACC) activity. Those results could be consistent with anxiety provocation and related amygdala activation, which has been found in the past, and the notion that the emotional value of an experience is stored in the amygdala.

Uher and colleagues used pictures of food and non-food aversive emotional stimuli to assess ill and recovered AN subjects. Food-stimulated medial prefrontal and ACC in both recovered and ill AN, but lateral prefrontal regions only in recovered AN. In controls, food was associated with occipital, basal ganglia, and lateral prefrontal activation. Aversive non-food stimuli activated occipital and dorsolateral prefrontal cortex in all three subject groups. In recovered AN patients, prefrontal cortex, ACC, and cerebellum were more highly activated compared with both controls and chronic AN after food. This suggested that higher ACC and medial prefrontal cortex activity in both ill and recovered AN subjects compared with controls may be a trait marker for AN. These are areas of executive function, decision-making, error monitoring, and reward expectancy. Such alterations could suggest heightened vigilance or processing activity in response to visual food stimuli.

Body image distortion is an integral part of AN pathophysiology. Studies have been done confronting three AN subjects and three controls with their own digitally distorted body images using a computer-based video technique and fMRI. AN patients had greater activation in the brain stem, right amygdala, and fusiform gyrus, again suggesting anxiety related to the body experience that is reflected by amygdala activity. In a follow-up study in a larger and more homogenous sample using the same paradigm, Wagner and colleagues found no amygdala activation but a hyper-responsiveness in brain areas belonging to the frontal visual system and the attention network (Brodman area 9) as well as inferior parietal lobule (Brodman area 40), including the anterior part of the intraparietal sulcus. The latter areas are specifically involved in visuospatial processing. This finding makes the involvement of the brain anxiety circuit less clear but may suggest that perceptual alterations may be related to the neglect phenomenon. In comparison, a study of a group of control women found left amygdala activation in relation to unpleasant body-related words, as well as contralateral parahippocampal activation that was negatively related to the *Eating Disorders Inventory* score. Thus, in young women, both controls and AN subjects may have somewhat similar anxiety reactions to their body images being distorted.

It is difficult to compare these studies, as the imaging modalities and tasks are not consistent and the groups of subjects are small. Still, it appears that temporal and cingulate activity are frequently different between AN and controls. Those regions are part of the emotion and anxiety processing network. Anxiety is a premorbid trait in AN, and a disturbance in those areas could reflect a biological trait-related correlate. Parietal cortical areas also seem to repeatedly distinguish AN from controls. In comparison, OCD also showed ACC and tempora-parietal activation in different studies. Future studies will need to determine whether there is a common neuronal network alteration in AN and OCD.

Receptor Imaging Studies

Neurotransmitters, such as 5-HT and dopamine, are distributed throughout the brain via specific neuronal pathways. Their influence on behavior is believed to be via action on specific receptors that are located mostly post-synaptically but also for some receptor types pre-synaptically in, for example, the midbrain. Radioligands exist for several of the serotonin receptor types. One of the most commonly assessed receptor type is the 5-HT2A receptor, which is involved in the regulation of feeding, mood, and anxiety, and in antidepressant action. Three studies have assessed 5-HT2A receptor binding in ill and recovered AN women. Ill subjects showed reduced binding in the left frontal, bilateral parietal, and occipital cortex. Recovered AN-R also had reduced 5-HT2A binding, most strongly in mesial temporal and parietal cortical areas as well as in the cingulate cortex. In another study, women recovered from AN-B/P had reduced 5-HT2A binding relative to controls in the left subgenual cingulate, left parietal, and right occipital cortex. In that study, 5-HT2A binding was positively related to harm avoidance and negatively to novelty seeking in cingulate and temporal regions, with negative relationships between 5-HT2A binding and drive for thinness.

Those findings further highlight the possibility of disturbances of the ACC and mesial temporal cortex in AN. Since these disturbances persist after recovery, it is possible they are trait disturbances. The ACC receives afferents from the amygdala and has direct projections to the premotor frontal cortex and other limbic regions. It plays a crucial role in initiation, motivation, and goal-directed behaviors as well as reward. The amygdala mediate the interpretation of fear and the representation of emotional stimuli values. One could state the hypothesis that AN patients have disturbed processing of emotional stimuli valence, resulting in poor flexibility in reevaluating actual danger of those stimuli and reduced adaptation to new situations. Future studies will need to determine whether relationships between 5-HT2A receptor activity and measures for anxiety, such as harm avoidance, can be replicated. This could be an exciting avenue for the link of neurochemistry and behavior.

Bulimia Nervosa

Bulimia nervosa (BN) is characterized by recurrent binge eating followed by behaviors to counteract weight gain, such as self-induced vomiting. Individuals with BN, usually at normal weight, present with a fear of gaining weight and food and body weight-related preoccupations. BN is usually associated with increased depressive and anxious feelings. Impulsive behaviors as well as cluster B—dramatic or erratic—behaviors are frequent.

Computed Tomography and Magnetic Resonance Imaging Studies

Only a few structural studies have been performed in BN. Pituitary abnormalities have been suggested, as well as cerebral atrophy and ventricular enlargement. No conclusions on etiology or impact of those structural lesions could have been drawn yet since those measures may be short-term dependent on nutritional intake.

Magnetic Resonance Spectroscopy Studies

A mixed group of AN and BN subjects had reduced prefrontal myo-inositol and lipid compounds compared with controls. However, it is unclear whether those findings were specific to either AN or BN or were related to both.

Positron Emission Tomography and Single Photon Emission Computed Tomography Studies: Resting Condition

Similar to findings in AN, rCGM in the resting state was reduced globally in BN compared with controls, with significantly reduced rCGM in the parietal cortex using PET. Interestingly, depressive symptoms in a bulimic group correlated with rCGM in the left anterolateral prefrontal cortex in one study. This finding has not been replicated. Another study investigated brain activity in BN versus depressed subjects and found that BN patients had reduced right frontal activation compared with controls and depressed subjects, but depressed subjects had reduced basal ganglia activity supporting different pathophysiology for BN and depression. In nine recovered (mean: 57 months) BN subjects rCBF was similar compared with 12 controls but correlated negatively with length of recovery, which could reflect either a scarring effect or possibly a return to premorbid lower rCBF. A follow-up study will need to clarify this finding.

It therefore appears that rCBF and rCGM alterations during the ill state remit with recovery, although pre- or post-illness alterations cannot be excluded based on the available data. Furthermore, BN and depression may be distinguished by different patterns of brain activity, which is important considering the frequent overlap in depressive symptoms.

Task-Activation Studies

Nozoe and colleagues found that BN patients had greater right inferior frontal and left temporal blood flow compared with controls before, but similar activity after a meal. BN subjects have increased liking for sweet stimuli compared with controls, and therefore, may have altered processing of taste stimuli. A fMRI study by Frank and colleagues using a glucose challenge, found in recovered BN subjects (seven BN, three AN-B/P) reduced ACC activity compared with six controls. The ACC is a cuneus area that is involved in error monitoring but also in the anticipation of reward. In this paradigm, where subjects knew which taste stimulus to expect, higher activity in controls could suggest higher reward expectation by controls than anticipated by BN-type subjects.

Receptor Imaging Studies

5-HT receptor alterations may have specific implications on behavior. Kaye and colleagues found reduced orbitofrontal 5-HT2A receptor binding in recovered BN subjects. Orbitofrontal alterations could reflect behavioral disturbances in BN that include impulsiveness and altered emotional processing. Altered orbitofrontal activity as found in borderline personality disorder could indicate a common area for impulse control disturbance. In addition, women with BN failed to show common correlations of age and 5-HT2A binding. This finding raises the possibility that women with BN may have alterations of developmental mechanisms of the 5-HT system. Another study reported on reduced 5-HT transporter binding in thalamus and hypothalamus in ill BN subjects. The 5-HT system has consistently been shown to be disturbed in ED, and reduced 5-HT transporter when ill may be related to altered brain 5-HT function, such as reduced 5-HT activity during the ill state. Reduced 5-HT2A activity after recovery could reflect a trait disturbance involved in alterations of mood, anxiety, and impulse control. Most recently, increased 5-HT1A receptor binding was found by Tiihonen and colleagues using PET in BN subjects in all studied brain regions, but most prominently in prefrontal, cingulate, and a parietal cortex area. Central 5-HT function is reduced in BN and increased 5-HT1A receptor binding could be a negative-feedback up-regulation. Higher 5-HT1A binding could also be related to the well-known phenomenon that BN patients require higher doses of selective serotonin reuptake inhibitors compared with, for example, patients being treated for depression. Those 5-HT receptor alterations and their implications on treatment will have to be further studied and the findings replicated.

Binge Eating Disorder

Binge eating disorder (BED) is a proposed diagnostic category. BED is characterized by BN-like symptoms, except that no compensatory measures are used. Very little is known about brain activity in BED. Karhunen and colleagues found that there may be a lateralization of blood flow in BED, with higher activity in the left hemisphere compared with the right in response to visual food presentation. Also, there was a linear correlation of hunger with left frontal/prefrontal cortical activity. The same group found reduced 5-HT transporter binding in the midbrain, that improved with fluoxetine and group psychotherapy, suggesting, at least in part, state-dependent serotonergic alterations.

Conclusion

Until recently, the assessment of psychiatric disorders has relied on subjective reports from patients, and biologic research has been limited by the inaccessibility of the living human brain. The emergence of brain imaging techniques raises the possibility to assess brain function in vivo and assess human behavior in conjunction with biological correlates. The eating disorders AN and BN are relatively homogeneous disorders. The new imaging methods give hope to the prospect of identifying biologic markers that will help categorize those disorders, and in turn, identify more effective treatments that could reduce morbidity associated with these frequently debilitating and deadly illnesses.

Studying eating disorders is complicated due to a relatively small prevalence and the many state-related (for example, hormonal) disturbances associated with these illnesses. Thus, it is difficult to assess factors that may be trait related and possibly pre-morbid. Studying subjects after long-term recovery may be our closest approximation to studying subjects premorbidly.

The most common structural abnormalities found in ill AN women are global reduction of gray matter and white matter which remit at least in part with recovery. Ill BN patients may have similar changes. Studies in depression found more specific regional volume changes, but we are not aware of similar changes with recovery in other disorders. It is possible that the explanation for reduction in brain mass when ill may be brain protein, fat, or fluid loss secondary to emaciation and dehydration. However, since some ED studies found relationships of brain volume with cortisol levels and cortisol related to brain cell death, it has to be assessed if hypercortisolism in ill AN patients is truly contributing to those findings.

Resting rCBF and rCGM showed mostly a general reduced cortical activity in the ill state that is most pronounced in temporal, parietal, or cingulate cortex. Very limited data suggest some persistence of these finding after recovery in both AN and BN. Whether these findings indicate involvement of the limbic system or are state- or trait-related or some complex combination of both remains unknown. Relatively few subjects have been studied, and there is a fair amount of inconsistencies among studies in terms of subject subgroups, state of illness, and other factors.

Functional MRI studies using visual stimuli of food or body image in AN suggested involvement of prefrontal, ACC, and parietal cortex. The only study in BN suggests altered ACC and cuneus activity in response to a sweet taste stimulus. This finding suggests that the decision-making network and that reward pathways may be differently activated in those tasks in BN. However, those studies have to be replicated. It is still unclear if ED subjects react differently to visual compared with oral high calorie stimuli, and if there are distinct alterations in the processing of taste stimuli, for example, for sweets compared with fats.

The receptor imaging studies that are available at this point show that reduced 5-HT2A receptor binding occurs in the ill state and persists after recovery from AN. BN subjects showed reduced 5-HT2A receptor activity when recovered and reduced 5-HT transporter binding when ill. They may have increased 5-HT1A receptor binding during the ill state. Such findings of 5-HT disturbances in ill and recovered subjects with ED may suggest a trait disturbance of the 5-HT system. Altered 5-HT receptor activity could be related to emotional disturbances such as increased depressive symptoms or anxiety.

Few studies have been done in ED in comparison with depressive disorders or OCD. The overlap and comorbidity of both major depression and OCD with ED require studies that will directly compare those disorders. ED and, in particular, AN are frequently debilitating with a high mortality. Studies comparing psychiatric disorders will help to find common pathways and distinct areas of disturbance that may identify targets for successful drug interventions.

Chapter 37

Effects of Laxatives, Ipecac, and Diet Supplements

Dangerous Substances

Laxatives

Each year between 400–500 million dollars are spent on laxatives. The use and abuse of laxatives among the general population is common. Reports of laxative abuse among high school students range from 3.5%–7% (40% of these patients use laxatives at least several times a week).

Laxative use and abuse among bulimic patients ranges from 40%–75% with about 15% abusing laxatives at least several times a day. Laxative abuse is not an efficient manner of promoting weight loss—it is ineffective. Individuals lose water, not weight. There is a false belief that laxatives will diminish calorie absorption.

Laxative abusers can develop life-threatening medical complications such as:

- A cathartic colon can develop (the colon becomes a big dilated tube that cannot function) and may require decompression or surgery.
- Failure to absorb important vitamins—like A, D, E, and K—occurs.

This chapter includes: "Dangerous Substances," reprinted with permission from the National Association of Anorexia Nervosa and Associated Disorders, http://www.anad.org; and, "Dietary Supplements–Adverse Event Reporting," U.S. Food and Drug Administration (FDA), December 2004.

- Repetitive diarrhea sometimes causes rectal prolapse (colon comes out of your rectum) and may need surgical repair.
- Watery diarrhea may cause life-threatening electrolyte imbalances.
- Potassium deficiency (an electrolyte that is lost with diarrhea or vomiting) can cause fatigability and muscle weakness.
- Other electrolytes are also lost (such as magnesium or phosphorous) which are important for your body, especially your heart, to function correctly.
- Individuals who abuse laxatives may also develop renal stones which are very painful.
- Laxative abusers are faced with periods of constipation (because they need the laxatives to move their bowels) and diarrhea.
- When they try to stop they may gain water weight and are driven to return to the use of laxatives.

There are laboratory tests that indicate if a patient has been using laxatives. Withdrawal from laxatives is an important first step in treatment. If withdrawal occurs on an outpatient basis, often it is done gradually. If problems arise where this cannot occur, hospitalization may be necessary and should be undertaken by an experienced physician

Ipecac

Ipecac is intended to induce vomiting in emergency situations only. One study showed that sporadic use of ipecac was as high as 28% in bulimic patients and about 3%–4% engaged in chronic regular abuse. Ipecac is extremely dangerous when used and abused. Effects may include:

- Dangerous myopathies (damage to muscles) including cardiomyopathies (damage to the heart muscle) can occur because the toxins in this substance can destroy muscles.
- Damage to the muscles can lead to weakness and neuritis.
- Damage to the heart muscle can be fatal.

Medical assessment, particularly of the cardiac status, should be done to rule out toxicity:

- An electrocardiogram and an echocardiogram should be considered.
- Be aware of possible ipecac abuse when patients complain of shortness of breath, fast heart rate or skipped beats, chest pain, or fainting episodes.

Diet Supplements and Other Herbal Products

People often think herbal products are safe because they are natural. This is not true. Herbal products are not regulated by the U.S. Food and Drug Administration (FDA) and therefore do not need to prove they are effective or safe. Moreover, these products could interfere with other medications to produce potentially dangerous interactions.

Ephedrine is a Chinese herb used as a central nervous system stimulant. When caffeine (guarana or cola nut which are often used as diuretics) is added, it becomes potentiated and is used for weight loss. Adverse effects include the following:

- increase in blood pressure
- headaches
- stroke
- sudden heart attack
- seizures
- death

Chromium picolinate is used for weight loss. It also is associated with the following effects:

- lowers the blood sugar
- may cause kidney damage
- destroys muscles
- impairs thinking

Yohimbine is used as a stimulant and may be in appetite suppressants. Is has been declared unsafe by the FDA. Adverse effects include the following:

- increase blood pressure
- anxiety

- rapid heart rate
- nausea and vomiting

Ginkgo biloba is used for gastrointestinal complaints (may act as a laxative). Adverse effects include the following:

- headache
- contact dermatitis
- stroke

Cascara is used as a laxative. Adverse effects include the following:

- severe vomiting
- electrolyte imbalance can lead to cardiac problems
- interacts with prescription drugs

Senna is used as a laxative. Adverse effects include the following:

- nausea
- abdominal cramping

St. John's wort is used for depression. It is often known as the over-the-counter Prozac. Adverse effects include the following:

- dry mouth
- constipation
- stomach distress
- confusion
- dizziness

Mixing St. John's wort with a prescription antidepressant (especially MAO inhibitors) may create additional problems.

Dietary Supplements: Adverse Event Reporting to the FDA

Report an Illness or Injury Associated with a Dietary Supplement

The FDA can be contacted to report general complaints or concerns about food products, including dietary supplements. You may telephone or write to FDA.

If you think you have suffered a serious harmful effect or illness from a dietary supplement, you or your health care provider can report this by calling FDA's MedWatch hotline or using the website. The MedWatch program allows for consumer or health care provider reporting of problems possibly caused by FDA-regulated products such as drugs, medical devices, medical foods, and dietary supplements. The identity of the patient is kept confidential.

Consumers may also report an adverse event or illness they believe to be related to the use of a dietary supplement by calling FDA or using the MedWatch website. FDA would like to know when a product causes a problem even if you are unsure the product caused the problem or even if you do not visit a doctor or clinic.

Additional Information

MedWatch
FDA Safety Information and Adverse Event Reporting Program
U.S. Food and Drug Administration
5600 Fishers Lane
Rockville, MD 20852-9787
Toll-Free: 800-332-1088
Fax: 800-332-0178
Website: http://www.fda.gov/medwatch

The form for voluntary reporting of adverse events, product problems, and product use errors is available at: http://www.fda.gov/medwatch/SAFETY/3500.pdf.

Part Four

Eating Disorders: Treatment and Recovery

Chapter 38

Treatment Options for Eating Disorders

Patients with eating disorders typically require a treatment team consisting of a primary care physician, dietitian, and a mental health professional knowledgeable about eating disorders. The multidisciplinary membership of the Academy for Eating Disorders reflects the consensus view that treatment must often involve clinicians from different health disciplines including psychologists, psychotherapists, physicians, dietitians, and nurses.

Research on the treatment of eating disorders is exploring how different treatments can be helpful for different types of eating disorders. The American Psychiatric Association has published a set of practice guidelines for the treatment of patients with eating disorders (American Psychiatric Association, Practice Guidelines for Eating Disorders, *American Journal of Psychiatry*, 2000).

There is general agreement that good treatment often requires a spectrum of treatment options. These options can range from basic educational interventions designed to teach nutritional and symptom management techniques to long-term residential treatment (living away from home in treatment centers).

Most individuals with eating disorders are treated on an outpatient basis after a comprehensive evaluation. Individuals with medical complications due to severe weight loss or due to the effects of

---

binge eating and purging may require hospitalization. Other individuals, for whom outpatient therapy has not been effective, may benefit from day hospital treatment, hospitalization, or residential placement.

Treatment is usually conducted in the least restrictive setting that can provide adequate safety for the individual. Many patients with eating disorders also have depression, anxiety disorders, drug and/or alcohol use disorders, and other psychiatric problems requiring treatment along with the eating disorder.

Initial Assessment

The initial assessment of individuals with eating disorders involves a thorough review of the patient's history, current symptoms, physical status, weight control measures, and other psychiatric issues or disorders such as depression, anxiety, substance abuse, or personality issues. Consultation with a physician and a registered dietitian is often recommended. The initial assessment is the first step in establishing a diagnosis and treatment plan.

Outpatient Treatment

Outpatient treatment for an eating disorder often involves a coordinated team effort between the patient, a psychotherapist, a physician, and a dietitian—yet, many patients are treated by their pediatrician or physician with or without a mental health professional's involvement. Similarly, many patients are seen and helped by generalist mental health clinicians without specialist involvement. Not all individuals, then, will receive a multidisciplinary approach, but the qualified clinician should have access to all of these resources.

Psychotherapy

There are several different types of outpatient psychotherapies with demonstrated effectiveness in patients with eating disorders. These include cognitive-behavioral therapy, interpersonal psychotherapy, family therapy, and behavioral therapy. Some of these therapies may be relatively short-term (for example, four months), but other psychotherapies may last years.

It is very difficult to predict who will respond to short-term treatments versus long-term treatments. Other therapies which some clinicians and patients have found to be useful include feminist therapies, psychodynamic psychotherapies, and various types of group therapy.

Psychopharmacology

Psychiatric medications have a demonstrated role in the treatment of patients with eating disorders. Most of the research to date has involved antidepressant medications such as fluoxetine (for example Prozac®); although some clinicians and patients have found that other types of medications may also be effective.

Nutritional Counseling

Regular contact with a registered dietitian can be an effective source of support and information for patients who are regaining weight or who are trying to normalize their eating behavior. Dietitians may help patients to gain a fundamental understanding of adequate nutrition and may also conduct dietary counseling which is a more specific process designed to help patients change the nature of their eating behavior.

Medical Treatment

Patients with eating disorders are subject to a variety of physical and medical concerns. Adequate medical monitoring is a cornerstone of effective outpatient treatment. Individuals with anorexia nervosa may be followed quite closely (for example, weekly or more often) because of the significant medical problems that this disorder poses for patients. Individuals with bulimia nervosa should be seen regularly, but may not require the intensive medical monitoring often seen in anorexia nervosa. Individuals with binge eating disorder may need medical treatment for a variety of complications from obesity such as diabetes and hypertension.

Day Hospital Care

Patients for whom outpatient treatment is ineffective may benefit from the increased structure provided by a day hospital treatment program. Generally, these programs are scheduled from three to eight hours a day and provide several structured eating sessions per day, along with various other therapies, including cognitive behavioral therapy, body image therapies, family therapy, and numerous other interventions. Day hospital treatment allows the patient to live at home when they are not in treatment, and often continue to work or attend school.

Inpatient Treatment

Inpatient treatment provides a structured and contained environment in which the patient with an eating disorder has access to clinical support 24-hours a day. Many programs are now affiliated with a day hospital program so that patients can step-up and step-down to the appropriate level of care depending on their clinical needs.

Although eating disorder patients can sometimes be treated on general psychiatric units with individuals experiencing other psychiatric disorders, such an approach often poses problems with monitoring and containing eating disorder symptoms. Therefore, most inpatient programs for eating disordered individuals only treat patients with anorexia nervosa, bulimia nervosa, binge eating disorder, or variants of these disorders.

Residential Care

Residential programs provide a treatment option for patients who require long-term treatment. This treatment option generally is reserved for individuals who have been hospitalized on several occasions, but have not been able to reach a significant degree of medical or psychological stability.

Chapter 39

Helping Someone Get Treatment for an Eating Disorder

First, understand that eating disorders are serious medical and psychological problems. They are not just fads, phases, or trivial eccentricities. If your friend or loved one had cancer, you would do everything you could to get her or him the finest professional care available. Eating disorders require that same level of treatment, and in fact eating disorders are like "soul cancer" because they so effectively destroy a person's body, mind, self-esteem, and relationships with friends and family. Individuals with eating disorders deserve and require professional evaluation, diagnosis, and treatment.

Eating disorders cripple the mind and heart with growing tumors of body dissatisfaction, perfectionism, and an overarching need for control. You cannot fix those things. That is a job for physicians, psychologists, and other mental health therapists who have been trained to work with these desperately needy, yet stubborn and defiant people who are doing the best they know how to take control of their lives in a world they find scary, lonely, and confusing.

Many factors contribute to the development of an eating disorder. Recovery means much more than replacing dieting, binge eating, and purging with healthy eating. It means identifying the underlying dynamics that have brought the person to disordered eating in the first place and then resolving them. The process requires skill, sensitivity,

---

"When You Want to Help a Friend or Loved One," used with permission of ANRED: Anorexia Nervosa and Related Eating Disorders, Inc. © 2006 ANRED. For additional information visit, http://www.anred.com.

and training—in other words, it's a job for medical and mental health professionals.

Does that mean there is nothing you can do to help? No, there is much you can do. You can be a friend, a parent, a spouse, a partner, a sibling—someone who cares—and there is great value in the support and encouragement you can provide in that role. What you cannot be is a trained clinician, and trained clinicians are what is required for recovery from an eating disorder. Therefore, your primary focus should be to encourage the person to talk things over with a physician or counselor. If after an evaluation, ongoing treatment is advised, encourage the person to begin it and stick with it until the problem is resolved.

Your biggest problem will be convincing the person to do this. Nothing will change until she or he admits having a problem and accepts help. At first she or he will deny there is a problem. The individual will fear weight gain and resist it mightily. She or he will be ashamed and not want to admit what they are doing. The eating disorder has been used to protect, hide, comfort, and empower the individual. In the beginning, at least, she or he will not want to give it up, and will see asking for help as some kind of shameful admission of inadequacy and entering treatment as loss of control. Arriving at a new and healthier perspective is the first challenge on the road to recovery.

Here are some suggestions to help you talk to an unhappy and defiant person.

If Your Child Is Younger Than 18 Years

Get professional help immediately. You have a legal and moral responsibility to get your child the needed care. Don't let tears, tantrums, or promises to do better stop you. Begin with a physical exam and psychological evaluation.

Hospitalize your child if the physician recommends you do so. People die from these disorders, and sometimes they need a structured time-out to break entrenched patterns.

Participate in family counseling if the physician or counselor asks you to do so. Children spend only a few hours a week with their counselors. The rest of the time they live with their families. You need as many tools as you can get to help your child learn new ways of coping with life, and family counseling is the place to get them.

If Your Friend Is Younger Than 18 Years

Tell a trusted adult—parent, teacher, coach, pastor, school nurse, school counselor—about your concern. If you don't, you may unwittingly help your friend avoid the treatment needed to get better.

Consider telling your friend's parents, even though it would be hard, why you are concerned. Your friend may be hiding unhealthy behaviors from them, and they deserve to know so they can arrange help and treatment. If you cannot bear to do this yourself, ask your parents or perhaps the school nurse for help.

If the Person Is 18 Years or Older

Recognize the boundaries. Legally the person is now an adult and can refuse treatment if they are not ready to change. Nevertheless, reach out. Tell her or him that you are concerned. Be gentle. Suggest that there has to be a better way to deal with life than starving and stuffing. Encourage professional help, but expect resistance and denial. You can lead a horse to water, but you can't make it drink—even when it is thirsty—if it is determined to follow its own path.

Information for Boyfriends and Girlfriends

If you are in love with someone with an eating disorder, by all means provide whatever support you can, but consider postponing any binding commitment until she or he is recovered. People with eating disorders can be physically and emotionally attractive. Their vulnerability and fragility can appeal to a partner's instincts to protect and help. This can be a trap.

Some people never do recover from an eating disorder. Don't link your life to a person with problems unless you are willing to put up with the problems for the rest of your life—or theirs. It might come to that. It is far wiser to wait until you can see that your life partner will be able to hold up her or his end of the commitment contract.

The kind of change required for recovery is extremely difficult. Kindness and love, as beautiful as they are, will not by themselves heal your beloved—professional treatment is needed too.

Things to Do

- Talk to the person when you are calm, not when you are frustrated or emotional. Be kind. Underneath the denial and bravado, the person is probably ashamed and fears criticism and rejection.

- Mention evidence you have heard or seen that suggests disordered eating. Don't dwell on appearance or weight. Instead talk about health, relationships (for example, withdrawal), and mood.
- Realize that the person will not change until she or he wants to.
- Provide information.
- Be supportive and caring. Be a good listener and don't give advice unless you are asked to do so. Even then be prepared to have it ignored.
- Continue to suggest professional help. Don't pester, but don't give up either.
- Ask: "Is doing what you are doing really working to get you what you want?"
- Talk about the advantages of recovery and a normal life.
- Agree that recovery is hard, but emphasize that many people have done it.
- If she or he is frightened to see a counselor, offer to go along the first time.
- Realize that recovery is the person's responsibility, not yours.
- Resist guilt. Do the best you can and then be gentle with yourself.

What Not to Do

- Never nag, plead, beg, bribe, threaten, or manipulate. These things don't work.
- Avoid power struggles. You will lose.
- Never criticize or shame. These tactics are cruel, and the person will withdraw.
- Don't pry. Respect privacy.
- Don't be a food monitor. You will create resentment and distance in the relationship.
- Don't try to control. The person will withdraw and ultimately outwit you.

- Don't waste time trying to reassure your friend that they are not fat—she or he will not be convinced.
- Don't get involved in endless conversations about weight, food, and calories. That just makes matters worse.
- Don't give advice unless asked.
- Don't expect the person to follow your advice even if she or he asked for it.
- Don't say, "You are too thin." Your friend will secretly celebrate.
- Don't say, "It's good you have gained weight." Your friend will lose it.
- Don't let the person always decide when, what, and where you will eat. She should not control everything, every time.
- Don't ignore stolen food and evidence of purging. Insist on responsibility.
- Don't overestimate what you can accomplish.

Friends and family members of people with eating disorders are concerned and want to help. They want information that they can pass along to their loved ones so they will stop their unhealthy food and weight behaviors. Unfortunately, information by itself is never enough to change behavior. Something else is needed. So what is that magic something? Well, first of all, it isn't magic. It is usually a long and difficult process that begins with the realization that starving and stuffing will never work to increase self-confidence, happiness, and satisfaction with oneself and one's life.

People with eating disorders aren't crazy, irrational, stupid, or dumb. Even if they can't, or won't, express themselves directly, they want to feel better about themselves. They also want to accomplish something, or get something, or avoid something, and because they don't know how to do so in forthright ways, or because they are too frightened or inexperienced to know how to attack their problems directly, they resort to working symbolically via food, weight, and eating. In addition, even though they want others to think they are strong and can handle anything, folks who use food and diets to try to work out other problems are emotionally fragile and easily hurt.

Confrontation and nagging create power struggles. You want the person to do things your way. She or he does not want to be manipulated or controlled. Even when you are right, your approach invites the person to rebel and stubbornly resist taking your good advice. As one person put it, "Even though I'm healthier now, I feel like I've lost and you've won. I hate it!"

Making changes, even minor ones, is hard, and giving up entrenched habits like starving, binge eating, and purging is overwhelming. That is why physicians and mental health therapists should be involved in the process. Friends and family members, as loving and filled with good intentions as they may be, do not have the training and experience to shepherd a person through the usually lengthy and always hard journey from eating disorder to health.

Don't forget to have fun with your friend or loved one. A movie, shopping trip, or a day at an amusement park can give the person a glimpse of some of the benefits of living and acting like normal people do. Don't spoil the event with lots of talk about food and weight.

And lastly, be aware of your limits and keep your expectations reasonable. You can be a resource person who provides friendship, support, and encouragement, but you cannot control her or make him change before she or he is ready.

Information about Psychiatric Commitment

Sometimes parents or spouses are so frightened that they want their loved one in treatment regardless of what has to happen to make that so. If your child is younger than 18 years, you do not need a legal commitment to place her or him into treatment. Just do it.

If your child or spouse is 18 years or older, and if you are considering commitment, talk to your attorney, but be aware that the process is difficult and may make treatment even more difficult, or even impossible, because of the anger, defiance, and resistance triggered by such loss of control. In addition, in the U.S., know that a commitment is difficult to obtain. Individual freedoms are protected fiercely, even the right to hang onto an untreated mental illness.

Information for Boyfriends, Husbands, and Other Pragmatists

Sometimes people with eating disorders ask their friends and partners to "be there for me." Most men and some women think that means finding an answer or solving the problem. Almost always, however, the person who asks really means "just listen and be supportive." This is very hard to do when the person is in medical danger—but it is all that you can do—which underscores the necessity of professional treatment focused on resolving underlying issues and changing behavior.

Information for Young Friends

Don't promise to keep secrets about your friend's self-destructive behavior. If you have already promised not to tell her or his parents, break that promise, and do it now. Yes, your friend will be angry, but you just might prevent a tragedy, and in so doing spare yourself a lifetime of guilt.

In Conclusion

When all is said and done, each of us must be responsible for the choices we make. We can support one another, encourage mature and rational thinking, provide information, and offer advice, but eventually each individual must decide what to do and how to do it. To live with honor and integrity takes courage. You cannot provide that for another person, just yourself.

To protect your own mental and physical health, you may find it necessary to take a break from the person you care about. Tell her or him that it's too frustrating and heartbreaking to watch the continuing self-abuse and rejection of your best advice and counsel. You might add that when she or he is ready to get help and make healthy changes, you will be back with support and encouragement.

Life is not a television show where some compassionate parent, friend, lover, pastor, counselor, or doctor says just the right thing so that the victim or sufferer sees the light and makes a 180-degree turn before the last commercial. Life is complicated and messy. We don't have maps or scripts to follow, but we do have multiple opportunities to choose wisdom and integrity over blind adherence to destructive patterns.

Chapter 40

Caring for Someone with an Eating Disorder

Although someone with an eating disorder will almost certainly need professional help, families and friends can provide invaluable help and support during recovery. However, home may feel like a battleground with parents or partners feeling that they have become the enemy. Long-standing friendships may come under pressure because of the changes in behavior that accompany an eating disorder.

The person with an eating disorder is likely to experience periods of depression, anger, hopelessness, and despair. It is important to remember it is the disorder that is taking over, and not the person who is changing.

The frustration you, your family, and friends experience almost always includes conflicting feelings of helplessness, despair, sympathy, anger, or resentment. You may feel that you should be able to help because you care for the person who is suffering—but you simply don't know what to do or say, perhaps because the person you care about is still not ready to admit they may have a problem.

You may feel very guilty about your child's or your partner's disorder, perhaps distressed by a friend's disorder—but instead of soul-searching for the reasons the eating disorder developed, be positive, try to gather useful information and plan what to do next. The sooner help is found, the better the outcome is likely to be. Be supportive when treatment is offered, and recognize that it may take some time

---

before the combination of treatment, people, and the sufferer's own attitude results in moves towards recovery.

Preventing the situation from becoming worse may not seem to be a very ambitious goal, but it is the first step to take. You can then try to help things improve. However, recovery is a step-by-step process that will include the odd step backwards as well as forwards. Being able to communicate without being judgemental or arguing is important. No relative or friend can single-handedly make someone recover, but your support is invaluable. What you say or do can help—or hinder—the recovery of someone with an eating disorder.

Trying to talk to someone you suspect has an eating disorder can be a daunting prospect. Recovery cannot begin in an atmosphere of secrecy or denial and the disorder will not go away by itself, so although talking about it may be difficult, it can often be an essential first step. When you first talk about your worries and concerns, try and prepare what you will say, and how you will say it. Find a time when neither of you are feeling angry or upset and somewhere you will not be interrupted. Try to explain that you have noticed the changes in their behavior, that you are concerned and want to help. Remember it's not about food, it's about feelings, so don't talk about diets and weight loss. Be honest about your own feelings and encourage the person you are helping to be honest about theirs.

You will also need help and support; however, don't swap roles with the person who is ill. Don't allow them to start acting as your carer, supporting your own distress and confusion. You should not allow them to be overburdened with your feelings as they will already have many mixed and guilty emotions to deal with.

Life must go on—try not to allow eating disorders to take over normal, everyday activities or to affect other relationships especially within the family. It can help if you try to keep something in your relationship which is unconnected with the eating disorder or food. You must look after yourself and show the person with anorexia or bulimia that taking care of your needs is acceptable. However, if you are part of the sufferer's immediate family, it is very important that you take part in family therapy sessions if they are offered as part of treatment.

Communicating with anyone and not just someone with an eating disorder means being a good listener and trying to understand what they may be struggling to say. Show you love and accept them for the person they are. Agree to disagree to avoid arguments and don't get hung up on issues such as commenting on their appearance.

For the family, there are practical things you can do to minimize anxiety at mealtimes. You and the person with the eating disorder can plan the menu for the following day, taking into account the kind of food that they might be willing to eat. Agree who will do the shopping and try to share the food preparation. If the sufferer is likely to binge, consider reducing the amount of food kept in stock.

It is important that you agree on behavior that will and will not be tolerated. This helps to establish clear boundaries. Things that you normally take for granted, like leaving food around or having a set of bathroom scales can cause problems for someone with an eating disorder, so try and identify these potential difficulties and discuss how you can deal with them together. Be united in your support as a family, or circle of friends, to prevent the eating disorder splitting a family or friendships.

Everyone who recovers from an eating disorder tells how important it was to have unconditional love and support from those who care about them, even when they knew their behavior was quite difficult to understand.

Chapter 41

Improving Care of Anorexia Nervosa Patients

Anorexia nervosa (AN), the oldest eating disorders subtype, was first described centuries ago. Its historical legacy has significant positives and negatives. The positives include improved diagnosis and research. The primary negative is hesitancy about changing historical thinking about AN, even though evidence-based studies suggest this is timely and imperative for improving patient care. Why have there been complexities in the diagnosis of AN?

Agreeing upon a Definition for Anorexia Nervosa

An agreement on a definition of AN comes first. AN is: (1) a disorder of abnormal eating behavior, (2) driven primarily by the internalization of the overvalued sociocultural belief in the benefits of slimming (predominantly among females) or shape change (predominantly among males), (3) sufficiently sustained in duration and severity to cause significant signs and symptoms of medical starvation as well as psychological and social change.

It is important to understand the psychopathology of overvalued beliefs. They are: (1) widely held sociocultural beliefs, (2) given ruling passion in small groups of individuals, often during crucial developmental years, (3) leading to risky or dangerous behaviors.

This chapter begins with "Revising the Diagnosis of Anorexia Nervosa Will Improve Patient Care," by Arnold E. Andersen, M.D. © 2006 Gurze Books. Reprinted with permission. It continues with "Prozac Not Effective Against Anorexia," copyright © 2006 ScoutNews, LLC. All rights reserved. Reprinted with permission.

AN is both a strategy to deal with emotional distress from a variety of sources (for example, existential fears of maturation, depressive or anxious mood, family functioning, decreased self-esteem, social acceptance), and an illness that has a life of its own once it is established. In addition, it has perhaps the highest premature mortality (12% to 19%) of any psychiatric disorder. AN is not a subset of another disorder, such as obsessive-compulsive disorder or psychosis, or major depressive illness, although it usually has from two to four companion comorbid disorders, some secondary to AN, some primary to it. Its hallmark psychopathological findings are: a morbid fear of fatness with a relentless drive for thinness, with frequent but not invariable distortion of body image. Many of its features, such as preoccupation with thoughts of food, emotional flattening or irritability, social isolation, and decreased sexual drive, are consequences of starvation, not part of the psychopathology of AN. These features have been reproduced in experimental starvation studies.

The high frequency of onset of AN during adolescence has primarily to do with the fact that the core challenge of adolescence is forming a personal identity, and slimming or shape change in this country are unfortunately very effective, albeit short-term, pseudo-solutions to forming a personal identity. In other words, just be thin and you will feel better about yourself; you can control something completely when everything is changing in ways you didn't ask for; you get more attention; and you have a method to deal with crummy moods. Unfortunately, AN is a good enough pseudo-solution to seem to solve all the issues it is asked to solve. There are no dumb reasons for developing AN.

Getting the Diagnosis Right

Although AN has been described as rare, it is as common as schizophrenia or childhood onset of type I diabetes. It is not a benign disorder, although it is highly treatable when done well. All of these are reasons to get the diagnosis right. The term diagnosis means thorough knowledge.

What kinds of knowledge are conferred by accurate diagnosis? An accurate diagnosis confers knowledge about: (1) what treatments to use; (2) what the future holds (pro-gnosis means future knowledge). In the ancient world, doctors were paid to tell a parent the probable outcome (prognosis) of an injured child, even when treatments were not effective. So why is there concern about the diagnosis of AN?

First, the historical nature of AN seems to make clinicians reluctant to make changes, even as evidence accumulates. AN has long been associated with (a) being female—even though the first cases involved a male and a female; and (b) amenorrhea (having been classified in the endocrine section of texts for more than 50 years).

At least two studies have demonstrated that amenorrhea is irrelevant to the diagnosis of AN. Patients meeting the core AN criteria (self-starvation, overvalued belief in the importance of slimness, sustained functional impairment medically, psychologically, and socially), whether or not they have a light menstrual bleed or none have the same clinical picture, the same natural course of illness, and the same response to treatment. In addition, requiring amenorrhea for the diagnosis is gender-biased. In the *International Classification of Diseases of the World Health Organization–10 (ICD–10)*, the diagnostic classification used by most of the world, uses the phrase "abnormality of reproductive hormone functioning," suggesting changes in estrogen or testosterone qualify as medical signs of AN. This is a better but still overly restricted appreciation of the global starvation changes that occur with AN. Requiring amenorrhea in the diagnosis of AN also ignores the data that some women lose periods soon after starting to diet, and some at very low weight have continued menstrual function. So, out with amenorrhea.

Misreading the Diagnostic and Statistical Manual of Mental Disorders (DSM–IV)

There is a slavish misreading of the *DSM-IV*'s supposed criterion of requiring weight less than 85% of norms for age and height for the diagnosis of AN. Normal weight, like height, is bell-curved in its distribution. A woman who is healthy at a self-regulating weight of, for example, 125% of the statistical average, and who diets, may have all the medical, psychological, and social symptoms of AN at 90% of normal or healthy weight, all of which are averages, not mandates. A straightforward reading of the *DSM-IV* is frustratingly ignored. The use of the 85% level is said to be *exempli gratia*, or an example. It is unbelievable how rigidly insurance companies, clinicians, and the media interpret this level.

Many mischievous as well as serious patient-unfriendly results occur when insistence on amenorrhea and a weight less than 85% of an average are required as part of the diagnosis of AN. The huge number of so-called atypical cases of eating disorders are, in fact, 75% of the time, AN misdiagnosed by relying on disproved or archaic criteria. Female patients are told if they have menstrual function and/or final diet-induced weight greater than 85% that they do not have AN, but rather have an atypical eating disorder. This confuses clinicians (How do you treat atypical cases?), and causes frequent denial of health insurance payment for diagnosis evaluation or treatment (We only reimburse AN and bulimia nervosa; also, atypical cases are not that serious.) These things shouldn't happen, but they do time and time again.

Resistance to Change

In the real world, there are some awkward factors to deal with in understanding resistance to change in diagnostic criteria. Some resistance to change comes from researchers invested in keeping overly narrow criteria because of the possible need to change diagnoses in research studies; emotional investments in archaic criteria, albeit out of date, are at times a personal reality. Politics as well as science affect the criteria in differing degrees (for example, diagnostic categories that had a brief half-life in previous *Diagnostic and Statistical Manual* editions).

More and more disorders are appreciated as being spectrum disorders, with a change from single rigid category on the dimension (high blood pressure vs. no high blood pressure) to a spectrum of severity. Now, a person with pre-hypertension is treated with the same vigor and method as the old "full" hypertensive.

Likewise, if a patient has the core features of AN: (1) self-induced starvation; (2) psychopathology of an overvalued belief in the benefits of slimming or shape change; (3) duration and severity of disorder sufficient to suffer functional impairment medically, psychologically, and socially, they have AN and need to be diagnosed as such, and treated as such.

Asthmatic patients are not told to go home and become more severely asthmatic before they qualify for treatment. Likewise, AN patients do not stop having AN because they exceed 85% of their normal weight or are at normal weight, any more than a hypertensive or diabetic patient loses his diagnosis because medical treatment produces normal blood pressure or normal glucose levels. If, after five years there are no signs of AN (normative cultural distress, for example, lip service to dieting is normal), then AN, like cancer, can be considered probably cured.

Thankfully, a transdiagnostic approach to AN at any level of severity, and whether or not they meet any current state-of-the-art evolving diagnostic criteria (*DSM–IV* or *ICD–10*), has been shown to lead to clinical improvement in the large majority of patients if applied integratively and for long enough to work the disorder out of a job. The myths of AN being always chronic, always severe, hard to treat, difficult to diagnose, and such, are all completely untrue. These myths have all the features of disorders clinicians most like to treat: (1) serious enough to absolutely require treatment; (2) responsive enough to have a high likelihood of cure, remission, not just improvement (up to 76% in the best-outcome series); and (3) challenging enough in research and treatment in both the psychosocial and biomedical areas to provoke new research efforts.

All the answers about AN are not in. But a simpler, clearer approach to diagnosis will benefit many of these patients. As with appendicitis, a clinician cannot treat what is not first accurately diagnosed. A quiet, persistent, noninflammatory insistence on recognizing AN as AN will benefit patients, and eventually the diagnostic criteria will come around to recognizing the criteria that are evidence-based and proven, and which need to be updated.

References

1. Garfinkel PE, Lin E, Goering P, et al. Should amenorrhea be necessary for the diagnosis of anorexia nervosa? Evidence from a Canadian community sample. *Br J Psychiatry* 1996; 168:500.

2. Andersen AE, Bowers B, Watson T. A slimming program for eating disorders not otherwise specified: reconceptualizing a confusing, residual diagnostic category. In: *Psych Clin N Am* June 2001:271.

3. Watson T, Andersen A. A critical examination of the amenorrhea and weight criteria for diagnosing anorexia. *Acta Psychiatr Scand* 2003;108:175.

4. Strober M, Freeman R, Morrell W. The long-term course of severe anorexia nervosa in adolescents: survival analysis of recovery, relapse, and outcome predictors over 10–15 years in a prospective study, *Int J Eat Disord* 1997;22:339.

Prozac Not Effective against Anorexia

A study found the antidepressant Prozac does not help women struggling with anorexia nervosa maintain a normal body weight, and it does not reduce their risk of relapsing, reported the *HealthDay News* on July 16, 2006. This revelation comes after years of prescribing the drug for patients suffering from the life-threatening eating disorder.

"People should not rely on medication which doesn't look terribly effective, but turn their attention to other treatments which may be more useful," said study lead author Dr. B. Timothy Walsh, a professor of psychiatry at New York State Psychiatric Institute at Columbia University Medical Center.

Dr. Onelia G. Lage, an associate professor of pediatrics at the University of Miami Miller School of Medicine, added that the finding "makes sense because anorexia is not a medically treated disease. So, yes, you're going to have relapse if the underlying family and psychological function continues to exist."

Anorexia nervosa, a disorder marked by extreme dieting and other behaviors to keep body weight abnormally low, has the highest mortality rate of any psychiatric illness. The disorder, which primarily affects women, also has a high rate of relapse, with some 30 percent to 50 percent of patients requiring re-hospitalization within one year of their initial discharge.

A sizable number of patients with the disorder are treated with antidepressants such as Prozac, even though there's little direct evidence to support the practice. Medical professionals have largely relied on indirect evidence.

"A lot of people with anorexia, even after they regain weight, have symptoms of anxiety and depression, and clearly fluoxetine (the generic name for Prozac) is useful for those people," Walsh explained. "Also, fluoxetine is clearly efficacious in the treatment of bulimia, and a number of people with anorexia have these symptoms." In addition, one small trial involving patients with anorexia found the drug did help prevent relapse.

For the new study, 93 women aged 16 to 45 with anorexia were randomly assigned to receive Prozac or a placebo. At the time of enrollment in the trial, the participants were completing intensive inpatient or day-program treatment at the New York State Psychiatric Institute or Toronto General Hospital. All had regained weight to a minimum body mass index (BMI, a ratio of weight to height) of 19 before they could be enrolled in the trial. A BMI ranging from 18.5 to 24.9 is considered normal weight.

According to the study, a similar percentage of women assigned to Prozac and the placebo maintained a BMI of at least 18.5 and remained in the study for a full year—26.5 percent in the Prozac group and 31.5 percent in the placebo group. There were also no significant differences in the amount of time it took to relapse. At one year, 45 percent of the placebo group and 43 percent of the Prozac group had not relapsed. The study results appeared in the June 14, 2006 issue of the *Journal of the American Medical Association*.

The findings don't rule out the possibility that drugs such as Prozac might work at a different point in time, for example, after a person has maintained a normal body weight for six months. Starting the drug when a patient is at a lower weight does not work, other trials have shown. The new results also don't shed light on effective treatments for younger patients. "The biggest problem we're having is with 9- to 12 year-olds," Lage said.

The age group in the trial was representative of most patients seeking treatment, Walsh said. And the bottom line, at least for this age group, is that approaches borrowed from other psychiatric disorders, such as depression and anxiety, do not work for anorexia. "It just doesn't respond like other disorders that you might think it is similar to," Walsh said. "That suggests to me that we need to think about the disorder in more innovative and fresher terms. We really need some new thinking, and thinking that is much more specific to anorexia as opposed to borrowing techniques from things that look similar."

Salvation may lie somewhere outside of drugs, Walsh said. "I'm afraid this study falls consistently in the long history of medication trials, almost none of which have been positive," he said. "We have yet to discover or identify an effective medication for anorexia."

Sources: B. Timothy Walsh, M.D., professor, psychiatry, New York State Psychiatric Institute at Columbia University Medical Center, New York City; Onelia G. Lage, M.D., associate professor, pediatrics, University of Miami Miller School of Medicine; June 14, 2006, *Journal of the American Medical Association*).

Additional Information

National Eating Disorders Association
603 Stewart St., Suite 803
Seattle, WA 98101
Toll-Free: 800-931-2237
Phone: 206-382-3587
Website: http://www.nationaleatingdisorders.org
E-mail: info@NationalEatingDisorders.org

Chapter 42

Bulimia Nervosa Treatment

The Treatment Experience

The treatment experience is different for each person. Following are some reflections about treatment from people who went through treatment for bulimia nervosa.

Mealtimes can be difficult not only during recovery, but for a long time—and even throughout the rest of a patient's life. Family members often are not sure how to act—should they congratulate the patient for eating food and encourage more eating? Should they take the

---

This chapter includes "What is treatment like?" "What treatments are used for bulimia nervosa?" and "Which treatments work best?" This information is excerpted from "ECRI's Bulimia Nervosa Resource Guide," © 2006 ECRI (formerly known as Emergency Care Research Institute). All Rights Reserved. Reprinted with permission. For additional information, visit www.bulimiaguide.org or www.ecri.org. This resource guide was produced by ECRI, a 40-year-old international non-profit health services research agency. ECRI's mission is to improve the quality, safety, and cost-effectiveness of healthcare. Recognized by the healthcare community worldwide as a trusted source of highly credible information with very strict conflict-of-interest rules, ECRI is designated as an Evidence-based Practice Center by the U.S. Agency for Healthcare Research and Quality, and as a Collaborating Center of the World Health Organization for Patient Safety, Risk Management, and Health Technology Assessment. This resource guide was funded in large part by the Hilda and Preston Davis Foundation and is available in print and online: www.bulimiaguide.org (free); in print (for a nominal shipping/handling cost) at National Eating Disorders Association online store www.nationaleatingdisorders.org. The guide is part of ECRI's National Patient Library ™ of evidence-based healthcare guides for consumers.

focus of attention completely off of food and talk about something else? One family found meal planning helpful. They decided with their recovering daughter which foods to eat and when to eat them. This was their only focus on food. They would "eat what was healthy and forget about it."

Staying busy after meals was important to get their daughter's mind off of what she had just consumed. The family would take walks or go shopping. Therapy helped this family work out how best to relate to their daughter. Although it was "not easy to sit with counselors and realize your faults as parents," said the mother, she felt that confronting her own role in the family was important to her daughter's recovery.

Another patient said it took her two years of intermittent treatment before she was truly comfortable at dinners. Mealtimes were tough during those two years; the family was not sure how to address the food issue. The patient's feelings towards food changed over time—from wanting to ignore it completely at meals to feeling comfortable talking about it.

The family had difficulty keeping up with the changes. And this caused tension. The patient described it this way. "You're trying not to think about [food], and you're feeling scrutinized about it." The family didn't go to therapy, although the patient felt it would have been helpful. Therapy can help the family and patient "figure out where you are on that continuum" of focusing on food or avoiding it, she said.

Another patient went in and out of treatment centers for five years and met a lot of other people in her situation. She observed that most of the patients, including her, had alienated or lost touch with old friends and bonded with each other in the center. This proved to be a double-edged sword. For this patient, the new-found friends were initially a lifeline to recovery because they understood each other. But some relationships eventually became a breeding ground for competition on weight loss or who would be the first to relapse and return to the treatment center.

"The intense bonding is just what you need in the moment, but later it can just hold you back," she said. She felt that staying friends with people who had not progressed as far in recovery as she had was holding back her own treatment. She also noted that because many people with eating disorders have abandonment issues, separating from friends made in treatment centers can be especially difficult. She maintains few relationships made during her recovery, and said that therapy was key to her ability to rebuild most of the friendships she had before starting treatment.

Treatment is a difficult process physically and emotionally. For one patient, the hardest part came after the treatment had started and her symptoms began to subside. She explained that for her, the disorder was about control—controlling her eating that later developed into controlling her emotions. She developed a "numb" feeling that "felt good" as her disorder progressed. However, as her treatment progressed and symptoms disappeared, her emotions returned and the numbness was gone. "The hardest thing was feeling the feelings," she said.

Treatments Used for Bulimia Nervosa

Standard bulimia nervosa treatments include medications (prescription drugs), various psychotherapies, nutrition therapy, other non-drug therapies and supportive or adjunct interventions such as yoga, art, massage, and movement therapy. Some novel treatments are currently under research, such as implantation of a device called a vagus nerve stimulator implanted at the base of the neck. This stimulator is currently in use to treat some forms of depression, and it is under research for treating obesity.

The most commonly used treatments—psychotherapy and medication—are delivered at various levels of inpatient and outpatient care, and in various settings depending on the severity of the illness and the treatment plan that has been developed for a particular patient. Bulimia nervosa can often be treated on an outpatient basis, although more severe cases may require inpatient residential treatment. The treatment plan should be developed by a multidisciplinary team in consultation with the patient, and family members as deemed appropriate by the patient and his or her team.

Types of Prescription Drug Therapy

Biochemical abnormalities in the brain and body have been associated with bulimia nervosa. Many types of prescription drugs have been used in treatment of bulimia nervosa, however, only one prescription drug (fluoxetine) actually has a labeled indication for bulimia nervosa. (This means that the manufacturer requested the U.S. Food and Drug Administration for permission to market the drug specifically for treatment of bulimia nervosa, and that FDA approved this request based on the evidence the manufacturer provided about the drug's efficacy for bulimia nervosa.)

Most prescription drug therapy used for treatment of the disorder is aimed at alleviating major depression, anxiety, or obsessive-compulsive disorder (OCD), which often co-exist with bulimia nervosa. Some prescription drug therapies are intended to make individuals feel full to try to prevent binge eating.

Anti-depressants are intended to try to reduce a patient's urge to binge and purge by treating depression, anxiety, and OCD. Generic and brand names of prescription drugs that have been used to treat bulimia nervosa are listed. Some of these anti-depressants also can exert other effects. Selective serotonin reuptake inhibitors (SSRIs) alleviate depression but may also play a role in making an individual feel full and possibly prevent binge eating.

Antidepressants

- tricyclics
  - amitriptyline (Elavil)
  - clomipramine (Anafranil)
  - desipramine (Norpramin, Pertofrane)
  - imipramine (Janimine, Tofranil)
  - nortriptyline (Aventyl, Pamelor)
- selective serotonin reuptake inhibitors (SSRIs)
  - citalopram (Celexa)
  - escitalopram (Lexapro)
  - fluoxetine (Prozac, Sarafem)
  - fluvoxamine (Luvox)
  - paroxetine (Paxil)
  - sertraline (Zoloft)
- monoamine oxidase inhibitors
  - brofaromine (Consonar)
  - isocarboxazid (Benzamide)
  - moclobemide (Manerix)
  - phenelzine (Nardil)
  - tranylcypromine (Parnate)
- tetracyclics
  - mianserin (Bolvidon)
  - mirtazapine (Remeron)

- modified cyclic antidepressants: trazodone (Desyrel)
- phenethylamine monoamine reuptake inhibitor: venlafaxine (Effexor)
- serotonin and noradrenaline reuptake inhibitor: duloxetine (Cymbalta)
- opioid antagonist: naltrexone (Intended to alleviate addictive behaviors such as the addictive drive to eat or binge eat.)
- antiemetic: ondansetron (Zofran) (Used to give sensation of satiety and fullness.)
- anticonvulsant: topiramate (Topamax) (May help regulate feeding behaviors.)
- other: lithium carbonate (Carbolith, Cibalith-S, Duralith, Eskalith, Lithane, Lithizine, Lithobid, Lithonate, Lithotabs) (This drug may be contraindicated for some patients with bulimia nervosa.)

Types of Psychotherapy

Several types of psychotherapy are used in individual and group settings and with families. A given psychologist may use several different approaches tailored to the situation. Cognitive behavior therapy (CBT) and behavior therapy (BT) have been used for many years as first-line treatment and are the most-used types of psychotherapy for this disorder.

CBT involves three overlapping phases. The first phase focuses on helping people to resist the urge to engage in the cycle of behavior by educating them about the dangers. The second phase introduces procedures to reduce dietary restraint and increase the regularity of eating. The last phase involves teaching people relapse-prevention strategies to help prepare them for possible setbacks. A course of individual CBT for bulimia nervosa usually involves 16 to 20, one hour sessions over four to five months. BT uses principles of learning to increase the frequency of desired behavior and decrease the frequency of problem behavior. When used to treat bulimia nervosa, BT focuses on teaching relaxation techniques and coping strategies that individuals can use instead of binge eating and purging or excessive exercise or fasting.

Individual psychotherapy includes the following:

- behavior therapy
- exposure with response prevention
- hypnotic-behavior therapy
- cognitive therapy
- cognitive analytic therapy
- cognitive behavior therapy (all forms)
- scheme-based cognitive therapy
- self-guided cognitive behavioral therapy
- dialectical behavior therapy
- psychodynamic therapy
- self psychology
- psychoanalysis
- interpersonal psychotherapy
- motivational enhancement therapy
- psychoeducation
- supportive therapy

Family therapy involves family members in psychotherapy sessions with and without the patient.

Group psychotherapy includes the following:

- cognitive behavioral therapy
- psychodynamic
- psychoeducational

Self-help groups include the following:

- ANAD (Anorexia Nervosa and Associated Disorders)
- 12-step approaches
- Eating Disorders Anonymous

Self-help groups are listed because they may be the only option available to people who have no insurance. However, self-help groups can also have negative affects on a person with an eating disorder if they are not well-moderated by a trained professional.

Other Types of Treatment

Many interventions that do not involve prescription drugs or psychotherapy have been used as adjuncts or supportive therapy. Some people consider some of these options to be "alternative or complementary therapy." Opinions differ about the role of many of these therapies in treatment. The approach taken in this guide is to identify all the treatments and interventions used with bulimia nervosa patients and then search for clinical trials that evaluated these treatments to see if there is any evidence of how well they work. The search results found that few or no well-conducted clinical studies have been done on these adjunct or alternative interventions for bulimia nervosa, so no one really knows whether or not they work or help patients.

Some of these interventions are used alone; others are used in conjunction with medications or psychotherapy. Some may be included as activities made available at residential treatment centers; others may be used in private therapists' offices. The following list includes treatments that are available and may be offered to patients, even though their effectiveness is unknown.

- creative arts therapies
    - art therapy
    - movement therapy
    - psychodrama
- nutritional counseling including individual, group, family, and mealtime support therapy
- other therapies
    - biofeedback
    - coaching
    - e-mailing for support or coaching
    - eye movement desensitization
    - exercise
    - guided imagery
    - journaling
    - mandometer
    - massage
    - meditation

- relaxation training
- vagus nerve stimulation
- yoga

Treatments That Work Best

Many different treatment approaches are used for bulimia nervosa. To know what really works best requires analyzing results of all the clinical trials that have been published on each treatment. Then, doctors and patients have the best information available to decide about treatment.

ECRI's analysis of all the available evidence found that medication used to treat bulimia nervosa reduced the frequency of binge eating and purging. Medication also lessened anxiety, depression, and eating disorder psychopathology (abnormal behavior). Cognitive behavioral therapy (CBT) reduced the frequency of purging, and it did so more effectively than medication. However, the effect of CBT on binge eating by itself, and on anxiety, depression, and eating disorder psychopathology is not clear from the available evidence. The effectiveness of other kinds of psychotherapy is also unclear at this time. More clinical research of high quality is needed to answer the questions that remain about how well CBT and other kinds of psychotherapy, and medications work for bulimia nervosa.

Trials on complementary therapies and alternative therapies for bulimia nervosa either did not exist or were of such poor quality that they could not be analyzed—so it was not possible to determine whether or not they work.

The first step in ECRI arriving at these conclusions was to identify all the trials that have published their results. The next step was to evaluate the quality of those studies to select those that provide the best evidence for analysis. This approach is known as "systematic review" because it involves a systematic, comprehensive approach to identifying and analyzing all available published clinical data. The systematic review addressed four key questions about the effectiveness of several prescription drugs, forms of psychotherapy, and other non-drug treatment options that have been used for treatment of bulimia nervosa. The four key questions addressed were:

1. Is drug therapy effective treatment for bulimia nervosa?
2. Is psychotherapy or other non-drug therapy effective treatment for bulimia nervosa?

3. Is psychotherapy therapy or other non-drug therapy more effective than drug therapy for the treatment of bulimia nervosa?

4. Is CBT (the most commonly used form of psychotherapy today) more effective than other types of psychotherapy for the treatment of bulimia nervosa?

ECRI's comprehensive searches for published clinical trials identified a total of 1,398 potentially relevant articles. Of those articles 181 merited more detailed examination to see if they contained data of sufficient quality for analysis. Finally selected were 71 relevant articles that described 48 randomized controlled trials. More than one article was published on some of the trials. Not all of the trials pertained to every key question: twenty-six trials addressed question one; fifteen trials addressed question two; six trials addressed question three; and thirteen trials addressed question four.

Whenever sufficient data were available, ECRI's analysts pooled data from several clinical trials using a statistical technique known as meta-analysis. For drug studies, they analyzed whether drugs were more effective than placebo (an inactive pill). For psychotherapy, they analyzed whether CBT (the therapy for which the most data were available) was better than no treatment and how it compared to drug therapy and other types of psychotherapies.

The effect of drug therapy and psychotherapy on each of these outcomes was analyzed:

- frequency of bulimic behavior (bingeing and compensatory behavior)
- patient quality of life
- mood and anxiety levels
- eating disorder psychopathology (for example, body image dissatisfaction and eating attitudes)
- personality and interpersonal functioning (for example, anxiety and depression measures, self-esteem measures, and family environment scales)
- patient mortality

ECRI did not formally evaluate the side effects of drug treatments for bulimia nervosa because drawing valid conclusions about drug safety requires a vast amount of data. Such a volume of data is not yet available on people with bulimia nervosa. However, manufacturers' drug labeling information does provide data on side effects that have been experienced by people taking the drugs that are often used to treat bulimia nervosa. Also included in the manufacturers' drug labeling information are important warnings associated with the use of the drug and its possible interactions with other drugs. Remember, however, that drug-labeling information is not specific to bulimia nervosa. Whether drug side effects differ in patients with bulimia nervosa compared to patients with other conditions is not known. Anyone taking medication should consult a physician or pharmacist about possible drug interactions.

For studies on the prescription drugs used to treat bulimia nervosa, ECRI first wanted to find out whether the various types of drugs that are used for bulimia nervosa differed from each other in effectiveness. Exploratory analyses were performed to examine this issue. It was found that different types of prescription drugs used in treatment did not appear to differ significantly in their effectiveness or acceptability to patients. Based on this analysis, data from studies on different types of prescription drugs was pooled into one analysis.

Studies on psychological treatments presented a different problem. Unlike individual drug studies, which studied only one drug, individual studies on psychological therapy often used more than one type of psychological therapy in a single trial. Psychological therapy was also delivered in individual and group settings, which could theoretically affect how well the therapy works. Thus, analysts had to adopt different analytic approaches to analyze data from these studies.

Is prescription drug therapy an effective treatment for bulimia nervosa?

The analysis found that drug therapy for bulimia nervosa reduced some patients' underlying anxiety and depression, eating-disorder psychopathology, and binge-eating and purging frequency. Whether or not drug therapy improved patients' quality of life could not be determined from the available data. These findings were obtained by pooling data from the 26 randomized controlled trials that compared drug therapy to a placebo (inactive pill). This is the type of comparison needed to learn whether drugs really work.

Is psychotherapy effective treatment for bulimia nervosa?

The analysis found that for some patients, CBT reduced purging behavior. However, the evidence was inconclusive on whether CBT improved patients' quality of life or reduced underlying eating disorder psychopathology, binge-eating behavior, or depression and anxiety. Also, determining whether the effectiveness of CBT changed when it was delivered in different formats could not be determined because too few studies were available to allow meaningful analysis of different CBT formats. This answer was obtained by pooling data from 11 randomized controlled trials that compared CBT to no therapy (individuals on a wait list).

Is psychotherapy more effective than prescription drug therapy for treatment of bulimia nervosa?

The analysis found that CBT was more effective than drug therapy for reducing purging behavior. The evidence was inconclusive on whether CBT was more effective than drug therapy for improving quality of life, reducing underlying eating disorder psychopathology, binge-eating behavior, or depression or anxiety. This answer was obtained by pooling data from six randomized controlled trials that compared the effectiveness of CBT to drug therapy. To better answer this question, more data from appropriately designed comparative studies are needed.

Is CBT, in particular, more effective than other types of psychotherapy for treatment of bulimia nervosa?

The results of this analysis were inconclusive because too few data were available. Data were available from 13 randomized controlled trials that compared CBT to other psychological therapies. The only comparisons that were made in more than one study were CBT versus behavioral therapy (three studies) and CBT versus interpersonal therapy (two studies). Pooled analyses were done where possible, but the data were insufficient to yield an answer. To satisfactorily answer this question, more data from appropriately designed controlled trials are needed.

Chapter 43

Nutrition Intervention in the Treatment of Eating Disorders

It is the position of the American Dietetic Association (ADA) that nutrition education and nutrition intervention, by a registered dietitian, is an essential component of the team treatment of patients with anorexia nervosa, bulimia nervosa, and eating disorders not otherwise specified (EDNOS) during assessment and treatment across the continuum of care.

Eating disorders are considered to be psychiatric disorders, but unfortunately they are remarkable for their nutrition and medical-related problems, some of which can be life-threatening. Eating disorders have the highest fatality of any psychiatric illness. As a general rule, eating disorders are characterized by abnormal eating patterns and cognitive distortions related to food and weight, which in turn result in adverse effects on nutrition status, medical complications, and impaired health status and function.

Many authors have noted that anorexia nervosa is detectable in all social classes, suggesting that higher socioeconomic status is not a major factor in the prevalence of anorexia and bulimia nervosa. A wide range of demographics is seen in eating disorder patients. The

---

Excerpted and reprinted from *Journal of the American Dietetic Association*, Volume 101:810, Bonnie A. Spear, Ph.D., R.D., and Eileen Stellefson Myers, MPH, R.D., FADA, "Nutrition intervention in the treatment of anorexia nervosa, bulimia nervosa, and eating disorder not otherwise specified (EDNOS)," p.810–819. Updated in October 2006 by Dr. David A. Cooke, M.D., Diplomate, American Board of Internal Medicine.

major characteristic of eating disorders are the disturbed body image in which one's body is perceived as being fat (even at normal or low weight), an intense fear of weight gain and becoming fat, and a relentless obsession to become thinner.

Diagnostic criteria for anorexia nervosa, bulimia nervosa, and eating disorders not otherwise specified (EDNOS) are identified in the fourth edition of the *Diagnostic and Statistical Manual of Mental Disorders (DSM-IV-TR)*. These clinical diagnoses are based on psychological, behavioral, and physiological characteristics.

It is important to note that patients cannot be diagnosed with both anorexia nervosa (AN) and bulimia nervosa (BN) at the same time. Patients with EDNOS do not fall into the diagnostic criterion for either AN or BN, but account for about 50% of the population with eating disorders. If left untreated and behaviors continue, the diagnosis may change to BN or AN. Binge eating disorder is currently classified within the EDNOS grouping.

Over a lifetime, an individual may meet diagnostic criteria for more than one of these conditions, suggesting a continuum of disordered eating. Attitudes and behaviors relating to food and weight overlap substantially. Nevertheless, despite attitudinal and behavioral similarities, distinctive patterns of comorbidity and risk factors have been identified for each of these disorders. Therefore, the nutritional and medical complications and therapy can differ significantly.

Because of the complex biopsychosocial aspects of eating disorders, the optimal assessment and ongoing management of these conditions appear to be under the direction of an interdisciplinary team consisting of professionals from medical, nursing, nutritional, and mental health disciplines. Medical nutrition therapy (MNT) provided by a registered dietitian trained in the area of eating disorders is an integral component of treatment and management of eating disorders.

Comorbid Illness and Eating Disorders

Patients with eating disorders may suffer from other psychiatric disorders as well as their eating disorder, which increases the complexity of treatment. Registered dietitians must understand the characteristics of these psychiatric disorders and the impact of these disorders on the course of treatment. The experienced dietitian knows to be in frequent contact with the mental health team member in order to have an adequate understanding of the patient's current status. Psychiatric disorders that are frequently seen in the eating disorder population include mood and anxiety disorders (such as depression or obsessive-compulsive disorder), personality disorders, and substance abuse disorders.

Abuse and trauma may precede the eating disorder in some patients. The registered dietitian must consult with the primary therapist on how to best handle the patient's recall of abuse or dissociative episodes that may occur during nutrition counseling sessions.

Role of the Treatment Team

The care of patients with eating disorder involves expertise and dedication of an interdisciplinary team. Since it is clearly a psychiatric disorder with major medical complications, psychiatric management is the foundation of treatment and should be instituted for all patients in combination with other treatment modalities. A physician familiar with eating disorders should perform a thorough physical exam. This may involve the patient's primary care provider, a physician specializing in eating disorders, or the psychiatrist caring for the patient. A dental exam should also be performed. Medication management and medical monitoring are the responsibilities of the physician(s) on the team. Psychotherapy is the responsibility of the clinician with credentials to provide psychotherapy. This task may be given to a social worker, a psychiatric nurse specialist (advanced practice nurse), psychologist, psychiatrist, a licensed professional counselor, or a master's level counselor. In inpatient and partial hospitalization settings, nurses monitor the status of the patient and dispense medications while recreation therapists and occupational therapists assist the patient in acquiring healthy daily living and recreational skills. The registered dietitian assesses the nutritional status, knowledge base, motivation, current eating, and behavioral status of the patient; develops the nutrition section of the treatment plan; implements the treatment plan; and supports the patient in accomplishing the goals set out in the treatment plan. Ideally, the dietitian has continuous contact with the patient throughout the course of treatment or, if this is not possible, refers the patient to another dietitian if the patient is transitioning from an inpatient to an outpatient setting.

Medical nutrition therapy and psychotherapy are two integral parts of the treatment of eating disorders. The dietitian working with eating disorder patients needs a good understanding of personal and professional boundaries. Unfortunately, this is not often taught in traditional training programs. Understanding of boundaries refers to recognizing and appreciating the specific tasks and topics that each member of the team is responsible for covering. Specifically, the role of the registered dietitian is to address the food and nutrition issues, the behavior associated with those issues, and assist the medical team member with monitoring lab values, vital signs, and physical symptoms associated with malnutrition. The psychotherapeutic issues are the focus of the psychotherapist or mental health team member.

Effective nutrition therapy for the patient with an eating disorder requires knowledge of motivational interviewing and cognitive behavioral therapy (CBT). The registered dietitian's communication style, both verbal and nonverbal, can significantly affect the patient's motivation to change. Motivational interviewing was developed because of the idea that individual's motivation arises from an interpersonal process. CBT identifies maladaptive cognitions and involves cognitive restructuring. Erroneous beliefs and thought patterns are challenged with more accurate perceptions and interpretations regarding dieting, nutrition, and the relationship between starvation and physical symptoms.

The trans-theoretical model of change suggests that an individual progresses through various stages of change and uses cognitive and behavioral processes when attempting to change health-related behavior. Stages include pre-contemplation, contemplation, preparation, action, and maintenance. Patients with eating disorders often progress along these stages with frequent backsliding along the way to recovery. The role of the nutritional therapist is to help move patients along the continuum until they reach the maintenance stage.

Medical Consequences and Intervention in Eating Disorders

Nutritional factors and dieting behaviors may influence the development and course of eating disorders. In the pathogenesis of anorexia nervosa, dieting or other purposeful changes in food choices can contribute enormously to the course of the disease because of the physiological and psychological consequences of starvation that perpetuate the disease and impede progress toward recovery. Higher prevalence rates among specific groups, such as athletes and patients with diabetes mellitus, support the concept that increased risk occurs with conditions in which dietary restraint or control of body weight assumes great importance. However, only a small proportion of individuals who diet or restrict intake develop an eating disorder. In many cases, psychological and cultural pressures must exist along with physical, emotional, and societal pressures for an individual to develop an eating disorder.

Anorexia Nervosa

Medical Symptoms

Essential to the diagnosis of anorexia nervosa (AN) is that patients weigh less than 85% of that expected. There are several ways to determine the less than 85th percentile. For adults (over 20 years of age) a body mass index (BMI) less than 18.5 is considered underweight and a BMI under 17.5 is diagnostic for AN. For postmenarchal adolescents and adults a standard formula to determine average body weight (ABW) for height can also be used (100 pounds for five feet of height plus five pounds for each inch over five feet tall for women). The 85th percentile of ABW can be diagnostic of AN. For children and young adults up to the age of 20 the percent of average weight-for-height can be calculated by using Centers for Disease Control and Prevention (CDC) growth charts or the CDC body mass index charts. Because children are still growing, the BMI increases with age in children and therefore the BMI percentiles must be used, not the actual numbers. Individuals with BMI less than the 10th percentile are considered underweight and BMI less than 5th percentile are at risk for AN. In all cases, the patient's body build, weight history, and stage of development (in adolescents) should be considered.

Physical symptoms can range from lanugo hair formation to life-threatening cardiac arrhythmias. Physical characteristics include lanugo hair on face and trunk; brittle, listless hair; cyanosis of hands and feet; and dry skin. Cardiovascular changes include bradycardia (heart rate less than 60 beats/min), hypotension (systolic less than 90 mm HG), and orthostatic hypotension. Many patients, as well as some health providers, attribute the low heart rate and low blood pressure to their physical fitness and exercise regimen. However, Nudel showed these lower vital signs actually altered cardiovascular responses to exercise in patients with AN. A reduced heart mass has also been associated with the reduced blood pressure and pulse rate. Cardiovascular complications have been associated with death in AN patients.

Anorexia nervosa can also significantly affect the gastrointestinal tract and brain mass of these individuals. Self-induced starvation can lead to delayed gastric emptying, decreased gut motility, and severe constipation. There is also evidence of structural brain abnormalities (tissue loss) with prolonged starvation, which appears early in the disease process and may be of substantial magnitude. While it is clear that some reversibility of brain changes occurs with weight recovery, it is uncertain whether complete reversibility is possible. To minimize the potential long-term physical complication of AN, early recognition and aggressive treatment is essential for young people who develop this illness.

Amenorrhea is a primary characteristic of AN. Amenorrhea is associated with a combination of hypothalamic dysfunction, weight loss, decreased body fat, stress, and excessive exercise. The amenorrhea appears to be caused by an alteration in the regulation of gonadotropin-releasing hormone. In AN, gonadotropins revert to prepubertal levels and patterns of secretion.

Osteopenia and osteoporosis, like brain changes, are serious and possibly irreversible medical complications of anorexia nervosa. This may be serious enough to result in vertebra compression and stress fractures. Study results indicate that some recovery of bone may be possible with weight restoration and recovery, but compromised bone density has been evident eleven years after weight restoration and recovery. In adolescents, more bone recovery may be possible. Unlike other conditions in which low circulating estrogen concentrations are associated with bone loss (for example, perimenopause), providing exogenous estrogen has not been shown to preserve or restore bone mass in the anorexia nervosa patient. Calcium supplementation alone or in combination with estrogen has not been observed to promote increased bone density. Adequate calcium intake may help to lessen bone loss. There is evidence that bisphosphonate drugs such as etidronate, alendronate, and risedronate may improve bone density in patients with anorexia nervosa. However, they are not FDA approved for this purpose, and data is quite limited. Only weight restoration has been definitively shown to increase bone density.

In patients with AN, laboratory values usually remain in normal ranges until the illness is far advanced, although true laboratory values may be masked by chronic dehydration. Some of the earliest lab abnormalities include bone marrow hypoplasia, including varying degrees of leukopenia and thrombocytopenia. Despite low-fat and low-cholesterol diets, patients with AN often have elevated cholesterol and abnormal lipid profiles. Reasons for this include mild hepatic dysfunction, decreased bile acid secretion, and abnormal eating patterns. Additionally, serum glucose tends to be low, secondary to a deficit of precursors for gluconeogenesis and glucose production. Patients with AN may have repeated episodes of hypoglycemia.

Despite dietary inadequacies, vitamin and mineral deficiencies are rarely seen in AN. This has been attributed to a decreased metabolic need for micronutrients in a catabolic state. Additionally, many patients take vitamin and mineral supplements, which may mask true deficiencies. Despite low iron intakes, iron deficiency anemia is rare. This may be due to decreased needs due to amenorrhea, decreased needs in a catabolic state, and altered states of hydration. Prolonged malnutrition leads to low levels of zinc, vitamin B_{12}, and folate. Any low nutrient levels should be treated appropriately with food and supplements as needed.

Medical and Nutritional Management

Treatment for anorexia nervosa may be inpatient or outpatient based, depending upon the severity and chronicity of both the medical and behavioral components of the disorder. No single professional or professional discipline is able to provide the necessary broad medical, nutritional, and psychiatric care necessary for patients to recover. Teams of professionals who communicate regularly must provide this care. This teamwork is necessary whether the individual is undergoing inpatient or outpatient treatment.

Although weight is a critical monitoring tool to determine a patient's progress, each program must individualize its own protocol for weighing the patient on an inpatient program. The protocol should include who will do the weighing, when the weighing will occur, and whether or not the patient is allowed to know their weight. In the outpatient setting, the team member weighing the patient may vary with the setting. In a clinic model, the nurse may weigh the patient as part of her responsibilities in taking vital signs. The patient then has the opportunity to discuss their reaction to the weight when seen by the registered dietitian. In a community outpatient model, the nutrition session is the appropriate place for weighing the patient, discussing reactions to weight and providing explanations for weight changes. In some cases such as a patient expressing suicidality, alternatives to the weight procedure may be used. For example, the patient may be weighed with their back to the scale and not told their weight, the mental health professional may do the weighing, or if the patient is medically stable the weight for that visit may be skipped. In such cases, there are many other tools to monitor the patient's medical condition, such as vital signs, emotional health, and laboratory measurements.

Outpatient

In AN the goals of outpatient treatment are to focus on nutritional rehabilitation, weight restoration, cessation of weight reduction behaviors, improvement in eating behaviors, and improvement in psychological and emotional state. Clearly weight restoration alone does not indicate recovery, and forcing weight gain without psychological support and counseling is contraindicated. Typically, the patient is terrified of weight gain and may be struggling with hunger and urges to binge, but the foods he or she allows himself or herself are too limited to enable sufficient energy intake. Individualized guidance and a meal plan that provides a framework for meals and snacks and food choices (but not a rigid diet) is helpful for most patients. The registered dietitian determines the individual caloric needs and with the patient develops a nutrition plan that allows the patient to meet these nutrition needs. In the early treatment of AN, this may be done on a gradual basis, increasing the caloric prescription in increments to reach the necessary caloric intake. MNT should be targeted at helping the patient understand nutritional needs as well as helping them begin to make wise food choices by increasing variety in diet and by practicing appropriate food behaviors. One effective counseling technique is CBT, which involves challenging erroneous beliefs and thought patterns with more accurate perceptions and interpretations regarding dieting, nutrition and the relationship between starvation and physical symptoms. In many cases, monitoring skinfolds can be helpful in determining composition of weight gain as well as being useful as an educational tool to show the patient the composition of any weight gain (lean body mass vs. fat mass). Percent body fat can be estimated from the sum of four skinfold measurements (triceps, biceps, subscapular and suprailiac crest) using the calculations of Durnin. This method has been validated against underwater weighing in adolescent girls with AN. Bioelectrical impedance analysis has been shown to be unreliable in patients with AN secondary to changes in intracellular and extracellular fluid changes and chronic dehydration.

The registered dietitian will need to recommend dietary supplements as needed to meet nutritional needs. In many cases, the registered dietitian will be the team member to recommend physical activity levels based on medical status, psychological status, and nutritional intake. Physical activity may need to be limited or initially eliminated with the compulsive exerciser who has AN so that weight restoration can be achieved. The counseling effort needs to focus on the message that exercise is an activity undertaken for enjoyment and fitness rather than a way to expend energy and promote weight loss. Supervised, low weight, strength training is less likely to impede weight gain than other forms of activity and may be psychologically helpful for patients. Nutrition therapy must be ongoing to allow the patient to understand his/her nutritional needs as well as to adjust and adapt the nutrition plan to meet the patient's medical and nutritional requirements.

During the refeeding phase (especially in the early refeeding process), the patient needs to be monitored closely for signs of refeeding syndrome. Refeeding syndrome is characterized by sudden and sometimes severe hypophosphatemia, sudden drops in potassium and magnesium, glucose intolerance, hypokalemia, gastrointestinal dysfunction, and cardiac arrhythmias (a prolonged QT interval is a contributing cause of the rhythm disturbances). Water retention during refeeding should be anticipated and discussed with the patient. Guidance with food choices to promote normal bowel function should be provided as well. A weight gain goal of one to two pounds per week for outpatient and two to three pounds for inpatients is recommended. In the beginning of therapy the registered dietitian will need to see the patient on a frequent basis. If the patient responds to medical, nutritional, and psychiatric therapy, nutrition visits may be less frequent. Refeeding syndrome can be seen in both the outpatient and inpatient settings and the patient should be monitored closely during the early refeeding process. Because more aggressive and rapid refeeding is initiated on the inpatient units, refeeding syndrome is more commonly seen in these units.

Inpatient

Although many patients may respond to outpatient therapy, others do not. Low weight is only one index of malnutrition; weight should never be used as the only criterion for hospital admission. Most patients with AN are knowledgeable enough to falsify weight through such strategies as excessive water or fluid intake. If body weight alone is used for hospital admission criteria, behaviors may result in acute hyponatremia or dangerous degrees of unrecognized weight loss. All criteria for admission should be considered. The criteria for inpatient admission include the following:

- severe malnutrition (weight less than 75% of expected weight for height)
- dehydration
- electrolyte disturbances
- cardiac dysrhythmia (including prolonged QT)

- physiological instability
    - severe bradycardia (fewer than 45 heartbeats per minute)
    - hypotension
    - hypothermia (less than 36° centigrade)
    - orthostatic changes (pulse and blood pressure)
- arrested growth and development
- failure of outpatient treatment
- acute food refusal
- uncontrollable binging and purging
- acute medical complication of malnutrition (for example; syncope, seizures, cardiac failure, pancreatitis)
- acute psychiatric emergencies (such as suicidal ideation or acute psychoses)
- comorbid diagnosis that interferes with the treatment of the eating disorder (such as severe depression, obsessive-compulsive disorder, severe family dysfunction).

The goals of inpatient therapy are the same as outpatient management; only the intensity increases. If admitted for medical instability, medical and nutrition stabilization is the first and most important goal of inpatient treatment. This is often necessary before psychological therapy can be optimally effective. Often, the first phase of inpatient treatment is on a medical unit to medically stabilize the patient. After medical stabilization, the patient can be moved to an inpatient psychiatric floor or discharged home to allow the patient to try outpatient treatment. If a patient is admitted for psychiatric instability but is medically stable, the patient should be admitted directly to a psychiatric floor or facility. The registered dietitian should guide the nutrition plan. The nutrition plan should help the patient, as quickly as possible, to consume a diet that is adequate in energy intake and nutritionally well-balanced.

The registered dietitian should monitor the energy intake as well as body composition to ensure that appropriate weight gain is achieved. As with outpatient therapy, MNT should be targeted at helping the patient understand nutritional needs as well as help the patient to begin to make wise food choices by increasing variety in diet and by practicing appropriate food behaviors. In very rare instances, enteral or parenteral feeding may be necessary. However, risks associated with aggressive nutrition support in these patients are substantial, including hypophosphatemia, edema, cardiac failure, seizures, aspiration of enteral formula, and death. Reliance on food as the primary method of weight restoration contributes significantly to successful long-term recovery —rather than enteral or parenteral nutrition support. The overall goal is to help the patient normalize eating patterns and learn that behavior change must involve planning and practicing with real food.

Partial Hospitalizations

Partial hospitalizations (day treatment) are increasingly utilized in an attempt to decrease the length of some inpatient hospitalizations and also for milder AN cases, in place of a hospitalization. Patients usually attend for seven to ten hours per day, and are served two meals and one to two snacks. During the day, they participate in medical and nutritional monitoring, nutrition counseling, and psychotherapy—both group and individual. The patient is responsible for one meal and any recommended snacks at home. The individual who participates in partial hospitalization must be motivated to participate and be able to consume an adequate nutritional intake at home as well as follow recommendations regarding physical activity.

Recovery

Recovery from AN takes time. Even after the patient has recovered medically, they may need ongoing psychological support to sustain the change. For patients with AN, one of their greatest fears is not being able to stop gaining weight after reaching a low, healthy weight. In long-term follow-up the registered dietitian's role is to assist the patient in reaching an acceptable healthy weight and to help the patient maintain this weight over time. The registered dietitian's counseling should focus on helping the patient to consume an appropriate, varied diet to maintain weight and appropriate body composition.

Bulimia Nervosa

Bulimia Nervosa (BN) occurs in approximately two to five percent of the population. Most patients with BN tend to be of normal weight or moderately overweight and therefore are often undetectable by appearance alone. The average onset of BN occurs between mid-adolescence and the late 20s with a great diversity of socioeconomic status. A full syndrome of BN is rare in the first decade of life. A biopsychosocial model seems best for explaining the etiology of BN. The individual at risk for the disorder may have a biological vulnerability to depression that is exacerbated by a chaotic and conflicting family and social role expectations. Society's emphasis on thinness often helps the person identify weight loss as the solution. Dieting then leads to binging, and the cyclical disorder begins. A subgroup of these patients exists where the binging proceeds dieting. This group tends to be of a higher body weight. The patient with BN has an eating pattern which is typically chaotic although rules of what should be eaten, how much, and what constitutes good and bad foods occupy the thought process for the majority of the patient's day.

Although the amount of food consumed that is labeled a binge episode is subjective, the criteria for bulimia nervosa requires other measures such as the feeling of out-of-control behavior during the bingeing. Although the diagnostic criteria for this disorder focuses on the binge and/or purge behavior, much of the time the person with BN is restricting her or his diet. The dietary restriction can be the physiological or psychological trigger to subsequent binge eating. Also, the trauma of breaking rules by eating something other than what was intended or more than what was intended may lead to self-destructive binge eating behavior. Any subjective or objective sensation of stomach fullness may trigger the person to purge. Common purging methods consist of self-induced vomiting with or without the use of syrup of ipecac, laxative use, diuretic use, and excessive exercise. Once purged, the patient may feel some initial relief; however, this is often followed by guilt and shame. Resuming normal eating commonly leads to gastrointestinal complaints such as bloating, constipation, and flatulence. This physical discomfort as well as the guilt from binging often results in a cyclical pattern as the patient tries to get back on track by restricting once again. Although the focus is on the food, the binge and/or purge behavior is often a means for the person to regulate and manage emotions and to medicate psychological pain.

Medical Symptoms

In the initial assessment, it is important to assess and evaluate for medical conditions that may play a role in the purging behavior. Conditions such as esophageal reflux disease (GERD) and *Helicobacter pylori* may increase the pain and the need for the patient to vomit.

Interventions for these conditions may help in reducing the vomiting and allow the treatment for BN to be more focused. Nutritional abnormalities for patients with BN depend on the amount of restriction during the non-binge episodes. It is important to note that purging behaviors do not completely prevent the utilization of calories from the binge; an average retention of 1200 calories occurs from binges of various sizes and contents.

Muscle weakness, fatigue, cardiac arrhythmias, dehydration, and electrolyte imbalance can be caused by purging, especially self-induced vomiting and laxative abuse. It is common to see hypokalemia and hypochloremic alkalosis as well as gastrointestinal problems involving the stomach and esophagus. Dental erosion from self-induced vomiting can be quite serious. Although laxatives are used to purge calories, they are quite ineffective. Chronic ipecac use has been shown to cause skeletal myopathy, electrocardiographic changes, and cardiomyopathy with consequent congestive heart failure, arrhythmia, and sudden death.

Medical and Nutritional Management of Bulimia Nervosa

As with AN, interdisciplinary team management is essential to care. The majority of patients with BN are treated in an outpatient or partial hospitalization setting. Indications for inpatient hospitalization include severe disabling symptoms that are unresponsive to outpatient treatment or additional medical problems such as uncontrolled vomiting, severe laxative abuse withdrawal, metabolic abnormalities or vital sign changes, suicidal ideations, or severe, concurrent substance abuse.

The registered dietitian's main role is to help develop an eating plan to help normalize eating for the patient with BN. The registered dietitian assists in the medical management of patients through the monitoring of electrolytes, vital signs, and weight, and monitors intake and behaviors, which sometimes allows for preventive interventions before biochemical index change. Most patients with BN desire some amount of weight loss at the beginning of treatment. It is not uncommon to hear patients say that they want to get well, but they also want to lose the "x" number of pounds that they feel is above what they should weigh. It is important to communicate to the patient that it is incompatible to diet and recover from the eating disorder at the same time. They must understand that the primary goal of intervention is to normalize eating patterns. Any weight loss that is achieved would occur as a result of a normalized eating plan and the elimination of binging. Helping patients combat food myths often requires specialized nutrition knowledge. The registered dietitian is uniquely qualified to provide scientific nutrition education. Given that there are so many fad diets and fallacies about nutrition, it is not uncommon for other members of the treatment team to be confused by the nutrition fallacies. Whenever possible, it is suggested that either formal or informal basic nutrition education inservice be provided for the treatment team.

Cognitive-behavioral therapy is now a well-established treatment modality for BN. A key component of the CBT process is nutrition education and dietary guidance. Meal planning, assistance with a regular pattern of eating, and rationale for and discouragement of dieting are all included in CBT. Nutrition education consists of teaching about body weight regulation, energy balance, effects of starvation, misconceptions about dieting and weight control, and the physical consequences of purging behavior. Meal planning consists of three meals a day, with one to three snacks per day prescribed in a structured fashion to help break the chaotic eating pattern that continues the cycle of binging and purging. Caloric intake should initially be based on the maintenance of weight to help prevent hunger since hunger has been shown to substantially increase the susceptibility to binging. One of the hardest challenges of normalizing the eating pattern of the person with BN is to expand the diet to include the patient's self-imposed forbidden or feared foods. CBT provides a structure to plan for and expose patients to these foods from least feared to most feared, while in a safe, structured, supportive environment. This step is critical in breaking the all or none behavior that goes along with the deprive-binge cycle.

Discontinuing purging and normalizing eating patterns are a key focus of treatment. Once accomplished, the patient is faced with fluid retention and needs much education and understanding of this temporary, yet disturbing phenomenon. Education consists of information about the length of time to expect the fluid retention and information on calorie conversion to body mass to provide evidence that the weight gain is not causing body mass gain. In some cases, utilization of skinfold measurements to determine percent body fat may be helpful in determining body composition changes. The patient must also be taught that continual purging or other methods of dehydration such as restricting sodium, or using diuretics or laxatives will prolong the fluid retention.

If the patient is laxative dependent, it is important to understand the protocol for laxative withdrawal to prevent bowel obstruction. The registered dietitian plays a key role in helping the patient eat a high fiber diet with adequate fluids while the physician monitors the slow withdrawal of laxatives and prescribes a stool softener.

A food record can be a useful tool in helping to normalize the patient's intake. Based on the patient's medical, psychological, and cognitive status, food records can be individualized with columns looking at the patient's thoughts and reactions to eating and/or not eating, to gather more information, and to educate the patient on the antecedents of her/his behavior. The registered dietitian is the expert in explaining to a patient how to keep a food record, reviewing food records, and understanding and explaining weight changes. Other members of the team may not be as sensitive to the fear of food recording or as familiar with strategies for reviewing the record as the registered dietitian. The registered dietitian can determine whether weight change is due to a fluid shift or a change in body mass.

Medication management is more effective in treating BN than in AN, especially with patients who present with comorbid conditions. Current evidence cites combined medication management and CBT as most effective in treating BN, although research continues to look at the effectiveness of other methods and combinations of methods of treatment.

Eating Disorders Not Otherwise Specified (EDNOS)

The large group of patients who present with EDNOS consists of subacute cases of AN or BN. The nature and intensity of the medical and nutritional problems and the most effective treatment modality will depend on the severity of impairment and the symptoms. These patients may have met all criteria for anorexia except that they have not missed three consecutive menstrual periods. Or, they may be of normal weight and purge without binging. Although the patient may not present with medical complications, they do often present with medical concerns.

EDNOS also includes Binge Eating Disorder (BED) which is listed separately in the appendix section of the *DSM IV* in which the patient has binging behavior without the compensatory purging seen in bulimia nervosa. It is estimated that prevalence of this disorder is one to two percent of the population. Binge episodes must occur at least twice a week and have occurred for at least six months. Most patients diagnosed with BED are overweight and suffer the same medical problems faced by the non-binging obese population such as diabetes, high blood pressure, high blood cholesterol levels, gallbladder disease, heart disease, and certain types of cancer.

The patient with binge eating disorder often presents with weight management concerns rather than eating disorder concerns. Although researchers are still trying to find the treatment that is the most helpful in controlling binge eating disorder, many treatment manuals exist utilizing the CBT model shown effective for bulimia nervosa. Whether weight loss should occur simultaneously with CBT or after a period of more stable, consistent eating is still being investigated.

In a primary care setting, it is the registered dietitian who often recognizes the underlying eating disorder before other members of the team who may resist a change of focus if the overall objective for the patient is weight loss. It is then the registered dietitian who must convince the primary care team and the patient to modify the treatment plan to include treatment of the eating disorder.

The Adolescent Patient

Eating disorders rank as the third most common chronic illness in adolescent females, with an incidence of up to five percent. The prevalence has increased dramatically over the past three decades. Large numbers of adolescents who have disordered eating do not meet the strict *DSM–IV–TR* criteria for either AN or BN but can be classified as EDNOS. In one study, more than half of the adolescents evaluated for eating disorders had subclinical disease, but suffered a similar degree of psychological distress as those who met strict diagnostic criteria. Diagnostic criteria for eating disorders such as *DSM–IV–TR* may not be entirely applicable to adolescents. The wide variability in the rate, timing, and magnitude of both height and weight gain during normal puberty, the absence of menstrual periods in early puberty along with the unpredictability of menses soon after menarche, and the lack of abstract concepts, limit the application of diagnostic criteria to adolescents.

Because of the potentially irreversible effects of an eating disorder on physical and emotional growth and development in adolescents, the onset and intensity of the intervention in adolescents should be lower than adults. Medical complications in adolescents that are potentially irreversible include: growth retardation if the disorder occurs before closure of the epiphyses, pubertal delay or arrest, and impaired acquisition of peak bone mass during the second decade of life increasing the risk of osteoporosis in adulthood.

Adolescents with eating disorders require evaluation and treatment focused on biological, psychological, family, and social features of these complex, chronic health conditions. The expertise and dedication of the members of a treatment team who work specifically with adolescents and their families are more important than the particular treatment setting. In fact, traditional settings such as a general psychiatric ward may be less appropriate than an adolescent medical unit. Smooth transition from inpatient to outpatient care can be facilitated by an interdisciplinary team that provides continuity of care in a comprehensive, coordinated, developmentally oriented manner. Adolescent health care specialists need to be familiar with working not only with the patient, but also with the family, school, coaches, and other agencies or individuals who are important influences on healthy adolescent development.

In addition to having skills and knowledge in the area of eating disorders, the registered dietitian working with adolescents needs skills and knowledge in the areas of adolescent growth and development, adolescent interviewing, special nutritional needs of adolescents, cognitive development in adolescents, and family dynamics. Since many patients with eating disorders have a fear of eating in front of others, it can be difficult for the patient to achieve adequate intake from meals at school. Since school is a major element in the life of adolescents, dietitians need to be able to help adolescents and their families work within the system to achieve a healthy and varied nutrition intake. The registered dietitian needs to be able to provide MNT to the adolescent as an individual but also work with the family while maintaining the confidentiality of the adolescent. In working with the family of an adolescent, it is important to remember that the adolescent is the patient and that all therapy should be planned on an individual basis. Parents can be included for general nutrition education with the adolescent present. It is often helpful to have the registered dietitian meet with adolescent patients and their parents to provide nutrition education and to clarify and answer questions. Parents are often frightened and want a quick fix. Educating the parents regarding the stages of the nutrition plan as well as explaining the hospitalization criteria may be helpful.

There is limited research in the long-term outcomes of adolescents with eating disorders. There appear to be limited prognostic indicators to predict outcome. Generally, poor prognosis has been reported when adolescent patients have been treated almost exclusively by mental health care professionals. Data from treatment programs based in adolescent medicine show more favorable outcomes. Reviews by Kriepe and colleagues showed a 71% to 86% satisfactory outcome when treated in adolescent-based programs. Strober and colleagues conducted a long-term prospective follow-up of severe AN patients admitted to the hospital. At follow-up, results showed that nearly 76% of the cohort met criteria for full recovery. In this study, approximately 30% of patients had relapses following hospital discharge. The authors also noted that the time to recovery ranged from 57 to 79 months.

Populations at High Risk

Specific population groups who focus on food or thinness such as athletes, models, culinary professionals, and young people who may be required to limit their food intake because of a disease state, are at risk for developing an eating disorder. Additionally, risks for developing an eating disorder may stem from predisposing factors such as a family history of mood, anxiety, or substance abuse disorders. A family history of an eating disorder or obesity, and precipitating factors such as the dynamic interactions among family members and societal pressures to be thin are additional risk factors.

The prevalence of formally diagnosable AN and BN in males is accepted to be from five to ten percent of all patients with an eating disorder. Young men who develop AN usually are members of subgroups (such as athletes, dancers, models, performers) that emphasize weight loss. The male anorexic is more likely to have been obese before the onset of the symptoms. Dieting may have been in response to past teasing or criticisms about his weight. Additionally, the association between dieting and sports activity is stronger among males. Both a dietary and activity history should be taken with special emphasis on body image, performance, and sports participation on the part of the male patient. These same young men should be screened for androgenic steroid use. The *DSM–IV–TR* diagnostic criterion for AN of being under the 85th percentile of ideal body weight is less useful in males. A focus on the BMI, non-lean body mass (percent body fat), and the height-weight ratio are far more useful in the assessment of the male with an eating disorder. Adolescent males below the 25th percentile for BMI, upper arm circumference, and subscapular and triceps skinfold thicknesses, should be considered to be in an unhealthy, malnourished state.

Hunger/Satiety Cues in Managing an Eating Disorder

With the emergence of the non-dieting approach to the treatment of disordered eating and obesity, it would seem that the use of hunger and/or satiety cues in managing an eating disorder may assist in resuming normal eating patterns. At this point in time, research suggests that eating-disordered patients have predominantly abnormal patterns of hunger and fullness, indicating a confusion of these concepts. Whether or not normal patterns of hunger and satiety resume after the normalization of weight and eating behaviors has yet to be determined.

Conclusion

Eating disorders are complex illnesses. To be effective in treating individuals who suffer from these illnesses, the expert interaction between professionals in many disciplines is required. The registered dietitian is an integral member of the treatment team and is uniquely qualified to provide the medical nutrition therapy for patients with eating disorders. The registered dietitian working with this population must understand the complexities and the long-term commitment involved. Entry-level dietetics provides the basics of assessment and nutrition counseling, but working with this population requires advanced level training, which may come from a combination of self-study, continuing education programs, and supervision by another experienced registered dietitian and/or an eating disorder therapist. Knowledge and practice using motivational interviewing and cognitive-behavioral therapy will enhance the effectiveness of counseling this population.

Chapter 44

Group Therapy for Eating Disorders

Treatment groups are an essential component of an eating disorders treatment program. There are a variety of different types of groups designed to support recovery. Groups vary in terms of both format and content. Some groups are more educational and may be run in a lecture style format, while others are discussion-based where participants are encouraged to discuss issues or process feelings. Still others may be expressive in nature in which participants are encouraged to work through issues or process feelings utilizing various activities or creative techniques. Finally, some treatment groups, such as meal groups and therapeutic outings give participants the opportunity to practice skills in a hands-on manner. All groups are considered integral to treatment.

Eating Disorders Issues Group

Eating disorders issues group is a discussion group in which issues relevant to eating disorders are discussed. Group leaders may provide a specific theme or topic, to which participants are encouraged to relate and share.

Dialectical Behavioral Therapy Group

Dialectical behavioral therapy group is an educational group that teaches participants skills in four important areas: mindfulness,

---

interpersonal effectiveness, emotional regulation, and distress tolerance. This group is specifically designed for individuals who have difficulties with self-harm, emotional dysregulation, and impulse control.

Cognitive Behavioral Therapy Group

Cognitive behavioral therapy (CBT) group provides participants the opportunity to examine connections between thoughts, feelings, and behaviors. CBT uses various exercises to modify maladaptive patterns.

Process Group

This group provides patients the opportunity to discuss and work through feelings, issues, and conflicts with which they are dealing. Patient or group leaders may propose themes for discussion. All group members are strongly encouraged to share. Group leaders help to maintain the focus of the discussion and provide a constructive, positive environment.

Expressive Therapy Group

This group provides patients with the opportunity to develop constructive means of expressing themselves as well as to explore possible relationships between their eating disorder symptoms and their emotions. Patients are supported as they engage in various forms of expression including art, music, poetry, writing, movement, psychodrama, and collage.

Body Image Group

This group enables patients to address and challenge distorted beliefs and esteem problems related to their bodies utilizing various experiential techniques, including mirror work.

Nutrition Group

This is an educational group in which patients learn about and discuss issues related to food, nutrition, metabolism, weight, and eating. In addition, patients work on planning menus, grocery outings, and cooking activities during group.

Multi-Family Therapy Group

This group provides family members and significant others an opportunity to examine and resolve dynamics related to the patient's eating disorder.

Meal Groups

Patients are supported by staff while eating an appropriate meal and are encouraged to discuss thoughts and feelings related to the meal during the post-meal segment of group. The focus of this group is to provide patients with support as they learn to cope with stressors related to food and eating.

Chapter 45

Virtual-Reality Therapy

Computer-Generated Cures

From Bethesda to Milan, virtual reality—VR for short—is being used to treat crippling disorders and soothe physical and mental anguish. The therapies have shown promise against stubborn conditions from eating disorders and addictions to phobias.

The technology is so promising that the National Institutes of Health's (NIH) National Institute on Drug Abuse (NIDA)—which had funded no virtual-reality research—now supports 16 such projects and has more grants in the pipeline. In February 2004, NIDA summoned scientists to a sort of VR-therapy showcase to consider the possibilities.

In a typical virtual-reality experience, a helmet blocks out the real world and immerses the patient in the sights and sounds of a three-dimensional (3-D) world supplied by computer software. The helmet positions goggle-size television screens close to each eye; the patient sees the screen views as a single 3-D image with realism and depth. The helmet's headphones supply sound; accessories such as joysticks and gloves let the patient manipulate the scene. This combined sensory input gives the patient the illusion of being in the virtual world.

Excerpted from "What Are You Afraid Of?" © 2004 Patricia Edmonds, reprinted with permission. Veteran journalist Patricia Edmonds (pattyedmonds2004@yahoo.com) has followed the progress of virtual reality (VR) therapy since the mid-1990s. A former assistant managing editor at National Public Radio (NPR), she's now a consultant and writer in northern Virginia.

Why does treating a disorder in a fake world translate to curing it in the real world? For reasons that we're still learning about, says VR-therapy expert Hunter Hoffman of the University of Washington's Human Interface Technology Lab. The basic principle is this: Experiences in the virtual world force patients to develop coping responses—responses that still serve them in real life.

With phobias, VR gradually and repeatedly exposes patients to what they fear until they learn to manage their anxiety. With eating disorders, it helps patients rethink often-distorted perceptions of their bodies. With pain management, the therapy is so attention-grabbing that it overrides even severe discomfort. With addiction—one of the newest frontiers—VR can artificially trigger patients' cravings (for cigarettes, alcohol, crack) and let them practice not giving in.

At universities and think tanks around the world, new VR-therapy applications are in development. And throughout the United States, counselors can treat anxiety and stress disorders in their offices with off-the-shelf therapy software from Virtually Better, a Georgia company founded by VR therapy pioneers Barbara Rothbaum and Larry Hodges.

When Bethesda psychologist Keith Saylor first reviewed VR-therapy software, he thought, "This is so cartoonish." More than five years later, he's used VR in combination with other techniques to treat more than 100 patients' fears of flying, heights, storms, and public speaking.

Among those who complete treatment, Saylor says, the success rate tops 80 percent. Because VR is part of regular 50-minute, $130 behavior-therapy sessions, it's covered for most patients whose insurance pays for behavioral health or psychological services.

One corner of Saylor's office houses the gear: a personal computer wired to a small platform, a curvy high-backed chair, and a helmet with stereo headphones and video goggles. If an assessment convinces Saylor that someone could benefit from VR therapy, he brings the patient here.

At one time, Saylor would have taken those patients on field trips—"in vivo" exposure therapy, where psychologists accompany patients as they gradually approach what they fear. But outings to tall buildings and airplanes are costly, and while airlines once let fearful flyers board parked planes as part of therapy, post-9/11 security has curtailed such practices.

In VR therapy, the patient can be "on a jet" while seated in Saylor's chair. As Saylor queues up the software, the patient sees a digital simulation of a familiar cabin view: aisle, overhead compartments, and seats. To the left, the view out the window is real video of tarmac—at Atlanta's Hartsfield-Jackson airport. Headphones deliver the hum of engines and a flight attendant's patter. The platform resonates with the ka-chunk of cargo-bay doors closing and the vibration of taxiing.

As patients experience the VR flight, Saylor asks how they're handling it on a 1-to-10 anxiety scale. If patients get too anxious, Saylor has only to click the program off. If they can talk themselves through the panic, the "flight" proceeds—and is replayed, with the patient feeling less fearful every time. Mastering phobias, Saylor says, is about "making friends with the things that you used to fear."

Rothbaum and Samantha Smith, a psychologist at DC's Walter Reed Army Hospital, compared fear-of-flying patients who did VR therapy with those who did traditional in-vivo exposure therapy. The findings: VR treatment did as well as traditional treatment in relieving fears—and six months after treatment, among both sets of patients, 14 out of 15 had successfully taken plane flights.

Tough-to-Treat Conditions

Virtual-reality tools show promise against other tough-to-treat conditions, too:

Smoking. At his Pittsburgh lab, researcher Steve Baumann guided smokers through two versions of a virtual world: one with no references to smoking and one littered with ashtrays, cigarette packs, and advertisements (which he customized to resemble the test subject's favorite brand). On a 1-to-100 scale, subjects reported a 15-point jump in their cravings in the smoky world as opposed to the smoke-free one.

Drug addiction. Rothbaum has developed a "virtual crack house," where addicts can be exposed to people or things that make them want to use. While the VR program could help addicts learn to fight their cravings, it also gives drugmakers a safe environment in which to test anti-craving medications. Similar VR programs are in development for abusers of alcohol and other substances.

Eating disorders. At the Istituto Auxologico Italiano near Milan, Italy, research professor Giuseppe Riva treats anorexia and bulimia patients with an inpatient program including VR.

Traditional eating disorder counseling aims to get patients to think and behave differently about their bodies. Riva's program reinforces that goal on several fronts. Showing patients virtual items and scenes from their everyday lives can help them identify—and avoid—things that spur destructive eating behaviors. And showing patients representations of themselves—computer-drawn avatars built to scale for their height, weight, and measurements—helps dispel, say, a gaunt girl's distorted view of how "fat" she is.

Riva says that while traditional eating-disorder therapies can require six to twelve months and lots of patient engagement to be effective, VR therapies can show "significant results after six weeks."

Though anorexia patients often can see photos of themselves and still deny how emaciated they look, researcher Azucena Garcia-Palacios says, "there's something about the computer that patients find an authoritative source of information." Garcia-Palacios is a member of a Spanish VR research team that collaborates with Riva's.

So when a VR-therapy program shows patients an average-size avatar and lets them digitally adjust it to be the size they think they are, patients often plump up the figure—and then can't deny the discrepancy when the computer shows them how skeletal their true-size avatar looks in comparison.

Virtual-Reality Research and Development

Like most promising technologies, VR has drawbacks. The chief obstacle, says Ro Nemeth-Coslett, cochair of the NIDA working group, is cyber-sickness—the nausea, dizziness, and eyestrain that older users, especially, can experience as they watch VR scenes.

Another issue: the availability and cost of the technology. Over the past decade, basic equipment has become easier to obtain and afford: An office setup like Saylor's can be put together for about $15,000, but more-sophisticated VR experiences would require computer-wired "cave" rooms that helmeted patients can walk around in—and only about a dozen of those exist in the United States.

NIDA, the NIH branch where most VR-therapy research and development is focused, has awarded about $3 million for it in the past two years. Although that's a fraction of the institute's nearly billion-dollar budget, NIDA's Dave Thomas says VR-therapy research ranks "among the fastest-growing NIDA-funded areas."

As the therapy goes into its second decade, innovations crowd the horizon. University of South Carolina (USC) researcher Skip Rizzo uses a "virtual classroom" to learn how screening out distractions may help students with attention deficit hyperactivity disorder. Researchers are testing whether VR worlds can help autistic children establish eye contact and focus their attention for longer periods.

Environments like Baumann's Smoker World may soon deliver smells as well as sights and sounds. As technology becomes cheaper, Thomas suggests, why not put VR gear in patients' homes, for 24/7 access to cyber "support groups" that help them resist alcohol, drugs, or overeating?

In the next decade, Nemeth-Coslett predicts, VR treatments will be possible "that we couldn't even imagine now." And they'll work, Hoffman predicts, because the technology will meld ever more powerfully with the key element in therapy: the patient's mind.

"The virtual world is not in the computer," Hoffman says. "The virtual world is in the person's brain. We're just helping people create the virtual world in their minds." And start healing.

Chapter 46

College Women May Benefit from Online Intervention

A long-term, large-scale study has found that an Internet-based intervention program may prevent some high risk, college-age women from developing an eating disorder. The study, funded by the National Institutes of Health's (NIH) National Institute of Mental Health (NIMH), was published in the August 2006 issue of the *Archives of General Psychiatry*.

The researchers conducted a randomized, controlled trial of 480 college-age women in the San Francisco Bay area and San Diego, California, who were identified in preliminary interviews as being at risk for developing an eating disorder. The trial included an eight-week, Internet-based, cognitive-behavioral intervention program called "Student Bodies," which had been shown to be effective in previous small-scale, short-term studies. The intervention aimed to reduce the participants' concerns about body weight and shape, enhance body image, promote healthy eating and weight maintenance, and increase knowledge about the risks associated with eating disorders.

The online program included reading and other assignments such as keeping an online body-image journal. Participants also took part in an online discussion group, moderated by clinical psychologists. Participants were interviewed immediately following the end of the online program, and annually for up to three years thereafter to determine their attitudes toward their weight and shape, and measure the onset of any eating disorders.

"College Women at Risk for Eating Disorder May Benefit From Online Intervention," News Release, National Institutes of Health (NIH), August 7, 2006.

"Eating disorders are complex and particularly difficult to treat. In fact, they have one of the highest mortality rates among all mental disorders," said NIMH Director Thomas Insel, M.D. "This study shows that innovative intervention can work, and offers hope to those trying to overcome these illnesses."

Over the course of a lifetime, about 0.5 to 3.7 percent of girls and women will develop anorexia nervosa, and about 1.1 to 4.2 percent will develop bulimia nervosa. About 0.5 percent of those with anorexia die each year as a result of their illness, making it one of the top psychiatric illnesses that lead to death.

Anorexia generally is characterized by a resistance to maintaining a healthy body weight, an intense fear of gaining weight, and other extreme behaviors that result in severe weight loss. People with anorexia see themselves as overweight even when they are dangerously thin. Bulimia generally is characterized by recurrent episodes of binge eating, followed by self-induced purging behaviors. People with bulimia often have normal weights, but like those with anorexia, they are intensely dissatisfied with their bodies. All eating disorders involve multiple biological, behavioral and social factors that are not well understood.

The intervention appeared to be most successful among overweight women who had elevated body mass index (BMI) of 25 or more at the start of the program. In fact, among these women in the intervention group, none developed an eating disorder after two years, while 11.9 percent of the women with comparable baseline BMI in the control group did develop an eating disorder during the same time frame. BMI is a reliable indicator of a person's body fat by measuring his or her weight and height.

The program also appeared to help women in the San Francisco Bay area who had some symptoms of an eating disorder at the start of the program, such as self-induced vomiting; laxative, diet pill or diuretic use; or excessive exercise. Of those in the intervention group with these characteristics, 14 percent developed an eating disorder within two years, while 30 percent of those with these characteristics in the control group developed an eating disorder during the same time frame.

The authors suggest that the intervention helped these high-risk women become less concerned about their weight and shape, while also helping them understand healthier eating and nutrition practices. "This is the first study to show that eating disorders can be prevented among high-risk groups," said lead author C. Barr Taylor, M.D., of Stanford University. "The study also provides evidence that elevated weight and shape concerns are causal risk factors for developing an eating disorder," he added.

The study suggests that relatively inexpensive options such as Internet-based interventions can have lasting effects on women at high risk of developing an eating disorder. However, the authors note that the results cannot be generalized widely because there were differences in the women's baseline characteristics and treatment responses between the two sites used in the study.

Also, the rate at which the women stuck with the program was very high—nearly 80 percent of the online program's Web pages were read—suggesting that the participants were unusually motivated. "Women who are less motivated may be less likely to participate in or stick with this type of long-term intervention," added Taylor.

In addition, women with restricted or no access to computers would not be able to benefit from an online intervention program. However, the authors conclude that such Internet-based programs may be a good first step in a diligent program designed to screen women for potential eating disorder risks.

Reference: Taylor CB, et al. Prevention of Eating Disorders in At-risk College-age Women. *Archives of General Psychiatry*. August 2006.

Chapter 47

Studies and Clinical Trials on Eating Disorders

Research Studies and Opportunities for Free Treatment

There are many ways to fight eating disorders. One way is to participate in research. Well-done studies help us understand why people become eating disordered, how they recover, and how treatment can be made more effective.

In addition, it's sad but true that treatment for an eating disorder is prohibitively expensive for many people, and insurance coverage tends to be minimal at best. Many research projects offer free treatment to qualified participants. Some even pay stipends, and procedures are supervised by clinical staff with professional credentials.

The treatment you receive in a study probably will not last for the several months, or even years, required to support full recovery, but it certainly can help you define the path you need to follow. And give you hope that recovery is possible.

Please note: The following contact information and brief project descriptions are offered for your information. If you are interested in any of these opportunities, evaluate potential benefits and possible risks. Be a wise consumer of medical and psychological services and procedures.

This chapter includes: Excerpts from "Research and Opportunities for Free Treatment," used with permission of ANRED: Anorexia Nervosa and Related Eating Disorders, Inc. © 2005 ANRED. For additional information, visit http://www.anred.com. Also, excerpts from "Clinical Trials: Eating Disorders," National Institute of Mental Health (NIMH), May 2006.

Center for Overcoming Problem Eating (COPE)
Department of Psychiatry
University of Pittsburgh Medical Center
3811 O'Hara Street
Pittsburgh, PA 15213
Toll-Free: 866-265-9289
Website: http://www.wpic.pitt.edu/research/anbnbrainimaging
E-mail: EDResearch@msx.upmc.edu

One of the oldest and most respected research programs in the U.S. is the Center for Overcoming Problem Eating (COPE) at the University of Pittsburgh Medical Center. COPE is exploring biological factors that may lead to eating disorders. They are using positive emission tomography (PET) scans and magnetic resonance imaging (MRI) (non-invasive and painless) to study brain activity. They need women 18-45 who have been recovered from anorexia nervosa or bulimia for at least one year. Participants will be required to complete a screening process, various questionnaires, and interviews. Must be medication free (birth control pills acceptable). The study requires travel to Pittsburgh, Pennsylvania, but travel expenses will be reimbursed. A stipend of up to $1200 will be paid on completion of the study.

Eating Disorders Clinic
New York State Psychiatric Institute (NYSPI)
1051 Riverside Dr.
New York, NY 10032
Phone: 212-543-5739
Website: http://www.nyspi.org/Kolb/index.htm
E-mail: EDRU@pi.cpmc.columbia.edu

Located at Columbia Presbyterian Medical Center, the NYSPI Eating Disorders Clinic offers free treatment to adolescent girls and women eligible for research who suffer from anorexia nervosa and bulimia nervosa. They also offer free treatment to men and women who suffer from binge eating disorder.

Genetic Study of Anorexia Nervosa in Families
Toll-Free: 888-895-3886
Website: http://www.wpic.pitt.edu/research/angenetics

The National Institute of Mental Health is sponsoring a multi-center, international study seeking to determine whether a gene or genes might predispose individuals to develop anorexia nervosa. They need families with at least two members (mothers, sisters, aunts, etc.)

who have or had anorexia nervosa, and who would be willing to participate. The study involves the completion of interviews, questionnaires, and a blood draw. Participants do not need to travel and will be paid upon completion of the study. Call or visit the website to find the clinic site nearest you.

Users Perceptions of the Effectiveness of ED Self-Help Websites

Department of Psychology
University of Alberta
Edmonton, AB T6G 2E9
Phone: 780-492-0970
Website: http://www.psych.ualberta.ca/%7ecaughell

An online questionnaire seeks to determine who uses different types of eating disorder self-help websites, whether users of these websites perceive the sites to be trustworthy and useful sources of social support, and how these factors relate to social support off-line. The questionnaire will take 15–20 minutes to complete and a summary of the results will be posted on the research site. Must be 18 years of age or older to participate.

Experiences in Treatment for Eating Disorders

Website: http://portal.bsu.edu/inqsit/inqsit.cgi/gorman

Canisius College; Buffalo, New York. Help improve eating disorders treatment. Researchers want to learn about the experiences of clients who have received treatment for an eating disorder. They hope to use this information to create a handbook to help beginning mental health therapists understand typical myths about treatment and frequent pitfalls. If you have been treated for an eating disorder, or if you have a friend or family member who has received treatment, you are invited to complete the questionnaire on the study's website. You will need 10–15 minutes, and when you are done, you can submit your responses online.

Eating Disorders Clinical Trials Information from the National Institute of Mental Health

Eating Disorders Clinic

New York State Psychiatric Institute (NYSPI)
1051 Riverside Dr.
New York, NY 10032

Phone: 212-543-5739
Website: http://www.nyspi.org/Kolb/index.htm
E-mail: EDRU@pi.cpmc.columbia.edu

Some of the clinical trials available through New York State Psychiatric Institute:

- **Determining the response to sipping beverages without swallowing in people with eating disorders.** This study will use a sipping and spitting exercise to better understand the brain's response to food intake in people with eating disorders. Females ages 16–45. Location: New York State Psychiatric Institute, New York, NY. Clinicaltrials.com identifier number: NCT00353548.
- **Brain function of self-regulation in women with bulimia nervosa.** This study will compare brain images of females with bulimia and females without eating disorders to better understand the brain's involvement with self-regulation. Ages 18–60. Location in New York, NY. Clinicaltrials.com identifier number: NCT00345943.
- **Serotonin transporter concentrations in women with a history of anorexia nervosa.** This study will compare the concentrations of serotonin transporter in the brains of women with a history of anorexia nervosa who are currently maintaining a normal weight to those of healthy women of normal weight. Ages 18–45. Location in New York, NY. Clinicaltrials.com identifier number: NCT00320684.
- **Cholecystokinin for reducing binge eating in people with bulimia nervosa.** Interventional study. This study will determine the effectiveness of administrating a dose of cholecystokinin during a binge eating episode in reducing this eating behavior in people with bulimia nervosa. Ages 18–55. Location in New York, NY. Clinicaltrials.com identifier number: NCT00308776.
- **Hormone release and stomach disturbances in people with binge eating disorder.** This study will determine whether the disturbances in cholecystokinin release and gastric emptying that occur in people with binge eating disorder are similar to those that occur in people with bulimia nervosa. Ages 18–60. Location in New York, NY. Clinicaltrials.com identifier number: NCT00307190.

- **Motivating factors that play a role in bulimia nervosa.** This study will compare the effects of binge eating to the reinforcing effects of frequently abused drugs by determining whether people with bulimia nervosa will exert effort to be able to binge eat. Ages 18–45. Location in New York, NY. Clinicaltrials.com identifier number: NCT00304174.
- **Effectiveness of antibiotic treatment for reducing binge eating and improving digestive function in people with bulimia nervosa.** This study will determine the effectiveness of the antibiotic erythromycin in enhancing gastrointestinal function and decreasing the frequency of binge eating in people with bulimia nervosa. Ages 18–55. Location in New York, NY. Clinical trials.com identifier number: NCT00304187.

Renfrew Center of Bryn Mawr
735 Old Lancaster Road
Bryn Mawr, PA 19010
Toll-Free: 800-RENFREW (736-3739)
Fax: 610-527-9361
Website: http://www.renfrewcenter.com/locations/bryn-mawr.asp

- **Effectiveness of a normalization of eating intervention program for treating women with eating disorders.** This study will evaluate the effectiveness of a new approach to a normalization of eating (NOE) program, based on principles of cognitive-behavioral therapy, in treating women with anorexia nervosa or bulimia nervosa. Ages 15–40. Locations in Bryn Mawr, PA; Philadelphia, PA. Clinicaltrials.com identifier number: NCT00272545.

Department of Psychology
Wesleyan University
207 High Street
Middletown, CT 06459-0408
Phone: 860-685-2760
Fax: 860-685-2761

- **Guided self-help treatment for binge eating disorder.** This study will determine the effectiveness of guided self-help (GSH) treatment in treating individuals with binge eating disorder (BED). Ages 18–50. Locations in Middletown, CT; Portland, OR. Clinicaltrials.com identifier number: NCT00158340.

Eating Disorder Program at the University of Chicago Hospitals
Department of Psychiatry, MC 3077
The University of Chicago
5841 S. Maryland Avenue
Chicago, IL 60637
Toll-Free: 888-824-0200
Phone: 773-834-5677
Website: http://www.uchospitals.edu/specialties/psychiatry

- **Effectiveness of family-based versus individual psychotherapy in treating adolescents with anorexia nervosa.** This study will compare the effectiveness of family-based therapy versus individual psychotherapy for the treatment of adolescent anorexia nervosa. Ages 12–18. Location in Chicago, IL. ClinicalTrials.gov identifier: NCT00149786.

Additional Information

Patient Recruitment
NIH Clinical Center
Bethesda, MD
Toll-Free: 800-411-1222
TTY: 866-411-1010
Website: http://www.cc.nih.gov/participate.shtml; or http://clinicaltrials.gov

Chapter 48

Effectiveness of Treatments for Eating Disorders

The RTI International–University of North Carolina at Chapel Hill Evidence-Based Practice Center (RTI-UNC EPC) conducted a systematic review of the literature on key questions concerning anorexia nervosa (AN), bulimia nervosa (BN), and eating disorders not otherwise specified (EDNOS) (focusing on binge eating disorder [BED]) to address questions posed by the American Psychiatric Association and Laureate Psychiatric Hospital through the Agency for Healthcare Research and Quality (AHRQ).

The evidence was systematically reviewed on two categories of issues—treatment and outcomes for AN, BN, and BED—in six key questions (KQs): (1) efficacy of treatment, (2) harms associated with treatment, (3) factors associated with the efficacy of treatment, (4) whether efficacy of treatment differs by sex, gender, age, race, ethnicity, or cultural group, (5) factors associated with outcomes, and (6) whether outcomes differ by sex, gender, age, race, ethnicity, or cultural group.

AN is marked by low body weight, fear of weight gain, disturbance in the way in which one's body size is perceived, denial of illness, or undue influence of weight on self-evaluation. Although amenorrhea is a diagnostic criterion, it is of questionable relevance.

BN is characterized by recurrent episodes of binge eating in combination with some form of compensatory behavior. Binge eating is the consumption of an uncharacteristically large amount of food by

---

Excerpts from "Management of Eating Disorders," Agency for Healthcare Research and Quality (AHRQ), AHRQ Publication No. 06–E010, April 2006.

social comparison coupled with a feeling of being out of control. Compensatory behaviors include self-induced vomiting; misuse of laxatives, diuretics, or other agents; fasting; and excessive exercise.

BED is marked by binge eating in the absence of compensatory behaviors, a series of associated features of binge eating, and marked distress regarding binge eating. Overweight and obesity are commonly seen in individuals with BED.

Although rigorous epidemiologic data are lacking in the United States, the mean prevalence of AN is 0.3 percent, of subthreshold AN 0.37 percent to 1.3 percent, of BN 1.0 percent, and of BED 0.7 percent to 3.0 percent. Mortality from AN is about 5 percent per decade of follow-up. Treatment for severe AN can involve inpatient or partial hospitalization in costly specialized settings. Inadequate insurance coverage often truncates the recommended duration of treatment. Treatment costs for AN are higher than those for obsessive-compulsive disorder and comparable to those for schizophrenia. In contrast, treatment for BN in the United States is typically on an outpatient basis.

Treatment Studies Results

Anorexia Nervosa

We divided the treatment literature into medication-only (generally in the context of clinical management or hospitalization), medication plus behavioral intervention, and behavioral intervention only for either adults or adolescents. The literature regarding medication treatments for AN is sparse and inconclusive. The vast majority of studies had small sample sizes and rarely had adequate statistical power to allow for definitive conclusions. Although studies did include medication administered during or after inpatient intervention, no AN studies that systematically combined medication with behavioral interventions met our inclusion criteria, revealing a substantial gap in the literature.

In the behavioral intervention literature, preliminary evidence suggests that cognitive behavioral therapy (CBT) may reduce relapse risk for adults with AN after weight restoration. Sufficient evidence does not exist to determine whether CBT has any effect during the acute phase of the illness, and one study, also requiring replication, showed that a manual-based treatment combining elements of sound clinical management and supportive psychotherapy by a specialist was more effective than CBT during the acute phase. Family therapy as currently conceptualized does not appear to be effective with adults with AN with longer duration of illness. Specific forms of family therapy initially focusing on parental control of nutrition is efficacious in treating AN in adolescents and leads to clinically meaningful weight gain and psychological change. The lack of follow-up data compromises our ability to determine the extent to which treatment gains are maintained.

Bulimia Nervosa

In medication trials, fluoxetine (60 milligrams (mg)/day) administered for six weeks to eighteen weeks reduced the core bulimia symptoms of binge eating and purging and associated psychological features in the short term. The 60 mg dose performs better than lower doses and is associated with prevention of relapse at one year. Evidence for the long-term effectiveness of relatively brief medication treatment does not exist. The optimal duration of treatment and the optimal strategy for maintenance of treatment gains are unknown.

Studies that combine drugs and behavioral interventions provide only preliminary evidence regarding the optimal combination of medication and psychotherapy or self-help. How best to treat individuals who do not respond to CBT or fluoxetine remains a major shortcoming of the literature. For behavioral interventions for BN, CBT administered individually or in group format is effective in reducing the core behavioral symptoms of binge eating and purging and psychological features in both the short and long term. Further evidence is required to establish the role for self-help in reducing bulimic behaviors.

Binge Eating Disorder

For BED, we addressed two critical outcomes—decrease in binge eating and decrease in weight in overweight individuals. Various medications were studied, including selective serotonin reuptake inhibitors (SSRIs); a combined serotonin, dopamine, and norepinephrine uptake inhibitor; tricyclic antidepressants; an anticonvulsant; and one appetite suppressant. In short-term trials, SSRIs led to greater rates of reduction in target eating, psychiatric and weight symptoms, and severity of illness than placebo controls. However, in the absence of clear endpoint data, and in the absence of data regarding abstinence from binge eating, we cannot judge the magnitude of the clinical impact of these interventions. Moreover, in the absence of follow-up data after drug discontinuation, we do not know whether observed changes in binge eating, depression, and weight persist. The combination of CBT plus medication may improve both binge eating and weight loss, although sufficient trials have not been done to determine definitively which medications are best at producing and maintaining weight loss. Moreover, the optimal duration of medication treatment for sustained weight loss has not yet been addressed empirically.

Collectively, clinical trials incorporating CBT for BED indicated that CBT decreases either the number of binge days or the actual number of reported binge episodes. CBT leads to greater rates of abstinence than does a waiting list control approach when administered either individually or in group format, and this abstinence persists for up to four months posttreatment. CBT also improves the psychological aspects of BED, such as ratings of restraint, hunger, and disinhibition. Results are mixed as to whether CBT improves self-rated depression in this population. Finally, CBT does not appear to produce decreases in weight.

Various forms of self-help were efficacious in decreasing binge days, binge eating episodes, and psychological features associated with BED. Self-help also led to greater abstinence from binge eating than waiting list; short-term abstinence rates approximate those seen in face-to-face psychotherapy trials.

Strength of Evidence in Treatment Literature

We graded the strength of the body of evidence for each question separately. For efficacy of treatment (KQ 1), we graded evidence for AN treatment as weak, that for BN medication and behavioral interventions as strong, and that for BED therapies as moderate. For harms associated with treatment (KQ 2), we graded medication interventions for BN and BED as consistently strong; the literatures for all AN interventions and all other BN and BED interventions were graded as weak to nonexistent because many studies failed to address harms associated with treatment. For factors associated with efficacy of treatment (KQ 3), with the exception of behavioral interventions for BN, which we graded as moderate, we graded the literature uniformly as weak. No published literature provided evidence on whether the efficacy of treatment for these conditions differs by sociodemographic factors (KQ 4). Overall, the literature on the treatment of AN in particular was deficient.

Managing Patients with Medication Alone

Managing individuals with AN with medication only is inappropriate, based on evidence reviewed here. No pharmacological intervention for AN has a significant impact on weight gain or the psychological features of AN. Although mood may improve with tricyclic antidepressants, this outcome is not associated with improved weight gain. Moreover, medication treatment for AN is associated with high dropout rates, suggesting that the currently available medications are not acceptable to individuals with AN.

For BN, good evidence indicates that fluoxetine (60 mg/day) reduces core bulimic symptoms of binge eating and purging and associated psychological features of the eating disorder in the short term. Based on two studies, the 60 mg dose performs better than lower doses and may contribute to decreased relapse at one year; however, patients do not tend to remain on the drug. Preliminary evidence exists for other second-generation antidepressants (trazodone and fluvoxamine), an anticonvulsant (topiramate), and a tricyclic antidepressant (desipramine). Preliminary evidence exists that monoamine oxidase inhibitors (MAOIs) are associated with decreased vomiting in the treatment of BN, although diet should be closely monitored.

Medication trials for BED have focused primarily on overweight individuals with BED. In these individuals, desired outcomes are twofold: weight loss and abstinence from binge eating. The majority of medication research for BED reflects short-term trials. Preliminary efficacy has been shown for selective serotonin reuptake inhibitors (SSRIs), one serotonin, dopamine, and norepinephrine uptake inhibitor, one tricyclic antidepressant, one anticonvulsant, and one appetite suppressant. In the absence of abstinence data and long-term follow-up, however, we do not know whether observed changes in binge eating, depression, and weight persist.

Managing Patients with Behavioral Interventions Alone

For adult AN, there is tentative evidence that CBT reduces relapse risk for adults with AN after weight restoration has been accomplished. By contrast, we do not know the extent to which CBT is helpful in the acutely underweight state, as one study found that a manual-based form of nonspecific supportive clinical management was more effective than CBT and interpersonal psychotherapy (IPT) in terms of global outcomes during the acute phase. No replications of these studies exist.

Family therapy as currently practiced has no supportive evidence for adults with AN and a comparatively long duration of illness. Overall, family therapy focusing on parental control of nutrition is efficacious in treating younger patients with AN; these approaches lead to clinically meaningful weight gain and psychological improvement. Although most studies of family therapy compared one variant of family therapy with another, two studies produced results suggesting that family therapy was superior to an individual therapy for adolescent patients with shorter duration of illness.

For BN, evidence for CBT is strong. Although IPT is also as effective, at 1-year follow-up, based on one study, symptomatic change appears to be more rapid with CBT. This factor decreases the time that patients are exposed to the symptoms of BN. Dialectical behavioral therapy (DBT) and guided imagery both show preliminary promise for BN patients.

For BED, CBT decreases the target symptom of binge eating. It does not, as currently delivered, promote weight loss in overweight patients. DBT may hold promise for BED patients as well.

Managing Patients with Combination Interventions

Although many of the medication trials for AN were conducted within the context of basic clinical management, no study that systematically studied medication plus psychotherapy for AN met our inclusion criteria.

For BN, the combined drug plus behavioral intervention studies provide only preliminary evidence regarding the optimal combination of medication and psychotherapy or self-help. Although some preliminary evidence exists for incremental efficacy with combined treatment, given the variety of designs used and lack of replication, evidence remains weak.

For BED, the combination of CBT plus medication may improve both binge eating and weight loss outcomes. Sufficient trials have not been done to determine definitively which medications are best at producing and maintaining weight loss in this population. Moreover, the optimal duration of medication treatment for abstinence from binge eating and sustained weight loss has not yet been addressed empirically, yet weight-loss effects of medication are generally known to cease when the medication is discontinued.

Managing Patients with Novel Interventions

Across the three disorders, we found evidence of various innovative approaches that seem to hold promise, especially for conditions as complex as these eating disorders. Nonetheless, nothing can be said definitively because the trials were small and inconclusive.

Reducing Mortality

The AN outcomes literature clearly and consistently identified that the risk of death is significantly higher in the AN population than would be expected in the population in general. Life-threatening complications of the disease include not only those directly related to weight loss and other physical problems but also a significantly elevated risk of suicide.

Studies were inconsistent concerning whether deceased patients had been included in the analysis sample at follow-up. Therefore, factors related to poor outcomes did not always include mortality risk. Several studies identified factors related to death versus all other outcomes. Only by including death with other outcome categories can we determine if factors related to death differ from factors related to other poor outcomes.

Individuals with BN and BED were not identified as being at elevated risk of death.

Conclusions

The literature regarding treatment efficacy and outcomes for AN, BN, and BED is of highly variable quality. For AN, the literature on medications was sparse and inconclusive. No studies combining medication with behavioral interventions met inclusion criteria. Evidence suggests that specific forms of family therapy are efficacious in treating adolescents, and preliminary evidence suggests that CBT may reduce relapse risk for adults after weight restoration and that a manual-based form of nonspecific supportive clinical management may be effective in underweight adults.

For BN, fluoxetine (60 mg/day) decreases the core bulimic symptoms of binge eating and purging and associated psychological features in the short term. CBT administered individually or in groups reduced core behavioral symptoms and psychological features in both the short and long term. How best to treat individuals who do not respond to CBT or fluoxetine remains unknown.

In BED, CBT reduced binge eating and leads to greater rates of abstinence when administered either individually or in group format, persisting for up to four months after treatment; however, CBT does not lead to weight loss in individuals with BED. Medications may also play a role in the treatment of BED although further research addressing how best to achieve both abstinence from binge eating and weight loss in overweight patients is required.

Higher levels of depression and compulsivity were associated with poorer outcomes in AN; increased mortality was associated with concurrent alcohol and substance use disorders. Only depression was consistently associated with poorer outcomes in BN; BN was not associated with an increased risk of mortality. Because of sparse data, we could reach no conclusions concerning BED outcomes. We uncovered weak to no evidence to address sociodemographic differences in either treatment or outcomes for any of these disorders.

The quality of the literature about treatment efficacy and outcome for AN, BN, and BED is highly variable. In the treatment literature, the largest deficiency rests with treatment efficacy for AN; we rated this literature as the weakest.

Future AN studies require large numbers of participants, multiple sites, clear delineation of the age of participants, and interventions that are tailored to the unique core pathology and medical sequelae of the illness. For BN, future studies should address novel treatments for the disorder, optimal duration of intervention, and optimal approaches for those who do not respond to medication or CBT. For BED, future studies require better explication of how best to target both binge eating and weight loss goals, optimal duration of intervention, and prevention of relapse.

For all three disorders, exploring additional treatment approaches is warranted. In addition, research teams should pay greater attention to factors influencing outcome, harms associated with treatment, and differential efficacy by age, sex, gender, race, ethnicity, and cultural group. Consensus definitions of remission, recovery, and relapse are essential. For both treatment and outcome literature, greater attention is required to the presentations currently grouped under the heading of EDNOS.

Outcome studies, especially for BN and BED, should emphasize population-based cohort studies with comparison groups and plan for adequate durations of follow-up. Ongoing psychiatric epidemiology studies should routinely include assessments of eating disorders. Epidemiologic studies of BMI and obesity trends should include assessments of eating disordered behavior. Population-based studies should include measures of disability and impairment associated with eating disorders. For both future treatment and outcome studies, researchers must carefully attend to issues of statistical power, research design, and sophistication and appropriateness of statistical analyses.

Chapter 49

Continuum of Care and a Typical Day in a Treatment Facility

Editor's Note: This information is offered as an example of care at a treatment facility for eating disorders.

The Pre-Admission Process

An assessment by telephone is conducted prior to admission to determine the appropriate entry level of care for each patient. The patient and her family members share information with a staff member responsible for intake. The staff person, in turn, provides program information, answers questions, addresses concerns, evaluates the patient's needs, begins to review financial issues, and offers guidance. The hospital has arrangements with many insurance carriers, but benefits vary greatly among plans, and most treatment requires preauthorization by the insurance company. Staff will investigate insurance benefits, which may provide full or partial payment. The goals during the admission process are for patients and families to know what to expect before arriving at the treatment center, to allay anxieties, and to make the transition as smooth and comfortable as possible.

The Residence

The residence is designed for individuals whose symptoms are so severe that they cannot safely function at a less restrictive level of care.

Excerpts from "The Klarman Eating Disorders Center at McLean Hospital," © 2004 McLean Hospital. Reprinted with permission.

Such symptoms might include excessive or rapid weight loss, metabolic disturbances, profound depression or risk of suicide, and/or severe, uncontrollable binge eating and/or purging. The residence ensures safety and encompasses psychological evaluation, medical observation, skilled nursing and nutritional services, supervision of daily activities (including meals and bathroom use), and intense behavioral and psychological therapies. Staff members work with each patient to establish a weight management contract that includes expectations of normalized eating behaviors, and for anorexia nervosa, consistent weight gain toward a normal weight range. When necessary, dietary supplementation and other medical approaches are employed.

The residence also provides education about eating disorders, refinement of symptom-management skills, relapse prevention, transition planning, and when indicated, a well-developed academic curriculum. The residence helps patients transition from a more acute phase to a focus on development of health and wellness skills and a positive self-image. Relapse prevention strategies and coping skills are emphasized.

Partial Hospital

Partial hospital services are fully integrated into the residence. At this level of care, the patient continues in all relevant treatment modalities during the day. The program continues through a supervised evening meal. Patients are then able to practice their newly acquired coping skills at home in the evening. The emphasis is on providing a smooth transition to home by learning and practicing the necessary skills that help reduce the potential for relapse. The goal of partial hospitalization is to provide a sufficient level of stability for the patient to succeed in outpatient treatment.

Outpatient Treatment

Referrals are made to qualified clinicians to address psychiatric, psychological, nutritional, and medical needs. The outpatient team will, whenever possible, consist of an individual therapist, a family therapist, and a nutritionist. Referral to a psychiatrist will be made if medications are recommended and the patient's primary care physician will be consulted if any medical issues arise.

Common Special Features of Eating Disorder Treatment Facilities

- A continuum of care with services provided in a building that is dedicated to the eating disorders program.

- Extensive resources to address coexisting conditions, such as substance abuse, depression, trauma-related disorders, anxiety disorders, and other comorbid psychiatric conditions.
- Medical services available 24 hours a day, seven days a week.
- A multidisciplinary clinical staff to address the variety of client needs.

A Typical Day

Patients may have a single bedroom or share a room with another patient; they are encouraged to bring familiar objects from home subject to approval by the nursing staff. There is an early morning wake-up time to complete activities of daily living followed by a supervised breakfast. After breakfast, lunch, and dinner there are post-meal therapy groups.

Programming varies depending on each patient's condition as well as the day of the week. The day typically consists of a variety of therapeutic groups or activities after breakfast. Following a supervised lunch, structured groups and activities continue. Additional groups or activities continue after a supervised dinner. Therapeutic groups and activities include individual psychotherapy, impulse control, relapse prevention, psychoeducation, and anger management groups, as well as nutrition, cooking, body image, and expressive therapy activities.

The day ends with a wrap-up group followed by lights out. Each day will provide opportunities for free time as well as time for making and receiving phone calls. The groups are designed to educate patients about their disorders, to support behavioral change, and to enhance motivation to achieve a healthy lifestyle for the future. School-age patients will typically have time to participate in the academic classroom. Meals are provided in a comfortable dining room. A full kitchen is typically located on the unit for meal preparation and cooking instruction. Other recreational and therapeutic activities off grounds, such as food shopping and restaurant outings, are part of the program.

Cognitive behavior therapy, or CBT, is a psychotherapeutic process in which the individual learns the interaction of thoughts, feelings, and behaviors. For example, if a person is experiencing anger or anxiety because of a life situation, she might employ binge eating as a coping response. CBT helps to identify the connections between thoughts that may trigger the emotion of anger and the behavior of binge eating.

The therapy assists the patient to modify the problematic thinking and learn behavioral skills to more effectively manage the distress.

Dialectical behavior therapy, or DBT, is a psychotherapeutic treatment model primarily designed for people who have trouble with emotion regulation and impulse control which results in self-destructive thoughts and/or behaviors. A form of cognitive behavior therapy, DBT focuses on improving skills to better manage emotional lability and impulsivity through the development of more effective coping skills and practical alternative strategies.

Chapter 50

Systems of Care for Families of Children with Mental Health Needs

Community-Based Care Leads to Meaningful Improvement

Children and youth with serious mental health needs make substantial improvements at home, at school, and in the community when served through systems of care that provide community-based services. Data released in May 2006 by the U.S. Substance Abuse and Mental Health Services Administration (SAMHSA) at a Capitol Hill briefing showed that children and youth in systems of care spend less time in inpatient care, experience fewer arrests, make improvements in their overall mental health, and do better in school than before enrollment.

A system of care for children's mental health is a coordinated network of community-based services and supports that are organized to meet the challenges of children and youth with serious mental health needs. Families and youth work in partnership with public and private organizations so services and supports are effective, build on the strengths of individuals, and address each person's cultural and linguistic needs.

"Children and youth with serious mental health needs and their families deserve the best care available," said SAMHSA Administrator

---

This chapter includes: Excerpts from "News Release: Community-Based Care Leads to Meaningful Improvement for Children and Youth with Severe Mental Health Needs," Substance Abuse and Mental Health Services Administration (SAMHSA), May 8, 2006; and excerpts from "Helping Children and Youth with Serious Mental Health Needs: Systems of Care," SAMHSA, 2006.

Charles Curie. "The systems of care approach is a proven approach that not only helps children thrive in their homes and communities, it is a wise investment of scarce resources."

The SAMHSA data suggest that systems of care save taxpayers money when compared to the traditional mental health service delivery systems. On average, systems of care save public health systems $2,776.85 per child in inpatient costs over the course of a year, and save juvenile justice systems $784.16 per child within the same time frame. Since its authorization in 1992, the program has funded a total of 121 programs across the United States that have helped transform the way in which treatment and care are provided to children with mental health needs and their families.

Helping Children and Youth with Serious Mental Health Needs

Why are systems of care needed?

Five to nine percent of children and youth between ages nine and seventeen have serious emotional disturbances that cause substantial functional impairment, and many do not receive the supports and services they need to reach their full potential at home, at school, and in their communities.

Children and youth with serious mental health needs and their families need supports and services from many different child- and family-serving agencies and organizations. Often, these agencies and organizations are serving the same children, youth, and families. By creating partnerships among these groups, systems of care are able to coordinate services and supports that meet the ever-changing needs of each child, youth, and family. Coordinated services and supports lead to improved outcomes for children, youth, and families, and help prevent the duplication of services for authorized care among government agencies.

What types of services are coordinated through systems of care?

Systems of care help parents and caregivers address the mental health needs of their children and youth while managing the demands of day-to-day living. Adequately meeting these needs requires multiple strategies and agencies. Some of the types of services that systems of care coordinate may include the following:

- care coordination (case or care management)
- child care
- community-based, inpatient psychiatric care
- counseling (individual, family, group, and youth)
- crisis residential care
- crisis outreach
- day treatment
- education/special education
- family support
- health care
- independent living supports
- legal services
- mental health information resources
- protection and advocacy
- psychiatric consultation
- recreation therapy
- residential treatment
- respite care
- self-help or support groups
- small therapeutic group care
- therapeutic foster care
- transition from youth to adult mental health services
- transportation
- tutoring
- vocational counseling

What are the outcomes of systems of care?

Systems of care have helped tens of thousands of children and youth with serious behavioral, emotional, and mental health needs make improvements in almost all aspects of their lives. One of the greatest accomplishments systems of care have made in helping children and youth with serious mental health needs is making services and supports family-driven and youth guided.

Family-driven means that families have a primary decision-making role in the care of their children and the policies and procedures governing care for children and youth in their community, State, tribe, territory, and Nation.

Youth-guided means that youth have the right to be empowered and educated decision-makers in their own care and the policies and procedures governing care for youth in their community, State, tribe, territory, and Nation.

In addition to the substantial roles children, youth, and families play in the care they receive, systems of care are successful because of the following reasons:

- Systems of care represent single points of contact for obtaining a comprehensive array of child, youth, and family services in homes and communities.
- Families work with service providers to develop, manage, deliver, and evaluate policies and programs.
- Services are delivered in the least restrictive, most natural environment appropriate for the needs of children, youth, and families.
- Agencies serving children, youth, and families establish partnerships to coordinate services and supports.
- Care management ensures that planned services and supports are delivered and continue to help children, youth, and families move through the system as their needs change.
- Systems of care include evidence-based treatments and interventions.
- All services and supports are selected and designed in ways that are responsive to families' beliefs, traditions, values, cultures, and languages.
- Systems of care are accountable for evaluating the outcomes of services for children, youth, and families.

Do national data support the effectiveness of systems of care?

National data collected for more than a decade confirm the experiences of children, youth, and caregivers: Systems of care work. Data from systems of care related to children, youth, and caregivers reflected the following:

- Children and youth improved on clinical outcomes after six months. Emotional and behavioral problems were reduced or remained stable for 89 percent of children and youth.
- Children and youth with suicide-related histories improved after six months. Almost 91 percent of children and youth with a history of suicide attempts or suicidal ideation improved or remained stable in their emotional and behavioral problems.
- Children and youth improved or remained stable on school-related outcomes after six months. School performance improved or remained the same for 75 percent of children and youth.
- Children and youth with co-occurring disorders improved after six months. Emotional and behavioral problems were reduced or remained stable for 89 percent of children and youth with co-occurring mental health and substance abuse diagnoses.
- System of care communities adopted a strength-based approach to planning services. Ninety-one percent used child and youth strengths to plan services. Also, eighty-five percent reported that children and youth helped plan services.
- Families/caregivers were satisfied with the cultural competence of service providers. More than 75 percent of families reported that they were satisfied with their providers' respect for their beliefs and values about mental health, understanding of their traditions, and ability to find services that acknowledged the positive traditions of their cultures.

Who can help my community establish a system of care?

The Center for Mental Health Services (CMHS) within the Substance Abuse and Mental Health Services Administration, U.S. Department of Health and Human Services, administers the Comprehensive Community Mental Health Services Program for Children and Their Families. Through Federal funding, this program supports States, communities, territories, and Tribal organizations and governments to develop, improve, or expand services to meet the needs of children and youth with serious mental health needs and their families. With Federal support, communities establish local systems of care that foster partnerships among a wide range of service and support providers.

Additional Information

Child, Adolescent, and Family Branch
Center for Mental Health Services
Substance Abuse and Mental Health Services Administration (SAMHSA)
1 Choke Cherry Road
Rockville, MD 20857
Phone: 240-276-1980
Fax: 240-276-1930
Website: http://www.systemsofcare.samhsa.gov

National Mental Health Information Center
Substance Abuse and Mental Health Services Administration (SAMHSA)
P.O. Box 42557
Washington, DC 20015
Toll-Free: 800-789-2647
Toll-Free TDD: 866-889-2647
Fax: 240-747-5470
Website: http://www.mentalhealth.samhsa.gov

Chapter 51

Understanding Health Insurance Issues and Their Effect on Benefits

Accessing the full benefits a patient is entitled to under his or her health plan contract requires understanding a few things about all the factors that affect access to care and reimbursement. Navigating the system to find out what the patient is entitled to receive also takes a lot of energy, and most patients entering treatment will not have the energy to see it through and need someone to do this, on their behalf. The information in this chapter is intended to provide the background needed to navigate the system as effectively as possible. This information reflects the experience of many patients, their families,

---

This information is excerpted from "ECRI's Bulimia Nervosa Resource Guide," For additional information, visit www.bulimiaguide.org or www.ecri.org. This resource guide was produced by ECRI, a 40-year-old international non-profit health services research agency. ECRI's mission is to improve the quality, safety, and cost-effectiveness of health care. Recognized by the health care community worldwide as a trusted source of highly credible information with very strict conflict-of-interest rules, ECRI is designated as an Evidence-based Practice Center by the U.S. Agency for Healthcare Research and Quality, and as a Collaborating Center of the World Health Organization for Patient Safety, Risk Management, and Health Technology Assessment. This resource guide was funded in large part by the Hilda and Preston Davis Foundation and is available in print and online: www.bulimiaguide.org (free); in print (for a nominal shipping/handling cost) at National Eating Disorders Association online store www.nationaleatingdisorders.org. The guide is part of ECRI's National Patient Library ™ of evidence-based health care guides for consumers.

and treatment centers in obtaining benefits to cover the cost of treatment of bulimia nervosa.

Because treatment usually involves mental health care and medical care aspects, a well-rounded care plan must address both types of care. The overall health care system has long treated medical care and mental health care separately. The result of that care model is that health insurers' benefits plans have often followed suit by separating mental health benefits (also called behavioral health benefits) from medical benefits. This split has created great difficulty for people with eating disorders, such as bulimia, who need an integrated care plan. Ways to steer through these difficulties are offered here in a seven step plan.

Another issue is the level of benefits for mental health care. For years, many health plans provided few or no mental health benefits. When they did, most subcontracted those benefits through "mental health carve-out" plans. Such plans are administered by behavioral health service companies that are separate from health plans. This approach made well-rounded care by a multidisciplinary care team very difficult to achieve. Even when a psychotherapist and medical doctor recognize the need for integrating services and case management, the health care delivery system may pose barriers that prevent that from happening.

When a service is provided by a doctor or facility, a billing code is needed to obtain reimbursement for services. Certain regulations govern how services must be coded. Different types of facilities and different health care professionals must use codes that apply to that type of facility and health professional. Also, if codes do not exist for certain services delivered in a particular setting, then facilities and health professionals have no way to bill for their services. Codes used for billing purposes are set up by various entities, such as the American Medical Association, U.S. Medicare program, and the World Health Organization's International Classification of Diseases. Thus, even a patient with good health insurance may face barriers to care simply because of the way our health care system is set up.

The system is slowly changing. Sporadic improvements have come about as a result of lawsuits and state legislation prompted by individuals, legislators, clinicians, support groups, and mental health advocacy groups. The U.S. federal government and most U.S. states have passed some form of mental health parity law. Generally these laws require insurers to provide a level of benefits for mental health care that is equivalent to medical benefits. These laws do, however, vary widely in their provisions.

Landmark lawsuits brought by families of patients with bulimia nervosa and/or anorexia in two states, Wisconsin in 1991, and Minnesota in 2001, were watershed events that set legal precedents about what insurers should cover for eating disorders. These lawsuits also raised public awareness of the problems faced by people seeking coverage for treatment of eating disorders. Nonetheless, the system today has a long way to go to improve access to care and adequate reimbursement for care for a sufficient period of time for a patient with bulimia nervosa or other eating disorder. Given that appropriate, well-integrated treatment for bulimia nervosa can easily cost more than $30,000 dollars per month, even with insurance, an insured individual is usually responsible for some portion of those costs.

The first line of decision-making about benefits at a health plan is typically made by a utilization review manager or case manager who reviews the requests for benefits submitted by a health care provider and determines whether the patient is entitled to benefits under the patient's contract. These decision-makers may have no particular expertise in the complex interrelated medical/mental health care needs for bulimia nervosa and other eating disorders. Claims can be rejected outright or approved for only part of the recommended treatment plan. Advance, adequate preparation on the part of the patient or the patients' support people is the best way to maximize benefits. Prepare to be persistent, assertive, and rational in explaining the situation and care needs. Early preparation can avert future coverage problems and situations that leave the patient holding the lion's share of bills.

Seven Steps to Maximize Insurance Benefits

Get Organized

If a bulimia patient's first encounter with the health care system is admission to an emergency room for a life-threatening situation with bulimia nervosa, whoever is going to deal with insurance issues on the patient's behalf will need to organize more quickly to figure out how to best access benefits. Patients who are seriously medically compromised will likely be in the hospital for a few days before discharge to a residential eating disorder center. Those few days are critical to negotiating reimbursement for the long-term care. If the situation is not an acute emergency and you want to find a treatment center, figure out whether you have authority to act on the patient's behalf or whether the patient must give you written authority to act on his or her behalf. If a child is 18 or older, parents will need the child's written permission to act on the child's behalf. Health care providers have forms that require signatures to allow free flow of communication and decision making. A spouse, partner, friend, or other person who wants to act on behalf of the patient will need to have the patient sign appropriate authorizations.

Read the Patient's Insurance Policy

Read the patient's insurance policy carefully to understand the available benefits. Obtain a copy of the "summary plan description" from the health plan's member's Web site (the specific plan that pertains to the insured), the insurer, or if the insurance plan is through work, from the employer's human resources department. Do not rely on general pamphlets or policy highlights. Read the detailed description of the benefits contract to find out what is covered and for how long. If you cannot understand the information, try talking with the human resources staff at the company that the insurance policy comes through, with an insurance plan representative, or with a billing or claims staff person where treatment will be sought. If hospital emergency care is not needed, make an appointment with a physician you trust to get a referral or directly contact an eating disorder treatment center to find out how to get a full assessment and diagnosis. The assessment should consider all related physical and psychological problems. There are four main reasons for doing this:

1. To obtain as complete a picture as possible about everything that is wrong.
2. To develop the best plan for treatment.
3. To obtain cost estimates before starting treatment.
4. To obtain the benefits the patient is entitled to under his or her contract for the type of care needed—for example, many insurers provide more coverage benefits for severe mental disorder diagnoses. Some insurers categorize bulimia nervosa as a severe disorder that qualifies for extensive inpatient and outpatient benefits, while others may not.

Medical benefits coverage may also come into play to treat associated medical conditions, so it is important to diagnose all physical illnesses present. Other mental conditions often co-exist with or underlie eating disorders and should be considered during the assessment, including depression, trauma, obsessive-compulsive disorder, anxiety, social phobias, and chemical dependence. These co-morbid conditions can affect eligibility for various benefits (and often can mean more benefits can be accessed) and eligibility for treatment centers.

Keep Careful and Complete Records

Keep careful and complete records of communications with the insurance company and health care providers for future reference as needed. Treatment for eating disorders such as bulimia nervosa often occurs over a long period of time. Maintaining a log book—whether computerized or in hard copy—can be important for future reference if there are questions about claims. Decide where all notes and documentation will be kept for easy access. Create a back-up copy of everything, and keep it in a safe and separate place. The log should contain notes taken of each conversation with an insurer or health care provider and should include the date, time, name, and title of person with whom you spoke, and their contact information. As a courtesy, you may wish to let these people know that you are keeping careful records of your conversations to help you and the patient remember what was discussed. If you decide to record any conversation, you must first inform and ask the permission of the person with whom you are speaking.

Call the Insurer to Discuss Benefits Options

With documentation in hand of the patient's diagnosis and the proposed care plan, it's a good idea to call the patient's insurance company before the patient enters a treatment program. Quite often, preauthorization for a treatment facility or health care provider is needed. Ask for a case manager who has credentials in eating disorders. This will improve your chance of getting one contact person to talk with over the term of treatment who understands the complexities of treatment. Confirm with the insurer that the patient has benefits for bulimia nervosa, anorexia, or other eating disorder treatment. Also ask about "in-network" and "out-of-network" benefits and the eating disorder facilities that have contracts with the patient's insurance company because this affects how much of the costs the patient is responsible for. If the insurer has no contract with certain treatment facilities, benefits may still be available, but may be considered out-of-network. In this case, the claims will be paid at a lower rate and the patient will have a larger share of the bill.

If the health insurance is through an employer and the patient had to quit work or take a leave of absence to get treatment, she or he may no longer be covered. Similarly, if the patient is a college student who had to drop out of school to seek treatment and was covered by school insurance or a parent's insurance policy, the student may no longer be covered. While many people with bulimia nervosa or other eating disorder continue working or attending school, some cannot. If this is the case, it is important to understand what happens with insurance. Most insurance policies cover students as long as they are enrolled in twelve credit hours per semester and attend classes. Experts in handling insurance issues for patients with eating disorders caution that patients who have dropped out of school should avoid trying to cover up that fact to maintain benefits because insurance companies will usually find out and then expect the patient to repay any benefits that were paid out.

If coverage has been lost, the student may be eligible to enroll in a Consolidated Omnibus Budget Reconciliation Act (COBRA) insurance program. COBRA is an Act of Congress that allows people who have lost insurance benefits to continue those benefits as long as they pay the full premium and qualify for the program. On the Internet, see www.cobrainsurance.com for more information. A person eligible for COBRA has only 30 days from the time of loss of benefits to enroll in a COBRA plan. It is critical that the sign up for COBRA be done or that option is lost. Be sure to get written confirmation of COBRA enrollment from the plan. If the student is not eligible for COBRA, an insurance company may offer a "conversion" plan for individual coverage.

If the patient is in the hospital and will be discharged to a residential treatment center, discuss how the medical and behavioral health components of benefits will work. Although a patient may be "medically stable" at discharge, she or he may not be nearly well enough to participate fully in psychotherapy at the residential center. The patient's medical condition, though not life-threatening at this point, affects mental health and ability to participate in treatment. Restoring physical health may take days or weeks. Therefore, before the patient is admitted to a residential eating disorder center or placed in outpatient treatment, contact the patient's health plan or employer (if applicable and the health plan is self-funded by the employer) and ask for the early claims for psychotherapy to be paid under the medical benefits instead of the behavioral health benefits. The language to use is: "Will you intercept psychotherapy claims and pay them under medical benefits until the patient is stable enough to participate fully and assist in her treatment?" Not all health plans will do this, but some do, so it is worth asking. Going this route can save the behavioral health benefits for the time when the patient is better able to take part in the psychotherapy.

Another way to get the most out of benefits is to find out whether chemical dependency or substance abuse benefits are included in the mental health day allotment or if it is a separate benefit. If it is separate and the patient does not really need this benefit, find out whether the insurer will "flex" the benefit to apply it for treating an eating disorder.

Determine the Authorizations for Care That the Insurer Requires

Find out the authorizations for care that the insurer requires for the patient to access care. Once insurance benefits are confirmed, be sure to obtain the health plan authorizations required for reimbursement for the care the patient will receive. Sometimes authorizations and referrals are sent electronically to the concerned parties. Always confirm that they have been sent and received by the appropriate parties. Ask for the level-of-care criteria the patient must meet to be eligible for the various levels of benefits. Again, keep a record of the authorizations received.

Communicate with Key Caregivers

Communicate with key caregivers to give any needed input and devise a treatment plan. Obtain the names of the people who will be providing care and have daily interactions with the patient (including lower level staff such as aides). Try to meet with or talk by phone to each caregiver on the team. Discuss the diagnosis (and whether there is more than one primary diagnosis), treatment options, and ask whether there is clinical evidence to support the recommended treatment and what that evidence is. This information can be useful when talking to the insurance company about benefits because insurance companies value evidence-based care.

Also ask how the treatment plan will be coordinated and managed, and who will do the coordination. People with bulimia nervosa often have close to normal body weights. However, serious, but less obvious medical conditions may also be present. These conditions include: osteoporosis, heart problems, kidney problems, brain abnormalities, diarrhea, reflux, nausea, malnutrition, and heartburn.

Ask for "letters of support" from the health care team. These letters should describe the treatment plan and reference the available evidence to support the treatment choice (such as an evidence report or evidence-based clinical practice guidelines). The letter should also include the rationale for each level of care, anticipated duration of care, the treatment center or setting in which care will be delivered. It is useful to use language that is used by insurance companies to have common ground. For example, it is important to point out care that is considered by the doctors to be “medically necessary” for the patient’s recovery. Documentation of this is useful to provide to the insurer when discussing reimbursement because it gives both you and the insurer a framework to discuss.

With regard to the health care providers, ask them how to and who can obtain copies of the patient’s medical records, who will provide progress reports, how often and to whom. Ask the health care provider (whether it is a facility or an individual therapist) for an itemization of the estimated costs of care, which costs will likely be paid by the insurer and which by the patient. Also ask how billing for reimbursement will be handled—ask whether you have to submit claims or whether the health care service provider submits the claims on the patient’s behalf.

Enlist Support

Enlist support from family members and friends you can count on. Make a list of people you can count on for moral support throughout the course of treatment. Keep their names, phone numbers, and e-mail addresses handy. For this list, identify people who can help the patient remain focused and provide helpful emotional support and encouragement while navigating the system to obtain care and while receiving care. Find out from each of them their availability (times, dates) for support and the kind of support they can offer. Also consider distributing that list among key people on the list so they know who is in your support network. Also, list key health care provider (facilities and health care providers) contact numbers on that list in the event of an emergency.

Chapter 52

Is Recovery from an Eating Disorder Possible?

Treatment and Recovery

Most people with eating disorders, especially in the beginning, resist treatment and behavior change. They cling to the illusion that if they just lose enough weight, they will feel good about themselves, improve their lives, and enjoy self-confidence and success. After a while, however, they begin to understand that the supposed benefits of thinness are only an illusion that will never bring them happiness. Starving, stuffing, purging, and other self-destructive behaviors will never lead to peace and a meaningful life. When people get to this point, and when they begin to look for better ways to build meaningful lives, recovery becomes a real possibility.

Unfortunately, even then there are challenges and obstacles to progress. Between 20 and 30 percent of people who enter treatment drop out too soon and relapse. Even those who stick with it usually have slips and lapses, leaving them discouraged, demoralized, and feeling like failures. Wanting a quick and easy solution to their problems, they too often give up when they find that recovery can take many months to several years of hard work before they are free of their destructive behaviors and in control of their lives. Recovery requires major commitments to (1) get into treatment, (2) stay in treatment, (3) make necessary lifestyle changes, and (4) resolve the underlying psychological

---

"Treatment and Recovery," used with permission of ANRED: Anorexia Nervosa and Related Eating Disorders, Inc. © 2005 ANRED. For additional information, visit http://www.anred.com.

and emotional issues that led to starving, binge eating, and/or purging in the first place.

Is recovery possible?

Yes, eating disorders are treatable, and lots of people recover from them. Recovery, however, as previously noted, is a difficult process that can take seven to ten years or even longer. Some people do better than others and make faster progress. The folks who do best, work with physicians and counselors who help them resolve both the medical and psychological issues that contribute to, or result from, disordered eating. (*International Journal of Eating Disorders*, 1997; 22:339 and *Eating Disorders*, 2000; 8:189)

About 80 percent of people with eating disorders who seek treatment either recover completely or make significant progress. Sadly, the rest remain chronic sufferers or they die.

What is recovery?

Recovery is much more than the abandonment of starving and stuffing. At minimum it includes the following:

- maintenance of normal or near-normal weight
- in women, regular menstrual periods (not triggered by medication)
- a varied diet of normal foods (not just low-cal, non-fat, non-sugar items)
- elimination or major reduction of irrational food fears
- age appropriate relationships with family members
- awareness of cultural demands for unrealistic thinness and effective ways of repudiating those demands
- one or more mutually satisfying friendships with healthy, normal people (Such friendships involve mutual give-and-take and a minimum of care taking and "parenting" behavior.)
- age-appropriate interest and participation in romantic relationships
- strong repertoire of problem-solving skills
- fun activities that have nothing to do with food, weight, or appearance
- understanding of the process of choices and consequences

A recovering person has a sense of self, plus goals, and a realistic plan for achieving them. She or he is moving towards building a meaningful, fulfilling, and satisfying life. She or he has also learned to be kind to self and others, forsaking perfectionism and confronting flaws and disorder with grace and understanding. A recovering person refuses to be driven by criticism and demands for unrealistic performance.

What is the best treatment for an eating disorder?

Because many factors contribute to the development of an eating disorder, and since every person's situation is different, the best treatment must be custom-tailored for each individual. The process begins with an evaluation by a physician or counselor. Recommendations include any or all of the following. In general, the more components included in the treatment plan, the faster the person will make progress.

- Hospitalization to prevent death, suicide, and medical crisis.
- Weight restoration to improve health, mood, and cognitive functioning. Note: An anorexic's fear of weight gain, especially forced weight gain in hospital, is a huge obstacle to treatment and recovery. Nevertheless, it is clear that the closer to normal weight is at the end of treatment, the better the chances of complete recovery. In study after study, low body weight is strongly correlated with treatment failure and relapse.
- Medication to relieve depression and anxiety.
- Dental work to repair damage and minimize future problems.
- Individual counseling to develop healthy ways of taking control of one's life. Cognitive behavioral therapy (CBT) has proved effective in treating bulimia and binge eating disorder. The counseling of choice for anorexia is determined by individual and family circumstances.
- Group counseling to learn how to manage relationships effectively.
- Family counseling to change old patterns and create healthier new ones.
- Nutrition counseling to debunk food myths and design healthy meals.
- Support groups to break down isolation and alienation. However, support groups by themselves are not sufficient treatment

for an eating disorder. To be effective, they must be integrated into a comprehensive treatment plan.

How long does it take to recover?

A few people who refuse professional treatment do eventually recover, but it may take several years or even decades. Most make little or no progress without help. Up to 20 percent do not survive.

People who do get into treatment, and stick with it, in general do much better. About half recover completely. Another 25 percent make significant progress. Unfortunately, the last 25 percent remain chronic sufferers, even with treatment, and a few die from consequences of their disordered behaviors.

With treatment, a few people recover in a year or less. For the vast majority, though, treatment and the recovery process take three to seven years, and in some cases even longer. Recovery takes however long it takes. For most people, changing entrenched food behaviors and resolving the issues that underlie them is a formidable challenge, perhaps the greatest challenge they will ever face.

Usually treatment is more intensive at the beginning: several therapy sessions a week and perhaps even hospitalization. As progress is made, sessions are scheduled less frequently until, at the end, there may be only two or three a year. Relapses, especially in the beginning, are to be expected. The person learns to cope with life without depending on food and weight manipulation but then encounters a problem. The new coping skills are overwhelmed, and the person, feeling frantic, resorts to old familiar patterns—binge eating, starving, or purging. A common scenario involves a person receiving treatment, leaving treatment, being successful for a while, relapsing, and then returning to treatment. The cycle may be repeated several times before recovery is stable. There should be no shame in these lapses. They are learning experiences that point out where more work needs to be done.

An outcome study at Rogers Memorial Hospital in Wisconsin indicates that in the case of anorexia nervosa, the longer the person remains in a hospital program, and the closer his or her weight is to normal at discharge, the greater the chances of long-term, stable recovery.

Where to Find Help

Finding a counselor, physician, and treatment team that you trust, and with whom you can work effectively, is an important part of the recovery process. Here are some tips to get you started.

- If you are in crisis, call 9-1-1 or a crisis hot line. (Find the number in the yellow pages under Crisis Intervention.) If it is safe to do so, go to a hospital emergency room and tell the staff what's going on. Be truthful. They are not mind readers.
- If you are not in crisis, ask your family doctor for an evaluation and referral to a counselor. Don't let embarrassment stop you from telling the physician all the details. Doctors, nurses, and counselors have heard the eating disorder story many times before.
- You can also ask people you trust, and who have been in your situation, for the names of physicians and counselors they found helpful.
- If you are a student, check with the school counseling center. Services may be low-cost or free.
- If your income is limited, or if your insurance will not cover treatment for eating disorders, look for community service agencies in the "Counselors" section of the yellow pages. The organizations listed there may not provide formal eating disorders programs, but they do offer basic assistance to people who have few other options.
- If you believe your insurance company is declining payment of a legitimate claim for eating disorders treatment, you may want to speak with an attorney. Sometimes insurance companies are open to negotiation, but unless you know how to do this, we recommend you let an attorney handle it for you. These discussions do not always lead to payment of claims, but some families have had success with them.

Questions to Ask a Counselor Before Counseling Begins

Your therapist or counselor will, in a sense, be your employee. You, or your insurance company, are paying him or her, so you might as well shop around for a good fit. If you want to work with someone who is warm and understanding, don't pick a person who works primarily in a corporate setting in problem-solving mode. Likewise, if you are ready for an action plan, you may not want a counselor who spends a lot of time examining feelings and emotions. The following are just some of the questions you can ask your potential "employee."

- What is your treatment approach?

- What can I expect to happen during sessions?
- How much experience have you had working with people who have eating disorders?
- What are your training, education, and licenses?
- How long do you think treatment will take?
- How often will we meet?
- If I think I need to, can I call you between sessions?
- What are your thoughts about using medications in the treatment of eating disorders?
- Could I be put in a hospital against my will? (This is a common fear. Get the facts at the beginning so you will know what to expect.)
- How much do sessions cost? Do you take insurance? What if my insurance will not cover all the costs of treatment?
- If I don't think I'm improving fast enough, I may feel like either you or I am failing. What can I do if that happens? (Be sure to ask this one. Don't just drop out if you get discouraged. Overcoming the times in treatment is a major victory.)

Chapter 53

Stages of Change and Milestones of Recovery

Stages of Change

Changing behavior is not just a simple matter of a black and white decision. There are many psychological theories which describe the components of change. To the outsider the need to change the overt problems of anorexia nervosa seems obvious, but the individual concerned typically does not share that view. Leaving eating disorders symptoms behind, or indeed changing any problematic behavior is a gradual process which involves passing through various stages. You may recognize these in yourself or in other people.

Stage 1. Pre-Contemplation

In this situation, the person with the eating disorder has only one mind and one thought set, and that is that anorexia nervosa is a solution and offers many rewards and no costs.

Stage 2. Contemplation

In this stage, the person is in two minds. She can see the costs and problems that anorexia nervosa brings, but she is also aware of the

---

This chapter begins with "Caring for Someone with an Eating Disorder and Stages of Change," by Prof. Janet Treasure, Dr. Ulrike Schmidt, and Gill Todd. It continues with "Milestones of Recovery in EDA,"

rewards and positive aspects. She will oscillate between these two positions and may seem very confused about what she wants.

Stage 3. Determination and Action

In this stage, the resolution of the conflict favors moving away from anorexia nervosa. The costs are seen to outweigh the benefits.

It is common for people to go through these various stages several times. Helping people negotiate these stages is not easy, however, there is some evidence from research that can help.

If your loved one is in stage one or two and you present the arguments for change in a strong confrontational manner (For example: "if you don't change you will die, your father will have another heart attack") this will only serve to stoke up the opposite point of view. Research has shown that when a therapist is confrontational then resistance to change and denial that there is a problem increases. On the other hand if the therapist is empathic and listens, resistance goes down.

The following story by the ancient Greek writer Aesop describes the type of approach that helps facilitate change when people are in stages one and two.

> "The sun and the wind were having a dispute as to who was the most powerful. They saw a man walking along and they challenged each other about which of them would be most successful at getting the man to remove his coat. The wind started first and blew up a huge gale; the coat flapped but the man only closed all his buttons and tightened up his belt. The sun tried next and shone brightly making the man sweat. He proceeded to take off his coat."

Milestones of Recovery

In recovery, pain and fear are faced without obsessing on food, weight, and body image. This does not mean a person never has food, weight, or body image issues. It merely means he or she can take it in stride when it happens. Recovery means developing healthy perspectives, knowing you will do better some days than others, knowing you will never be perfect at anything including recovery, and knowing recovery is not freedom from trouble and pain, but freedom from getting stuck in feelings of uselessness and self-pity.

Eating disordered individuals binged, starved, purged, and obsessed in an effort to manage unwelcome emotions. The solution to an eating disorder has to do with accepting thoughts and feelings, and finding safe and responsible ways to express them. There is no magic about recovery. When a person takes responsibility for understanding needs and getting them met, he or she can walk free. It sounds so simple, but it is hard work, especially at first.

Recovery means rebuilding trust with oneself and others, taking careful risks to learn what is safe and good. As careful self-honesty and self-disclosure is practiced, perspective is regained. Perspective enables one to see options and make careful, responsible choices in life. As careful self-expression is learned, one regains lost authenticity, peace, and power. The process is usually gradual and halting. New attitudes and behaviors are alien, and it is hard to feel safe and keep perspective. It is hard to remember one is aiming for balance, not perfection. It is very important to claim successes in achieving balance and attaining perspective, in identifying personal needs and in developing more resilient relationships with ourselves, with others, and with food. This is just where "milestones of recovery" comes in.

Milestones

A "milestone of recovery" is a self-defined marker on a journey in recovery. It is essential to recognize that even on the worst days things are done that are right and good and supportive of personal recovery. Milestones—which take myriad and often surprising forms—are bright spots in group meetings that inspire people with their honesty and reality. Individuals find, often in retrospect, that milestones express how the principles of the program are working in our lives. The principles—embodied in the 12 Steps of Eating Disorders Anonymous (EDA)—include **h**onesty, **e**quality, **a**ccountability, **l**ove, **t**rust and **hu**mility (HEALTH: the EDA motto).

Suggestions for Building Recovery

- Eat when hungry, stop when moderately full. Consistent nutrition is essential for recovery. Recovery is about feelings, not food, but trust cannot be built when bingeing, purging, or starving.
- Get basic needs met first. If hungry, eat. If angry, find a safe outlet. If lonely, reach out. If tired, sleep. If ashamed, talk about it. Be an adult. This takes training and practice.
- Ask others for input and make your own decisions.
- When anxious, get physical, get outside, pray. Then deal with the problem head-on.

- Be open with others. Honesty restores integrity.
- Develop willingness to look at things differently. Recovery is not rigid.
- Go to 12-step meetings, read the literature, and work the steps with a sponsor or buddy.
- Be proactive and plan your recovery.

Examples of Milestones

- "I ate pizza last night for the first time in three years and it was great!"
- "I took responsibility and let go of one of my boyfriends."
- "I refused to let my wife tell me what to think about this issue."
- "I'm looking at how miserable I am, and I need to know what I'm getting from staying stuck. Maybe if I know what works about it, I can make a different plan to get those needs met."
- "I thought about what might make me happy and decided to take dance lessons."
- "I forgave my friend for disappointing me. I felt very mature about that."
- "Ugh! I'm obsessing again, but at least I know it, and I'm being open about it."
- "I finally weaned myself off laxatives. It's been twelve years since I've gone without them for this long."
- "I was feeling very hurt and rejected, and I said so calmly without expecting any particular response."
- "My need for security always seems to conflict with my need for self-expression. It makes me mad and I want to escape. But, I realized I'll never be safe until I allow myself to have and express ugly thoughts."
- "I screamed what I was thinking on paper, and then I found I could talk about it calmly without blaming."
- "I wanted to run and hide by being really busy, but I sat down and asked myself what I was afraid of. I made a new plan. My fears evaporated, and I felt terrific."
- "I was sad yesterday and I just let myself be sad."

Chapter 54

Tips for Recovery from an Eating Disorder

Self-Help Tips

Recovery from an eating disorder demands maturity. What is maturity? Here is one definition:

> Maturity is the ability to control our impulses, to think beyond the moment, and consider how our words and our actions will affect ourselves and others before we act. (Source: Jeanne Phillips, "Dear Abby," May 2005.)

In the U.S., and in other developed countries as well, we are influenced by many forces that encourage us to be immature, to act (buy, eat, drink, be sexual) on the spur of the moment, when opportunity presents itself. When we do so, without forethought or reflection, we often regret our actions and choices later, when it is either too late to change our minds or extremely difficult to do so.

Nonetheless, recovery demands that we grow up, that we resist the many destructive messages that society—often in the form of advertising—crams down our throat in attempts to get us to spend our money "perfecting" ourselves. Recovery insists that we consciously choose to examine our thoughts and behaviors, following only those

---

This chapter begins with "Self-Help Tips," used with permission of ANRED: Anorexia Nervosa and Related Eating Disorders, Inc. © 2005 ANRED. For additional information, visit http://www.anred.com. It continues with text from "Suggestions for Recovery" and "Holiday Help," © 2002 Eating Disorders Anonymous.

that lead to health and personal growth without harming anyone else in the process.

You already know that we live in a thin-obsessed society. The cultural ideals held up for us to emulate are either stick-thin with surgically enhanced breasts (female) or powerful with clear muscle definition (male). It's no wonder that so many people develop eating disorders when they try to achieve these unrealistic—and often unhealthy—images of "perfection."

Almost always, professional help is required for recovery from an eating disorder, to support development of the necessary maturity, but if you want to try to help yourself, here are some suggestions. If you are not in medical danger, try them for a week. If, after seven days, you can't shake your preoccupations with food and weight, and especially if you don't make any progress towards changing harmful behaviors, get help from a resource person—a parent, school nurse, school counselor, family physician, or mental health counselor. These people can be great allies in your struggle for health and happiness. Don't avoid being honest with them because of guilt or embarrassment.

Note: if you have even the smallest suspicion that you are in medical danger, consult a physician immediately. Eating disorders can kill, and if you are already in trouble, you need medical attention, not self-help tips.

Anorexia Nervosa

- Don't diet—never, ever. Instead design a meal plan that gives your body all the nutrition it needs for health and growth.
- Get 30 to 60 minutes of exercise or physical activity three to five days a week. More than that is too much if you have an eating disorder. Be safe. Ask your physician to okay your meal plans and exercise schedule before you begin.
- Ask someone you trust for an honest, objective opinion of your weight. If they say you are normal weight or thin, believe them.
- When you start to get overwhelmed by "feeling fat," push beyond the anxiety and ask yourself what you are really afraid of. Then take steps to deal with the threat, if it is real, or dismiss it if it is not real.

Bulimia Nervosa and Binge Eating Disorder

- Don't let yourself get too hungry, too angry, too frustrated, too lonely, too tired, or too bored. Don't let yourself get pulled in too many directions by too many people, too many demands, and too many responsibilities. All these states are powerful binge triggers. Watch for them, and when they first appear, deal with them in a healthy manner instead of letting the tension build until bingeing and purging become the only release you can think of.

- Stay comfortably busy and avoid unstructured time. Empty time is too easily filled with binge food.
- Make sure you get enough sleep, at least seven hours every night.
- Don't diet. Dieting means depriving yourself of nourishment and pleasure. Dieting and deprivation are powerful triggers of binge eating. Note: A healthy meal plan, one that manages weight and reduces risks of medical problems, is not dieting in the usual sense of deprivation. A healthy meal plan respects nutritional needs and is flexible enough to include reasonable amounts of fun foods.
- Make sure that every day you spend time with friends and loved ones—in person is best; phone and e-mail can substitute, but only once in a while. Enjoy being with people you love and those who love you. It sounds corny, but hugs really are healing.
- Take control of your life. Make choices thoughtfully and deliberately. Make your living situation safe and comfortable. Choose every day to bring pleasure into your life, at least for a few minutes.
- Every day do something fun, something relaxing, something energizing.
- Monitor your self-talk. Challenge self-critical nagging. Deliberately choose to change the subject and count your blessings to combat negative thoughts about yourself, your appearance, your abilities, and your accomplishments.
- Keep tabs on your feelings. Several times a day ask yourself how you feel. If you get off track, do whatever the situation requires to get back to your comfort zone.

A reminder: If these tips don't work for you in seven days, talk over your situation with a resource person—physician, counselor, or therapist. If you have even the smallest suspicion you are in medical danger, don't wait one day longer. Talk to a physician immediately.

Suggestions for Recovery

Priority Activities of First Three Months of Recovery

- Make sure you are medically stable. Consult a doctor.
- Get support: a counselor and nutritionist (both trained eating disorders specialists), and join an eating disorders support group(s).
- Read recovery literature.

Additional Suggestions

Keep it simple (pick a few new activities each month).

- Keep things simple.
- Make a list of self-soothing activities, and do one or two a day.
- Practice being honest with yourself and others; validate your feelings.
- Give yourself permission to eat.
- Practice eating when hungry, stopping when moderately full.
- Let go of second-guessing your choices.
- Attend a variety of meetings (online and in person, if possible).
- Make outreach calls.
- Find a sponsor or partner, contact regularly.
- Work 12-step program with a sponsor or partner.
- Keep a journal.

Beyond the First Three Months in Recovery

- Continue with priority activities and the advice of your physician, counselor, and nutritionist.
- Accept a service position at one of your regular support group meetings.
- Make use of daily meditation literature, five minutes helps a lot.
- Help others—ask program members to coffee, or a movie.

Try New Ways of Thinking

- Focus on solutions to your issues.

- Focus on what is working.
- Check out your thinking with others.
- Take responsibility for your choices.
- Do not blame others (It does not help to perceive yourself as a victim).
- Cultivate a sense of humor.
- Keep an open mind.
- Keep being honest.
- Express your feelings safely.
- Think about bringing balance into your life.
- Express gratitude.
- Notice what is right and good in your world.
- Be willing to change your mind.
- Be willing to change your behavior.
- See yourself as recovering.
- Be gentle with yourself.
- Practice compassion with yourself and others.
- Rely on yourself; trust your inner resources.
- Treat yourself as if you are your best friend.
- Approve of yourself: Your best is good enough.
- Confront ill attitudes and behaviors in yourself.
- Identify ruts; plan new ways to think and act.

Try New Behaviors

- Make a list of what your eating disorder does for you, and come up with alternatives that deliver the same result.
- When feeling down or uncomfortable, ask: "What would I be doing if I felt better?" and then do it.
- Be on time. Stop the internal stress cycle that tardiness creates.
- Refrain from gossip of all types: find a safe outlet to discuss interpersonal problems.
- Explore new ways to communicate and set boundaries; you will be taking care of yourself and your self-esteem will benefit.

- When angry, ask: "What would make me feel heard and validated?" and do it.
- Afraid of rejection? Plan how to comfort yourself when you get it.
- Talk about your mistakes and what you want to do differently next time.
- Be wary of setting unrealistic expectations. Talk with others before deciding what is realistic. Be flexible in your thinking.
- Perfectionism is a barrier to all progress. Let go of it.

Help for Recovery Focused Holidays

The holidays can be a very difficult time for those dealing with eating disorders. The emphasis on spending time with family members, the focus on an endless variety of foods and eating traditions, as well as strong emotions, can present a number of challenges to recovery.

Take a deep breath and ask yourself what kind of holiday you want to have? What would you like to have different from past years, what enjoyment do you miss from past holidays? Who do you feel more positive and energetic when you are around, and who leaves you feeling drained, self-critical?

Here are a few tools to help you have a more peaceful and recovery focused holiday.

1. Predict times of high stress and places that cause you high stress, in other words, be prepared and make choices about where you will attend and where you won't go ahead of time and stick to your plans.
2. Plan self-care time, time to regenerate and relax and refocus on your recovery. This may be talking a walk, going to the movies, attending a meeting, calling a friend in recovery, meditation time, or anything else that gives you a time out to recharge.
3. Plan to eat three meals a day to help reduce the chance of a binge or focusing on food too much. Allow yourself to continue your regular recovery routine.
4. Plan to continue your regular exercise routine. This will allow you to maintain the structure you have created.

5. Allow yourself some treats. Deprivation is not self-care and is more likely to lead to resentment, binges, or further restrictions.

6. Make a phone list and carry it with you so you can make support calls whenever you need to. This can also be a form of service work as you reach out to others in their recovery who may need support as well.

7. Think about doing some volunteer work or 12-step work to reach out to others and be able to let go of the self-focus that can sabotage recovery.

8. Consider making an extra effort to begin each day with some prayer and meditation, even if just for ten minutes. This can set the tone for the day and be something that can help you to find your balance again quicker when needed later in the day.

9. Make a plan about boundaries that may need to be set with others. This can include food boundaries "Thanks for your concern, but I won't get into a debate about my weight. Please leave it up to me to decide about the portions and foods I will eat."

10. Make use of coping or positive self-talk statements. This can include: "I have a right to say no;" "I know I can handle this situation;" "I am honoring my recovery by making this choice;" "I am worth taking special care of myself during this season;" and, "I don't have to do this perfectly but can focus on doing a few positive healthy things each day." You can also follow this up with a gratitude list at the end of each day, no matter how small it may be.

11. Remind yourself if you binge, purge, overeat, or restrict, that this behavior will decrease with healthier attitudes and eating practices. This can help you to not punish or beat yourself up around relapses.

Remember that it is only you that remains responsible for your health and recovery, not family, friends, partners, or sponsors.

Additional Information

ANRED: Anorexia Nervosa and Related Eating Disorders, Inc.
Website: http://www.anred.com

Eating Disorders Anonymous
P.O. Box 55876
Phoenix, AZ 85078-5876
Website: http://www.eatingdisordersanonymous.org
E-mail: info@eatingdisordersanonymous.org

Chapter 55

Value of a Support Group in Recovery from an Eating Disorder

Value of a Support Group

Research

The National Association of Anorexia Nervosa and Associated Disorders (ANAD) has conducted a study of its support groups in the United States and South Africa. Two types of survey forms were sent to support groups, one for the leaders and one for members. The leaders' survey inquired into group process, format, content, and the historical development of the group, whereas the group participant questionnaire focuses on participants' perceptions of group effectiveness and on aspects of group leadership and process which they perceive as helpful to their recovery process. The research project was developed and completed by Vivian Hanson Meehan and Laura DeJarnett, ANAD Research Associate.

The purpose of ANAD support groups—the first one in the nation began in 1976—is to provide helping and sharing meetings for individuals affected by eating disorders and their family members. For thousands of participants, these groups are and have been a valuable adjunct to therapy. Responses are included from groups in 25 states and one foreign country, South Africa.

This chapter includes: "Value of a Support Group," reprinted with permission from the National Association of Anorexia Nervosa and Associated Disorders, http://www.anad.org. Also, "What You Can Expect from OA" is reprinted with permission from Overeaters Anonymous, http://www.oa.org.

Although a great deal has been known about ANAD support groups, this is the first study that documents the crucial importance of these programs in many different communities and areas. The following quote is an example of a statement from a group member who benefited from the positive power of coming together to work through their issues with other recovering people:

> "ANAD has been a big part of my recovery. I have 11 months of freedom from bingeing, purging, starving, over-exercising, and using diet pills. I am focusing more on being healthy rather than being skinny. I have more confidence in myself and my ability to overcome this disease. I feel stronger and I am very grateful for how far I've come." —Recovering eating disorder sufferer

Leaders and members in almost 400 groups in most states and 15 foreign countries often do much more than attend meetings. Large numbers make educational and prevention presentations at schools and organizations in their communities. They help mobilize efforts to draw attention to the dangers of eating disorders, and they lead efforts to pass legislation through state and federal governments to assure adequate treatment for eating disorders.

The age range of study participants was 14–62 years old with the median age being 31.5 years old. Attendees reported a broad range of illnesses with which they are coping: thirty-two percent are anorexic, twenty-seven percent are bulimic, eight percent are compulsive eaters, and thirty-three percent are a combination of these problems. Fifty-six percent of the attendees were female, while forty-four percent were male.

Socioeconomic backgrounds differed considerably. Some lived at or below the poverty level whereas most make a modest living. A few reported household incomes of over $75,000.

Results

In response to questions about the importance of ANAD groups to their recovery, 77 percent state that the groups are an important aspect of their recovery while 93 percent reported they would recommend their groups to others with eating disorders. An additional 20 percent felt their group was somewhat helpful. Other advantages of the group were that 78 percent said they had the ability to talk with leaders when they were feeling down, and 68 percent said they could talk with other members of their group when they were looking for additional support. Fifty-three percent reported that they are in frequent contact with other group members.

Sixty-one percent gave the following reason for becoming involved in an ANAD support group: desire for help in recovery, need for additional support, and desire for a better understanding of the illness. Another 35 percent joined upon the recommendation of a therapist, treatment facility, or family member support. The chief reasons for missing or discontinuing attendance were work, family, or school conflicts with the meetings.

While the style of content of the group meetings varied considerably, 89 percent relied upon interactional discussions as the main procedure for meetings. Thirty-eight percent used the ANAD eight-step guide, *Applying New Attitudes and Directions*, for meetings and 29 percent used educational presentations in their meetings. Spiritual aspects of recovery are discussed in 67 percent of the groups. Family members attend 48 percent of the groups. Seventy-one percent of the groups meet every week and another nine percent meet every other week. Phone chain lists (exchange of phone numbers by members for additional support between meetings) are used by 87 percent of the groups. Seventy-seven percent said the phone chain gave them extra support and comfort to talk with others who understand what they're going through. Nine percent said the phone list helps them to stop when they are tempted to binge or purge or starve.

Groups in the United States and South Africa responded similarly to questions about their groups. The responses from South Africa and the United States indicated a general similarity in group meeting content and approach in coping with and overcoming eating disorders.

1. Topics discussed in the group are self-esteem, body image, recovery, family, relationships, and depression.

2. Focus of group is recovery, health, reasons behind eating disorders, and goals.

3. Benefits of group include sharing, support, letting members know they are not alone, and being in a safe haven.

4. Positive elements of the group are honesty, support, empathy, and education.

5. Negative elements of the group are that some members focus on the negative, some are not committed, and some monopolize group time.

What You Can Expect from Overeaters Anonymous (OA)

After years of struggling with your weight and obsessing about food, you have decided to give Overeaters Anonymous a try. You can find an OA meeting in your area by checking OA's online meeting locator or by calling or e-mailing the World Service Office (WSO). Call the contact person to confirm the day, time, and location of the meeting to make sure the information has not changed.

When you arrive at the meeting, you will find men and women who share a common malady—compulsive eating—and have found a common solution: the Twelve Steps and Twelve Traditions of Overeaters Anonymous. You will see anywhere from three to thirty people at the meeting. An average meeting has about ten people. You will be warmly welcomed.

The meeting usually opens with the Serenity Prayer, and you may hear a reading called "Our Invitation to You," which describes the disease of compulsive overeating and the Twelve-Step solution. Meeting formats may vary, but all OA groups are the same in that they seek recovery on three levels—physical, emotional, and spiritual—through the Twelve Steps, and the only requirement for membership is a desire to stop eating compulsively.

You may hear a speaker open the meeting and speak for 10 to 15 minutes about what life was like before OA, what happened, and what he or she is like now; or someone might read from OA or AA (Alcoholics Anonymous) literature. Other members will share their experience, strength, and hope. You will have an opportunity to introduce yourself as a newcomer, if you like. You will find that you are not alone, that there is a way out of your desperation. Because anonymity is a critical principle of the OA program, you are assured that what you share will be held in confidence. This provides the safety you need to share your experiences honestly.

You may recognize your own story when you listen to others share. Listening will help you find others who have what you want, whether it be weight loss, clarity, joy, or recovery from the obsession. You may want to ask someone to be your sponsor. A sponsor will help you work the Steps of the program to achieve the recovery you seek.

When members share, you may hear them refer to a Higher Power or to God. OA is not a religious program and does not subscribe to any specific religious ideology. It is a program that practices spiritual principles, and members individually approach these principles with a Higher Power of their understanding.

A list may be passed around for all to sign their names and phone numbers, so people can offer each other support between meetings. Someone from the meeting you attend may call you to answer any questions you may have about the program, and you will also have an opportunity to get phone numbers yourself to reach out for help. The telephone is an important tool in OA for getting and giving support and reminding you that you are not alone.

Meetings usually last between one and two hours, and they often include a break. During the break, feel free to ask questions and pick up some OA literature to help you learn about the program. By asking for help, you are taking an important step toward recovery. Because OA is self-supporting through member contributions, a basket will be passed for donations.

You will notice that some members volunteer to help keep the meeting going, such as the group secretary, the treasurer, and greeters. Members find that doing service in OA helps keep them from eating compulsively. Service is important to their recovery and allows them to give back to the fellowship that has saved their lives. Service opportunities exist in all levels of the group, from making coffee and setting up chairs at a meeting to being on the Board of Trustees.

The meeting usually closes with a reading like the OA Promise, "I Put My Hand in Yours." If you find that the meeting you attended does not feel right, try a different group at another time and location. It is a good idea to attend at least six meetings before deciding on a meeting that is right for you.

What you won't find at OA meetings are weigh-ins, packaged meals, dues, fees, "shoulds," "musts," or judgment. What you will find at meetings is:

- Acceptance of you—as you are now, as you were, as you will be.
- Understanding of the problems you now face—problems almost certainly shared by others in the group.
- Communication that comes as the natural result of our mutual understanding and acceptance.
- Recovery from your illness.
- Power to enter a new way of life through the acceptance and understanding of yourself, the practice of the Twelve-Step recovery program, the belief in a power greater than yourself, and the support and companionship of the group.

Additional Information

Overeaters Anonymous
World Service Office
P.O. Box 44020
Rio Rancho, NM 87174-4020
Phone: 505-891-2664
Fax: 505-891-4320
Website: http://www.oa.org
E-mail: info@oa.org

To find a meeting of Overeaters Anonymous, visit http://www.oa.org/all_about_meetings.htm.

Chapter 56

Eating Disorder Relapse Prevention

The road to recovery is usually long and hard. No one travels it gracefully. There are many slips, trips, and lapses. Those who eventually do recover learn to pick themselves up when they fall, brush off the dust, and keep going. By doing so, they keep temporary lapses from turning into full-blown relapses. Following are things to do when relapse threatens.

Anorexia Nervosa Relapse Prevention

It sounds simplistic, but it is true: if no one ever dieted there would be no anorexia nervosa. Instead of dieting, design a meal plan that gives your body all the nutrition it needs for normal growth and health. If you want to work towards a healthy weight, then limit (but don't eliminate) your intake of fatty and sugary foods and refined carbohydrates. Eat lots of whole grains, fruits, vegetables, and enough dairy and protein foods to maintain strong bones and healthy muscles and organs. Also get 30 to 60 minutes of exercise or physical activity three to five days a week. Unless you are working under the supervision of a coach or trainer, anything more rigorous is excessive.

When you start to get overwhelmed by "feeling fat," instead of dwelling on your appearance, ask yourself how your life would be better if you were thinner. What would you have then that you don't have

---

"Relapse Prevention," used with permission of ANRED: Anorexia Nervosa and Related Eating Disorder, Inc. © 2006 ANRED. For additional information visit, http://www.anred.com.

now? Friends? Self-confidence? Love? Control? The admiration of others? Their acceptance? Success and status?

Then realize that being unhealthily thin will bring you none of these things, only a fragile illusion of success that has to be constantly reinforced with even more weight loss. All of the items listed in the preceding paragraph are legitimate goals of healthy people, but working to achieve them directly is much more effective than trying to be successful by losing weight. If weight loss brought happiness, then starving Third World children would be ecstatic with joy. They are not. They are miserable and depressed, just like people who have anorexia nervosa.

Accept that your body shape is determined in part by genetics. Accept that you may never have a totally flat stomach. Even if you are very thin, your internal organs will give your belly a certain roundness, especially after you eat. That's normal, especially if people in your family tend to store fat in the midsection.

If you feel yourself slipping back into unhealthy habits, call your therapist and schedule an appointment. Returning to counseling in no way means you have failed. It means only that it's time to reevaluate and fine tune your recovery plan.

Bulimia Nervosa and Binge Eating Disorder Relapse Prevention

Never ever let yourself get so hungry that the urge to binge is overwhelming. People who recover from bulimia say that they eat regularly. Because they are never ravenous, they have no physical reason to binge eat. Hunger is the most powerful binge trigger there is. It is a recognized fact that the longer one has dieted, and the more severely calories have been restricted, the higher the risk of binge eating.

Never ever deprive yourself of good-tasting food, even if it has more fat and calories than "safe" diet foods. If you refuse to eat appealing foods that you really want, you will feel deprived and crave them. Then you are vulnerable to bingeing. Remember Adam and Eve in the Garden of Eden? The one food they were not supposed to eat was the one they could not stay away from.

Until you have achieved some balance and perspective, stay away from temptation. Don't go to all-you-can-eat salad bars. If ice cream is a binge trigger, don't keep it in your freezer. When you want potato salad, for example, or rocky road ice cream, go to a sit-down restaurant and order a single portion, ideally as part of a balanced meal.

By doing so, you accomplish three things: you avoid depriving yourself; you avoid the urges to binge created by deprivation; and you also learn how to integrate normal food into a reasonable and healthy meal plan.

When you do feel powerful urges to binge, postpone the act for thirty minutes. Surely you can wait half an hour. During that time think about what is going on in your life. What stresses are you facing? What is missing right now from your life that you need in order to be happy and avoid the looming binge? Make a list of things you could you do instead of binge eating to deal with your situation. If you are truly committed to recovery, at least some of the time you will choose one of these healthier behaviors instead of binge food.

Take charge of your life. Stop using words like, "I wish," "I want," "I hope," and "I can't." They are weak victim words. Say instead things like, "I choose," even if you are choosing to binge. Say, "I will," even if the thing you will do is vomit. These are words that express responsibility, power, and control. If you can choose to binge, then by implication at some future time you can choose not to binge. If you will vomit, then next week or next month or next year you can choose to say, "I won't vomit."

If you feel yourself slipping back into unhealthy habits, call your therapist and schedule an appointment. Returning to counseling in no way means you have failed. It means only that it's time to reevaluate and fine tune your recovery plan.

Relapse Prevention Tips for Everyone

Nourish yourself physically, emotionally, and spiritually. Accept that everyone has needs, legitimate needs, and you don't need to be ashamed of yours. Learn how to meet your needs in healthy, responsible ways. If you make yourself feel needy, you will be tempted to look for comfort in diet books or the refrigerator. Especially make sure that every day you spend time with friends. In person is best, but phone calls and e-mail are better than nothing.

Also every day spend time doing things you are good at, things you can take pride in, things that demonstrate your competency and abilities. Allow yourself to enjoy your accomplishments and refuse to listen to the nagging inner voice that insists you could do better if only you tried harder.

Schedule something to look forward to every day, something that's fun and pleasurable. Watch comedy videos and laugh out loud at outrageous jokes. Play something—a board game, a computer game, a musical instrument, tapes or compact disks. Go outside and enjoy the birds, trees, flowers, and fresh air. If you live in the middle of a big city, go to a park. Make something with your own hands. Figure out how to give yourself a fun break from the daily routine, and then do it.

Keep tabs on your feelings. Several times during the day, especially in the first stages of recovery, take time out and ask yourself how you feel. If you notice rising stress, anger, anxiety, fear, sadness—and even strong joy—be alert to the possibility that you may try to dull these strong emotions by turning to, or away from, food. Find a better way of dealing with your feelings such as talking them over with a trusted friend.

Do something meaningful every day, something that gives you a sense of having made the world a better place, if only in some small way. If you do this consistently, you will build a sense of your dignity, value, and ability to make a difference in your world.

The 12-step folks have a useful formula. When they feel on the verge of falling into old behaviors, they say HALT (**H**ungry, **A**ngry, **L**onely, **T**ired). Then they ask, "Am I too hungry, too angry, too lonely, or too tired?" All of those states are strong binge triggers. Additional triggers for people with eating disorders seem to be boredom and unstructured time. If you find yourself stressed by any of these feelings, figure out a healthier and more effective way of dealing with them than binge eating or starving.

If you feel yourself slipping back into unhealthy habits, call your therapist and schedule an appointment. Returning to counseling in no way means you have failed. It means only that it's time to reevaluate and fine tune your recovery plan.

Healthy Lifestyle Insulates against Major Relapse

Get at least eight hours of sleep every night, more if you need it. Sleep deprivation seems to impair the way the human body uses insulin, which can lead to overweight and possible problems with blood sugar.

Do thirty to sixty minutes of physical activity every day. It does not have to be done all at one time, and routine activities such as climbing stairs and yard maintenance count.

Nurture supportive relationships with friends, family members, and romantic partners. Enjoy being with people you like and who like you back.

Deliberately make choices. Don't make the mistake of thinking that you are the victim of forces over which you have no control. As soon as you realize you are making choices, you can decide to choose other possibilities.

Do something fun every day. Let yourself experience pleasure too. When you play and enjoy yourself, you don't have to turn to diet books or binge food for release from daily stress.

No smoking. Anything. Ever.

If you use alcohol, no more than two standard servings per day for males and one standard serving per day for females.

No abuse of prescription drugs or use of recreational drugs. In addition to hurting your body, these substances impair brain function and muddy your thoughts. If you want to be healthy and free of relapses, you need your wits about you. If you are dependent on alcohol or other drugs, get treatment and get clean. Many people with eating disorders are also chemically dependent.

Eat a nutritious breakfast every morning. Ninety-six percent of individuals who lose weight and keep it off eat breakfast every day, according to Ann Yelmokas McDermot, a nutrition scientist at Tufts University (U.S. Department of Agriculture (USDA) Nutrition Research Center).

Important for everyone: Wear your seat belt when in a car. No unprotected sex unless you are in a strictly monogamous relationship. Insist on counseling or leave relationships if you are being physically, sexually, or emotionally abused. Also, get counseling if you have painful issues in your past that have not been resolved.

Part Five

Healthy Weight Control and Dieting

Chapter 57

Healthy Eating

Chapter Contents

Section 57.1

Dietary Guidelines for Americans

"Finding Your Way to a Healthier You: Based on the Dietary Guidelines for Americans," U.S. Department of Agriculture (USDA), 2005.

Feel Better, Stay Healthy

Feel better today. Stay healthy for tomorrow. Here's how: The food and physical activity choices you make every day affect your health—how you feel today, tomorrow, and in the future. The science-based advice of the *Dietary Guidelines for Americans, 2005* in this section highlights how to:

- Make smart choices from every food group.
- Find your balance between food and physical activity.
- Get the most nutrition out of your calories.

You may be eating plenty of food, but not eating the right foods that give your body the nutrients you need to be healthy. You may not be getting enough physical activity to stay fit and burn those extra calories. Eating right and being physically active aren't just a diet or a program—they are keys to a healthy lifestyle. With healthy habits, you may reduce your risk of many chronic diseases such as heart disease, diabetes, osteoporosis, and certain cancers, and increase your chances for a longer life.

Make Smart Choices from Every Food Group

The best way to give your body the balanced nutrition it needs is by eating a variety of nutrient-packed foods every day. Just be sure to stay within your daily calorie needs.

A healthy eating plan is one that:

- emphasizes fruits, vegetables, whole grains, and fat-free or low-fat milk and milk products;

- includes lean meats, poultry, fish, beans, eggs, and nuts;
- is low in saturated fats, trans fats, cholesterol, salt (sodium), and added sugars.

Eating Out

Don't give in when you eat out and are on the go. It is important to make smart food choices and watch portion sizes wherever you are—at the grocery store, at work, in your favorite restaurant, or running errands. Try these tips:

- At the store, plan ahead by buying a variety of nutrient-rich foods for meals and snacks throughout the week.
- When grabbing lunch, have a sandwich on whole grain bread and choose low-fat or fat-free milk, water, or other drinks without added sugars.
- In a restaurant, opt for steamed, grilled, or broiled dishes instead of those that are fried or sautéed.
- On a long commute or shopping trip, pack some fresh fruit, cut-up vegetables, string cheese sticks, or a handful of unsalted nuts to help you avoid impulsive, less healthful snack choices.

Mix Choices within Each Food Group

- **Focus on fruits.** Eat a variety of fruits—whether fresh, frozen, canned, or dried—rather than fruit juice for most of your fruit choices. For a 2,000-calorie diet, you will need two cups of fruit each day (for example, one small banana, one large orange, and 1/4 cup of dried apricots or peaches).
- **Vary your veggies.** Eat more dark green veggies, such as broccoli, kale, and other dark leafy greens; orange veggies, such as carrots, sweet potatoes, pumpkin, and winter squash; and beans and peas, such as pinto beans, kidney beans, black beans, garbanzo beans, split peas, and lentils.
- **Get your calcium-rich foods.** Drink three cups of low-fat or fat-free milk every day—or an equivalent amount of low-fat yogurt or low-fat cheese (1½ ounces of cheese equals one cup of milk). For kids aged 2 to 8, it's two cups of milk. If you don't or can't consume milk, choose lactose-free milk products and calcium-fortified foods and beverages.

- **Make half your grains whole.** Eat at least three ounces of whole-grain cereals, breads, crackers, rice, or pasta every day. One ounce is about one slice of bread, one cup of breakfast cereal, or ½ cup of cooked rice or pasta. Look to see that grains such as wheat, rice, oats, or corn are referred to as whole in the list of ingredients.
- **Go lean with protein.** Choose lean meats and poultry. Bake it, broil it, or grill it. And vary your protein choices—with more fish, beans, peas, nuts, and seeds.
- **Know the limits on fats, salt, and sugars.** Read the Nutrition Facts label on foods. Look for foods low in saturated fats and trans fats. Choose and prepare foods and beverages with little salt (sodium) or added sugars (caloric sweeteners).

Food and Physical Activity Balance

Find your balance between food and physical activity. Becoming a healthier you is not just about eating healthy—it's also about physical activity. Regular physical activity is important for your overall health and fitness. It also helps you control body weight by balancing the calories you take in as food with the calories you expend each day.

- Be physically active for at least 30 minutes most days of the week.
- Increasing the intensity or the amount of time that you are physically active can have even greater health benefits and may be needed to control body weight. About 60 minutes a day may be needed to prevent weight gain.
- Children and teenagers should be physically active for 60 minutes every day, or almost every day.

If you eat 100 more food calories a day than you burn, you'll gain about one pound in a month. That's about ten pounds in a year. The bottom line is that to lose weight, it's important to reduce calories and increase physical activity.

Get the Most Nutrition from Calories

Get the most nutrition out of your calories. There is a right number of calories for you to eat each day. This number depends on your age, activity level, and whether you're trying to gain, maintain, or lose weight. You could use up the entire amount on a few high-calorie items, but chances are you won't get the full range of vitamins and nutrients your body needs to be healthy.

Choose the most nutritionally rich foods you can from each food group each day—those packed with vitamins, minerals, fiber, and other nutrients but lower in calories. Pick foods like fruits, vegetables, whole grains, and fat-free or low-fat milk and milk products more often.

Know the Facts about Nutrition

Most packaged foods have a Nutrition Facts label. For a healthier you, use this tool to make smart food choices quickly and easily. Try these tips:

- Keep these low: saturated fats, trans fats, cholesterol, and sodium.
- Get enough of these: potassium, fiber, vitamins A and C, calcium, and iron.
- Use the % Daily Value (DV) column when possible: 5% DV or less is low, 20% DV or more is high.

Check servings and calories. Look at the serving size and how many servings you are actually consuming. If you double the servings you eat, you double the calories and nutrients, including the % DV.

Make your calories count. Look at the calories on the label and compare them with what nutrients you are also getting to decide whether the food is worth eating. When one serving of a single food item has over 400 calories per serving, it is high in calories.

Don't sugarcoat it. Since sugars contribute calories with few, if any, nutrients, look for foods and beverages low in added sugars. Read the ingredient list and make sure that added sugars are not one of the first few ingredients. Some names for added sugars (caloric sweeteners) include sucrose, glucose, high fructose corn syrup, corn syrup, maple syrup, and fructose.

Know your fats. Look for foods low in saturated fats, trans fats, and cholesterol to help reduce the risk of heart disease (5% DV or less is low, 20% DV or more is high). Most of the fats you eat should be polyunsaturated and monounsaturated fats. Keep total fat intake between 20% to 35% of calories.

Reduce sodium (salt), increase potassium. Research shows that eating less than 2,300 milligrams of sodium (about one tsp of salt) per day may reduce the risk of high blood pressure. Most of the sodium people eat comes from processed foods, not from the saltshaker. Also look for foods high in potassium, which counteracts some of sodium's effects on blood pressure.

Food Safety

Play it safe with food. Know how to prepare, handle, and store food safely to keep you and your family safe:

- Clean hands, food contact surfaces, fruits, and vegetables. To avoid spreading bacteria to other foods, meat and poultry should not be washed or rinsed.
- Separate raw, cooked, and ready-to-eat foods while shopping, preparing, or storing.
- Cook meat, poultry, and fish to safe internal temperatures to kill microorganisms.
- Chill perishable foods promptly and thaw foods properly.

Alcohol

If you choose to drink alcohol, do so in moderation. Moderate drinking means up to one drink a day for women and up to two drinks for men. Twelve ounces of regular beer, five ounces of wine, or 1½ ounces of 80-proof distilled spirits count as a drink for purposes of explaining moderation. Remember that alcoholic beverages have calories but are low in nutritional value.

Generally, anything more than moderate drinking can be harmful to your health. And some people, or people in certain situations, shouldn't drink at all. If you have questions or concerns, talk to your doctor or healthcare provider.

Section 57.2

Fundamentals of Feeding Children

In our culture, like so many others, food and feeding is equated with love and nurturing. The feeding process, when done in a mutually respecting manner, is one of the quickest ways of building and maintaining a positive, trusting relationship. But so often what starts out as a symbol of love and nurturing, ends up for many parents as a power struggle at the dinner table.

One such scenario may be fueled by concerns that a child is not eating enough. The parent is concerned that the child is undernourished and on the verge of starvation. Here begins the all too common mealtime activity between parents and child of gentle coaxing, begging, pleading, and outright bribery. It is not uncommon for the frustrated parent to resort to an unsuccessful attempt at making their child eat. These scenes will often finally culminate in a test of wills, and what might appear to be a standoff.

Under these circumstances, one of two things may happen. Either the child unwillingly accepts the food—or flatly refuses it. The parent involved may feel frustrated or inadequate. She or he may feel like a total failure at the seemingly simple task of feeding their child with love and good sense. Even more devastating is the feeling of personal rejection, especially if the child accepts the same food from someone else.

Children do not like to see the person who guides and loves them frustrated or despairing of them. The child also does not enjoy having to go to bed scared or defiant as a way of showing that their caregiver is not listening to their needs.

Feeding Relationships

The above scenario is an example of a feeding relationship gone wrong. Generally speaking, a feeding relationship is created when a caregiver prepares and offers food to a child. The child responds to the offer by accepting or rejecting the offer. The nature of the relationship is further re-enforced when the caregiver in turn responds to the child in a more or less supportive manner which then leads to a counter move by the child and so on. Over time, the predominant feelings, whether positive or negative, that result from these feeding interactions will determine whether this is a positive, respectful, and supportive feeding relationship, or one more likely to result in a negative relationship with food for the child, and potentially also a negative relationship between the caregiver and the child.

Common Feeding or Eating Problems

There is convincing evidence to suggest that 25–30% of children are affected by feeding or eating problems, which in turn often impacts both physical and emotional growth and development. Common problems include poor food acceptance at all ages, under-eating or overeating compared to actual physiological or emotional need, vomiting or gagging at the sight of certain foods, failure to progress appropriately to solids and table foods (in the absence of a medical explanation), excessive finickiness, and what can be characterized as unacceptable behaviors by the child at mealtimes.

These can be frustrating issues for parents to deal with. Part of the frustration comes from not knowing if or when it is appropriate to intervene in the situation, or to let it run its course. After all, what toddler do you know who is not a picky eater at some stage? Who ever said teenagers are supposed to love vegetables? The dislike of broccoli is genetic, isn't it?

In order to encourage physical growth and healthy psychosocial development, it is important to be able to distinguish between normal versus problematic feeding and eating behaviors. The other frustrating aspect of opening Pandora's box and asking whether or not there is a problem, is, if it is determined that there is a problem, then what do you do about it? (We are ever mindful of the fact that forced feeding is unethical and illegal in Canada. But so too is letting a child starve). No wonder parents caught in these feeding dilemmas feel like they are in a Catch-22 situation.

Here then are my top five most often overlooked fundamentals about children's eating and feeding children. These are taken from my experience working as an outpatient dietitian in the eating disorders clinic and the out-patient pediatric department of a large urban hospital, as well as in my private practice. In addition to overlooking these fundamentals, parents frequently experience some level of difficulty in honoring the principle known as the Division of Responsibility in Feeding. Ellen Satter, the foremost clinician and author in the area of feeding children, developed the Division of Responsibility in Feeding over 30 years ago. The principle holds that parents (caregivers) are responsible for selecting, preparing, and offering food to their children. They are also responsible for determining mealtime structure such as times and place where the meals and snacks will be eaten. The child's responsibility is to choose to eat from the selection offered, or to choose not to eat. When the Division of Responsibility is blurred, a mealtime struggle often results.

Five Fundamentals about Children's Eating

Children Depend on Adults in Order to Achieve Their Eating Competence

Children will take the easy way out if they are not offered the appropriate level of eating mastery challenges at the right time. Awareness of the different levels of food mastery expectations and how they apply to a child's growth, development, and sense of confidence is key to helping the child become successful at the task of eating. For instance, the timing of the transition to solid foods, as well as the pace of the increase in textures, will set the stage for future acceptance or rejection of new foods and new textures. If you are struggling with a picky eater, regardless of age, it is still not too late to provide them with the opportunity to achieve eating competence. The learning opportunity will be enhanced if presented in a neutral, supportive environment.

Children Need to Know That They Will Be Fed

Given today's rushed lifestyle, the importance of predictability and structure in children's meal and snack times is often overlooked. When much uncertainty surrounds feeding, and if feeding doesn't correspond with their hunger, the industrious child will load up at every opportunity, in defense of the next perceived famine. Predictable meal and snack times also help to regulate physiological hunger and satiety cues.

Children Are Erratic about Their Eating

Even though you have developed a reliable schedule of meal and snack times, depending on your child's age and level of development, erratic eating behavior may occur from time to time. The best advice

I can give is to not panic and automatically stock up on children's vitamin supplements, or worse, try to force them to eat as much as you think they should be hungry for. There is much evidence to support the idea that children regulate their intake over time in order to meet their physiological needs. Continue with your role in the division of responsibility in feeding. That is, keep offering the balanced meal and snack selections you have always offered, and trust that their current and future intake, along with their nutrient stores, will allow for the overall balance that they need to grow.

Children Need to Feel in Control of Their Eating

Fear of the unfamiliar is natural at first. However, children are more prone to experimenting with new food if they know they have an out—that is, there are no significant performance expectations of them regarding these new foods. Therefore, eliminating pressure might in fact serve to pique their curiosity about these foods sooner than you might expect.

Offering food, as opposed to pressuring children to eat, is an extension of your earlier acknowledgement (when they were infants) that they, not you, are in the best position to determine what and how much they are hungry for. This simple but profound act of trust validates the child's sole right and responsibility for determining what and how much they are hungry for, based on their own internally regulated needs. As well, it provides them with the freedom to act accordingly, without fear of reprisal from peers, family members, or the society at large. In my work with clients struggling with eating disorders, it is not surprising to learn that for many, their struggles for control, over their food as well as other aspects of their lives, began at the dinner table at a very early age.

Children Will Accomplish More with Their Eating When the Feeder Does Less

The way the feeder approaches food and eating has a major effect on the likelihood that the nutritional or skill-building goals of the feeding session will be achieved. For instance, children will often shut down and abandon the feeding process if and when the feeder becomes overly involved, or continually undermines their efforts to become an active participant in the process. The role of the feeder is to be:

- present at meal times;
- to provide positive modeling;

- to provide a pleasant meal environment for all;
- to support and encourage current eating skills;
- to gently assist or guide the building of new food mastery skills.

If the feeder is rigid or overly involved in the feeding process, the messages to the child becomes "I don't believe you are capable of figuring this out for yourself. If you cannot get it perfect, then your efforts are not good enough," and "getting nutrition into you is more important to me than your feelings," certainly not the kind of messages that promote high self esteem.

Thus it is clear that the early context in which we are fed can lead to a sense of pleasure, experimentation, and efficacy over our eating behavior. Conversely, poor attention to the needs and wants of a child with regard to eating and autonomy may create ongoing problems with over- or under-control of eating. It is important to keep perspective on the eating behaviors of children in your care, and to focus on their general well-being. Normal eating is not a science: it fluctuates with the energy and emotional needs of the individual.

References and Suggested Reading

Coloroso, B. 1995. *Kids Are Worth It!* Somerville House Publishing. Toronto, Ontario.

Hirschmann, J. R. and L. Zaphiropoulos. 1993. *Preventing Childhood Eating Problems. A practical, positive approach to raising children free of food & weight conflicts.* Gurze Books. Carlsbad: California.

Linscheid, T. R 1986. Disturbance of eating and feeding in D. Drotar (ed.), *New directions in failure to thrive: Implications for research and practice* (pp. 191–218). New York: Plenum.

Satter, E. 1995. Feeding Dynamics: Helping Children to Eat Well. *Journal of Pediatric Health Care July–August.* (pp. 178–184).

Satter, E. 2000. *Child of Mine, Feeding With Love and Food Sense.* Bull Publishing Company. Palo Alto: California.

Satter, E. 1987. *How To Get Your Kid to Eat ....But Not Too Much.* Bull Publishing Company. Palo Alto: California.

Satter, E. 1999. *Secrets of Feeding a Healthy Family.* Kelcy Press. Madison: Wisconsin.

Section 57.3

Eating Well as We Age: Tips for Senior Adults

U.S. Food and Drug Administration (FDA), FDA 05–1107C, 2005.

Eating Well

Many older people have trouble eating well. This section tells why. Then it gives ideas on what you can do about it. Using the food label is one way to eat well. There are others.

Cannot Chew

Do you have trouble chewing? If so, you may have trouble eating foods such as meat, fresh fruits, and vegetables. Table 57.1 offers some suggestions about foods to try to help overcome a problem with chewing.

Table 57.1. Foods to Try for Chewing Problems

Instead of:	Try:
fresh fruit	fruit juices and soft canned fruits, such as applesauce, peaches, and pears
raw vegetables	vegetable juices and creamed and mashed cooked vegetables
meat	ground meat, eggs, milk, cheese, yogurt, and foods made with milk, such as pudding and cream soups
sliced bread	cooked cereals, rice, bread pudding, and soft cookies

Upset Stomach

Too much gas and other stomach problems may make you stay away from foods you think cause the problem. This means you could be missing out on important nutrients, such as vitamins, calcium, fiber, and protein. Table 57.2 offers some suggestions of foods to try if you are having stomach problems.

Table 57.2. Foods to Try for Upset Stomach

Instead of:	Try:
milk	milk foods that may not bother you, such as cream soups, pudding, yogurt, and cheese
vegetables such as cabbage and broccoli	vegetable juices and other vegetables, such as green beans, carrots, and potatoes
fresh fruit	fruit juices and soft canned fruits

If You Cannot Shop

You may have problems shopping for food. Maybe you can't drive anymore. You may have trouble walking or standing for a long time. Possible solutions may include:

- Ask the local food store to bring groceries to your home. Some stores deliver free. Sometimes there is a charge.
- Ask your church or synagogue for volunteer help. Or sign up for help with a local volunteer center.
- Ask a family member or neighbor to shop for you. Or pay someone to do it. Some companies let you hire home health workers for a few hours a week. These workers may shop for you, and do other things. Look for these companies in the Yellow Pages of the phone book under "Home Health Services."

If You Cannot Cook

You may have problems with cooking. It may be hard for you to hold cooking utensils and pots and pans. Or you may have trouble standing for a long time. Possible solutions may include:

- Use a microwave oven to cook frozen dinners, other frozen foods, and foods made up ahead of time by the store.
- Take part in group meal programs, offered through senior citizen programs. Or have meals brought to your home.
- Move to a place where someone else will cook, such as a family member's home or a home for senior citizens. To find out about senior citizen group meals and home-delivered meals, call Eldercare Locator services at 800-677-1116. These meals cost little or no money.

If You Have No Appetite

Older people who live alone sometimes feel lonely at mealtimes. This feeling can make you lose your appetite. Or you may not feel like making meals for just yourself. Maybe your food has no flavor or tastes bad. This could be caused by medicines you are taking. Possible solutions may include:

- Eat with family and friends.
- Take part in group meal programs, offered through senior citizen programs.
- Ask your doctor if your medicines could be causing appetite or taste problems. If so, ask about changing medicines.
- Increase the flavor of food by adding spices and herbs.

Money Problems

Not having enough money to buy enough food can keep you from eating well. Possible solutions include:

- Buy low-cost food, such as dried beans and peas, rice, and pasta. Or buy foods that contain these items, such as split pea soup, canned beans, and rice.
- Use coupons for money off on foods you like.
- Buy foods on sale. Also buy store-brand foods. They often cost less.
- Find out if your local church or synagogue offers free or low-cost meals.
- Take part in group meal programs, offered through local senior citizen programs. Or have meals brought to your home.
- Get food stamps. Call the food stamp office listed under your county government in the blue pages of the phone book.

Read Food Labels

Look for words that say something healthy about the food. Examples are: "Low Fat," "Cholesterol Free," and "Good Source of Fiber." Also look for words that tell about the relation of food to a disease. A low-fat food may say: "While many factors affect heart disease, diets low in saturated fat and cholesterol may reduce the risk of this disease." The words may be on the front or side of the food package. The FDA makes sure these words are true.

Look for Nutrition Facts

Most food labels tell what kinds and amounts of vitamins, minerals, protein, fat, and other nutrients are in food. This information is called "Nutrition Facts."

- Look at the serving size.
- Find the % Daily Value (DV). The numbers underneath tell how much of each nutrient listed is in one serving.
- About 100% of each nutrient every day is usually healthful. If you're on a special diet, such as a low-sodium or low-fat diet, use the % numbers to pick low-sodium and low-fat food.

Additional Information

U.S. Food and Drug Administration (FDA)
5600 Fishers Lane
Rockville, MD 20857
Toll-Free: 888-INFO-FDA (463-6332)
Website: http://www.fda.gov

Chapter 58

Energy Balance: Appropriate Calorie Intake

Energy is another word for calories. What you eat and drink is energy taken in. What you burn through physical activity is energy put out.

You burn a certain number of calories just by breathing and digesting. A big person burns more calories every day than a small person. You also burn a certain number of calories through your daily routine. For example, children burn calories being students. Adults burn calories being office workers, kindergarten teachers, construction workers, stay-at-home parents, and everything in between. People with active lifestyles burn more than those with not-so-active lifestyles.

- The same amount of energy in and energy out over time = weight stays the same
- More in than out over time = weight gain
- More out than in over time = weight loss

Your energy taken in and put out does not have to balance exactly every day. It's the balance over time that determines whether you can maintain a healthy weight in the long run. And, because children need energy to grow properly, energy balance in children happens when the amount of energy taken in and energy put out supports natural growth without promoting excess weight gain.

"Learn It: What Is Energy Balance?" National Heart, Lung, and Blood Institute (NHLBI), June 2005.

To give you a sense of how many calories—energy taken in—you and your family need see the Table 58.1. This table shows the calorie level health experts recommend by gender and age level, also factoring in a person's overall level of physical activity.

Estimated Calorie Requirements

Table 58.1 shows the estimated amounts of calories needed to maintain energy balance for various gender and age groups at three different levels of physical activity. The estimates are rounded to the nearest 200 calories and were determined using the Institute of Medicine (IOM) equation.

Energy Balance in Real Life

Here's an example of how you can balance your "lifestyle budget." If you know you're going to a party and may eat more high-calorie foods than you normally would, then eat fewer calories for a few days beforehand so it balances out. Or, you can increase your physical activity for the few days before or after the party so you can burn off the extra energy. This same idea also applies to your children. If they will be going to a birthday party where you know they will be eating cake and ice cream and other foods high in fat and added sugar, help them balance their calories the day before and after the party and provide opportunities for them to be more active.

Here's another way of looking at energy balance in real life. Eating just 150 calories more a day than you burn in activity can lead to a gain of five pounds over six months, or ten pounds a year. If you don't want this to happen, or you want to lose the extra weight, you can either reduce your energy taken in or increase your energy put out. Doing both is the best idea.

For example, to reduce energy taken in by 150 calories (for a 150 pound person):

- drink water instead of a 12-ounce regular soda;
- downsize a medium french fries to a small, or substitute a salad.

To increase energy put out by 150 calories:

- shoot hoops for 30 minutes;
- walk two miles in 30 minutes.

Table 58.1. Estimated Calorie Requirements (in Kilocalories) for Each Gender and Age Group at Three Levels of Physical Activity[a]

		Activity Level [b, c, d]		
Gender	**Age (years)**	**Sedentary[b]**	**Moderately Active[c]**	**Active[d]**
Child	2–3	1,000	1,000–1400e	1,000–1,400[e]
Female	4–8	1,200	1,400–1,600	1,400–1,800
	9–13	1,600	1,600–2,000	1,800–2,200
	14–18	1,800	2,000	2,400
	19–30	2,000	2,000–2,200	2,400
	31–50	1,800	2,000	2,400
	51+	1,600	1,800	2,000–2,200
Male	4–8	1,400	1,400–1,600	1,600–2,000
	9–13	1,800	1,800–2,200	2,000–2,600
	14–18	2,200	2,400–2,800	2,800–3,200
	19–30	2,400	2,600–2,800	3,000
	31–50	2,200	2,400–2,600	2,800–3,000
	51+	2,000	2,200–2,400	2,400–2,800

Source: HHS/USDA Dietary Guidelines for Americans, 2005

[a] These levels are based on Estimated Energy Requirements (EER) from the Institute of Medicine Dietary Reference Intakes macronutrients report, 2002, calculated by gender, age, and activity level for reference-sized individuals. “Reference size,” as determined by IOM, is based on median height and weight for ages up to age 18 years of age and median height and weight for that height to give a BMI of 21.5 for adult females and 22.5 for adult males.

[b] Sedentary means a lifestyle that includes only the light physical activity associated with typical day-to-day life.

[c] Moderately active means a lifestyle that includes physical activity equivalent to walking about 1.5 to 3 miles per day at 3 to 4 miles per hour, in addition to the light physical activity associated with typical day-to-day life.

[d] Active means a lifestyle that includes physical activity equivalent to walking more than 3 miles per day at 3 to 4 miles per hour, in addition to the light physical activity associated with typical day-to-day life.

[e] The calorie ranges shown are to accommodate needs of different ages within the group. For children and adolescents, more calories are needed at older ages. For adults, fewer calories are needed at older ages.

Additional Information

National Heart, Lung, and Blood Institute
P.O. Box 30105
Bethesda, MD 20824-0105
Phone: 301-592-8573
TTY: 240-629-3255
Fax: 240-629-3246
Website: http://www.nhlbi.nih.gov
E-mail: nhlbiinfo@nhlbi.nih.gov

We Can! (Ways to Enhance Children's Activity and Nutrition)
Website: http://www.nhlbi.nih.gov/health/public/heart/obesity/wecan

National program with practical tools, tips, and activities aimed at improving food choices, increasing physical activity and reducing screen time for children.

Chapter 59

Relationship between Eating Disorders and Obesity

Eating disorders and obesity are usually seen as very different problems, but actually share many similarities. In fact, eating disorders, obesity, and other weight-related disorders may overlap as girls move from one problem, such as unhealthy dieting, to another, such as obesity.

Eating disorders and obesity are part of a range of weight-related problems. These problems include anorexia nervosa, bulimia nervosa, anorexic and bulimic behaviors, unhealthy dieting practices, binge eating disorder, and obesity. Adolescent girls may suffer from more than one disorder or may progress from one problem to another at varying degrees of severity. It is important to understand this range of weight-related problems in order to avoid causing one disorder, such as bulimia, while trying to prevent another, such as obesity.[1]

Body dissatisfaction and unhealthy dieting practices are linked to the development of eating disorders, obesity, and other problems. High numbers of adolescent girls are reporting that they are dissatisfied with their bodies and are trying to lose weight in unhealthy ways, including skipping meals, fasting, and using tobacco. A smaller number of girls are even resorting to more extreme methods such as self-induced vomiting, diet pills, and laxative use.[2]

These attitudes and behaviors place girls at a greater risk for eating disorders, obesity, poor nutrition, growth impairments, and emotional

---

"Eating Disorders and Obesity: How Are They Related?" Office on Women's Health, October 2005.

problems such as depression.[3] Research shows, for example, that overweight girls are more concerned about their weight, more dissatisfied with their bodies, and more likely to diet than their normal-weight peers.[4]

Binge eating is common among people with eating disorders and people who are obese. People with bulimia binge eat and then purge by vomiting, using laxatives, or other means. Binge eating that is not followed by purging may also be considered an eating disorder and can lead to weight gain. More than one-third of obese individuals in weight-loss treatment programs report difficulties with binge eating.[5] This type of eating behavior contributes to feelings of shame, loneliness, poor self-esteem, and depression.[6] Conversely, these kinds of feelings can cause binge eating problems.[7] A person may binge or overeat for emotional reasons, including stress, depression, and anxiety.[8]

Depression, anxiety, and other mood disorders are associated with both eating disorders and obesity. Adolescents who are depressed may be at an increased risk of becoming obese. One recent study found that depressed adolescents were two times more likely to become obese at the one year follow-up than teens who did not suffer from depression.[9] In addition, many people with eating disorders suffer from clinical depression, anxiety, personality or substance abuse disorders, or in some cases obsessive-compulsive disorder.[10] Therefore, a mental health professional may need to be involved in treating an adolescent who is obese or suffers from an eating disorder or other weight-related problem.

The environment may contribute to both eating disorders and obesity. The mass media, family, and peers may be sending children and adolescents mixed messages about food and weight that encourage disordered eating.[11] Today's society idealizes thinness and stigmatizes fatness, yet high-calorie foods are widely available and heavily advertised.[12] At the same time, levels of physical activity are at record lows as television and computers replace more active leisure activities, travel by automobile has replaced walking, and many communities lack space for walking and recreation.[13]

Health Risks

> "Most teens don't suffer from either anorexia or obesity. They are more likely to engage in disordered eating behaviors such as bingeing, purging, and dieting. These behaviors are associated with serious physical and emotional health problems. We've got to get back to three square meals a day, healthy meal planning,

nutritious snacks, and regular physical activity."[14] —Richard Kreipe, M.D., Chief, Division of Adolescent Medicine, University of Rochester Medical Center

Eating disorders may lead to the following concerns:

- stunted growth
- delayed menstruation
- damage to vital organs such as the heart and brain
- nutritional deficiencies, including starvation
- cardiac arrest
- emotional problems such as depression and anxiety

Obesity increases the risk for the following:

- high blood pressure
- stroke
- cardiovascular disease
- gallbladder disease
- diabetes
- respiratory problems
- arthritis
- cancer
- emotional problems such as depression and anxiety

"Changing habits is never easy, but switching to a healthier diet and regular physical activity will bring children and their families many benefits, including improved health, more energy, and a better quality of life."[15] —Jonelle C. Rowe, M.D., Office on Women's Health

Help Adolescents Develop Healthy Eating Attitudes and Behaviors

Be a positive role model. Children look to parents and other adult caregivers as they develop their own attitudes and behaviors toward eating and weight. For example, children of overweight parents are more likely to be overweight than their peers. Also, daughters of mothers who diet are more likely to diet than other girls.[16] Teach young people how to eat healthily through your own actions. Avoid unhealthy habits such as skipping meals to lose weight, complaining about your body, or using food as a reward.

Help children learn to control their own eating. Parents and other adults can help children get in touch with their feelings of hunger and fullness. For example, encourage young people to stop eating when satisfied. Avoid forcing children to eat certain foods, requiring that they clean their plates, or forbidding particular foods, as it may even increase their preference for and intake of those foods.[17] Studies show that when mothers try to restrict their children's food, the children actually tend to eat more when they are not being supervised.[18]

Offer young people a variety of healthy foods at meal and snack times. Plan meals in advance, and make sure they include vegetables, whole grains, protein, and other foods that are low in sugar and saturated fat. Pack a healthy school lunch for your child. Keep plenty of healthy snacks such as nuts and fruit available at home.

Eat dinner together as a family most days of the week. Meals are an important social activity, and eating together helps parents and caregivers keep track of what young people are eating, as well as their activities and moods. Make mealtime a relaxed and enjoyable occasion.

Be aware of your child's emotional health. Depression, anxiety, and other mood disorders are associated with obesity, eating disorders, and other weight-related problems. Consult a mental health professional if you think your child may be suffering from a more serious emotional problem than typical adolescent mood swings.

Provide opportunities for children to participate in sports, dance, swimming, or other physical activities. Take your child regularly to parks, beaches, and other places where he or she can be physically active. Take walks, hikes, or bike rides as a family. Keep exercise clothing and equipment available. Limit and monitor time spent watching television, which encourages sedentary behavior and exposes children to junk food advertisements. Remove televisions from kids' bedrooms.

Counteract harmful media messages about body image. Watch television with children and talk about messages regarding body image.

Discuss how advertisers use thin models to market products and manipulate photos and other images to make bodies look perfect. Praise the child for his or her talents and abilities, and encourage a focus on health rather than on appearance.

Don't be afraid to seek help. Take your child to a family doctor if you think he or she has a weight-related problem. A doctor can suggest ways to maintain a healthy weight, assess your child for any underlying emotional problems, or recommend a program that promotes healthy food choices and exercise. Many of these programs include family members, so you may benefit personally from it too.

Did you know?

- In American high schools, 30 percent of girls and 16 percent of boys schools suffer from disordered eating, including bingeing, vomiting, fasting, laxative and diet pill use, and compulsive exercise.[19]
- Childhood obesity has more than tripled in the last 30 years. By the year 2000, 15 percent of children and adolescents ages 6 to 19 were obese.[20]
- Studies suggest that about 70 percent of overweight adolescents will become obese adults.[21]
- A personal or family history of obesity is a risk factor for later development of bulimia.[22]
- The average child in the U.S. watches 10,000 television advertisements for food each year, 95% of which are for foods in one of four categories: sugared cereals, candy, fast foods, and soft drinks.[23]

The Diet Trap

- The risk for obesity may be 324 percent greater for adolescent girls who describe themselves as dieters than girls who do not diet.[24]
- Up to one in four 11-year-old girls have already tried to diet at least once.[25]
- Children who diet may actually end up gaining more weight in the long term than children who do not diet. This is because

dieting may cause a cycle of restrictive eating, followed by overeating or binge eating.[26]

- People who are obese or at risk of becoming obese are more likely to use unhealthy weight loss practices, such as vomiting and using diet pills or laxatives.[27]
- Disordered eating and dieting have been linked to serious risk-taking behaviors such as drug, alcohol and tobacco use, delinquency, unprotected sexual activity, dating violence, and suicide attempts.[28]

> "...the potential consequences of body dissatisfaction and unhealthy weight control behaviors are of considerable public health significance, because these negative cognitions and behaviors are associated with the development of both eating disorders and obesity."[29] —Dianne Neumark-Sztainer, Ph.D., M.P.H., R.D., Division of Epidemiology, University of Minnesota School of Public Health

Definitions

Anorexia nervosa is self-starvation. People with this disorder eat very little even though they are thin. They have an intense and overpowering fear of body fat and weight gain.

Binge eating disorder means eating large amounts of food in a short period of time, usually alone, without being able to stop when full. The overeating and bingeing are often accompanied by feeling out of control and followed by feelings of depression, guilt, or disgust.

Body image is how you see yourself when you look in the mirror or picture yourself in your mind.

Bulimia nervosa is characterized by cycles of binge eating and purging, either by vomiting or taking laxatives or diuretics (water pills). People with bulimia have a fear of body fat even though their size and weight may be normal.

Disordered eating refers to troublesome eating behaviors, such as restrictive dieting, bingeing, or purging, which occur less frequently or are less severe than those required to meet the full criteria for the diagnosis of an eating disorder.

Obesity means having an abnormally high proportion of body fat. A person is considered obese if he or she has a body mass index (BMI) of 30 or greater. BMI is calculated by dividing a person's weight in kilograms by height in meters squared.

Overweight refers to an excess of body weight compared to set standards. The excess weight may come from muscle, bone, fat, or body water. A person can be overweight without being obese (for example, athletes who have a lot of muscle). However, many people who are overweight are considered obese due to excess fat on their bodies. A person may be considered overweight if he or she has a BMI of 25–29.9.

End Notes

1. Neumark-Sztainer, D. "Obesity and Eating Disorder Prevention: An Integrated Approach?" *Adolescent Medicine*, Feb;14(1): 159–73 (Review), 2003.
2. Neumark-Sztainer, D., Story, M., Hannan, P.J., et al. "Weight-Related Concerns and Behaviors Among Overweight and Non-Overweight Adolescents: Implications for Preventing Weight-Related Disorders." *Archives of Pediatrics and Adolescent Medicine*, Feb;156(2):171–8, 2002.
3. Neumark-Sztainer, D. "Obesity and Eating Disorder Prevention: An Integrated Approach?" 2003.
4. Burrows, A., Cooper, M. "Possible Risk Factors in the Development of Eating Disorders in Overweight Pre-Adolescent Girls." *International Journal of Obesity and Related Metabolic Disorders*, Sept;26(9):1268–1273, 2002; Davison, K.K., Markey, C.N., Birch, L.L. "Etiology of Body Dissatisfaction and Weight Concerns Among 5-year-old Girls." *Appetite*, Oct;35(2):143–151, 2000; Vander Wal, J.S., Thelen, M.H. "Eating and Body Image Concerns Among Obese and Average-Weight Children." *Addictive Behavior*, Sept–Oct;25(5):775–778, 2000.
5. Yanovski, S.Z. "Binge Eating in Obese Persons." In Fairburn, C.G., Brownell, K.D. (eds), *Eating Disorders and Obesity, 2nd ed*. New York: Guilford Press, 403–407, 2002.
6. Waller, G. "The Psychology of Binge Eating." In Fairburn, C.G., Brownell, K.D. (eds) *Eating Disorders and Obesity, 2nd ed*. New York: Guilford Press, 98–102, 2002.

7. Fairburn, C., *Overcoming Binge Eating*. New York: The Guilford Press, 1995, pp. 80–99.

8. Goodman, E, Whitaker, R. "A Prospective Study of the Role of Depression in the Development and Persistence of Adolescent Obesity." *Pediatrics*. 2002 Sep;110(3):497–504. Lumeng JC, Gannon K, Cabral HJ, Frank DA, Zuckerman B. "Association between clinically meaningful behavior problems and overweight in children." *Pediatrics*. 2003 Nov;112(5):1138–45.

9. Goodman, E., Whitaker, R.C. "A Prospective Study of the Role of Depression in the Development and Persistence of Adolescent Obesity." *Pediatrics*. Sep;110(3):497–504, 2002.

10. National Mental Health Association. "Teen Eating Disorders." 1997.

11. Irving, L.M., Neumark-Sztainer, D. "Integrating the Prevention of Eating Disorders and Obesity: Feasible or Futile?" *Preventive Medicine*, 34:299–309, 2002. Stice, E. "Sociocultural Influences on Body Image and Eating Disturbance." In Fairburn, C.G., Brownell, K.D. (eds) *Eating Disorders and Obesity, 2nd ed*. New York: Guilford Press, 103–107, 2002.

12. Battle, E.K., Brownell, K.D. "Confronting a Rising Tide of Eating Disorders and Obesity: Treatment vs. Prevention and Policy." *Addictive Behavior*, 21:755–65 (Review), 1996.

13. French, S.A, Story, M., Jeffery, R. "Environmental Influences on Eating and Physical Activity." *Annual Review of Public Health*, 22:309–35 (Review), 2001.

14. Kreipe, R. Personal communication. November 9, 2003.

15. Rowe, J.C. Personal communication. October 31, 2003.

16. Steinberg, A.B., Phares, V. "Family Functioning, Body Image, and Eating Disturbances." In Thompson, J.K., Smolak, L. (eds), *Body Image, Eating Disorders, and Obesity in Youth*. Washington, DC: American Psychological Association, 127–147, 2001.

17. Fisher, J.O., Birch, L.L. "Early Experience with Food and Eating: Implications for the Development of Eating Disorders." In Thompson, J.K., Smolak, L. (eds), *Body Image, Eating Disorders, and Obesity in Youth*. Washington, DC: American Psychological Association, 23–39, 2001.

18. Birch, L. "Acquisition of Food Preferences and Eating Patterns in Children." In Fairburn, C.G., Brownell, K.D. (eds), *Eating Disorders and Obesity, 2nd ed.* New York: Guilford Press, 75–79, 2002.

19. Austin, B., Ziyadeh, N., Leliher, A., Zachary, A. & Forman, S. "Screening High School Students for Eating Disorders: Results of a National Initiative." *Journal of Adolescent Health*, 28(2), 96, 2001.

20. Ogden, C.L., Flegal, K.M., Carroll, M.D., Johnson, C.L. "Prevalence and Trends in Overweight Among US Children and Adolescents, 1999-2000." *JAMA.* 2002;288:1728–1732.

21. Dietz, W.H. "Medical Consequences of Obesity in Children and Adolescents." In Fairburn, C.G., Brownell, K.D., (eds), *Eating Disorders and Obesity, 2nd ed.* New York: Guilford Press, 473–476, 2002.

22. Fairburn, C.G., Stice, E., Cooper, Z., Doll, H.A., Norman, P.A., O'Connor, M.E. "Understanding Persistence in Bulimia Nervosa: A 5-year Naturalistic Study." *Journal of Consulting and Clinical Psychology*, Feb;71(1):103–9, 2003.

23. Brownell, K.D. "The Environment and Obesity." In Fairburn, C.G., Brownell, K.D. (eds) *Eating Disorders and Obesity, 2nd ed.* New York: Guilford Press, 403–407, 2002.

24. Stice, E., Cameron, R.P., Killen, J.D., et al. "Naturalistic Weight-Reduction Efforts Prospectively Predict Growth in Relative Weight and Onset of Obesity among Female Adolescents." *Journal of Consulting and Clinical Psychology*, Dec;67(6):967–74, 1999.

25. Hill, A.J. "Prevalence and Demographics of Dieting." In Fairburn, C.G., Brownell, K.D. (eds) *Eating Disorders and Obesity, 2nd ed.* New York: Guilford Press, 80–83, 2002.

26. Field, A.E., Austin, S.B., Taylor, C.B., Malspeis, S., Rosner, B., Rockett, H.R., Gillman, M.W., Colditz, G.A. "Relation Between Dieting and Weight Change Among Preadolescents and Adolescents." *Pediatrics*, Oct;112(4):900–6, 2003.

27. Neumark-Sztainer, D., Story, M., Falkner, N.H., et al. "Sociodemographic and Personal Characteristics of Adolescents Engaged in Weight Loss and Weight/Muscle Gain Behaviors: Who

is Doing What?" *Preventive Medicine*, 28:40, 1999. Neumark-Sztainer, D., Story, M., French, S., Hannan, P., Resknick, M., Blum, R.W. "Psychosocial Concerns and Health-Compromising Behaviors among Overweight and Non-overweight Adolescents." *Obesity Research*, May;5(3):237–49, 1997.

28. Neumark-Sztainer, D., Story, M., French, S.A. "Covariations of an Unhealthy Weight Loss Behaviors and Other High-Risk Behaviors among Adolescents." *Archives of Pediatric Adolescent Medicine*, 150(3), 304–308, 1996.

29. Neumark-Sztainer, D. "Obesity and Eating Disorder Prevention: An Integrated Approach?" 2003.

Additional Information

American Dietetic Association
120 S. Riverside Plaza, Suite 2000
Chicago, IL 60606-6995
Toll-Free: 800-877-1600
Website: http://www.eatright.org

Body Positive
P.O. Box 7801
Berkeley, CA 94707
Phone: 510-528-0101
Fax: 510-558-0979
Website: http://www.thebodypositive.org
E-mail: info@thebodypositive.org

National Eating Disorders Association (NEDA)
603 Stewart St. Suite 803
Seattle, WA 98101
Toll-Free: 800-931-2237
Phone: 206-382-3587
Website: http://www.nationaleatingdisorders.org
E-mail: info@NationalEatingDisorders.org

National Heart, Lung, and Blood Institute (NHLBI)
P.O. Box 30105
Bethesda, MD 20824-0105
Phone: 301-592-8573
TTY: 240-629-3255

Fax: 240-629-3246
Website: http://www.nhlbi.nih.gov
E-mail: nhlbiinfo@nhlbi.nih.gov

National Institute of Diabetes and Digestive and Kidney Diseases (NIDDK)
National Institutes of Health
Building 31, Room 9A06
31 Center Drive, MSC 2560
Bethesda, MD 20892-2560
Toll-Free: 800-891-5390
Website: http://www.niddk.nih.gov

National Women's Health Information Center (NWHIC)
8270 Willow Oaks Corporate Drive
Fairfax, VA 22031
Toll-Free: 800-994-9662
Toll-Free TDD: 888-220-5446
Website: http://www.4woman.gov

Weight-Control Information Network (WIN)
1 Win Way
Bethesda, MD 20892-3665
Toll-Free: 877-946-4627
Phone: 202-828-1025
Fax: 202-828-1028
Website: http://win.niddk.nih.gov
E-mail: win@info.niddk.nih.gov

Chapter 60

Supervised Weight Loss Is Not Linked to Eating Disorders in Overweight Adults

Dieting, defined as the intentional and sustained restriction of caloric intake to reduce body weight or change body shape, does not appear to cause eating disorders or other psychological dysfunction in overweight and obese adults. The National Task Force on Prevention and Treatment of Obesity reached this conclusion as a result of a comprehensive literature review. Empirical studies evaluating weight loss treatment, very low calorie diets (VLCD), weight cycling, prescription medications, and non-dieting approaches do not support concerns that dieting may lead to or worsen eating disorders in overweight and obese adults, the task force reported in the September 25, 2000 *Archives of Internal Medicine*.

Such concerns about the relationship of dieting to eating disorders originated with an experiment conducted during World War II with normal weight subjects. Young men who ate a semi-starvation diet for six months developed negative emotional reactions including depression, irritability, and anger, and a few engaged in binge eating behavior that persisted even after they had free access to food. These results are often assumed to apply to overweight and obese adults, among whom binge eating disorder (BED) is the most common eating disorder. A key question for the task force was whether weight-loss treatment leads to increased binge eating in these individuals. Obese adults

---

"Dieting Not Linked to Eating Disorders in Overweight Adults," Weight-Control Information Network (WIN), National Institute of Diabetes and Digestive and Kidney Diseases (NIDDK), 2001. Reviewed in October 2006 by Dr. David A. Cooke, M.D., Diplomate, American Board of Internal Medicine.

enrolled in weight-loss programs that focus on moderate energy restriction, increased physical activity, and group or individual counseling are unlikely to develop binge eating problems, concluded several studies. In contrast, the data suggest that this type of treatment reduces binge eating in those who had recurrent binge eating episodes prior to program enrollment.

Several studies looked at the effect of VLCD ranging from 400 to 800 calories per day on the development of binge eating as a compensatory response to psychological or physiological deprivation. Two studies reported no increase in binge eating among those who were classified as non-binge eaters prior to treatment, and found improvement in eating behavior among binge eaters. One investigation found an increase in self-reported binge eating behavior in previous non-binge eaters after twelve weeks on a liquid diet, although caloric content of these self-reported binge episodes was not collected. Several cross-sectional studies found a consistent, positive link between weight cycling and binge eating. It is unclear from these reports, however, if weight cycling caused the binge eating or if binge eaters were more likely to weight cycle. One study found that weight-cycling women with BED reported greater psychological distress, depression, and lower self-esteem than weight cyclers without BED. Overall, weight cycling does not seem to be associated with clinically significant psychopathologic conditions.

Does dieting and weight loss in overweight and obese adults cause psychological problems, as early studies suggest? Numerous studies conducted over the last twenty-five years show reductions in symptoms of depression and anxiety—or at least no worsening of these conditions—in obese patients undergoing supervised weight loss treatment. Almost half of the men and women enrolled in the National Weight Control Registry (a registry of people who have lost at least thirty pounds and maintained the loss for more than a year) lost weight on their own without a formal program. Measures of mood, distress, restraint, disinhibition, binge eating, and purging among these individuals indicate that many people who have lost weight through a variety of methods do not experience significant psychological distress or disordered eating behaviors.

Non-dieting approaches to weight control have become more common in response to the generally poor results of long-term weight-loss programs. These approaches focus on helping people recognize and eat in response to the body's natural hunger and satiety signals, and increase self-esteem and positive body image through self-acceptance. Non-dieting approaches appear to result in improved self-esteem, mood, and eating behavior—changes that are comparable to those of traditional weight loss treatments. However, these approaches do not seem to lead to clinically significant short- or long-term weight loss or improvement in weight-related illnesses like hypertension or type 2 diabetes.

Based on these studies, the task force concluded that dieting does not induce eating disorders or other psychological dysfunction in overweight and obese adults. It also found that such concerns should not discourage overweight adults from eating fewer calories and being more active to lose a moderate amount of weight or prevent additional weight gain.

The full report appeared in the September 25, 2000 issue of *Archives of Internal Medicine.*

Additional Information

Weight-Control Information Network (WIN)
1 Win Way
Bethesda, MD 20892-3665
Toll-Free: 877-946-4627
Phone: 202-828-1025
Fax: 202-828-1028
Website: http://win.niddk.nih.gov
E-mail: win@info.niddk.nih.gov

Chapter 61

Effective Weight Management Techniques

Weight Management Techniques

Effective weight control involves multiple techniques and strategies including dietary therapy, physical activity, behavior therapy, pharmacotherapy, and surgery as well as combinations of these strategies. Relevant treatment strategies can also be used to foster long-term weight control.

Some strategies such as modifying dietary intake and physical activity can also have impact on obesity-related comorbidities or risk factors. A low calorie diet modifies calorie intake and reduces saturated fat, total fat, and cholesterol intake in order to help lower high blood cholesterol levels. The diet also includes the current recommendations for sodium, calcium, and fiber intakes. Increased physical activity is not only important for weight loss and weight-loss maintenance but also impacts other comorbidities and risk factors such as high blood pressure, and high blood cholesterol levels. Reducing body weight in overweight and obese patients not only helps reduce the risk of these comorbidities from developing but also helps in their management.

Weight management techniques need to take into account the needs of individual patients so they should be culturally sensitive and

---

Excerpted from, "The Practical Guide: Identification, Evaluation, and Treatment of Overweight and Obesity in Adults," National Heart, Lung, and Blood Institute (NHLBI) 2000. Updated in October 2006 by Dr. David A. Cooke, M.D., Diplomate, American Board of Internal Medicine.

incorporate the patient's perspectives and characteristics. Treatment of overweight, obesity, and eating disorders is to be taken seriously since it involves treating an individual's disease over the long term as well as making modifications to a way of life for entire families.

Dietary Therapy

Dietary therapy includes instructing patients in the modification of their diets to achieve appropriate caloric intake. Some patients need to reduce caloric intake and others need to maintain or increase caloric intake. A diet that is individually planned to help create a deficit of 500 to 1,000 kcal/day should be an integral part of any program aimed at achieving a weight loss of one to two pounds per week. A key element of the current recommendation is the use of a moderate reduction in caloric intake, which is designed to achieve a slow, but progressive, weight loss. Ideally, caloric intake should be reduced only to the level that is required to maintain weight at a desired level. If this level of caloric intake is achieved, excess weight will gradually decrease. In practice, somewhat greater caloric deficits are used in the period of active weight loss, but diets with a very low calorie content are to be avoided. Finally, the composition of the diet should be modified to minimize other cardiovascular risk factors.

Despite widespread media attention given to particular kinds of popular weight-loss diets (for example, low fat diets or low carbohydrate diets), there is little evidence that any one type of diet is superior. Most direct comparison studies have found fairly similar degrees of weight loss, as well as similar and high drop-out rates. Low-fat diets have been shown to reduce cardiovascular risk with long-term use. It is unclear what effects other popular kinds of diets (such as the Atkins diet) have on long-term health, as no available studies longer than one to two years duration have been performed.

Successful weight management is more likely to occur when consideration is given to a patient's food preferences in tailoring a particular diet. Care should be taken to ensure that all of the recommended dietary allowances are met; this may require the use of a dietary or vitamin supplement. Dietary education is necessary for all weight management diets. Educational efforts should pay particular attention to the following topics:

- energy value of different foods
- food composition—fats, carbohydrates (including dietary fiber), and proteins

- evaluation of nutrition labels to determine caloric content and food composition
- new habits of purchasing
- food preparation
- avoiding overconsumption of high-calorie foods (both high-fat and high-carbohydrate foods)
- adequate water intake
- appropriate portion sizes
- limiting alcohol consumption

Physical Activity

Physical activity should be an integral part of weight-loss therapy and weight maintenance. Initially, moderate levels of physical activity for 30 to 45 minutes, three to five days per week, should be encouraged.

An increase in physical activity is an important component of weight-loss therapy, although it will not lead to a substantially greater weight loss than diet alone over six months. Most weight loss occurs because of decreased caloric intake. Sustained physical activity is most helpful in the prevention of weight regain. In addition, physical activity is beneficial for reducing risks for cardiovascular disease and type 2 diabetes. The practitioner must decide whether exercise testing for cardiopulmonary disease is needed before embarking on a new physical activity regimen. This decision should be based on a patient's age, symptoms, and concomitant risk factors.

For most obese patients, physical activity should be initiated slowly, and the intensity should be increased gradually. Initial activities may be increasing small tasks of daily living such as taking the stairs or walking or swimming at a slow pace. With time—depending on progress, the amount of weight lost, and functional capacity—the patient may engage in more strenuous activities. Some of these include fitness walking, cycling, rowing, cross-country skiing, aerobic dancing, and jumping rope. Jogging provides a high-intensity aerobic exercise, but it can lead to orthopedic injury. If jogging is desired, the patient's ability to do this must first be assessed. The availability of a safe environment for the jogger is also a necessity. Competitive sports, such as tennis and volleyball, can provide an enjoyable form of physical activity for many, but again, care must be taken to avoid injury, especially in older people.

A moderate amount of physical activity can be achieved in a variety of ways. People can select activities that they enjoy and that fit into their daily lives. Because amounts of activity are functions of duration, intensity, and frequency, the same amounts of activity can be obtained in longer sessions of moderately intense activities (such as brisk walking) as in shorter sessions of more strenuous activities (such as running).

A regimen of daily walking is an attractive form of physical activity for many people. The patient can start by walking ten minutes, three days a week, and can build to 30 to 45 minutes of more intense walking at least three days a week and increase to most, if not all, days. With this regimen, an additional 100 to 200 kcal/day of physical activity can be expended. Caloric expenditure will vary depending on the individual's body weight and the intensity of the activity.

This regimen can be adapted to other forms of physical activity, but walking is particularly attractive because of its safety and accessibility. With time, a larger weekly volume of physical activity can be performed that would normally cause a greater weight loss if it were not compensated by a higher caloric intake.

- For the beginner, or someone who leads a very sedentary lifestyle, very light activity would include increased standing activities, room painting, pushing a wheelchair, yard work, ironing, cooking, and playing a musical instrument.
- Light activity would include slow walking (24 min/mile), garage work, carpentry, house cleaning, child care, golf, sailing, and recreational table tennis.
- Moderate activity would include walking a 15-minute mile, weeding and hoeing a garden, carrying a load, cycling, skiing, tennis, and dancing.
- High activity would include jogging a mile in 10 minutes, walking with a load uphill, tree felling, heavy manual digging, basketball, climbing, and soccer.
- Other key activities would include flexibility exercises to attain full range of joint motion, strength or resistance exercises, and aerobic conditioning.

Behavior Therapy

Behavior therapy provides methods for overcoming barriers to compliance with dietary therapy and/or increased physical activity, and these methods are important components of weight management and weight-loss treatment. The importance of individualizing behavioral strategies to the needs of the patient must be emphasized for behavior therapy, as it was for diet and exercise strategies.

In addition, the practitioner must assess the patient's motivation to enter weight management therapy and the patient's readiness to implement the plan. Then the practitioner can take appropriate steps to motivate the patient for treatment.

Pharmacotherapy

The purpose of weight loss and weight maintenance is to reduce health risks. If weight is regained, health risks increase. A majority of patients who lose weight regain it, so the challenge to the patient

Table 61.1. Examples of Moderate Amounts of Physical Activity

Common Chores	Sporting Activities
Washing and waxing a car for 45–60 minutes	Playing volleyball for 45–60 minutes
Washing windows or floors for 45–60 minutes	Playing touch football for 45 minutes
Gardening for 30–45 minutes	Walking 20 min/mile
Wheeling self in wheelchair for 30–40 minutes	Basketball (shooting baskets) for 30 minutes
Pushing a stroller 1½ miles in 30 minutes	Bicycling 5 miles in 30 minutes
Raking leaves for 30 minutes	Dancing fast (social) for 30 minutes
Walking 2 miles in 30 minutes	Water aerobics for 30 minutes
Shoveling snow for 15 minutes	Swimming laps for 20 minutes
Stair walking for 15 minutes	Basketball (playing a game) for 15–20 minutes Jumping rope for 15 minutes Running 1½ miles in 15 minutes

A moderate amount of physical activity is roughly equivalent to physical activity that uses approximately 150 calories of energy per day, or 1,000 calories per week.

† Some activities can be performed at various intensities; the suggested durations correspond to expected intensity of effort.

and the practitioner is to maintain a healthy weight. Because of the tendency to regain weight after weight loss, the use of long-term medication to aid in the treatment of obesity may be indicated for carefully selected patients.

The drugs used to promote weight loss have been anorexiants or appetite suppressants. Three classes of anorexiant drugs have been developed, all of which affect neurotransmitters in the brain. They may be designated as follows: (1) those that affect catecholamines, such as dopamine and norepinephrine; (2) those that affect serotonin; and (3) those that affect more than one neurotransmitter. These drugs work by increasing the secretion of dopamine, norepinephrine, or serotonin into the synaptic neural cleft, by inhibiting the reuptake of these neurotransmitters into the neuron, or by a combination of both mechanisms. Sibutramine inhibits the reuptake of norepinephrine and serotonin. Orlistat is not an appetite suppressant and has a different mechanism of action; it blocks about one-third of fat absorption. Very few trials longer than six months have been done with any of these drugs.

There are few long-term studies that evaluate the safety or efficacy of most currently approved weight-loss medications. Only patients who are at increased medical risk because of their weight should use weight-loss medications; they should not be used for cosmetic weight loss.

There is great interest in weight-loss drugs among consumers. Because of the possibility of serious adverse effects, it is incumbent upon the practitioner to use drug therapy with caution. Herbal medications are not recommended as part of a weight-loss program. These preparations have unpredictable amounts of active ingredients and unpredictable—and potentially harmful—effects.

Drugs should be used only as part of a comprehensive program that includes behavior therapy, diet, and physical activity. Appropriate monitoring for side effects must be continued while drugs are part of the regimen. The purpose of these visits is to monitor weight, blood pressure, and pulse, discuss side effects, conduct laboratory tests, and answer the patient's questions.

Weight-Loss Surgery

Weight-loss surgery is an option for weight reduction in patients with clinically severe obesity, such as a BMI greater than or equal to 40, or a BMI greater than or equal to 35 with comorbid conditions. Weight-loss surgery should be reserved for patients in whom other methods of treatment have failed and who have clinically severe obesity (once commonly referred to as morbid obesity). Weight-loss surgery provides medically significant sustained weight loss for more than five years in most patients. Two types of operations have proven to be effective: those that restrict gastric volume (banded gastroplasty) and those that, in addition to limiting food intake, also alter digestion (Roux-en-Y gastric bypass).

Lifelong medical monitoring after surgery is a necessity. An integrated program that provides guidance on diet, physical activity, and psychosocial concerns before and after surgery is necessary. Most patients fare remarkably well with reversal of diabetes, control of hypertension, marked improvement in mobility, return of fertility, cure of pseudotumor cerebri, and significant improvement in quality of life.

Chapter 62

Body Mass Index (BMI) and Waist Circumference

Assessing Your Risk

The body mass index (BMI) is a measure of your weight relative to your height and waist circumference measures abdominal fat. Combining these with information about your additional risk factors yields your risk for developing obesity-associated diseases.

Body Mass Index (BMI)

BMI is a reliable indicator of total body fat, which is related to the risk of disease and death. The score is valid for both men and women but it does have some limits. The limits are:

- It may overestimate body fat in athletes and others who have a muscular build.
- It may underestimate body fat in older persons and others who have lost muscle mass.

To use the BMI table, find the appropriate height in the left-hand column labeled Height. Move across to a given weight. The number at the top of the column is the BMI at that height and weight. Pounds have been rounded off.

"Aim for a Healthy Weight: Assess Your Risk," National Heart, Lung, and Blood Institute (NHLBI), December 2004.

Table 62.1. *Body Mass Index Table (Source: Excerpted from "The Practical Guide: Identification, Evaluation, and Treatment of Overweight and Obesity in Adults," National Heart, Lung, and Blood Institute (NHLBI), NIH Publication Number 00-4084, October 2000.)*

BMI	19	20	21	22	23	24	25	26	27	28	29	30	31	32	33	34	35
Height (inches)								Body Weight (pounds)									
58	91	96	100	105	110	115	119	124	129	134	138	143	148	153	158	162	167
59	94	99	104	109	114	119	124	128	133	138	143	148	153	158	163	168	173
60	97	102	107	112	118	123	128	133	138	143	148	153	158	163	168	174	179
61	100	106	111	116	122	127	132	137	143	148	153	158	164	169	174	180	185
62	104	109	115	120	126	131	136	142	147	153	158	164	169	175	180	186	191
63	107	113	118	124	130	135	141	146	152	158	163	169	175	180	186	191	197
64	110	116	122	128	134	140	145	151	157	163	169	174	180	186	192	197	204
65	114	120	126	132	138	144	150	156	162	168	174	180	186	192	198	204	210
66	118	124	130	136	142	148	155	161	167	173	179	186	192	198	204	210	216
67	121	127	134	140	146	153	159	166	172	178	185	191	198	204	211	217	223
68	125	131	138	144	151	158	164	171	177	184	190	197	203	210	216	223	230
69	128	135	142	149	155	162	169	176	182	189	196	203	209	216	223	230	236
70	132	139	146	153	160	167	174	181	188	195	202	209	216	222	229	236	243
71	136	143	150	157	165	172	179	186	193	200	208	215	222	229	236	243	250
72	140	147	154	162	169	177	184	191	199	206	213	221	228	235	242	250	258
73	144	151	159	166	174	182	189	197	204	212	219	227	235	242	250	257	265
74	148	155	163	171	179	186	194	202	210	218	225	233	241	249	256	264	272
75	152	160	168	176	184	192	200	208	216	224	232	240	248	256	264	272	279
76	156	164	172	180	189	197	205	213	221	230	238	246	254	263	271	279	287

BMI	36	37	38	39	40	41	42	43	44	45	46	47	48	49	50	51	52	53	54
58	172	177	181	186	191	196	201	205	210	215	220	224	229	234	239	244	248	253	258
59	178	183	188	193	198	203	208	212	217	222	227	232	237	242	247	252	257	262	267
60	184	189	194	199	204	209	215	220	225	230	235	240	245	250	255	261	266	271	276
61	190	195	201	206	211	217	222	227	232	238	243	248	254	259	264	269	275	280	285
62	196	202	207	213	218	224	229	235	240	246	251	256	262	267	273	278	284	289	295
63	203	208	214	220	225	231	237	242	248	254	259	265	270	278	282	287	293	299	304
64	209	215	221	227	232	238	244	250	256	262	267	273	279	285	291	296	302	308	314
65	216	222	228	234	240	246	252	258	264	270	276	282	288	294	300	306	312	318	324
66	223	229	235	241	247	253	260	266	272	278	284	291	297	303	309	315	322	328	334
67	230	236	242	249	255	261	268	274	280	287	293	299	306	312	319	325	331	338	344
68	236	243	249	256	262	269	276	282	289	295	302	308	315	322	328	335	341	348	354
69	243	250	257	263	270	277	284	291	297	304	311	318	324	331	338	345	351	358	365
70	250	257	264	271	278	285	292	299	306	313	320	327	334	341	348	355	362	369	376
71	257	265	272	279	286	293	301	308	315	322	329	338	343	351	358	365	372	379	386
72	265	272	279	287	294	302	309	316	324	331	338	346	353	361	368	375	383	390	397
73	272	280	288	295	302	310	318	325	333	340	348	355	363	371	378	386	393	401	408
74	280	287	295	303	311	319	326	334	342	350	358	365	373	381	389	396	404	412	420
75	287	295	303	311	319	327	335	343	351	359	367	375	383	391	399	407	415	423	431
76	295	304	312	320	328	336	344	353	361	369	377	385	394	402	410	418	426	435	443

For adults, overweight and obesity ranges are determined by using weight and height to calculate a number called the body mass index (BMI). BMI is used because, for most people, it correlates with their amount of body fat.

- An adult who has a BMI below 18.5 is considered underweight.
- An adult who has a BMI between 18.5 and 24.9 is considered normal.
- An adult who has a BMI between 25 and 29.9 is considered overweight.
- An adult who has a BMI of 30 or higher is considered obese.

Waist Circumference

Determine your waist circumference by placing a measuring tape snugly around your waist. It is a good indicator of your abdominal fat

Table 62.2. Classification of Overweight and Obesity by BMI, Waist Circumference, and Associated Disease Risks

			Disease Risk Relative to Normal Weight and Waist Circumference	
Weight	**BMI (kg/m2)**	**Obesity Class**	**Men** 102 cm (40 in) or less **Women** 88 cm (35 in) or less	**Men** greater than 102 cm (40 in) **Women** greater than 88 cm (35 in)
Underweight	under 18.5			
Normal	18.5–24.9			
Overweight	25.0–29.9		Increased	High
Obesity	30.0–34.9	I	High	Very High
	35.0–39.9	II	Very High	Very High
Extreme Obesity	40.0+	III	Extremely High	Extremely High

*Disease risk for type 2 diabetes, hypertension, and cardiovascular disease (CVD).

Increased waist circumference can also be a marker for increased risk even in persons of normal weight.

which is another predictor of your risk for developing risk factors for heart disease and other diseases. This risk increases with a waist measurement of over 40 inches in men and over 35 inches in women. Table 62.2 provides you with an idea of whether your BMI combined with your waist circumference increases your risk for developing obesity associated diseases or conditions.

Other Risk Factors

Besides being overweight or obese, there are additional risk factors to consider including the following:

- high blood pressure (hypertension)
- high LDL-cholesterol (bad cholesterol)
- low HDL-cholesterol (good cholesterol)
- high triglycerides
- high blood glucose (sugar)
- family history of premature heart disease
- physical inactivity
- cigarette smoking

Assessment

For people who are considered obese (BMI greater than or equal to 30) or those who are overweight (BMI of 25 to 29.9) and have two or more risk factors, the guidelines recommend weight loss. Even a small weight loss (just ten percent of your current weight) will help to lower your risk of developing diseases associated with obesity. Patients who are overweight, do not have a high waist measurement, and have less than two risk factors may need to prevent further weight gain rather than lose weight.

Talk to your doctor to see if you are at an increased risk and if you should lose weight. Your doctor will evaluate your BMI, waist measurement, and others risk factors for heart disease. People who are overweight or obese have a greater chance of developing high blood pressure, high blood cholesterol or other lipid disorders, type 2 diabetes, heart disease, stroke, and certain cancers, and even a small weight loss (just ten percent of your current weight) will help to lower your risk of developing those diseases.

Additional Information

National Heart, Lung, and Blood Institute

P.O. Box 30105
Bethesda, MD 20824-0105
Phone: 301-592-8573
TTY: 240-629-3255
Fax: 240-629-3246
Website: http://www.nhlbi.nih.gov
E-mail: nhlbiinfo@nhlbi.nih.gov

Weight-Control Information Network (WIN)

1 Win Way
Bethesda, MD 20892-3665
Toll-Free: 877-946-4627
Phone: 202-828-1025
Fax: 202-828-1028
Website: http://win.niddk.nih.gov
E-mail: win@info.niddk.nih.gov

Chapter 63

Weight Loss and Nutrition Myths

The information in this chapter will help clear up confusion about weight loss, nutrition, and physical activity. It may also help you make healthy changes in your eating and physical activity habits. If you have questions not answered here, or if you want to lose weight, talk to your health care provider. A registered dietitian, or other qualified health professional can give you advice on how to follow a healthy eating plan, lose weight safely, and keep it off.

Diet Myths

Myth: Fad diets work for permanent weight loss.

Fact: Fad diets are not the best way to lose weight and keep it off. Fad diets often promise quick weight loss or tell you to cut certain foods out of your diet. You may lose weight at first on one of these diets. But diets that strictly limit calories or food choices are hard to follow. Most people quickly get tired of them and regain any lost weight.

Fad diets may be unhealthy because they may not provide all of the nutrients your body needs. Also, losing weight at a very rapid rate (more than three pounds a week after the first couple weeks) may increase your risk for developing gallstones (clusters of solid material in the gallbladder that can be painful). Diets that provide less than

---

Weight-Control Information Network (WIN), National Institute of Diabetes and Digestive and Kidney Diseases (NIDDK), NIH Publication No. 04–4561, updated March 2006.

800 calories per day also could result in heart rhythm abnormalities, which can be fatal.

- **Tip:** Research suggests that losing ½ to 2 pounds a week by making healthy food choices, eating moderate portions, and building physical activity into your daily life is the best way to lose weight and keep it off. By adopting healthy eating and physical activity habits, you may also lower your risk for developing type 2 diabetes, heart disease, and high blood pressure.

Myth: High-protein, low-carbohydrate diets are a healthy way to lose weight.

Fact: The long-term health effects of a high-protein, low-carbohydrate diet are unknown. But getting most of your daily calories from high-protein foods like meat, eggs, and cheese is not a balanced eating plan. You may be eating too much fat and cholesterol, which may raise heart disease risk. You may be eating too few fruits, vegetables, and whole grains, which may lead to constipation due to lack of dietary fiber. Following a high-protein, low-carbohydrate diet may also make you feel nauseous, tired, and weak.

Eating fewer than 130 grams of carbohydrate a day can lead to the buildup of ketones (partially broken-down fats) in your blood. A buildup of ketones in your blood (called ketosis) can cause your body to produce high levels of uric acid, which is a risk factor for gout (a painful swelling of the joints) and kidney stones. Ketosis may be especially risky for pregnant women and people with diabetes or kidney disease.

- **Tip:** High-protein, low-carbohydrate diets are often low in calories because food choices are strictly limited, so they may cause short-term weight loss. But a reduced-calorie eating plan that includes recommended amounts of carbohydrate, protein, and fat will also allow you to lose weight. By following a balanced eating plan, you will not have to stop eating whole classes of foods, such as whole grains, fruits, and vegetables—and miss the key nutrients they contain. You may also find it easier to stick with a diet or eating plan that includes a greater variety of foods.

Myth: Starches are fattening and should be limited when trying to lose weight.

Fact: Many foods high in starch, like bread, rice, pasta, cereals, beans, fruits, and some vegetables (like potatoes and yams), are low in fat and calories. They become high in fat and calories when eaten in large portion sizes or when covered with high-fat toppings like butter, sour cream, or mayonnaise. Foods high in starch (also called complex carbohydrates) are an important source of energy for your body.

- **Tip:** A healthy eating plan is one that:
  - emphasizes fruits, vegetables, whole grains, and fat-free or low-fat milk and milk products;
  - includes lean meats, poultry, fish, beans, eggs, and nuts;
  - is low in saturated fats, trans fat, cholesterol, salt (sodium), and added sugars.

Myth: Certain foods, like grapefruit, celery, or cabbage soup, can burn fat and make you lose weight.

Fact: No foods can burn fat. Some foods with caffeine may speed up your metabolism (the way your body uses energy, or calories) for a short time, but they do not cause weight loss.

- **Tip:** The best way to lose weight is to cut back on the number of calories you eat and be more physically active.

Myth: Natural or herbal weight-loss products are safe and effective.

Fact: A weight-loss product that claims to be natural or herbal is not necessarily safe. These products are not usually scientifically tested to prove that they are safe or that they work. For example, herbal products containing ephedra (now banned by the U.S. Government) have caused serious health problems and even death. Newer products that claim to be ephedra-free are not necessarily danger-free, because they may contain ingredients similar to ephedra.

- **Tip:** Talk with your health care provider before using any weight-loss product. Some natural or herbal weight-loss products can be harmful.

Meal Myths

Myth: "I can lose weight while eating whatever I want."

Fact: To lose weight, you need to use more calories than you eat. It is possible to eat any kind of food you want and lose weight. You need to limit the number of calories you eat every day and/or increase your daily physical activity. Portion control is the key. Try eating smaller amounts of food and choosing foods that are low in calories.

- **Tip:** When trying to lose weight, you can still eat your favorite foods—as long as you pay attention to the total number of calories that you eat.

Myth: Low-fat or nonfat means no calories.

Fact: A low-fat or nonfat food is often lower in calories than the same size portion of the full-fat product. But many processed low-fat or nonfat foods have just as many calories as the full-fat version of the same food or even more calories. They may contain added sugar, flour, or starch thickeners to improve flavor and texture after fat is removed. These ingredients add calories.

- **Tip:** Read the Nutrition Facts Panel on a food package to find out how many calories are in a serving. Check the serving size too, it may be less than you are used to eating.

Myth: Fast foods are always an unhealthy choice, and you should not eat them when dieting.

Fact: Fast foods can be part of a healthy weight-loss program with a little bit of know-how.

- **Tip:** Avoid supersize combo meals, or split one with a friend. Sip on water or nonfat milk instead of soda. Choose salads and grilled foods, like a grilled chicken breast sandwich or small hamburger. Try a fresco taco (with salsa instead of cheese or sauce) at taco stands. Fried foods, like French fries and fried chicken, are high in fat and calories, so order them only once in a while, order a small portion, or split an order with a friend. Also, use only small amounts of high-fat, high-calorie toppings, like regular mayonnaise, salad dressings, bacon, and cheese.

Myth: Skipping meals is a good way to lose weight.

Fact: Studies show that people who skip breakfast and eat fewer times during the day tend to be heavier than people who eat a healthy breakfast and eat four or five times a day. This may be because people who skip meals tend to feel hungrier later on, and eat more than they normally would. It may also be that eating many small meals throughout the day helps people control their appetites.

- **Tip:** Eat small meals throughout the day that include a variety of healthy, low-fat, low-calorie foods.

Myth: Eating after 8 p.m. causes weight gain.

Fact: It does not matter what time of day you eat. It is what and how much you eat and how much physical activity you do during the whole day that determines whether you gain, lose, or maintain your weight. No matter when you eat, your body will store extra calories as fat.

- **Tip:** If you want to have a snack before bedtime, think first about how many calories you have eaten that day. And try to avoid snacking in front of the television at night it may be easier to overeat when you are distracted by the television.

Physical Activity Myth

Myth: Lifting weights is not good to do if you want to lose weight, because it will make you bulk up.

Fact: Lifting weights or doing strengthening activities like push-ups and crunches on a regular basis can actually help you maintain or lose weight. These activities can help you build muscle, and muscle burns more calories than body fat. So if you have more muscle, you burn more calories—even sitting still. Doing strengthening activities two or three days a week will not bulk you up. Only intense strength training, combined with a certain genetic background, can build very large muscles.

- **Tip:** In addition to doing at least 30 minutes of moderate-intensity physical activity (like walking two miles in 30 minutes) on most days of the week, try to do strengthening activities two to three days a week. You can lift weights, use large rubber bands (resistance bands), do push-ups or sit-ups, or do household or garden tasks that make you lift or dig.

Food Myths

Myth: Nuts are fattening and you should not eat them if you want to lose weight.

Fact: In small amounts, nuts can be part of a healthy weight-loss program. Nuts are high in calories and fat. However, most nuts contain healthy fats that do not clog arteries. Nuts are also good sources of protein, dietary fiber, and minerals including magnesium and copper.

- **Tip:** Enjoy small portions of nuts. One-half ounce of nuts has about 270 calories.

Myth: Eating red meat is bad for your health and makes it harder to lose weight.

Fact: Eating lean meat in small amounts can be part of a healthy weight-loss plan. Red meat, pork, chicken, and fish contain some cholesterol and saturated fat (the least healthy kind of fat). They also contain healthy nutrients like protein, iron, and zinc.

- **Tip:** Choose cuts of meat that are lower in fat and trim all visible fat. Lower fat meats include pork tenderloin and beef round steak, tenderloin, sirloin tip, flank steak, and extra lean ground beef. Also, pay attention to portion size. Three ounces of meat or poultry is the size of a deck of cards.

Myth: Dairy products are fattening and unhealthy.

Fact: Low-fat and nonfat milk, yogurt, and cheese are just as nutritious as whole milk dairy products, but they are lower in fat and calories. Dairy products have many nutrients your body needs. They offer protein to build muscles and help organs work properly, and calcium to strengthen bones. Most milks and some yogurts are fortified with vitamin D to help your body use calcium.

- **Tip:** *The Dietary Guidelines for Americans* recommends consuming three cups per day of fat-free or low-fat milk or equivalent milk products. If you cannot digest lactose (the sugar found in dairy products), choose low-lactose or lactose-free dairy products, or other foods and beverages that offer calcium and vitamin D.
    - Calcium: fortified fruit juice, soy-based beverage, or tofu made with calcium sulfate; canned salmon; dark leafy greens like collards or kale
    - Vitamin D: fortified fruit juice, soy-based beverage, or cereal (getting some sunlight on your skin also gives you a small amount of vitamin D

Myth: Going vegetarian means you are sure to lose weight and be healthier.

Fact: Research shows that people who follow a vegetarian eating plan, on average, eat fewer calories and less fat than non-vegetarians. They also tend to have lower body weights relative to their heights than non-vegetarians. Choosing a vegetarian eating plan with a low fat content may be helpful for weight loss. But vegetarians—like non-vegetarians—can make food choices that contribute to weight gain, like eating large amounts of high-fat, high-calorie foods or foods with little or no nutritional value.

Vegetarian diets should be as carefully planned as non-vegetarian diets to make sure they are balanced. Nutrients that non-vegetarians normally get from animal products, but that are not always found in a vegetarian eating plan, are iron, calcium, vitamin D, vitamin B_{12}, zinc, and protein.

- **Tip:** Choose a vegetarian eating plan that is low in fat and that provides all of the nutrients your body needs. Food and beverage sources of nutrients that may be lacking in a vegetarian diet are listed.
    - Iron: cashews, spinach, lentils, garbanzo beans, fortified bread or cereal
    - Calcium: dairy products, fortified soy-based beverages or fruit juices, tofu made with calcium sulfate, collard greens, kale, broccoli
    - Vitamin D: fortified foods and beverages including milk, soy-based beverages, fruit juices, or cereal
    - Vitamin B_{12}: eggs, dairy products, fortified cereal or soy-based beverages, tempeh, miso (tempeh and miso are foods made from soybeans)
    - Zinc: whole grains (especially the germ and bran of the grain), nuts, tofu, leafy vegetables (spinach, cabbage, lettuce)
    - Protein: eggs, dairy products, beans, peas, nuts, seeds, tofu, tempeh, soy-based burgers

Additional Information

American Dietetic Association
120 S. Riverside Plaza, Suite 2000
Chicago, IL 60606-6995
Toll-Free: 800-877-1600
Website: http://www.eatright.org

Federal Trade Commission
CRC-240
Washington, DC 20580
Toll-Free: 877-FTC-HELP (382-4357)
Phone: 202-326-2222
Website: http://www.ftc.gov

If you don't know whether or not to believe a weight-loss or nutrition claim, check it out. The Federal Trade Commission has information on deceptive weight-loss advertising claims.

Weight-Control Information Network (WIN)
1 Win Way
Bethesda, MD 20892-3665
Toll-Free: 877-946-4627
Phone: 202-828-1025
Fax: 202-828-1028
Website: http://win.niddk.nih.gov
E-mail: win@info.niddk.nih.gov

Chapter 64

Choosing Safe Weight-Loss Programs

Choosing a weight-loss program may be a difficult task. You may not know what to look for in a weight-loss program or what questions to ask. This chapter can help you talk to your health care professional about weight loss and get the best information before choosing a program.

Talk with Your Health Care Professional

If your health care provider tells you that you should lose weight and you want to find a weight-loss program to help you, look for one that is based on regular physical activity and an eating plan that is balanced, healthy, and easy to follow.

You may want to talk with your doctor or other health care professional about controlling your weight before you decide on a weight-loss program. Even if you feel uncomfortable talking about your weight with your doctor, remember that he or she is there to help you improve your health. Here are some tips:

- Tell your provider that you would like to talk about your weight. Share your concerns about any medical conditions you have or medicines you are taking.
- Write down your questions in advance.

"Choosing a Safe and Successful Weight-Loss Program," Weight-Control Information Network (WIN), National Institute of Diabetes and Digestive and Kidney Diseases (NIDDK), NIH Publication No. 03–3700, revised February 2006.

- Bring pen and paper to take notes.
- Bring a friend or family member along for support if this will make you feel more comfortable.
- Make sure you understand what your health care provider is saying. Ask questions if there is something you do not understand.
- Ask for other sources of information like brochures or websites.
- If you want more support, ask for a referral to a registered dietitian, a support group, or a commercial weight-loss program.
- Call your provider after your visit if you have more questions or need help.

Ask Questions

Find out as much as you can about your health needs before joining a weight-loss program. Here are some questions you might want to ask your health care provider.

About Your Weight

- Do I need to lose weight? Or should I just avoid gaining more?
- Is my weight affecting my health?
- Could my excess weight be caused by a medical condition such as hypothyroidism or by a medicine I am taking? (Hypothyroidism is when your thyroid gland does not produce enough thyroid hormone, a condition that can slow your metabolism—how your body creates and uses energy.)

About Weight Loss

- What should my weight-loss goal be?
- How will losing weight help me?

About Nutrition and Physical Activity

- How should I change my eating habits?
- What kinds of physical activity can I do?
- How much physical activity do I need?

About Treatment

- Should I take weight-loss medicine?
- What about weight-loss surgery?
- Could a weight-loss program help me?

A Responsible and Safe Weight-Loss Program

If your health care provider tells you that you should lose weight and you want to find a weight-loss program to help you, look for one that is based on regular physical activity and an eating plan that is balanced, healthy, and easy to follow. Weight-loss programs should encourage healthy behaviors that help you lose weight and that you can stick with every day. Safe and effective weight-loss programs should include the following components:

- Healthy eating plans that reduce calories but do not forbid specific foods or food groups.
- Tips to increase moderate-intensity physical activity.
- Tips on healthy behavior changes that also keep your cultural needs in mind.
- Slow and steady weight loss. Depending on your starting weight, experts recommend losing weight at a rate of ½ to 2 pounds per week. Weight loss may be faster at the start of a program.
- Medical care if you are planning to lose weight by following a special formula diet, such as a very low-calorie diet.
- A plan to keep the weight off after you have lost it.

Get Familiar with the Program

Gather as much information as you can before deciding to join a program. Professionals working for weight-loss programs should be able to answer the following questions.

What does the weight-loss program consist of?

- Does the program offer one-on-one counseling or group classes?
- Do you have to follow a specific meal plan or keep food records?

- Do you have to purchase special food, drugs, or supplements?
- Does the program help you be more physically active, follow a specific physical activity plan, or provide exercise instruction?
- Does the program teach you to make positive and healthy behavior changes?
- Is the program sensitive to your lifestyle and cultural needs?

What are the staff qualifications?

- Who supervises the program?
- What type of weight-management training, experience, education, and certifications do the staff have?

Does the product or program carry any risks?

- Could the program hurt you?
- Could the recommended drugs or supplements harm your health?
- Do participants talk with a doctor?
- Does a doctor run the program?
- Will the program's doctors work with your personal doctor if you have a medical condition such as high blood pressure or are taking prescribed drugs?

How much does the program cost?

- What is the total cost of the program?
- Are there other costs, such as weekly attendance fees, or food and supplement purchases?
- Are there fees for a follow-up program after you lose weight?
- Are there other fees for medical tests?

What results do participants typically have?

- How much weight does an average participant lose, and how long does he or she keep the weight off?
- Does the program offer publications or materials that describe what results participants typically have?

If you are interested in finding a weight-loss program near you, ask your health care provider for a referral or contact your local hospital.

Additional Information

Weight-Control Information Network (WIN)
1 Win Way
Bethesda, MD 20892-3665
Toll-Free: 877-946-4627
Phone: 202-828-1025
Fax: 202-828-1028
Website: http://win.niddk.nih.gov
E-mail: win@info.niddk.nih.gov

Chapter 65

Develop Healthy Exercise Habits

Compulsive Exercise

Rachel and her cheerleading team practice three to five times a week. Rachel feels a lot of pressure to keep her weight down—as head cheerleader, she wants to set an example to the team. So she adds extra daily workouts to her regimen. But lately, Rachel has been feeling worn out, and she has a hard time just making it through a regular team practice. You may think you can't get too much of a good thing, but in the case of exercise, a healthy activity can sometimes turn into an unhealthy compulsion. Rachel is a good example of how an overemphasis on physical fitness or weight control can become unhealthy. Read on to find out more about compulsive exercise and its effects.

Too Much of a Good Thing?

We all know the benefits of exercise, and it seems that everywhere we turn, we hear that we should exercise more. The right kind of exercise does many great things for your body and soul: It can strengthen your heart and muscles, lower your body fat, and reduce your risk of many diseases.

This information was provided by TeensHealth, one of the largest resources online for medically reviewed health information written for parents, kids, and teens. For more articles like this one, visit www.TeensHealth.org, or www.KidsHealth.org.

Many teens who play sports have higher self-esteem than their less active pals, and exercise can even help keep the blues at bay because of the endorphin rush it can cause. Endorphins are naturally produced chemicals that affect your sensory perception. These chemicals are released in your body during and after a workout and they go a long way in helping to control stress.

So how can something with so many benefits have the potential to cause harm? Lots of people start working out because it is fun or it makes them feel good, but exercise can become a compulsive habit when it is done for the wrong reasons.

Some people start exercising with weight loss as their main goal. Although exercise is part of a safe and healthy way to control weight, many people may have unrealistic expectations. We are bombarded with images from advertisers of the ideal body: young and thin for women; strong and muscular for men. To try to reach these unreasonable ideals, people may turn to diets, and for some, this may develop into eating disorders such as anorexia and bulimia. And some people who grow frustrated with the results from diets alone may overexercise to speed up weight loss.

Some athletes may also think that repeated exercise will help them to win an important game. Like Rachel, they add extra workouts to those regularly scheduled with their teams without consulting their coaches or trainers. The pressure to succeed may also lead these people to exercise more than is healthy. The body needs activity but it also needs rest. Over-exercising can lead to injuries like fractures and muscle strains.

Are You a Healthy Exerciser?

Fitness experts recommend that teens do at least 60 minutes of moderate to vigorous physical activity every day. Most young people exercise much less than this recommended amount (which can be a problem for different reasons), but some—such as athletes—do more.

Experts say that repeatedly exercising beyond the requirements for good health is an indicator of compulsive behavior. Some people need more than the average amount of exercise, of course—such as athletes in training for a big event. But several workouts a day, every day, when a person is not in training is a sign that the person is probably overdoing it.

People who are exercise dependent also go to extremes to fit activity into their lives. If you put workouts ahead of friends, homework, and other responsibilities, you may be developing a dependence on exercise.

If you are concerned about your own exercise habits or a friend's, ask yourself the following questions. Do you:

- force yourself to exercise, even if you don't feel well;
- prefer to exercise rather than being with friends;
- become very upset if you miss a workout;
- base the amount you exercise on how much you eat;
- have trouble sitting still because you think you're not burning calories;
- worry that you'll gain weight if you skip exercising for a day?

If the answer to any of these questions is yes, you or your friend may have a problem. What should you do?

How to Get Help

The first thing you should do if you suspect that you are a compulsive exerciser is get help. Talk to your parents, doctor, a teacher or counselor, a coach, or another trusted adult. Compulsive exercise, especially when it is combined with an eating disorder, can cause serious and permanent health problems, and in extreme cases, death.

Because compulsive exercise is closely related to eating disorders, help can be found at community agencies specifically set up to deal with anorexia, bulimia, and other eating problems. Your school's health or physical education department may also have support programs and nutrition advice available. Ask your teacher, coach, or counselor to recommend local organizations that may be able to help.

You should also schedule a checkup with a doctor. Because our bodies go through so many important developments during the teen years, guys and girls who have compulsive exercise problems need to see a doctor to make sure they are developing normally. This is especially true if the person also has an eating disorder. Female athlete triad, a condition that affects girls who overexercise and restrict their eating because of their sports, can cause a girl to stop having her period. Medical help is necessary to resolve the physical problems associated with overexercising before they cause long-term damage to the body.

Make a Positive Change

Changes in activity of any kind—eating or sleeping, for example—can often be a sign that something else is wrong in your life. Girls and guys who exercise compulsively may have a distorted body image and low self-esteem. They may see themselves as overweight or out of shape even when they are actually a healthy weight.

Compulsive exercisers need to get professional help for the reasons described above. But there are also some things that you can do to help you take charge again:

- Work on changing your daily self-talk. When you look in the mirror, make sure you find at least one good thing to say about yourself. Be more aware of your positive attributes.
- When you exercise, focus on the positive, mood-boosting qualities.
- Give yourself a break. Listen to your body and give yourself a day of rest after a hard workout.
- Control your weight by exercising and eating moderate portions of healthy foods. Don't try to change your body into an unrealistically lean shape. Talk with your doctor, dietitian, coach, athletic trainer, or other adult about what a healthy body weight is for you and how to develop healthy eating and exercise habits.

Exercise and sports are supposed to be fun and keep you healthy. Working out in moderation will do both.

Chapter 66

Avoid Laxative and Enema Abuse

By abusing laxatives and enemas, some people with eating disorders try to rush food through their bodies before the calories can be absorbed. These practices are harmful, even potentially fatal, and they are not an effective weight-loss method.

I have been using laxatives and enemas to control my weight. My mother says I am putting myself in danger. Is she just trying to scare and control me?

Listen to your mother. This time she is right. Laxatives and enemas have no place in modern health care except in medical conditions monitored by physicians.

People with eating disorders abuse laxatives because they believe they can remove food from their bodies before the calories are absorbed. (They can't.) Also, many are constipated. The little bit of food they allow themselves does not provide enough bulk to stimulate regular bowel movements.

The misuse of laxatives and enemas can cause serious, sometimes irreversible, sometimes fatal problems. Many people can kick the laxative or enema habit, even after long-term use. To manage problems, work with a physician.

"Laxatives and Enemas: Not the Way to Go," information used with permission of ANRED: Anorexia Nervosa and Related Eating Disorders, Inc. © 2006 ANRED. For additional information, visit http://www.anred.com.

Why can't laxatives help me control my weight? After I use the bathroom, I always weigh less than I did before.

A healthy bowel receives food residue from the stomach and small intestine. As the bowel fills, bulky fecal matter stimulates nerve endings causing muscle contractions that expel the residue from the body in a bowel movement. Laxatives and enemas artificially stimulate nerve endings in the large bowel, which is also called the colon. The colon is one of the last structures in the digestive tract. By the time food arrives there, nothing is left but indigestible fiber and other non-nutritive material.

Laxatives remove lots of water from the colon as well as food residue. The scales indicate weight loss after a laxative-induced bowel movement, but it is false weight loss. The ounces or pounds return as the body rehydrates after liquid intake. If the person refuses to drink liquids, she or he risks dehydration which can lead to fainting spells, irregular heartbeat, and in some cases death.

Laxatives and enemas cannot stimulate the small intestine, the part of the gastrointestinal tract where food is digested and where nutrients and calories are absorbed. The small intestine does not even have the kinds of nerves that occur in the colon and respond to artificial stimulation.

In one experiment, a group of laxative abusers ate a high calorie meal. A group of normal people ate the same food, which totaled several thousand calories. The laxative abusers took their purgatives of choice. The normal people let nature take its course. Researchers collected all the material passed in bowel movements and tested it for calorie content. Even after consuming thousands of calories and massive amounts of laxatives, the laxative abusers managed to remove only about 100 extra calories from their bodies, the amount found in one small cookie.

How can I hurt myself by continuing to use laxatives and enemas?

- You can upset your electrolyte balance. Electrolytes are minerals like sodium and potassium that are dissolved in the blood and other body fluids. They must be present in very specific amounts and exact ratios for proper functioning of nerves and muscles, including the heart muscle. Laxatives and enemas (and also forced vomiting) can upset this balance by flushing essential minerals out of the body, resulting in muscle cramps, tremors, spasms, irregular heartbeat, and in some cases cardiac arrest. The heart stops, and unless the person receives immediate emergency medical treatment, she or he dies.

- Laxatives and enemas (and also vomiting) remove needed fluid from the body. The resulting dehydration can lead to tremors, weakness, blurry vision, fainting spells, kidney damage, and in some cases death. Severe dehydration requires medical treatment. Drinking fluid may not hydrate cells and tissues quickly enough to prevent organ damage or death.
- Laxatives irritate intestinal nerve endings, which in turn stimulate muscle contractions that move the irritant through the gut and out of the body. After a while the nerve endings no longer respond to stimulation. The person must now take greater and greater amounts of laxatives to produce bowel movements. She or he has become laxative dependent and without artificial stimulation may not have any bowel movements at all.
- Laxatives and enemas strip away protective mucus that lines the colon, leaving it vulnerable to infection.
- Enemas can stretch the colon, which over time becomes a limp sack with no muscle tone. No longer can it generate the muscle contractions necessary to move fecal matter out of the body.
- Laxatives abusers seem to have more trouble with the following problems than do nonusers: irritable bowel syndrome (rectal pain, gas, and episodes of constipation and diarrhea) and bowel tumors (both benign and cancerous).

How can I stop the laxative and enema habit?

Ask your doctor for help. Don't let shyness or embarrassment stop you.

Take one step at a time or one big leap. As your doctor advises, either taper off or go cold turkey. Expect to be anxious when time passes with no bowel movement and increasing feelings of fullness, bloat, and discomfort. Your body needs time to regulate itself and relearn how to respond to natural cues. Be reassured that most people who stick with their doctor's recommendations manage to stop laxatives and enemas and resume normal functioning after an initial period of discomfort.

Get enough fiber. Make sure you eat enough food, especially high-fiber items like whole grains, fresh fruits, and fresh vegetables. Eat the skin and peels too; they are usually high in fiber. An inexpensive, effective way to increase fiber in your diet is to add a few spoonfuls of unprocessed bran to soups, stews, and cereals. Don't go overboard with bran, however. It can generate intestinal gas which will increase your discomfort.

Combine a hot beverage and exercise. Drink a hot beverage (lemon juice in hot water is good), and then walk briskly for thirty minutes. The hot liquid and muscle movements in your legs and abdomen will help stimulate muscle contractions in the intestines.

Drink enough water. Drink lots of water during the day. Doctors recommend eight to ten glasses. Don't count caffeine beverages in your total; caffeine pulls water out of your body instead of adding it to cells and tissues.

Walk in the morning. Before breakfast, take a walk. Walking gets your intestinal muscles working so they can move the contents of your gastrointestinal tract along and out of your body. A cup of hot water and lemon juice helps get things going too. Eat breakfast. After breakfast, sit on the toilet for 5–10 minutes. Breakfast initiates a reflex that triggers the intestines to evacuate their contents.

Let your therapist help you deal with the anxiety that this recovery process may create. Remember that the human body has tremendous powers of restoration, but they sometimes take a while to kick in. Best wishes for health and happiness.

Chapter 67

How Sleep Affects Weight

Are the sleepless counting doughnuts and pies instead of sheep? "Americans sleep less than they used to, and this could be part of the reason why more of us are now overweight," says David Dinges, Chief of the Division of Sleep and Chronobiology at the University of Pennsylvania School of Medicine.

Over the past 40 years, Americans have cut their snooze time by one to two hours a night. We now sleep less than people in any other industrialized country. And researchers are discovering that sleep affects hormones that regulate satiety, hunger, and how efficiently you burn calories.

Too little sleep may make you hungry, especially for calorie-dense foods, and may prime your body to try to hold on to the calories you eat. It may also boost your insulin levels, which increases the risk of heart disease and diabetes.

The Sleep-Weight Link

"Obesity is obviously a very complex issue, and no one is suggesting that lack of sleep is the cause of the obesity epidemic," says Carl Hunt, director of the National Center on Sleep Disorders Research at the National Institutes of Health in Bethesda, Maryland. "But new

---

research certainly supports the idea that sleeping less may be a previously unknown but important contributor to the obesity epidemic in the U.S."

The link between sleep and weight was first noticed in the 1990s, when European researchers were puzzling over why so many children were getting heavier. "They were surprised to discover that it wasn't how much television a child watched, but how much sleep the child got, that best predicted whether he or she was overweight," says Dinges. "The less children slept, the heavier they were."

Researchers in the U.S. are finding the same link in adults. In the Wisconsin Sleep Cohort Study, which tracks the sleep habits of nearly 3,000 middle-aged state government employees, those who reported that they typically slept less than eight hours a night were more likely to be overweight.[1] And researchers at Columbia University in New York City found that people who slept six hours a night were 23 percent more likely to be obese than people who slept between seven and nine hours. Those who slept five hours were 50 percent more likely—while those who slept four hours or less were 73 percent more likely—to be obese.

The connection between hours slept and weight wasn't significant for people 60 and older, says James Gangwisch, a psychiatric epidemiologist at Columbia, "probably because the sleep problems that are so common in older people obscure the link." (The analysis hasn't yet been published.)

Leapin' Leptin

Why would people who sleep less weigh more? "The results are somewhat counterintuitive," says Gangwisch, since people burn more calories when they're awake. "We think it has more to do with what happens to your body when you deprive it of sleep, as opposed to the amount of physical activity you get."

What happens involves two hormones: Leptin, which is released by fat cells, signals the brain to stop eating. Ghrelin (pronounced GRELL-lin), which is made in the stomach, is a signal to keep eating. The two influence whether you go for a second helping or push yourself away from the table. "Studies have shown that leptin levels are lower and ghrelin levels are higher in people who sleep fewer hours," says Gangwisch.

In the Wisconsin Sleep Cohort Study, those who slept for five hours had 15 percent lower leptin levels and 15 percent higher ghrelin levels than those who slept for eight hours.[1] While the study wasn't designed to prove whether sleep deprivation causes changes in leptin and ghrelin levels, new research at the University of Chicago suggests that it does.

When Eve Van Cauter and co-workers limited 12 healthy young men to just four hours of sleep for two consecutive nights, their leptin levels were 18 percent lower and their ghrelin levels were 28 percent higher than after two nights of sleeping for ten hours.[2]

"The combination of low leptin and high ghrelin is likely to increase appetite," says Wisconsin Sleep Cohort Study researcher Emmanuel Mignot of Stanford University (though "short sleepers may also have more time to overeat," he points out). In fact, the men in Van Cauter's study said that they were more hungry—and that they'd be more likely to eat salty foods like chips and nuts; sweets like cake, candy, and ice cream; and starchy foods like bread, cereal, and potatoes—after four hours of sleep than after ten hours.

Compounding the problem: the brain interprets a drop in leptin as a sign of starvation. So it responds not only by boosting hunger, but by burning fewer calories. That means you put on more weight even if you don't eat any more food.

Sweet Dreams

Sleep deprivation may stimulate more than your appetite. "It also affects insulin resistance and blood glucose levels, which are two important components of the metabolic syndrome," says Carl Hunt of the National Center on Sleep Disorders Research. The metabolic syndrome, also called insulin resistance syndrome, is a cluster of symptoms that increases the risk of heart attack, stroke, and diabetes. Signs of the syndrome are abdominal obesity, low high density lipoprotein (HDL) (good) cholesterol, and elevated (though not necessarily high) triglycerides, blood pressure, and blood sugar.

When the University of Chicago's Eve Van Cauter and her colleagues limited 11 healthy men in their 20s to four hours of sleep for six straight nights, "it brought them to a nearly prediabetic state." Their bodies were 40 percent less able to clear glucose from their blood and 30 percent slower in releasing insulin than when they were allowed to sleep for twelve hours.[3] In fact, four hours of sleep for six consecutive nights gave the young men the insulin sensitivity of 70- or 80-year-olds.

"We didn't expect to see a change of that magnitude," says Van Cauter. (Insulin is a hormone that lets glucose, or blood sugar, enter the body's cells, where the sugar is burned for energy. When people are insulin insensitive, or insulin resistant, their insulin doesn't work efficiently.) "The consensus that prevailed until recently was that sleep is for the brain, not for the rest of the body," says Van Cauter. "But sleep really affects everything. We are not wired biologically for sleep deprivation. We're the only animal that intentionally sleeps less than we need to."

Sleepus Interruptus

Sleep less, weigh more. If true, that's not good news for the estimated 15 million Americans with sleep apnea. Sleep apnea (pronounced APP-knee-uh) typically occurs when the soft tissue in the rear of the throat relaxes too much during sleep, partially blocking the passage and cutting off the flow of air. The result: loud snoring and labored breathing. If the passage closes entirely, no air can get through and breathing stops until the brain rouses the person enough to gasp for air.

According to the American Sleep Apnea Association in Washington, DC, some people with untreated apnea stop breathing hundreds of times during the night, often for a minute or longer. When they do fall back to sleep, it's generally to a lighter, fragmented, less restful stage that leaves them drowsy the next day.

It's not a minor problem: the number of Americans who have sleep apnea equals the number who have diabetes. And, like those with diabetes, "the majority don't know it or aren't being properly treated," says Sleep Apnea Association president Rochelle Goldberg. What's more, apnea "increases your risk for developing high blood pressure, coronary heart disease, and diabetes, for suffering strokes, and for having accidents during the day." How? "Obstructed breathing produces an arousal response that revs up the body into a 'fight-or-flight' stance," she explains. To divert blood to high-priority sites, the blood vessels constrict and the heart rate increases. "Since the oxygen supply is cut off at the same time, the circulatory system can be damaged, especially if it happens again and again every night."

And it's not just the blood vessels that pay. People with severe sleep apnea—that means at least 15 breathing disruptions an hour—suffer a loss of motor skills, attention, and concentration that's equal to an additional five years of aging.[4] "Men are twice as likely as women to have sleep apnea," says Goldberg, "because the tissues in their throats are usually larger and thus more likely to cause obstruction." Ditto for people who are overweight. Even so, "you can be thin as a rail and still have the airway characteristics that cause apnea," says Goldberg.

It's a Snore

People with sleep apnea are more likely to snore, and to snore loudly. "If someone snores and wonders whether they have sleep apnea, they should answer a few questions," says Goldberg.

- If the snoring is pretty much every night, is there any irregular breathing or pauses between the snores?
- Do you wake with some frequency at night, even if just to go to the bathroom?
- Do you still feel tired the next day after what seemed like a good night's sleep?
- Do you have trouble concentrating and working through simple tasks during the day?
- Do you have headaches while you sleep or when you wake up?

"The most effective treatment for sleep apnea is CPAP, or continuous positive airway pressure," says Goldberg. It's a machine with a mask that attaches over the face and keeps the air passage open by forcing air through the nose and mouth throughout the night. Not everyone can tolerate it. Dental appliances and surgery work about half the time, while drugs and supplements don't work at all, says Goldberg.

References

1. *PLoS Med.* 1: e62 2004 (Epub.).
2. *Ann. Intern. Med.* 141: 846, 2004.
3. *Lancet* 354: 1435, 1999.
4. *Amer. J. Respir. Crit. Care Med.* 156: 1813, 1997.

Part Six

Additional Help and Information

Chapter 68

Glossary of Terms Related to Eating Disorders

Abuse: Misuse, wrong use, especially excessive use, of anything. Also, injurious, harmful, or offensive treatment, as in child abuse or sexual abuse.

Alexithymia: Difficulty in recognizing and describing one's emotions, defining them in terms of somatic sensations or behavioral reactions.

Amenorrhea: Absence or abnormal cessation of the menses.

Anorexia: Diminished appetite; aversion to food.

Anorexia nervosa: A mental disorder manifested by extreme fear of becoming obese and an aversion to food, usually occurring in young women and often resulting in life-threatening weight loss, accompanied by a disturbance in body image, hyperactivity, and amenorrhea.

Anxiety: Fear or apprehension or dread of impending danger and accompanied by restlessness, tension, tachycardia, and dyspnea unattached to a clearly identifiable stimulus.

Behavior therapy: An offshoot of psychotherapy involving the use of procedures and techniques associated with research in the fields

---

Definitions in this chapter are from *Stedman's Medical Dictionary 27th Edition*.

of conditioning and learning for the treatment of a variety of psychologic conditions; distinguished from psychotherapy because specific symptoms (such as phobia, enuresis, high blood pressure) are selected as the target for change, planned interventions or remedial steps to extinguish or modify these symptoms are then employed, and the progress of changes is continuously and quantitatively monitored.

Body dysmorphic disorder: A psychosomatic (somatoform) disorder characterized by preoccupation with some imagined defect in appearance in a normal-appearing person.

Body image: Personal conception of one's own body as distinct from one's actual anatomic body or the conception other persons have of it.

Body mass index: An anthropometric measure of body mass, defined as weight in kilograms divided by height in meters squared; a method of determining caloric nutritional status.

Bulimia nervosa: A chronic morbid disorder involving repeated and secretive episodic bouts of eating characterized by uncontrolled rapid ingestion of large quantities of food over a short period of time (binge eating), followed by self-induced vomiting, use of laxatives or diuretics, fasting, or vigorous exercise in order to prevent weight gain; often accompanied by feelings of guilt, depression, or self-disgust.

Cardiac dysrhythmia: Any abnormality in the rate, regularity, or sequence of cardiac activation.

Cognitive therapy: Any of a variety of techniques in psychotherapy that utilizes guided self-discovery, imaging, self-instruction, symbolic modeling, and related forms of explicitly elicited cognitions as the principal mode of treatment.

Comorbidity: A concomitant but unrelated pathologic or disease process; usually used in epidemiology to indicate the coexistence of two or more disease processes.

Crisis intervention: A psychotherapeutic technique directed at counseling at the time of an acute life crisis and limited in aim to helping resolve the crisis.

Diagnostic and Statistical Manual of Mental Disorders (DSM): A system of classification, published by the American Psychiatric Association, that divides recognized mental disorders into clearly defined categories based on sets of objective criteria. Representing a majority view (rather than a consensus) of hundreds of contributors and consultants, *DSM* is widely recognized as a diagnostic standard and widely used for reporting, coding, and statistical purposes. Briefly stated, the axes are I, clinical disorders; II, personality disorders and mental retardation; III, general medical disorders; IV, psychosocial and environmental stressors; and V, overall level of functioning.

Diet:

1. Food and drink in general.
2. A prescribed course of eating and drinking in which the amount and kind of food, as well as the times at which it is to be taken, are regulated for therapeutic purposes.
3. Reduction of caloric intake so as to lose weight.
4. To follow any prescribed or specific diet.

Eating disorders: A group of mental disorders including anorexia nervosa, bulimia nervosa, pica, and rumination disorder of infancy.

Emaciation: Becoming abnormally thin from extreme loss of flesh.

Emetic:

1. Relating to or causing vomiting.
2. An agent that causes vomiting, such as ipecac syrup.

Enema: A rectal injection for clearing out the bowel, or administering drugs or food.

Family therapy: A type of group psychotherapy in which a family in conflict meets as a group with the therapist and explores its relationships and processes; focus is on the resolution of current interactions between members rather than on individual members.

Intervention: An action or ministration that produces an effect or that is intended to alter the course of a pathologic process.

Ketosis: A condition characterized by the enhanced production of ketone bodies, as in diabetes mellitus or starvation.

Labile: In psychology or psychiatry, denoting free and uncontrolled mood or behavioral expression of the emotions.

Laxative: Mildly cathartic; having the action of loosening the bowels without pain or violent action.

Malnutrition: Faulty nutrition resulting from malabsorption, poor diet, or overeating.

Nutrition:

1. A function of living plants and animals, consisting in the taking in and metabolism of food material whereby tissue is built up and energy liberated.
2. The study of the food and liquid requirements of human beings or animals for normal physiologic function, including energy, need, maintenance, growth, activity, reproduction, and lactation.

Osteoporosis: Reduction in the quantity of bone or atrophy of skeletal tissue. Women who become amenorrheic because of rigorous athletic exercise and dietary restriction or eating disorders are at risk of osteoporosis.

Phobia: Any objectively unfounded morbid dread or fear that arouses a state of panic. The word is used as a combining form in many terms expressing the object that inspires the fear.

Pica: A perverted appetite for substances not fit as food or of no nutritional value such as clay, dried paint, starch, or ice.

Psychoanalysis: A method of psychotherapy, designed to bring preconscious and unconscious material to consciousness primarily through the analysis of transference and resistance; an integrated body of observations and theories on personality development, motivation, and behavior; and an institutionalized school of psychotherapy, as in jungian or freudian psychoanalysis.

Purge: To cause a copious evacuation of the bowels.

Self-regulation: A three-stage strategy patients are taught to use in order to end risky health-associated behaviors such as smoking and overeating: (1) self-monitoring (self-observation), the first stage in self-regulation involves the individual's deliberately attending to and recording his or her own behavior; (2) self-evaluation, the second stage, in which the individual assesses what was learned by self-monitoring, such as how often and where one smokes, and uses those observational data to establish health goals or criteria; and (3) self-reinforcement, the third stage, in which the individual rewards himself or herself for each behavioral success on the road to that goal, thereby enhancing the chance of reaching it.

Starvation: Lengthy and continuous deprivation of food.

Supportive therapy: Psychotherapy aiming at bolstering the patient's psychologic defenses and providing reassurance, as in crisis intervention, rather than probing provocatively into the patient's conflicts.

Therapy: The treatment of disease or disorder by any method.

Chapter 69

Online Resources for More Information about Eating Disorders

When searching on the internet, try using directory sites of respected organizations, rather than doing blind searches with a search engine. The following websites and search engines provide reliable information, resources, and internet links for further research about eating disorders.

Academy for Eating Disorders
Website: http://www.aedweb.org

Promotes excellence in research, treatment, education, and prevention of eating disorders.

ANRED: Anorexia Nervosa and Related Eating Disorders, Inc.
Website: http://www.anred.com

Provides reliable information about eating disorders, self-help tips, and prevention and recovery.

Body Positive
Website: http://www.bodypositive.com

Promotes positive body image and acceptance of the body you have.

Online listings in this chapter are from sources deemed reliable. All contact information was verified and updated in November 2006.

Bulimia Nervosa Resource Guide
Website: http://www.bulimiaguide.org

Comprehensive resource guide about bulimia nervosa.

Caringonline
Website: http://www.caringonline.com/index.html

Introduction to eating disorders topics and current news.

Dads and Daughters
Website: http://www.dadsanddaughters.org/

Provides resources and support for building good relationships between fathers and daughters.

Eating Disorder Foundation
Website: http://www.eatingdisorderfoundation.org

General information about eating disorders and a list of support groups available in Colorado.

Eating Disorder Referral and Information Center
Website: http://www.edreferral.com

Offers a comprehensive database of eating disorder information and resources including lists of treatment professionals.

Eating Disorders Recovery Center
Website: http://www.addictions.net

Offers general information about eating disorders and specifics about treatment available at their Richmond Heights, MO treatment facility.

Focus Adolescent Services
Website: http://www.focusas.com/EatingDisorders.html

General information about eating disorders and many links for further research.

Massachusetts Eating Disorder Association
Website: http://www.medainc.org

Focuses on prevention and treatment of eating disorders.

National Association of Anorexia Nervosa and Associated Disorders (ANAD)
Website: http://www.anad.org

Offers help for individuals struggling with eating disorders including resources and referrals.

National Eating Disorders Association (NEDA)
Website: http://www.edap.org

Provides general information, links, resources, and hotline information.

Overeaters Anonymous
Website: http://www.oa.org/index.htm

Offers support for individuals struggling with obesity and binge eating along with support group listings.

Something Fishy Website on Eating Disorders
Website: http://www.somethingfishy.org

Works to raise awareness about eating disorders and provide support for individuals and their families.

Chapter 70

Additional Resources for Information about Eating Disorders

American Association for Marriage and Family Therapy
112 S. Alfred St.
Alexandria, VA 22314
Phone: 703-838-9808
Fax: 703-838-9805
Website: http://www.aamft.org

American Dietetic Association
120 S. Riverside Plaza, Ste. 2000
Chicago, IL 60606-6995
Toll-Free: 800-877-1600
Website: http://www.eatright.org

American Psychiatric Association
1000 Wilson Blvd., Suite 1825
Arlington, VA 22209-3902
Phone: 703-907-7300
Fax: 703-907-1085
Website: http://www.psych.org
E-mail: apa@psych.org

American Psychological Association
750 First St., NE
Washington, DC 20002-4242
Toll-Free: 800-374-2721
Phone: 202-336-5500
TDD/TTY: 202-336-6123
Website: http://www.apa.org

Body Positive
P.O. Box 7801
Berkeley, CA 94707
Phone: 510-528-0101
Fax: 510-558-0979
Website: http://
www.thebodypositive.org
E-mail: info@thebodypositive
.org

Resources in this chapter were compiled from several sources deemed reliable. All contact information was verified and updated in November 2006.

Child, Adolescent, and Family Branch
Center for Mental Health Services
Substance Abuse and Mental Health Services Administration (SAMHSA)
1 Choke Cherry Road
Rockville, MD 20857
Phone: 240-276-1980
Fax: 240-276-1930
Website: http://www.systemsofcare.samhsa.gov

Eating Disorders Anonymous
P.O. Box 55876
Phoenix, AZ 85078-5876
Website: http://www.eatingdisordersanonymous.org
E-mail: info@eatingdisordersanonymous.org

Eating Disorders Coalition
611 Pennsylvania Ave., SE #423
Washington, DC 20003-4303
Phone: 202-543-9570
Website: http://www.eatingdisorderscoalition.org

GirlsHealth.gov
8270 Willow Oaks Corporate Dr.
Suite 301
Fairfax, VA 22031
Website: http://www.4girls.gov

MedWatch
FDA Safety Information and Adverse Event Reporting Program
U.S. Food and Drug Administration
5600 Fishers Lane
Rockville, MD 20852-9787
Toll-Free: 800-332-1088
Fax: 800-332-0178
Website: http://www.fda.gov/medwatch

National Association of Anorexia Nervosa and Associated Disorders
Box 7
Highland Park, IL 60035
Phone: 847-831-3438
Fax: 847-433-4632
Website: http://www.anad.org

National Eating Disorders Association (NEDA)
603 Stewart St., Suite 803
Seattle, WA 98101
Toll-Free: 800-931-2237
Phone: 206-382-3587
Website: http://www.nationaleatingdisorders.org
E-mail: info@NationalEatingDisorders.org

National Heart, Lung, and Blood Institute (NHLBI)
P.O. Box 30105
Bethesda, MD 20824-0105
Phone: 301-592-8573
TTY: 240-629-3255
Fax: 240-629-3246
Website: http://www.nhlbi.nih.gov
E-mail: nhlbiinfo@nhlbi.nih.gov

National Institute of Diabetes and Digestive and Kidney Diseases (NIDDK)
National Institutes of Health
Building 31, Room 9A06
31 Center Drive, MSC 2560
Bethesda, MD 20892-2560
Toll-Free: 800-891-5390
Website: http://www.niddk.nih.gov

National Institute of Mental Health (NIMH)
6001 Executive Boulevard
Room 8184, MSC 9663
Bethesda, MD 20892-9663
Toll-Free: 866-615-6464
Toll-Free TTY: 866-415-8051
Phone: 301-443-4513
Fax: 301-443-4279
Website: http://www.nimh.nih.gov
E-mail: nimhinfo@nih.gov

National Institute on Alcohol Abuse and Alcoholism (NIAAA)
5635 Fishers Lane, MSC 9304
Bethesda, MD 20892-9304
Website: http://www.niaaa.nih.gov

National Mental Health Association (NMHA)
2000 N. Beauregard St., 6th Floor
Alexandria, VA 22311
Toll-Free: 800-969-6642
Toll-Free TTY: 800-433-5959
Phone: 703-684-7722
Fax: 703-684-5968
Website: http://www.nmha.org

National Mental Health Information Center
Substance Abuse and Mental Health Services Administration (SAMHSA)
P.O. Box 42557
Washington, DC 20015
Toll-Free: 800-789-2647
Toll-Free TDD: 866-889-2647
Fax: 240-747-5470
Website: http://www.mentalhealth.samhsa.gov

National Women's Health Information Center (NWHIC)
8270 Willow Oaks Corporate Dr.
Fairfax, VA 22031
Toll-Free: 800-994-9662
Toll-Free TDD: 888-220-5446
Website: http://www.4woman.gov

Office on Women's Health
Department of Health and Human Services
200 Independence Ave., SW
Room 712E
Washington, DC 20201
Toll-Free: 800-994-9662
Toll-Free TDD: 888-220-5446
Phone: 202-690-7650
Fax: 202-205-2631
Website: http://www.4woman.gov

Osteoporosis and Related Bone Diseases
National Resource Center
2 AMS Circle
Bethesda, MD 20892-3676
Toll-Free: 800-624-2663
Phone: 202-223-0344
TTY: 202-466-4315
Fax: 202-293-2356
Website: http://www.osteo.org
E-mail:
NIAMSBONEINFO@mail.nih.gov

Overeaters Anonymous
World Service Office
Phone: 505-891-2664
Website: http://www.oa.org

Society for Adolescent Medicine
1916 Copper Oaks Circle
Blue Springs, MO 64015
Phone: 816-224-8010
Fax: 816-224-8009
Website: http://
www.adolescenthealth.org
E-mail:
sam@adolescenthealth.org

Students Against Destructive Decisions (SADD)
SADD National Office
255 Main Street
Marlborough, MA 01752
Toll-Free: 877-SADD-INC (723-3462)
Fax: 508-481-5759
Website: http://www.sadd.org
E-mail: info@sadd.org

Substance Abuse and Mental Health Services Administration (SAMHSA)
1 Choke Cherry Rd.
Rockville, MD 20857
Toll-Free Crisis: 800-273-8255
Toll-Free TTY Crisis: 800-799-4889
Phone: 240-276-2130
Website: http://www.samhsa.gov
Mental Health Services Locator:
http://mentalhealth.samhsa.gov/databases

Weight-Control Information Network (WIN)
1 Win Way
Bethesda, MD 20892-3665
Toll-Free: 877-946-4627
Phone: 202-828-1025
Fax: 202-828-1028
Website: http://
win.niddk.nih.gov
E-mail: win@info.niddk.nih.gov

Index

Index

Page numbers followed by 'n' indicate a footnote. Page numbers in *italics* indicate a table or illustration.

A

B

C

D

H

M

N

T

X

Y

Z

Health Reference Series

COMPLETE CATALOG

List price $87 per volume. **School and library price $78 per volume.**

Adolescent Health Sourcebook, 2nd Edition

Basic Consumer Health Information about the Physical, Mental, and Emotional Growth and Development of Adolescents, Including Medical Care, Nutritional and Physical Activity Requirements, Puberty, Sexual Activity, Acne, Tanning, Body Piercing, Common Physical Illnesses and Disorders, Eating Disorders, Attention Deficit Hyperactivity Disorder, Depression, Bullying, Hazing, and Adolescent Injuries Related to Sports, Driving, and Work

Along with Substance Abuse Information about Nicotine, Alcohol, and Drug Use, a Glossary, and Directory of Additional Resources

Edited by Joyce Brennfleck Shannon. 683 pages. 2006. 978-0-7808-0943-7.

"It is written in clear, nontechnical language aimed at general readers. . . . Recommended for public libraries, community colleges, and other agencies serving health care consumers."

—*American Reference Books Annual, 2003*

"Recommended for school and public libraries. Parents and professionals dealing with teens will appreciate the easy-to-follow format and the clearly written text. This could become a 'must have' for every high school teacher." —*E-Streams, Jan '03*

"A good starting point for information related to common medical, mental, and emotional concerns of adolescents." —*School Library Journal, Nov '02*

"This book provides accurate information in an easy to access format. It addresses topics that parents and caregivers might not be aware of and provides practical, useable information."

—*Doody's Health Sciences Book Review Journal, Sep-Oct '02*

"Recommended reference source."

—*Booklist, American Library Association, Sep '02*

AIDS Sourcebook, 3rd Edition

Basic Consumer Health Information about Acquired Immune Deficiency Syndrome (AIDS) and Human Immunodeficiency Virus (HIV) Infection, Including Facts about Transmission, Prevention, Diagnosis, Treatment, Opportunistic Infections, and Other Complications, with a Section for Women and Children, Including Details about Associated Gynecological Concerns, Pregnancy, and Pediatric Care

Along with Updated Statistical Information, Reports on Current Research Initiatives, a Glossary, and Directories of Internet, Hotline, and Other Resources

Edited by Dawn D. Matthews. 664 pages. 2003. 978-0-7808-0631-3.

"The 3rd edition of the *AIDS Sourcebook*, part of Omnigraphics' *Health Reference Series*, is a welcome update. . . . This resource is highly recommended for academic and public libraries."

—*American Reference Books Annual, 2004*

"Excellent sourcebook. This continues to be a highly recommended book. There is no other book that provides as much information as this book provides."

—*AIDS Book Review Journal, Dec-Jan '00*

"Recommended reference source."

—*Booklist, American Library Association, Dec '99*

Alcoholism Sourcebook, 2nd Edition

Basic Consumer Health Information about Alcohol Use, Abuse, and Dependence, Featuring Facts about the Physical, Mental, and Social Health Effects of Alcohol Addiction, Including Alcoholic Liver Disease, Pancreatic Disease, Cardiovascular Disease, Neurological Disorders, and the Effects of Drinking during Pregnancy

Along with Information about Alcohol Treatment, Medications, and Recovery Programs, in Addition to Tips for Reducing the Prevalence of Underage Drinking, Statistics about Alcohol Use, a Glossary of Related Terms, and Directories of Resources for More Help and Information

Edited by Amy L. Sutton. 653 pages. 2006. 978-0-7808-0942-0.

"This title is one of the few reference works on alcoholism for general readers. For some readers this will be a welcome complement to the many self-help books on the market. Recommended for collections serving general readers and consumer health collections."

—*E-Streams, Mar '01*

"This book is an excellent choice for public and academic libraries."

—*American Reference Books Annual, 2001*

"Recommended reference source."

—*Booklist, American Library Association, Dec '00*

"Presents a wealth of information on alcohol use and abuse and its effects on the body and mind, treatment, and prevention." —*SciTech Book News, Dec '00*

"Important new health guide which packs in the latest consumer information about the problems of alcoholism." —*Reviewer's Bookwatch, Nov '00*

SEE ALSO *Drug Abuse Sourcebook*

Allergies Sourcebook, 2nd Edition

Basic Consumer Health Information about Allergic Disorders, Triggers, Reactions, and Related Symptoms, Including Anaphylaxis, Rhinitis, Sinusitis, Asthma, Dermatitis, Conjunctivitis, and Multiple Chemical Sensitivity

Along with Tips on Diagnosis, Prevention, and Treatment, Statistical Data, a Glossary, and a Directory of Sources for Further Help and Information

Edited by Annemarie S. Muth. 598 pages. 2002. 978-0-7808-0376-3.

"This book brings a great deal of useful material together. . . . This is an excellent addition to public and consumer health library collections."
—*American Reference Books Annual, 2003*

"This second edition would be useful to laypersons with little or advanced knowledge of the subject matter. This book would also serve as a resource for nursing and other health care professions students. It would be useful in public, academic, and hospital libraries with consumer health collections." —*E-Streams, Jul '02*

Alternative Medicine Sourcebook

SEE Complementary & Alternative Medicine Sourcebook

Alzheimer's Disease Sourcebook, 3rd Edition

Basic Consumer Health Information about Alzheimer's Disease, Other Dementias, and Related Disorders, Including Multi-Infarct Dementia, AIDS Dementia Complex, Dementia with Lewy Bodies, Huntington's Disease, Wernicke-Korsakoff Syndrome (Alcohol-Related Dementia), Delirium, and Confusional States

Along with Information for People Newly Diagnosed with Alzheimer's Disease and Caregivers, Reports Detailing Current Research Efforts in Prevention, Diagnosis, and Treatment, Facts about Long-Term Care Issues, and Listings of Sources for Additional Information

Edited by Karen Bellenir. 645 pages. 2003. 978-0-7808-0666-5.

"This very informative and valuable tool will be a great addition to any library serving consumers, students and health care workers."
—*American Reference Books Annual, 2004*

"This is a valuable resource for people affected by dementias such as Alzheimer's. It is easy to navigate and includes important information and resources."
—*Doody's Review Service, Feb '04*

"Recommended reference source."
—*Booklist, American Library Association, Oct '99*

SEE ALSO *Brain Disorders Sourcebook*

Arthritis Sourcebook, 2nd Edition

Basic Consumer Health Information about Osteoarthritis, Rheumatoid Arthritis, Other Rheumatic Disorders, Infectious Forms of Arthritis, and Diseases with Symptoms Linked to Arthritis, Featuring Facts about Diagnosis, Pain Management, and Surgical Therapies

Along with Coping Strategies, Research Updates, a Glossary, and Resources for Additional Help and Information

Edited by Amy L. Sutton. 593 pages. 2004. 978-0-7808-0667-2.

"This easy-to-read volume is recommended for consumer health collections within public or academic libraries." —*E-Streams, May '05*

"As expected, this updated edition continues the excellent reputation of this series in providing sound, usable health information. . . . Highly recommended."
—*American Reference Books Annual, 2005*

"Excellent reference." —*The Bookwatch, Jan '05*

Asthma Sourcebook, 2nd Edition

Basic Consumer Health Information about the Causes, Symptoms, Diagnosis, and Treatment of Asthma in Infants, Children, Teenagers, and Adults, Including Facts about Different Types of Asthma, Common Co-Occurring Conditions, Asthma Management Plans, Triggers, Medications, and Medication Delivery Devices

Along with Asthma Statistics, Research Updates, a Glossary, a Directory of Asthma-Related Resources, and More

Edited by Karen Bellenir. 609 pages. 2006. 978-0-7808-0866-9.

"A worthwhile reference acquisition for public libraries and academic medical libraries whose readers desire a quick introduction to the wide range of asthma information." —*Choice, Association of College & Research Libraries, Jun '01*

"Recommended reference source."
—*Booklist, American Library Association, Feb '01*

"Highly recommended." —*The Bookwatch, Jan '01*

"There is much good information for patients and their families who deal with asthma daily."
—*American Medical Writers Association Journal, Winter '01*

"This informative text is recommended for consumer health collections in public, secondary school, and community college libraries and the libraries of universities with a large undergraduate population."
—*American Reference Books Annual, 2001*

Attention Deficit Disorder Sourcebook

Basic Consumer Health Information about Attention Deficit/Hyperactivity Disorder in Children and Adults,

Including Facts about Causes, Symptoms, Diagnostic Criteria, and Treatment Options Such as Medications, Behavior Therapy, Coaching, and Homeopathy

Along with Reports on Current Research Initiatives, Legal Issues, and Government Regulations, and Featuring a Glossary of Related Terms, Internet Resources, and a List of Additional Reading Material

Edited by Dawn D. Matthews. 470 pages. 2002. 978-0-7808-0624-5.

"Recommended reference source."
—*Booklist, American Library Association, Jan '03*

"This book is recommended for all school libraries and the reference or consumer health sections of public libraries." —*American Reference Books Annual, 2003*

Back & Neck Sourcebook, 2nd Edition

Basic Consumer Health Information about Spinal Pain, Spinal Cord Injuries, and Related Disorders, Such as Degenerative Disk Disease, Osteoarthritis, Scoliosis, Sciatica, Spina Bifida, and Spinal Stenosis, and Featuring Facts about Maintaining Spinal Health, Self-Care, Pain Management, Rehabilitative Care, Chiropractic Care, Spinal Surgeries, and Complementary Therapies

Along with Suggestions for Preventing Back and Neck Pain, a Glossary of Related Terms, and a Directory of Resources

Edited by Amy L. Sutton. 633 pages. 2004. 978-0-7808-0738-9.

"Recommended . . . an easy to use, comprehensive medical reference book." —*E-Streams, Sep '05*

"The strength of this work is its basic, easy-to-read format. Recommended." —*Reference and User Services Quarterly, American Library Association, Winter '97*

Blood & Circulatory Disorders Sourcebook, 2nd Edition

Basic Consumer Health Information about the Blood and Circulatory System and Related Disorders, Such as Anemia and Other Hemoglobin Diseases, Cancer of the Blood and Associated Bone Marrow Disorders, Clotting and Bleeding Problems, and Conditions That Affect the Veins, Blood Vessels, and Arteries, Including Facts about the Donation and Transplantation of Bone Marrow, Stem Cells, and Blood and Tips for Keeping the Blood and Circulatory System Healthy

Along with a Glossary of Related Terms and Resources for Additional Help and Information

Edited by Amy L. Sutton. 659 pages. 2005. 978-0-7808-0746-4.

"Highly recommended pick for basic consumer health reference holdings at all levels."
—*The Bookwatch, Aug '05*

"Recommended reference source."
—*Booklist, American Library Association, Feb '99*

"An important reference sourcebook written in simple language for everyday, non-technical users. "
—*Reviewer's Bookwatch, Jan '99*

Brain Disorders Sourcebook, 2nd Edition

Basic Consumer Health Information about Acquired and Traumatic Brain Injuries, Infections of the Brain, Epilepsy and Seizure Disorders, Cerebral Palsy, and Degenerative Neurological Disorders, Including Amyotrophic Lateral Sclerosis (ALS), Dementias, Multiple Sclerosis, and More

Along with Information on the Brain's Structure and Function, Treatment and Rehabilitation Options, Reports on Current Research Initiatives, a Glossary of Terms Related to Brain Disorders and Injuries, and a Directory of Sources for Further Help and Information

Edited by Sandra J. Judd. 625 pages. 2005. 978-0-7808-0744-0.

"Highly recommended pick for basic consumer health reference holdings at all levels."
—*The Bookwatch, Aug '05*

"Belongs on the shelves of any library with a consumer health collection." —*E-Streams, Mar '00*

"Recommended reference source."
—*Booklist, American Library Association, Oct '99*

SEE ALSO *Alzheimer's Disease Sourcebook*

Breast Cancer Sourcebook, 2nd Edition

Basic Consumer Health Information about Breast Cancer, Including Facts about Risk Factors, Prevention, Screening and Diagnostic Methods, Treatment Options, Complementary and Alternative Therapies, Post-Treatment Concerns, Clinical Trials, Special Risk Populations, and New Developments in Breast Cancer Research

Along with Breast Cancer Statistics, a Glossary of Related Terms, and a Directory of Resources for Additional Help and Information

Edited by Sandra J. Judd. 595 pages. 2004. 978-0-7808-0668-9.

"This book will be an excellent addition to public, community college, medical, and academic libraries."
—*American Reference Books Annual, 2006*

"It would be a useful reference book in a library or on loan to women in a support group."
—*Cancer Forum, Mar '03*

"Recommended reference source."
—*Booklist, American Library Association, Jan '02*

"This reference source is highly recommended. It is quite informative, comprehensive and detailed in na-

ture, and yet it offers practical advice in easy-to-read language. It could be thought of as the 'bible' of breast cancer for the consumer." —*E-Streams, Jan '02*

"From the pros and cons of different screening methods and results to treatment options, *Breast Cancer Sourcebook* provides the latest information on the subject."
—*Library Bookwatch, Dec '01*

"This thoroughgoing, very readable reference covers all aspects of breast health and cancer. . . . Readers will find much to consider here. Recommended for all public and patient health collections."
—*Library Journal, Sep '01*

SEE ALSO *Cancer Sourcebook for Women, Women's Health Concerns Sourcebook*

Breastfeeding Sourcebook

Basic Consumer Health Information about the Benefits of Breastmilk, Preparing to Breastfeed, Breastfeeding as a Baby Grows, Nutrition, and More, Including Information on Special Situations and Concerns Such as Mastitis, Illness, Medications, Allergies, Multiple Births, Prematurity, Special Needs, and Adoption

Along with a Glossary and Resources for Additional Help and Information

Edited by Jenni Lynn Colson. 388 pages. 2002. 978-0-7808-0332-9.

"Particularly useful is the information about professional lactation services and chapters on breastfeeding when returning to work. . . . *Breastfeeding Sourcebook* will be useful for public libraries, consumer health libraries, and technical schools offering nurse assistant training, especially in areas where Internet access is problematic."
—*American Reference Books Annual, 2003*

SEE ALSO *Pregnancy & Birth Sourcebook*

Burns Sourcebook

Basic Consumer Health Information about Various Types of Burns and Scalds, Including Flame, Heat, Cold, Electrical, Chemical, and Sun Burns

Along with Information on Short-Term and Long-Term Treatments, Tissue Reconstruction, Plastic Surgery, Prevention Suggestions, and First Aid

Edited by Allan R. Cook. 604 pages. 1999. 978-0-7808-0204-9.

"This is an exceptional addition to the series and is highly recommended for all consumer health collections, hospital libraries, and academic medical centers."
—*E-Streams, Mar '00*

"This key reference guide is an invaluable addition to all health care and public libraries in confronting this ongoing health issue."
—*American Reference Books Annual, 2000*

"Recommended reference source."
—*Booklist, American Library Association, Dec '99*

SEE ALSO *Dermatological Disorders Sourcebook*

Cancer Sourcebook, 5th Edition

Basic Consumer Health Information about Major Forms and Stages of Cancer, Featuring Facts about Head and Neck Cancers, Lung Cancers, Gastrointestinal Cancers, Genitourinary Cancers, Lymphomas, Blood Cell Cancers, Endocrine Cancers, Skin Cancers, Bone Cancers, Metastatic Cancers, and More

Along with Facts about Cancer Treatments, Cancer Risks and Prevention, a Glossary of Related Terms, Statistical Data, and a Directory of Resources for Additional Information

Edited by Karen Bellenir. 1,102 pages. 2007. 978-0-7808-0947-5.

"With cancer being the second leading cause of death for Americans, a prodigious work such as this one, which locates centrally so much cancer-related information, is clearly an asset to this nation's citizens and others."
—*Journal of the National Medical Association, 2004*

"This title is recommended for health sciences and public libraries with consumer health collections."
—*E-Streams, Feb '01*

". . . can be effectively used by cancer patients and their families who are looking for answers in a language they can understand. Public and hospital libraries should have it on their shelves."
—*American Reference Books Annual, 2001*

"Recommended reference source."
—*Booklist, American Library Association, Dec '00*

SEE ALSO *Breast Cancer Sourcebook, Cancer Sourcebook for Women, Pediatric Cancer Sourcebook, Prostate Cancer Sourcebook*

Cancer Sourcebook for Women, 3rd Edition

Basic Consumer Health Information about Leading Causes of Cancer in Women, Featuring Facts about Gynecologic Cancers and Related Concerns, Such as Breast Cancer, Cervical Cancer, Endometrial Cancer, Uterine Sarcoma, Vaginal Cancer, Vulvar Cancer, and Common Non-Cancerous Gynecologic Conditions, in Addition to Facts about Lung Cancer, Colorectal Cancer, and Thyroid Cancer in Women

Along with Information about Cancer Risk Factors, Screening and Prevention, Treatment Options, and Tips on Coping with Life after Cancer Treatment, a Glossary of Cancer Terms, and a Directory of Resources for Additional Help and Information

Edited by Amy L. Sutton. 715 pages. 2006. 978-0-7808-0867-6.

"An excellent addition to collections in public, consumer health, and women's health libraries."
—*American Reference Books Annual, 2003*

"Overall, the information is excellent, and complex topics are clearly explained. As a reference book for the consumer it is a valuable resource to assist them to make informed decisions about cancer and its treatments." —*Cancer Forum, Nov '02*

"Highly recommended for academic and medical reference collections." —*Library Bookwatch, Sep '02*

"This is a highly recommended book for any public or consumer library, being reader friendly and containing accurate and helpful information."

—*E-Streams, Aug '02*

"Recommended reference source."

—*Booklist, American Library Association, Jul '02*

SEE ALSO *Breast Cancer Sourcebook, Women's Health Concerns Sourcebook*

Cancer Survivorship Sourcebook

Basic Consumer Health Information about the Physical, Educational, Emotional, Social, and Financial Needs of Cancer Patients from Diagnosis, through Cancer Treatment, and Beyond, Including Facts about Researching Specific Types of Cancer and Learning about Clinical Trials and Treatment Options, and Featuring Tips for Coping with the Side Effects of Cancer Treatments and Adjusting to Life after Cancer Treatment Concludes

Along with Suggestions for Caregivers, Friends, and Family Members of Cancer Patients, a Glossary of Cancer Care Terms, and Directories of Related Resources

Edited by Karen Bellenir. 650 pages. 2007. 978-0-7808-0985-7.

Cardiovascular Diseases & Disorders Sourcebook, 3rd Edition

Basic Consumer Health Information about Heart and Vascular Diseases and Disorders, Such as Angina, Heart Attacks, Arrhythmias, Cardiomyopathy, Valve Disease, Atherosclerosis, and Aneurysms, with Information about Managing Cardiovascular Risk Factors and Maintaining Heart Health, Medications and Procedures Used to Treat Cardiovascular Disorders, and Concerns of Special Significance to Women

Along with Reports on Current Research Initiatives, a Glossary of Related Medical Terms, and a Directory of Sources for Further Help and Information

Edited by Sandra J. Judd. 713 pages. 2005. 978-0-7808-0739-6.

"This updated sourcebook is still the best first stop for comprehensive introductory information on cardiovascular diseases."

—*American Reference Books Annual, 2006*

"Recommended for public libraries and libraries supporting health care professionals."

—*E-Streams, Sep '05*

"This should be a standard health library reference."

—*The Bookwatch, Jun '05*

"Recommended reference source."

—*Booklist, American Library Association, Dec '00*

". . . comprehensive format provides an extensive overview on this subject."

—*Choice, Association of College & Research Libraries*

Caregiving Sourcebook

Basic Consumer Health Information for Caregivers, Including a Profile of Caregivers, Caregiving Responsibilities and Concerns, Tips for Specific Conditions, Care Environments, and the Effects of Caregiving

Along with Facts about Legal Issues, Financial Information, and Future Planning, a Glossary, and a Listing of Additional Resources

Edited by Joyce Brennfleck Shannon. 600 pages. 2001. 978-0-7808-0331-2.

"Essential for most collections."

—*Library Journal, Apr 1, 2002*

"An ideal addition to the reference collection of any public library. Health sciences information professionals may also want to acquire the *Caregiving Sourcebook* for their hospital or academic library for use as a ready reference tool by health care workers interested in aging and caregiving." —*E-Streams, Jan '02*

"Recommended reference source."

—*Booklist, American Library Association, Oct '01*

Child Abuse Sourcebook

Basic Consumer Health Information about the Physical, Sexual, and Emotional Abuse of Children, with Additional Facts about Neglect, Munchausen Syndrome by Proxy (MSBP), Shaken Baby Syndrome, and Controversial Issues Related to Child Abuse, Such as Withholding Medical Care, Corporal Punishment, and Child Maltreatment in Youth Sports, and Featuring Facts about Child Protective Services, Foster Care, Adoption, Parenting Challenges, and Other Abuse Prevention Efforts

Along with a Glossary of Related Terms and Resources for Additional Help and Information

Edited by Dawn D. Matthews. 620 pages. 2004. 978-0-7808-0705-1.

"A valuable and highly recommended resource for school, academic and public libraries whether used on its own or as a starting point for more in-depth research." —*E-Streams, Apr '05*

"Every week the news brings cases of child abuse or neglect, so it is useful to have a source that supplies so much helpful information. . . . Recommended. Public and academic libraries, and child welfare offices."

—*Choice, Association of College & Research Libraries, Mar '05*

"Packed with insights on all kinds of issues, from foster care and adoption to parenting and abuse prevention."

—*The Bookwatch, Nov '04*

SEE ALSO: *Domestic Violence Sourcebook*

Childhood Diseases & Disorders Sourcebook

Basic Consumer Health Information about Medical Problems Often Encountered in Pre-Adolescent Children, Including Respiratory Tract Ailments, Ear Infections, Sore Throats, Disorders of the Skin and Scalp, Digestive and Genitourinary Diseases, Infectious Diseases, Inflammatory Disorders, Chronic Physical and Developmental Disorders, Allergies, and More

Along with Information about Diagnostic Tests, Common Childhood Surgeries, and Frequently Used Medications, with a Glossary of Important Terms and Resource Directory

Edited by Chad T. Kimball. 662 pages. 2003. 978-0-7808-0458-6.

"This is an excellent book for new parents and should be included in all health care and public libraries."
—*American Reference Books Annual, 2004*

SEE ALSO: *Healthy Children Sourcebook*

Colds, Flu & Other Common Ailments Sourcebook

Basic Consumer Health Information about Common Ailments and Injuries, Including Colds, Coughs, the Flu, Sinus Problems, Headaches, Fever, Nausea and Vomiting, Menstrual Cramps, Diarrhea, Constipation, Hemorrhoids, Back Pain, Dandruff, Dry and Itchy Skin, Cuts, Scrapes, Sprains, Bruises, and More

Along with Information about Prevention, Self-Care, Choosing a Doctor, Over-the-Counter Medications, Folk Remedies, and Alternative Therapies, and Including a Glossary of Important Terms and a Directory of Resources for Further Help and Information

Edited by Chad T. Kimball. 638 pages. 2001. 978-0-7808-0435-7.

"A good starting point for research on common illnesses. It will be a useful addition to public and consumer health library collections."
—*American Reference Books Annual, 2002*

"Will prove valuable to any library seeking to maintain a current, comprehensive reference collection of health resources. . . . Excellent reference."
—*The Bookwatch, Aug '01*

"Recommended reference source."
—*Booklist, American Library Association, Jul '01*

Communication Disorders Sourcebook

Basic Information about Deafness and Hearing Loss, Speech and Language Disorders, Voice Disorders, Balance and Vestibular Disorders, and Disorders of Smell, Taste, and Touch

Edited by Linda M. Ross. 533 pages. 1996. 978-0-7808-0077-9.

"This is skillfully edited and is a welcome resource for the layperson. It should be found in every public and medical library."
—*Booklist Health Sciences Supplement, American Library Association, Oct '97*

Complementary & Alternative Medicine Sourcebook, 3rd Edition

Basic Consumer Health Information about Complementary and Alternative Medical Therapies, Including Acupuncture, Ayurveda, Traditional Chinese Medicine, Herbal Medicine, Homeopathy, Naturopathy, Biofeedback, Hypnotherapy, Yoga, Art Therapy, Aromatherapy, Clinical Nutrition, Vitamin and Mineral Supplements, Chiropractic, Massage, Reflexology, Crystal Therapy, Therapeutic Touch, and More

Along with Facts about Alternative and Complementary Treatments for Specific Conditions Such as Cancer, Diabetes, Osteoarthritis, Chronic Pain, Menopause, Gastrointestinal Disorders, Headaches, and Mental Illness, a Glossary, and a Resource List for Additional Help and Information

Edited by Sandra J. Judd. 657 pages. 2006. 978-0-7808-0864-5.

"Recommended for public, high school, and academic libraries that have consumer health collections. Hospital libraries that also serve the public will find this to be a useful resource." —*E-Streams, Feb '03*

"Recommended reference source."
—*Booklist, American Library Association, Jan '03*

"An important alternate health reference."
—*MBR Bookwatch, Oct '02*

"A great addition to the reference collection of every type of library." —*American Reference Books Annual, 2000*

Congenital Disorders Sourcebook, 2nd Edition

Basic Consumer Health Information about Nonhereditary Birth Defects and Disorders Related to Prematurity, Gestational Injuries, Congenital Infections, and Birth Complications, Including Heart Defects, Hydrocephalus, Spina Bifida, Cleft Lip and Palate, Cerebral Palsy, and More

Along with Facts about the Prevention of Birth Defects, Fetal Surgery and Other Treatment Options, Research Initiatives, a Glossary of Related Terms, and Resources for Additional Information and Support

Edited by Sandra J. Judd. 647 pages. 2006. 978-0-7808-0945-1.

"Recommended reference source."
—*Booklist, American Library Association, Oct '97*

SEE ALSO *Pregnancy & Birth Sourcebook*

Contagious Diseases Sourcebook

Basic Consumer Health Information about Infectious Diseases Spread by Person-to-Person Contact through

Direct Touch, Airborne Transmission, Sexual Contact, or Contact with Blood or Other Body Fluids, Including Hepatitis, Herpes, Influenza, Lice, Measles, Mumps, Pinworm, Ringworm, Severe Acute Respiratory Syndrome (SARS), Streptococcal Infections, Tuberculosis, and Others

Along with Facts about Disease Transmission, Antimicrobial Resistance, and Vaccines, with a Glossary and Directories of Resources for More Information

Edited by Karen Bellenir. 643 pages. 2004. 978-0-7808-0736-5.

"This easy-to-read volume is recommended for consumer health collections within public or academic libraries." —*E-Streams, May '05*

"This informative book is highly recommended for public libraries, consumer health collections, and secondary schools and undergraduate libraries."
—*American Reference Books Annual, 2005*

"Excellent reference." —*The Bookwatch, Jan '05*

Death & Dying Sourcebook, 2nd Edition

Basic Consumer Health Information about End-of-Life Care and Related Perspectives and Ethical Issues, Including End-of-Life Symptoms and Treatments, Pain Management, Quality-of-Life Concerns, the Use of Life Support, Patients' Rights and Privacy Issues, Advance Directives, Physician-Assisted Suicide, Caregiving, Organ and Tissue Donation, Autopsies, Funeral Arrangements, and Grief

Along with Statistical Data, Information about the Leading Causes of Death, a Glossary, and Directories of Support Groups and Other Resources

Edited by Joyce Brennfleck Shannon. 653 pages. 2006. 978-0-7808-0871-3.

"Public libraries, medical libraries, and academic libraries will all find this sourcebook a useful addition to their collections."
—*American Reference Books Annual, 2001*

"An extremely useful resource for those concerned with death and dying in the United States."
—*Respiratory Care, Nov '00*

"Recommended reference source."
—*Booklist, American Library Association, Aug '00*

"This book is a definite must for all those involved in end-of-life care." —*Doody's Review Service, 2000*

Dental Care & Oral Health Sourcebook, 2nd Edition

Basic Consumer Health Information about Dental Care, Including Oral Hygiene, Dental Visits, Pain Management, Cavities, Crowns, Bridges, Dental Implants, and Fillings, and Other Oral Health Concerns, Such as Gum Disease, Bad Breath, Dry Mouth, Genetic and Developmental Abnormalities, Oral Cancers, Orthodontics, and Temporomandibular Disorders

Along with Updates on Current Research in Oral Health, a Glossary, a Directory of Dental and Oral Health Organizations, and Resources for People with Dental and Oral Health Disorders

Edited by Amy L. Sutton. 609 pages. 2003. 978-0-7808-0634-4.

"This book could serve as a turning point in the battle to educate consumers in issues concerning oral health."
—*American Reference Books Annual, 2004*

"Unique source which will fill a gap in dental sources for patients and the lay public. A valuable reference tool even in a library with thousands of books on dentistry. Comprehensive, clear, inexpensive, and easy to read and use. It fills an enormous gap in the health care literature." —*Reference & User Services Quarterly, American Library Association, Summer '98*

"Recommended reference source."
—*Booklist, American Library Association, Dec '97*

Depression Sourcebook

Basic Consumer Health Information about Unipolar Depression, Bipolar Disorder, Postpartum Depression, Seasonal Affective Disorder, and Other Types of Depression in Children, Adolescents, Women, Men, the Elderly, and Other Selected Populations

Along with Facts about Causes, Risk Factors, Diagnostic Criteria, Treatment Options, Coping Strategies, Suicide Prevention, a Glossary, and a Directory of Sources for Additional Help and Information

Edited by Karen Bellenir. 602 pages. 2002. 978-0-7808-0611-5.

"*Depression Sourcebook* is of a very high standard. Its purpose, which is to serve as a reference source to the lay reader, is very well served."
—*Journal of the National Medical Association, 2004*

"Invaluable reference for public and school library collections alike." —*Library Bookwatch, Apr '03*

"Recommended for purchase."
—*American Reference Books Annual, 2003*

Dermatological Disorders Sourcebook, 2nd Edition

Basic Consumer Health Information about Conditions and Disorders Affecting the Skin, Hair, and Nails, Such as Acne, Rosacea, Rashes, Dermatitis, Pigmentation Disorders, Birthmarks, Skin Cancer, Skin Injuries, Psoriasis, Scleroderma, and Hair Loss, Including Facts about Medications and Treatments for Dermatological Disorders and Tips for Maintaining Healthy Skin, Hair, and Nails

Along with Information about How Aging Affects the Skin, a Glossary of Related Terms, and a Directory of Resources for Additional Help and Information

Edited by Amy L. Sutton. 645 pages. 2005. 978-0-7808-0795-2.

"... comprehensive, easily read reference book."
—*Doody's Health Sciences Book Reviews, Oct '97*

SEE ALSO *Burns Sourcebook*

Diabetes Sourcebook, 3rd Edition

Basic Consumer Health Information about Type 1 Diabetes (Insulin-Dependent or Juvenile-Onset Diabetes), Type 2 Diabetes (Noninsulin-Dependent or Adult-Onset Diabetes), Gestational Diabetes, Impaired Glucose Tolerance (IGT), and Related Complications, Such as Amputation, Eye Disease, Gum Disease, Nerve Damage, and End-Stage Renal Disease, Including Facts about Insulin, Oral Diabetes Medications, Blood Sugar Testing, and the Role of Exercise and Nutrition in the Control of Diabetes

Along with a Glossary and Resources for Further Help and Information

Edited by Dawn D. Matthews. 622 pages. 2003. 978-0-7808-0629-0.

"This edition is even more helpful than earlier versions. . . . It is a truly valuable tool for anyone seeking readable and authoritative information on diabetes."
—*American Reference Books Annual, 2004*

"An invaluable reference." —*Library Journal, May '00*

Selected as one of the 250 "Best Health Sciences Books of 1999." —*Doody's Rating Service, Mar-Apr '00*

"Provides useful information for the general public."
—*Healthlines, University of Michigan Health Management Research Center, Sep/Oct '99*

"... provides reliable mainstream medical information . . . belongs on the shelves of any library with a consumer health collection." —*E-Streams, Sep '99*

"Recommended reference source."
—*Booklist, American Library Association, Feb '99*

Diet & Nutrition Sourcebook, 3rd Edition

Basic Consumer Health Information about Dietary Guidelines and the Food Guidance System, Recommended Daily Nutrient Intakes, Serving Proportions, Weight Control, Vitamins and Supplements, Nutrition Issues for Different Life Stages and Lifestyles, and the Needs of People with Specific Medical Concerns, Including Cancer, Celiac Disease, Diabetes, Eating Disorders, Food Allergies, and Cardiovascular Disease

Along with Facts about Federal Nutrition Support Programs, a Glossary of Nutrition and Dietary Terms, and Directories of Additional Resources for More Information about Nutrition

Edited by Joyce Brennfleck Shannon. 633 pages. 2006. 978-0-7808-0800-3.

"This book is an excellent source of basic diet and nutrition information." —*Booklist Health Sciences Supplement, American Library Association, Dec '00*

"This reference document should be in any public library, but it would be a very good guide for beginning students in the health sciences. If the other books in this publisher's series are as good as this, they should all be in the health sciences collections."
—*American Reference Books Annual, 2000*

"This book is an excellent general nutrition reference for consumers who desire to take an active role in their health care for prevention. Consumers of all ages who select this book can feel confident they are receiving current and accurate information." —*Journal of Nutrition for the Elderly, Vol. 19, No. 4, 2000*

SEE ALSO *Digestive Diseases & Disorders Sourcebook, Eating Disorders Sourcebook, Gastrointestinal Diseases & Disorders Sourcebook, Vegetarian Sourcebook*

Digestive Diseases & Disorders Sourcebook

Basic Consumer Health Information about Diseases and Disorders that Impact the Upper and Lower Digestive System, Including Celiac Disease, Constipation, Crohn's Disease, Cyclic Vomiting Syndrome, Diarrhea, Diverticulosis and Diverticulitis, Gallstones, Heartburn, Hemorrhoids, Hernias, Indigestion (Dyspepsia), Irritable Bowel Syndrome, Lactose Intolerance, Ulcers, and More

Along with Information about Medications and Other Treatments, Tips for Maintaining a Healthy Digestive Tract, a Glossary, and Directory of Digestive Diseases Organizations

Edited by Karen Bellenir. 335 pages. 2000. 978-0-7808-0327-5.

"This title would be an excellent addition to all public or patient-research libraries."
—*American Reference Books Annual, 2001*

"This title is recommended for public, hospital, and health sciences libraries with consumer health collections." —*E-Streams, Jul-Aug '00*

"Recommended reference source."
—*Booklist, American Library Association, May '00*

SEE ALSO *Eating Disorders Sourcebook, Gastrointestinal Diseases & Disorders Sourcebook*

Disabilities Sourcebook

Basic Consumer Health Information about Physical and Psychiatric Disabilities, Including Descriptions of Major Causes of Disability, Assistive and Adaptive Aids, Workplace Issues, and Accessibility Concerns

Along with Information about the Americans with Disabilities Act, a Glossary, and Resources for Additional Help and Information

Edited by Dawn D. Matthews. 616 pages. 2000. 978-0-7808-0389-3.

"It is a must for libraries with a consumer health section." —*American Reference Books Annual, 2002*

"A much needed addition to the Omnigraphics *Health Reference Series.* A current reference work to provide people with disabilities, their families, caregivers or those who work with them, a broad range of information in one volume, has not been available until now. . . . It is recommended for all public and academic library reference collections." —*E-Streams, May '01*

"An excellent source book in easy-to-read format covering many current topics; highly recommended for all libraries." —*Choice, Association of College & Research Libraries, Jan '01*

"Recommended reference source."
—*Booklist, American Library Association, Jul '00*

Domestic Violence Sourcebook, 2nd Edition

Basic Consumer Health Information about the Causes and Consequences of Abusive Relationships, Including Physical Violence, Sexual Assault, Battery, Stalking, and Emotional Abuse, and Facts about the Effects of Violence on Women, Men, Young Adults, and the Elderly, with Reports about Domestic Violence in Selected Populations, and Featuring Facts about Medical Care, Victim Assistance and Protection, Prevention Strategies, Mental Health Services, and Legal Issues

Along with a Glossary of Related Terms and Resources for Additional Help and Information

Edited by Dawn D. Matthews. 628 pages. 2004. 978-0-7808-0669-6.

"Educators, clergy, medical professionals, police, and victims and their families will benefit from this realistic and easy-to-understand resource."
—*American Reference Books Annual, 2005*

"Recommended for all collections supporting consumer health information. It should also be considered for any collection needing general, readable information on domestic violence." —*E-Streams, Jan '05*

"This sourcebook complements other books in its field, providing a one-stop resource . . . Recommended."
—*Choice, Association of College & Research Libraries, Jan '05*

"Interested lay persons should find the book extremely beneficial. . . . A copy of ***Domestic Violence and Child Abuse Sourcebook*** should be in every public library in the United States."
—*Social Science & Medicine, No. 56, 2003*

"This is important information. The Web has many resources but this sourcebook fills an important societal need. I am not aware of any other resources of this type." —*Doody's Review Service, Sep '01*

"Recommended reference source."
—*Booklist, American Library Association, Apr '01*

"Important pick for college-level health reference libraries." —*The Bookwatch, Mar '01*

"Because this problem is so widespread and because this book includes a lot of issues within one volume, this work is recommended for all public libraries."
—*American Reference Books Annual, 2001*

SEE ALSO *Child Abuse Sourcebook*

Drug Abuse Sourcebook, 2nd Edition

Basic Consumer Health Information about Illicit Substances of Abuse and the Misuse of Prescription and Over-the-Counter Medications, Including Depressants, Hallucinogens, Inhalants, Marijuana, Stimulants, and Anabolic Steroids

Along with Facts about Related Health Risks, Treatment Programs, Prevention Programs, a Glossary of Abuse and Addiction Terms, a Glossary of Drug-Related Street Terms, and a Directory of Resources for More Information

Edited by Catherine Ginther. 607 pages. 2004. 978-0-7808-0740-2.

"Commendable for organizing useful, normally scattered government and association-produced data into a logical sequence."
—*American Reference Books Annual, 2006*

"This easy-to-read volume is recommended for consumer health collections within public or academic libraries." —*E-Streams, Sep '05*

"An excellent library reference."
—*The Bookwatch, May '05*

"Containing a wealth of information, this book will be useful to the college student just beginning to explore the topic of substance abuse. This resource belongs in libraries that serve a lower-division undergraduate or community college clientele as well as the general public." —*Choice, Association of College & Research Libraries, Jun '01*

"Recommended reference source."
—*Booklist, American Library Association, Feb '01*

SEE ALSO *Alcoholism Sourcebook*

Ear, Nose & Throat Disorders Sourcebook, 2nd Edition

Basic Consumer Health Information about Disorders of the Ears, Hearing Loss, Vestibular Disorders, Nasal and Sinus Problems, Throat and Vocal Cord Disorders, and Otolaryngologic Cancers, Including Facts about Ear Infections and Injuries, Genetic and Congenital Deafness, Sensorineural Hearing Disorders, Tinnitus, Vertigo, Ménière Disease, Rhinitis, Sinusitis, Snoring, Sore Throats, Hoarseness, and More

Along with Reports on Current Research Initiatives, a Glossary of Related Medical Terms, and a Directory of Sources for Further Help and Information

Edited by Sandra J. Judd. 659 pages. 2006. 978-0-7808-0872-0.

"Overall, this sourcebook is helpful for the consumer seeking information on ENT issues. It is recommended for public libraries."

—*American Reference Books Annual, 1999*

"Recommended reference source."

—*Booklist, American Library Association, Dec '98*

Eating Disorders Sourcebook, 2nd Edition

Basic Consumer Health Information about Anorexia Nervosa, Bulimia Nervosa, Binge Eating, Compulsive Exercise, Female Athlete Triad, and Other Eating Disorders, Including Facts about Body Image and Other Cultural and Age-Related Risk Factors, Prevention Efforts, Adverse Health Effects, Treatment Options, and the Recovery Process

Along with Guidelines for Healthy Weight Control, a Glossary, and Directories of Additional Resources

Edited by Joyce Brennfleck Shannon. 585 pages. 2007. 978-0-7808-0948-2.

"Recommended for health science libraries that are open to the public, as well as hospital libraries. This book is a good resource for the consumer who is concerned about eating disorders." —*E-Streams, Mar '02*

"This volume is another convenient collection of excerpted articles. Recommended for school and public library patrons; lower-division undergraduates; and two-year technical program students."

—*Choice, Association of College & Research Libraries, Jan '02*

"Recommended reference source."

—*Booklist, American Library Association, Oct '01*

SEE ALSO *Diet & Nutrition Sourcebook, Digestive Diseases & Disorders Sourcebook, Gastrointestinal Diseases & Disorders Sourcebook*

Emergency Medical Services Sourcebook

Basic Consumer Health Information about Preventing, Preparing for, and Managing Emergency Situations, When and Who to Call for Help, What to Expect in the Emergency Room, the Emergency Medical Team, Patient Issues, and Current Topics in Emergency Medicine

Along with Statistical Data, a Glossary, and Sources of Additional Help and Information

Edited by Jenni Lynn Colson. 494 pages. 2002. 978-0-7808-0420-3.

"Handy and convenient for home, public, school, and college libraries. Recommended."

— *Choice, Association of College & Research Libraries, Apr '03*

"This reference can provide the consumer with answers to most questions about emergency care in the United States, or it will direct them to a resource where the answer can be found."

—*American Reference Books Annual, 2003*

"Recommended reference source."

— *Booklist, American Library Association, Feb '03*

Endocrine & Metabolic Disorders Sourcebook

Basic Information for the Layperson about Pancreatic and Insulin-Related Disorders Such as Pancreatitis, Diabetes, and Hypoglycemia; Adrenal Gland Disorders Such as Cushing's Syndrome, Addison's Disease, and Congenital Adrenal Hyperplasia; Pituitary Gland Disorders Such as Growth Hormone Deficiency, Acromegaly, and Pituitary Tumors; Thyroid Disorders Such as Hypothyroidism, Graves' Disease, Hashimoto's Disease, and Goiter; Hyperparathyroidism; and Other Diseases and Syndromes of Hormone Imbalance or Metabolic Dysfunction

Along with Reports on Current Research Initiatives

Edited by Linda M. Shin. 574 pages. 1998. 978-0-7808-0207-0.

"Omnigraphics has produced another needed resource for health information consumers."

—*American Reference Books Annual, 2000*

"Recommended reference source."

— *Booklist, American Library Association, Dec '98*

Environmental Health Sourcebook, 2nd Edition

Basic Consumer Health Information about the Environment and Its Effect on Human Health, Including the Effects of Air Pollution, Water Pollution, Hazardous Chemicals, Food Hazards, Radiation Hazards, Biological Agents, Household Hazards, Such as Radon, Asbestos, Carbon Monoxide, and Mold, and Information about Associated Diseases and Disorders, Including Cancer, Allergies, Respiratory Problems, and Skin Disorders

Along with Information about Environmental Concerns for Specific Populations, a Glossary of Related Terms, and Resources for Further Help and Information

Edited by Dawn D. Matthews. 673 pages. 2003. 978-0-7808-0632-0.

"This recently updated edition continues the level of quality and the reputation of the numerous other volumes in Omnigraphics' *Health Reference Series.*"

— *American Reference Books Annual, 2004*

"An excellent updated edition."

— *The Bookwatch, Oct '03*

"Recommended reference source."

— *Booklist, American Library Association, Sep '98*

"This book will be a useful addition to anyone's library." — *Choice Health Sciences Supplement, Association of College & Research Libraries, May '98*

". . . a good survey of numerous environmentally induced physical disorders . . . a useful addition to anyone's library."

— *Doody's Health Sciences Book Reviews, Jan '98*

Ethnic Diseases Sourcebook

Basic Consumer Health Information for Ethnic and Racial Minority Groups in the United States, Including General Health Indicators and Behaviors, Ethnic Diseases, Genetic Testing, the Impact of Chronic Diseases, Women's Health, Mental Health Issues, and Preventive Health Care Services

Along with a Glossary and a Listing of Additional Resources

Edited by Joyce Brennfleck Shannon. 664 pages. 2001. 978-0-7808-0336-7.

"Recommended for health sciences libraries where public health programs are a priority."

—E-Streams, Jan '02

"Not many books have been written on this topic to date, and the *Ethnic Diseases Sourcebook* is a strong addition to the list. It will be an important introductory resource for health consumers, students, health care personnel, and social scientists. It is recommended for public, academic, and large hospital libraries."

—American Reference Books Annual, 2002

"Recommended reference source."

—Booklist, American Library Association, Oct '01

"Will prove valuable to any library seeking to maintain a current, comprehensive reference collection of health resources. . . . An excellent source of health information about genetic disorders which affect particular ethnic and racial minorities in the U.S."

—The Bookwatch, Aug '01

Eye Care Sourcebook, 2nd Edition

Basic Consumer Health Information about Eye Care and Eye Disorders, Including Facts about the Diagnosis, Prevention, and Treatment of Common Refractive Problems Such as Myopia, Hyperopia, Astigmatism, and Presbyopia, and Eye Diseases, Including Glaucoma, Cataract, Age-Related Macular Degeneration, and Diabetic Retinopathy

Along with a Section on Vision Correction and Refractive Surgeries, Including LASIK and LASEK, a Glossary, and Directories of Resources for Additional Help and Information

Edited by Amy L. Sutton. 543 pages. 2003. 978-0-7808-0635-1.

". . . a solid reference tool for eye care and a valuable addition to a collection."

—American Reference Books Annual, 2004

Family Planning Sourcebook

Basic Consumer Health Information about Planning for Pregnancy and Contraception, Including Traditional Methods, Barrier Methods, Hormonal Methods, Permanent Methods, Future Methods, Emergency Contraception, and Birth Control Choices for Women at Each Stage of Life

Along with Statistics, a Glossary, and Sources of Additional Information

Edited by Amy Marcaccio Keyzer. 520 pages. 2001. 978-0-7808-0379-4.

"Recommended for public, health, and undergraduate libraries as part of the circulating collection."

—E-Streams, Mar '02

"Information is presented in an unbiased, readable manner, and the sourcebook will certainly be a necessary addition to those public and high school libraries where Internet access is restricted or otherwise problematic." *—American Reference Books Annual, 2002*

"Recommended reference source."

—Booklist, American Library Association, Oct '01

"Will prove valuable to any library seeking to maintain a current, comprehensive reference collection of health resources. . . . Excellent reference."

—The Bookwatch, Aug '01

SEE ALSO *Pregnancy & Birth Sourcebook*

Fitness & Exercise Sourcebook, 3rd Edition

Basic Consumer Health Information about the Physical and Mental Benefits of Fitness, Including Cardiorespiratory Endurance, Muscular Strength, Muscular Endurance, and Flexibility, with Facts about Sports Nutrition and Exercise-Related Injuries and Tips about Physical Activity and Exercises for People of All Ages and for People with Health Concerns

Along with Advice on Selecting and Using Exercise Equipment, Maintaining Exercise Motivation, a Glossary of Related Terms, and a Directory of Resources for More Help and Information

Edited by Amy L. Sutton. 663 pages. 2007. 978-0-7808-0946-8.

"This work is recommended for all general reference collections."

—American Reference Books Annual, 2002

"Highly recommended for public, consumer, and school grades fourth through college." *—E-Streams, Nov '01*

"Recommended reference source."

—Booklist, American Library Association, Oct '01

"The information appears quite comprehensive and is considered reliable. . . . This second edition is a welcomed addition to the series."

—Doody's Review Service, Sep '01

Food Safety Sourcebook

Basic Consumer Health Information about the Safe Handling of Meat, Poultry, Seafood, Eggs, Fruit Juices, and Other Food Items, and Facts about Pesticides, Drinking Water, Food Safety Overseas, and the Onset, Duration, and Symptoms of Foodborne Illnesses, Including Types of Pathogenic Bacteria, Parasitic Protozoa, Worms, Viruses, and Natural Toxins

Along with the Role of the Consumer, the Food Handler, and the Government in Food Safety; a Glossary, and Resources for Additional Help and Information

Edited by Dawn D. Matthews. 339 pages. 1999. 978-0-7808-0326-8.

"This book is recommended for public libraries and universities with home economic and food science programs."
—*E-Streams, Nov '00*

"Recommended reference source."
—*Booklist, American Library Association, May '00*

"This book takes the complex issues of food safety and foodborne pathogens and presents them in an easily understood manner. [It does] an excellent job of covering a large and often confusing topic."
—*American Reference Books Annual, 2000*

■

Forensic Medicine Sourcebook

Basic Consumer Information for the Layperson about Forensic Medicine, Including Crime Scene Investigation, Evidence Collection and Analysis, Expert Testimony, Computer-Aided Criminal Identification, Digital Imaging in the Courtroom, DNA Profiling, Accident Reconstruction, Autopsies, Ballistics, Drugs and Explosives Detection, Latent Fingerprints, Product Tampering, and Questioned Document Examination

Along with Statistical Data, a Glossary of Forensics Terminology, and Listings of Sources for Further Help and Information

Edited by Annemarie S. Muth. 574 pages. 1999. 978-0-7808-0232-2.

"Given the expected widespread interest in its content and its easy to read style, this book is recommended for most public and all college and university libraries."
—*E-Streams, Feb '01*

"Recommended for public libraries."
—*Reference & User Services Quarterly, American Library Association, Spring 2000*

"Recommended reference source."
—*Booklist, American Library Association, Feb '00*

"A wealth of information, useful statistics, references are up-to-date and extremely complete. This wonderful collection of data will help students who are interested in a career in any type of forensic field. It is a great resource for attorneys who need information about types of expert witnesses needed in a particular case. It also offers useful information for fiction and nonfiction writers whose work involves a crime. A fascinating compilation. All levels."
—*Choice, Association of College & Research Libraries, Jan '00*

"There are several items that make this book attractive to consumers who are seeking certain forensic data. . . . This is a useful current source for those seeking general forensic medical answers."
—*American Reference Books Annual, 2000*

Gastrointestinal Diseases & Disorders Sourcebook, 2nd Edition

Basic Consumer Health Information about the Upper and Lower Gastrointestinal (GI) Tract, Including the Esophagus, Stomach, Intestines, Rectum, Liver, and Pancreas, with Facts about Gastroesophageal Reflux Disease, Gastritis, Hernias, Ulcers, Celiac Disease, Diverticulitis, Irritable Bowel Syndrome, Hemorrhoids, Gastrointestinal Cancers, and Other Diseases and Disorders Related to the Digestive Process

Along with Information about Commonly Used Diagnostic and Surgical Procedures, Statistics, Reports on Current Research Initiatives and Clinical Trials, a Glossary, and Resources for Additional Help and Information

Edited by Sandra J. Judd. 681 pages. 2006. 978-0-7808-0798-3.

". . . very readable form. The successful editorial work that brought this material together into a useful and understandable reference makes accessible to all readers information that can help them more effectively understand and obtain help for digestive tract problems."
—*Choice, Association of College & Research Libraries, Feb '97*

SEE ALSO *Diet & Nutrition Sourcebook, Digestive Diseases & Disorders Sourcebook, Eating Disorders Sourcebook*

■

Genetic Disorders Sourcebook, 3rd Edition

Basic Consumer Health Information about Hereditary Diseases and Disorders, Including Facts about the Human Genome, Genetic Inheritance Patterns, Disorders Associated with Specific Genes, Such as Sickle Cell Disease, Hemophilia, and Cystic Fibrosis, Chromosome Disorders, Such as Down Syndrome, Fragile X Syndrome, and Turner Syndrome, and Complex Diseases and Disorders Resulting from the Interaction of Environmental and Genetic Factors, Such as Allergies, Cancer, and Obesity

Along with Facts about Genetic Testing, Suggestions for Parents of Children with Special Needs, Reports on Current Research Initiatives, a Glossary of Genetic Terminology, and Resources for Additional Help and Information

Edited by Karen Bellenir. 777 pages. 2004. 978-0-7808-0742-6.

"This text is recommended for any library with an interest in providing consumer health resources."
—*E-Streams, Aug '05*

"This is a valuable resource for anyone wishing to have an understandable description of any of the topics or disorders included. The editor succeeds in making complex genetic issues understandable."
—*Doody's Book Review Service, May '05*

"A good acquisition for public libraries."
—*American Reference Books Annual, 2005*

"Excellent reference." —*The Bookwatch, Jan '05*

"Recommended reference source."
—*Booklist, American Library Association, Apr '01*

"Important pick for college-level health reference libraries." —*The Bookwatch, Mar '01*

■

Head Trauma Sourcebook

Basic Information for the Layperson about Open-Head and Closed-Head Injuries, Treatment Advances, Recovery, and Rehabilitation

Along with Reports on Current Research Initiatives

Edited by Karen Bellenir. 414 pages. 1997. 978-0-7808-0208-7.

Headache Sourcebook

Basic Consumer Health Information about Migraine, Tension, Cluster, Rebound and Other Types of Headaches, with Facts about the Cause and Prevention of Headaches, the Effects of Stress and the Environment, Headaches during Pregnancy and Menopause, and Childhood Headaches

Along with a Glossary and Other Resources for Additional Help and Information

Edited by Dawn D. Matthews. 362 pages. 2002. 978-0-7808-0337-4.

"Highly recommended for academic and medical reference collections." —*Library Bookwatch, Sep '02*

■

Healthy Aging Sourcebook

Basic Consumer Health Information about Maintaining Health through the Aging Process, Including Advice on Nutrition, Exercise, and Sleep, Help in Making Decisions about Midlife Issues and Retirement, and Guidance Concerning Practical and Informed Choices in Health Consumerism

Along with Data Concerning the Theories of Aging, Different Experiences in Aging by Minority Groups, and Facts about Aging Now and Aging in the Future; and Featuring a Glossary, a Guide to Consumer Help, Additional Suggested Reading, and Practical Resource Directory

Edited by Jenifer Swanson. 536 pages. 1999. 978-0-7808-0390-9.

"Recommended reference source."
—*Booklist, American Library Association, Feb '00*

SEE ALSO *Physical & Mental Issues in Aging Sourcebook*

■

Healthy Children Sourcebook

Basic Consumer Health Information about the Physical and Mental Development of Children between the Ages of 3 and 12, Including Routine Health Care, Preventative Health Services, Safety and First Aid, Healthy Sleep, Dental Care, Nutrition, and Fitness, and Featuring Parenting Tips on Such Topics as Bedwetting, Choosing Day Care, Monitoring TV and Other Media, and Establishing a Foundation for Substance Abuse Prevention

Along with a Glossary of Commonly Used Pediatric Terms and Resources for Additional Help and Information.

Edited by Chad T. Kimball. 647 pages. 2003. 978-0-7808-0247-6.

"It is hard to imagine that any other single resource exists that would provide such a comprehensive guide of timely information on health promotion and disease prevention for children aged 3 to 12."
—*American Reference Books Annual, 2004*

"The strengths of this book are many. It is clearly written, presented and structured."
—*Journal of the National Medical Association, 2004*

SEE ALSO *Childhood Diseases & Disorders Sourcebook*

■

Healthy Heart Sourcebook for Women

Basic Consumer Health Information about Cardiac Issues Specific to Women, Including Facts about Major Risk Factors and Prevention, Treatment and Control Strategies, and Important Dietary Issues

Along with a Special Section Regarding the Pros and Cons of Hormone Replacement Therapy and Its Impact on Heart Health, and Additional Help, Including Recipes, a Glossary, and a Directory of Resources

Edited by Dawn D. Matthews. 336 pages. 2000. 978-0-7808-0329-9.

"A good reference source and recommended for all public, academic, medical, and hospital libraries."
—*Medical Reference Services Quarterly, Summer '01*

"Because of the lack of information specific to women on this topic, this book is recommended for public libraries and consumer libraries."
—*American Reference Books Annual, 2001*

"Contains very important information about coronary artery disease that all women should know. The information is current and presented in an easy-to-read format. The book will make a good addition to any library." —*American Medical Writers Association Journal, Summer '00*

"Important, basic reference."
—*Reviewer's Bookwatch, Jul '00*

SEE ALSO *Cardiovascular Diseases & Disorders Sourcebook, Women's Health Concerns Sourcebook*

■

Hepatitis Sourcebook

Basic Consumer Health Information about Hepatitis A, Hepatitis B, Hepatitis C, and Other Forms of Hepatitis, Including Autoimmune Hepatitis, Alcoholic Hepatitis, Nonalcoholic Steatohepatitis, and Toxic Hepatitis, with

Facts about Risk Factors, Screening Methods, Diagnostic Tests, and Treatment Options

Along with Information on Liver Health, Tips for People Living with Chronic Hepatitis, Reports on Current Research Initiatives, a Glossary of Terms Related to Hepatitis, and a Directory of Sources for Further Help and Information

Edited by Sandra J. Judd. 597 pages. 2005. 978-0-7808-0749-5.

"Highly recommended."
—*American Reference Books Annual, 2006*

Household Safety Sourcebook

Basic Consumer Health Information about Household Safety, Including Information about Poisons, Chemicals, Fire, and Water Hazards in the Home

Along with Advice about the Safe Use of Home Maintenance Equipment, Choosing Toys and Nursery Furniture, Holiday and Recreation Safety, a Glossary, and Resources for Further Help and Information

Edited by Dawn D. Matthews. 606 pages. 2002. 978-0-7808-0338-1.

"This work will be useful in public libraries with large consumer health and wellness departments."
—*American Reference Books Annual, 2003*

"As a sourcebook on household safety this book meets its mark. It is encyclopedic in scope and covers a wide range of safety issues that are commonly seen in the home." —*E-Streams, Jul '02*

Hypertension Sourcebook

Basic Consumer Health Information about the Causes, Diagnosis, and Treatment of High Blood Pressure, with Facts about Consequences, Complications, and Co-Occurring Disorders, Such as Coronary Heart Disease, Diabetes, Stroke, Kidney Disease, and Hypertensive Retinopathy, and Issues in Blood Pressure Control, Including Dietary Choices, Stress Management, and Medications

Along with Reports on Current Research Initiatives and Clinical Trials, a Glossary, and Resources for Additional Help and Information

Edited by Dawn D. Matthews and Karen Bellenir. 613 pages. 2004. 978-0-7808-0674-0.

"Academic, public, and medical libraries will want to add the *Hypertension Sourcebook* to their collections."
—*E-Streams, Aug '05*

"The strength of this source is the wide range of information given about hypertension."
—*American Reference Books Annual, 2005*

Immune System Disorders Sourcebook, 2nd Edition

Basic Consumer Health Information about Disorders of the Immune System, Including Immune System Function and Response, Diagnosis of Immune Disorders, Information about Inherited Immune Disease, Acquired Immune Disease, and Autoimmune Diseases, Including Primary Immune Deficiency, Acquired Immunodeficiency Syndrome (AIDS), Lupus, Multiple Sclerosis, Type 1 Diabetes, Rheumatoid Arthritis, and Graves' Disease

Along with Treatments, Tips for Coping with Immune Disorders, a Glossary, and a Directory of Additional Resources.

Edited by Joyce Brennfleck Shannon. 671 pages. 2005. 978-0-7808-0748-8.

"Highly recommended for academic and public libraries." —*American Reference Books Annual, 2006*

"The updated second edition is a 'must' for any consumer health library seeking a solid resource covering the treatments, symptoms, and options for immune disorder sufferers. . . . An excellent guide."
—*MBR Bookwatch, Jan '06*

Infant & Toddler Health Sourcebook

Basic Consumer Health Information about the Physical and Mental Development of Newborns, Infants, and Toddlers, Including Neonatal Concerns, Nutrition Recommendations, Immunization Schedules, Common Pediatric Disorders, Assessments and Milestones, Safety Tips, and Advice for Parents and Other Caregivers

Along with a Glossary of Terms and Resource Listings for Additional Help

Edited by Jenifer Swanson. 585 pages. 2000. 978-0-7808-0246-9.

"As a reference for the general public, this would be useful in any library." —*E-Streams, May '01*

"Recommended reference source."
—*Booklist, American Library Association, Feb '01*

"This is a good source for general use."
—*American Reference Books Annual, 2001*

Infectious Diseases Sourcebook

Basic Consumer Health Information about Non-Contagious Bacterial, Viral, Prion, Fungal, and Parasitic Diseases Spread by Food and Water, Insects and Animals, or Environmental Contact, Including Botulism, E. Coli, Encephalitis, Legionnaires' Disease, Lyme Disease, Malaria, Plague, Rabies, Salmonella, Tetanus, and Others, and Facts about Newly Emerging Diseases, Such as Hantavirus, Mad Cow Disease, Monkeypox, and West Nile Virus

Along with Information about Preventing Disease Transmission, the Threat of Bioterrorism, and Current Research Initiatives, with a Glossary and Directory of Resources for More Information

Edited by Karen Bellenir. 634 pages. 2004. 978-0-7808-0675-7.

"This reference continues the excellent tradition of the *Health Reference Series* in consolidating a wealth of information on a selected topic into a format that is easy to use and accessible to the general public."
—*American Reference Books Annual, 2005*

"Recommended for public and academic libraries."
—*E-Streams, Jan '05*

Injury & Trauma Sourcebook

Basic Consumer Health Information about the Impact of Injury, the Diagnosis and Treatment of Common and Traumatic Injuries, Emergency Care, and Specific Injuries Related to Home, Community, Workplace, Transportation, and Recreation

Along with Guidelines for Injury Prevention, a Glossary, and a Directory of Additional Resources

Edited by Joyce Brennfleck Shannon. 696 pages. 2002. 978-0-7808-0421-0.

"This publication is the most comprehensive work of its kind about injury and trauma."
—*American Reference Books Annual, 2003*

"This sourcebook provides concise, easily readable, basic health information about injuries. . . . This book is well organized and an easy to use reference resource suitable for hospital, health sciences and public libraries with consumer health collections."
—*E-Streams, Nov '02*

"Practitioners should be aware of guides such as this in order to facilitate their use by patients and their families."
—*Doody's Health Sciences Book Review Journal, Sep-Oct '02*

"Recommended reference source."
—*Booklist, American Library Association, Sep '02*

"Highly recommended for academic and medical reference collections."
—*Library Bookwatch, Sep '02*

Kidney & Urinary Tract Diseases & Disorders Sourcebook

SEE *Urinary Tract & Kidney Diseases & Disorders Sourcebook*

Learning Disabilities Sourcebook, 2nd Edition

Basic Consumer Health Information about Learning Disabilities, Including Dyslexia, Developmental Speech and Language Disabilities, Non-Verbal Learning Disorders, Developmental Arithmetic Disorder, Developmental Writing Disorder, and Other Conditions That Impede Learning Such as Attention Deficit/Hyperactivity Disorder, Brain Injury, Hearing Impairment, Klinefelter Syndrome, Dyspraxia, and Tourette's Syndrome

Along with Facts about Educational Issues and Assistive Technology, Coping Strategies, a Glossary of Related Terms, and Resources for Further Help and Information

Edited by Dawn D. Matthews. 621 pages. 2003. 978-0-7808-0626-9.

"The second edition of Learning Disabilities Sourcebook far surpasses the earlier edition in that it is more focused on information that will be useful as a consumer health resource."
—*American Reference Books Annual, 2004*

"Teachers as well as consumers will find this an essential guide to understanding various syndromes and their latest treatments. [An] invaluable reference for public and school library collections alike."
—*Library Bookwatch, Apr '03*

Named "Outstanding Reference Book of 1999."
—*New York Public Library, Feb '00*

"An excellent candidate for inclusion in a public library reference section. It's a great source of information. Teachers will also find the book useful. Definitely worth reading."
—*Journal of Adolescent & Adult Literacy, Feb 2000*

"Readable . . . provides a solid base of information regarding successful techniques used with individuals who have learning disabilities, as well as practical suggestions for educators and family members. Clear language, concise descriptions, and pertinent information for contacting multiple resources add to the strength of this book as a useful tool."
—*Choice, Association of College & Research Libraries, Feb '99*

"Recommended reference source."
—*Booklist, American Library Association, Sep '98*

"A useful resource for libraries and for those who don't have the time to identify and locate the individual publications."
—*Disability Resources Monthly, Sep '98*

Leukemia Sourcebook

Basic Consumer Health Information about Adult and Childhood Leukemias, Including Acute Lymphocytic Leukemia (ALL), Chronic Lymphocytic Leukemia (CLL), Acute Myelogenous Leukemia (AML), Chronic Myelogenous Leukemia (CML), and Hairy Cell Leukemia, and Treatments Such as Chemotherapy, Radiation Therapy, Peripheral Blood Stem Cell and Marrow Transplantation, and Immunotherapy

Along with Tips for Life During and After Treatment, a Glossary, and Directories of Additional Resources

Edited by Joyce Brennfleck Shannon. 587 pages. 2003. 978-0-7808-0627-6.

"Unlike other medical books for the layperson, . . . the language does not talk down to the reader. . . . This volume is highly recommended for all libraries."
—*American Reference Books Annual, 2004*

". . . a fine title which ranges from diagnosis to alternative treatments, staging, and tips for life during and after diagnosis."
—*The Bookwatch, Dec '03*

Liver Disorders Sourcebook

Basic Consumer Health Information about the Liver and How It Works; Liver Diseases, Including Cancer, Cirrhosis, Hepatitis, and Toxic and Drug Related Diseases; Tips for Maintaining a Healthy Liver; Laboratory Tests, Radiology Tests, and Facts about Liver Transplantation

Along with a Section on Support Groups, a Glossary, and Resource Listings

Edited by Joyce Brennfleck Shannon. 591 pages. 2000. 978-0-7808-0383-1.

"A valuable resource."
—*American Reference Books Annual, 2001*

"This title is recommended for health sciences and public libraries with consumer health collections."
—*E-Streams, Oct '00*

"Recommended reference source."
—*Booklist, American Library Association, Jun '00*

■

Lung Disorders Sourcebook

Basic Consumer Health Information about Emphysema, Pneumonia, Tuberculosis, Asthma, Cystic Fibrosis, and Other Lung Disorders, Including Facts about Diagnostic Procedures, Treatment Strategies, Disease Prevention Efforts, and Such Risk Factors as Smoking, Air Pollution, and Exposure to Asbestos, Radon, and Other Agents

Along with a Glossary and Resources for Additional Help and Information

Edited by Dawn D. Matthews. 678 pages. 2002. 978-0-7808-0339-8.

"This title is a great addition for public and school libraries because it provides concise health information on the lungs."
—*American Reference Books Annual, 2003*

"Highly recommended for academic and medical reference collections." —*Library Bookwatch, Sep '02*

SEE ALSO *Respiratory Diseases & Disorders Sourcebook*

■

Medical Tests Sourcebook, 2nd Edition

Basic Consumer Health Information about Medical Tests, Including Age-Specific Health Tests, Important Health Screenings and Exams, Home-Use Tests, Blood and Specimen Tests, Electrical Tests, Scope Tests, Genetic Testing, and Imaging Tests, Such as X-Rays, Ultrasound, Computed Tomography, Magnetic Resonance Imaging, Angiography, and Nuclear Medicine

Along with a Glossary and Directory of Additional Resources

Edited by Joyce Brennfleck Shannon. 654 pages. 2004. 978-0-7808-0670-2.

"Recommended for hospital and health sciences libraries with consumer health collections."
—*E-Streams, Mar '00*

"This is an overall excellent reference with a wealth of general knowledge that may aid those who are reluctant to get vital tests performed."
—*Today's Librarian, Jan '00*

"A valuable reference guide."
—*American Reference Books Annual, 2000*

■

Men's Health Concerns Sourcebook, 2nd Edition

Basic Consumer Health Information about the Medical and Mental Concerns of Men, Including Theories about the Shorter Male Lifespan, the Leading Causes of Death and Disability, Physical Concerns of Special Significance to Men, Reproductive and Sexual Concerns, Sexually Transmitted Diseases, Men's Mental and Emotional Health, and Lifestyle Choices That Affect Wellness, Such as Nutrition, Fitness, and Substance Use

Along with a Glossary of Related Terms and a Directory of Organizational Resources in Men's Health

Edited by Robert Aquinas McNally. 644 pages. 2004. 978-0-7808-0671-9.

"A very accessible reference for non-specialist general readers and consumers." —*The Bookwatch, Jun '04*

"This comprehensive resource and the series are highly recommended."
—*American Reference Books Annual, 2000*

"Recommended reference source."
—*Booklist, American Library Association, Dec '98*

■

Mental Health Disorders Sourcebook, 3rd Edition

Basic Consumer Health Information about Mental and Emotional Health and Mental Illness, Including Facts about Depression, Bipolar Disorder, and Other Mood Disorders, Phobias, Post-Traumatic Stress Disorder (PTSD), Obsessive-Compulsive Disorder, and Other Anxiety Disorders, Impulse Control Disorders, Eating Disorders, Personality Disorders, and Psychotic Disorders, Including Schizophrenia and Dissociative Disorders

Along with Statistical Information, a Special Section Concerning Mental Health Issues in Children and Adolescents, a Glossary, and Directories of Resources for Additional Help and Information

Edited by Karen Bellenir. 661 pages. 2005. 978-0-7808-0747-1.

"Recommended for public libraries and academic libraries with an undergraduate program in psychology."
—*American Reference Books Annual, 2006*

"Recommended reference source."
—*Booklist, American Library Association, Jun '00*

Mental Retardation Sourcebook

Basic Consumer Health Information about Mental Retardation and Its Causes, Including Down Syndrome, Fetal Alcohol Syndrome, Fragile X Syndrome, Genetic Conditions, Injury, and Environmental Sources

Along with Preventive Strategies, Parenting Issues, Educational Implications, Health Care Needs, Employment and Economic Matters, Legal Issues, a Glossary, and a Resource Listing for Additional Help and Information

Edited by Joyce Brennfleck Shannon. 642 pages. 2000. 978-0-7808-0377-0.

"Public libraries will find the book useful for reference and as a beginning research point for students, parents, and caregivers."
—*American Reference Books Annual, 2001*

"The strength of this work is that it compiles many basic fact sheets and addresses for further information in one volume. It is intended and suitable for the general public. This sourcebook is relevant to any collection providing health information to the general public."
—*E-Streams, Nov '00*

"From preventing retardation to parenting and family challenges, this covers health, social and legal issues and will prove an invaluable overview."
—*Reviewer's Bookwatch, Jul '00*

Movement Disorders Sourcebook

Basic Consumer Health Information about Neurological Movement Disorders, Including Essential Tremor, Parkinson's Disease, Dystonia, Cerebral Palsy, Huntington's Disease, Myasthenia Gravis, Multiple Sclerosis, and Other Early-Onset and Adult-Onset Movement Disorders, Their Symptoms and Causes, Diagnostic Tests, and Treatments

Along with Mobility and Assistive Technology Information, a Glossary, and a Directory of Additional Resources

Edited by Joyce Brennfleck Shannon. 655 pages. 2003. 978-0-7808-0628-3.

". . . a good resource for consumers and recommended for public, community college and undergraduate libraries." —*American Reference Books Annual, 2004*

Muscular Dystrophy Sourcebook

Basic Consumer Health Information about Congenital, Childhood-Onset, and Adult-Onset Forms of Muscular Dystrophy, Such as Duchenne, Becker, Emery-Dreifuss, Distal, Limb-Girdle, Facioscapulohumeral (FSHD), Myotonic, and Ophthalmoplegic Muscular Dystrophies, Including Facts about Diagnostic Tests, Medical and Physical Therapies, Management of Co-Occurring Conditions, and Parenting Guidelines

Along with Practical Tips for Home Care, a Glossary, and Directories of Additional Resources

Edited by Joyce Brennfleck Shannon. 577 pages. 2004. 978-0-7808-0676-4.

"This book is highly recommended for public and academic libraries as well as health care offices that support the information needs of patients and their families."
—*E-Streams, Apr '05*

"Excellent reference." —*The Bookwatch, Jan '05*

Obesity Sourcebook

Basic Consumer Health Information about Diseases and Other Problems Associated with Obesity, and Including Facts about Risk Factors, Prevention Issues, and Management Approaches

Along with Statistical and Demographic Data, Information about Special Populations, Research Updates, a Glossary, and Source Listings for Further Help and Information

Edited by Wilma Caldwell and Chad T. Kimball. 376 pages. 2001. 978-0-7808-0333-6.

"The book synthesizes the reliable medical literature on obesity into one easy-to-read and useful resource for the general public."
—*American Reference Books Annual, 2002*

"This is a very useful resource book for the lay public."
—*Doody's Review Service, Nov '01*

"Well suited for the health reference collection of a public library or an academic health science library that serves the general population." —*E-Streams, Sep '01*

"Recommended reference source."
—*Booklist, American Library Association, Apr '01*

"Recommended pick both for specialty health library collections and any general consumer health reference collection." —*The Bookwatch, Apr '01*

Oral Health Sourcebook

***SEE** Dental Care & Oral Health Sourcebook*

Osteoporosis Sourcebook

Basic Consumer Health Information about Primary and Secondary Osteoporosis and Juvenile Osteoporosis and Related Conditions, Including Fibrous Dysplasia, Gaucher Disease, Hyperthyroidism, Hypophosphatasia, Myeloma, Osteopetrosis, Osteogenesis Imperfecta, and Paget's Disease

Along with Information about Risk Factors, Treatments, Traditional and Non-Traditional Pain Management, a Glossary of Related Terms, and a Directory of Resources

Edited by Allan R. Cook. 584 pages. 2001. 978-0-7808-0239-1.

"This would be a book to be kept in a staff or patient library. The targeted audience is the layperson, but the therapist who needs a quick bit of information on a particular topic will also find the book useful."
—*Physical Therapy, Jan '02*

"This resource is recommended as a great reference source for public, health, and academic libraries, and is another triumph for the editors of Omnigraphics."
—*American Reference Books Annual, 2002*

"Recommended for all public libraries and general health collections, especially those supporting patient education or consumer health programs."
—*E-Streams, Nov '01*

"Will prove valuable to any library seeking to maintain a current, comprehensive reference collection of health resources. . . . From prevention to treatment and associated conditions, this provides an excellent survey."
—*The Bookwatch, Aug '01*

"Recommended reference source."
—*Booklist, American Library Association, Jul '01*

SEE ALSO *Healthy Aging Sourcebook, Physical & Mental Issues in Aging Sourcebook, Women's Health Concerns Sourcebook*

Pain Sourcebook, 2nd Edition

Basic Consumer Health Information about Specific Forms of Acute and Chronic Pain, Including Muscle and Skeletal Pain, Nerve Pain, Cancer Pain, and Disorders Characterized by Pain, Such as Fibromyalgia, Shingles, Angina, Arthritis, and Headaches

Along with Information about Pain Medications and Management Techniques, Complementary and Alternative Pain Relief Options, Tips for People Living with Chronic Pain, a Glossary, and a Directory of Sources for Further Information

Edited by Karen Bellenir. 670 pages. 2002. 978-0-7808-0612-2.

"A source of valuable information. . . . This book offers help to nonmedical people who need information about pain and pain management. It is also an excellent reference for those who participate in patient education."
—*Doody's Review Service, Sep '02*

"Highly recommended for academic and medical reference collections." —*Library Bookwatch, Sep '02*

"The text is readable, easily understood, and well indexed. This excellent volume belongs in all patient education libraries, consumer health sections of public libraries, and many personal collections."
—*American Reference Books Annual, 1999*

"The information is basic in terms of scholarship and is appropriate for general readers. Written in journalistic style . . . intended for non-professionals. Quite thorough in its coverage of different pain conditions and summarizes the latest clinical information regarding pain treatment." —*Choice, Association of College and Research Libraries, Jun '98*

"Recommended reference source."
—*Booklist, American Library Association, Mar '98*

Pediatric Cancer Sourcebook

Basic Consumer Health Information about Leukemias, Brain Tumors, Sarcomas, Lymphomas, and Other Cancers in Infants, Children, and Adolescents, Including Descriptions of Cancers, Treatments, and Coping Strategies

Along with Suggestions for Parents, Caregivers, and Concerned Relatives, a Glossary of Cancer Terms, and Resource Listings

Edited by Edward J. Prucha. 587 pages. 1999. 978-0-7808-0245-2.

"An excellent source of information. Recommended for public, hospital, and health science libraries with consumer health collections." —*E-Streams, Jun '00*

"Recommended reference source."
—*Booklist, American Library Association, Feb '00*

"A valuable addition to all libraries specializing in health services and many public libraries."
—*American Reference Books Annual, 2000*

SEE ALSO *Childhood Diseases & Disorders Sourcebook, Healthy Children Sourcebook*

Physical & Mental Issues in Aging Sourcebook

Basic Consumer Health Information on Physical and Mental Disorders Associated with the Aging Process, Including Concerns about Cardiovascular Disease, Pulmonary Disease, Oral Health, Digestive Disorders, Musculoskeletal and Skin Disorders, Metabolic Changes, Sexual and Reproductive Issues, and Changes in Vision, Hearing, and Other Senses

Along with Data about Longevity and Causes of Death, Information on Acute and Chronic Pain, Descriptions of Mental Concerns, a Glossary of Terms, and Resource Listings for Additional Help

Edited by Jenifer Swanson. 660 pages. 1999. 978-0-7808-0233-9.

"This is a treasure of health information for the layperson." — *Choice Health Sciences Supplement, Association of College & Research Libraries, May '00*

"Recommended for public libraries."
—*American Reference Books Annual, 2000*

"Recommended reference source."
—*Booklist, American Library Association, Oct '99*

SEE ALSO *Healthy Aging Sourcebook*

Podiatry Sourcebook, 2nd Edition

Basic Consumer Health Information about Disorders, Diseases, Deformities, and Injuries that Affect the Foot and Ankle, Including Sprains, Corns, Calluses, Bunions, Plantar Warts, Plantar Fasciitis, Neuromas, Clubfoot, Flat Feet, Achilles Tendonitis, and Much More

Along with Information about Selecting a Foot Care Specialist, Foot Fitness, Shoes and Socks, Diagnostic Tests and Corrective Procedures, Financial Assistance for Corrective Devices, a Glossary of Related Terms, and a Directory of Resources for Additional Help and Information

Edited by Ivy L. Alexander. 543 pages. 2007. 978-0-7808-0944-4.

"Recommended reference source."
—*Booklist, American Library Association, Feb '02*

"There is a lot of information presented here on a topic that is usually only covered sparingly in most larger comprehensive medical encyclopedias."
—*American Reference Books Annual, 2002*

Pregnancy & Birth Sourcebook, 2nd Edition

Basic Consumer Health Information about Conception and Pregnancy, Including Facts about Fertility, Infertility, Pregnancy Symptoms and Complications, Fetal Growth and Development, Labor, Delivery, and the Postpartum Period, as Well as Information about Maintaining Health and Wellness during Pregnancy and Caring for a Newborn

Along with Information about Public Health Assistance for Low-Income Pregnant Women, a Glossary, and Directories of Agencies and Organizations Providing Help and Support

Edited by Amy L. Sutton. 626 pages. 2004. 978-0-7808-0672-6.

"Will appeal to public and school reference collections strong in medicine and women's health. . . . Deserves a spot on any medical reference shelf."
—*The Bookwatch, Jul '04*

"A well-organized handbook. Recommended."
—*Choice, Association of College & Research Libraries, Apr '98*

"Recommended reference source."
—*Booklist, American Library Association, Mar '98*

"Recommended for public libraries."
—*American Reference Books Annual, 1998*

SEE ALSO *Breastfeeding Sourcebook, Congenital Disorders Sourcebook, Family Planning Sourcebook*

Prostate & Urological Disorders Sourcebook

Basic Consumer Health Information about Urogenital and Sexual Disorders in Men, Including Prostate and Other Andrological Cancers, Prostatitis, Benign Prostatic Hyperplasia, Testicular and Penile Trauma, Cryptorchidism, Peyronie Disease, Erectile Dysfunction, and Male Factor Infertility, and Facts about Commonly Used Tests and Procedures, Such as Prostatectomy, Vasectomy, Vasectomy Reversal, Penile Implants, and Semen Analysis

Along with a Glossary of Andrological Terms and a Directory of Resources for Additional Information

Edited by Karen Bellenir. 631 pages. 2005. 978-0-7808-0797-6.

Prostate Cancer Sourcebook

Basic Consumer Health Information about Prostate Cancer, Including Information about the Associated Risk Factors, Detection, Diagnosis, and Treatment of Prostate Cancer

Along with Information on Non-Malignant Prostate Conditions, and Featuring a Section Listing Support and Treatment Centers and a Glossary of Related Terms

Edited by Dawn D. Matthews. 358 pages. 2001. 978-0-7808-0324-4.

"Recommended reference source."
—*Booklist, American Library Association, Jan '02*

"A valuable resource for health care consumers seeking information on the subject. . . . All text is written in a clear, easy-to-understand language that avoids technical jargon. Any library that collects consumer health resources would strengthen their collection with the addition of the *Prostate Cancer Sourcebook.*"
—*American Reference Books Annual, 2002*

SEE ALSO *Men's Health Concerns Sourcebook*

Reconstructive & Cosmetic Surgery Sourcebook

Basic Consumer Health Information on Cosmetic and Reconstructive Plastic Surgery, Including Statistical Information about Different Surgical Procedures, Things to Consider Prior to Surgery, Plastic Surgery Techniques and Tools, Emotional and Psychological Considerations, and Procedure-Specific Information

Along with a Glossary of Terms and a Listing of Resources for Additional Help and Information

Edited by M. Lisa Weatherford. 374 pages. 2001. 978-0-7808-0214-8.

"An excellent reference that addresses cosmetic and medically necessary reconstructive surgeries. . . . The style of the prose is calm and reassuring, discussing the many positive outcomes now available due to advances in surgical techniques."
—*American Reference Books Annual, 2002*

"Recommended for health science libraries that are open to the public, as well as hospital libraries that are open to the patients. This book is a good resource for the consumer interested in plastic surgery."
—*E-Streams, Dec '01*

"Recommended reference source."
—*Booklist, American Library Association, Jul '01*

Rehabilitation Sourcebook

Basic Consumer Health Information about Rehabilitation for People Recovering from Heart Surgery, Spinal Cord Injury, Stroke, Orthopedic Impairments, Amputation, Pulmonary Impairments, Traumatic Injury, and More, Including Physical Therapy, Occupational Therapy, Speech/Language Therapy, Massage Therapy, Dance Therapy, Art Therapy, and Recreational Therapy

Along with Information on Assistive and Adaptive Devices, a Glossary, and Resources for Additional Help and Information

Edited by Dawn D. Matthews. 531 pages. 1999. 978-0-7808-0236-0.

"This is an excellent resource for public library reference and health collections."
—*American Reference Books Annual, 2001*

"Recommended reference source."
—*Booklist, American Library Association, May '00*

Respiratory Diseases & Disorders Sourcebook

Basic Information about Respiratory Diseases and Disorders, Including Asthma, Cystic Fibrosis, Pneumonia, the Common Cold, Influenza, and Others, Featuring Facts about the Respiratory System, Statistical and Demographic Data, Treatments, Self-Help Management Suggestions, and Current Research Initiatives

Edited by Allan R. Cook and Peter D. Dresser. 771 pages. 1995. 978-0-7808-0037-3.

"Designed for the layperson and for patients and their families coping with respiratory illness. . . . an extensive array of information on diagnosis, treatment, management, and prevention of respiratory illnesses for the general reader." —*Choice, Association of College & Research Libraries, Jun '96*

"A highly recommended text for all collections. It is a comforting reminder of the power of knowledge that good books carry between their covers."
—*Academic Library Book Review, Spring '96*

"A comprehensive collection of authoritative information presented in a nontechnical, humanitarian style for patients, families, and caregivers."
—*Association of Operating Room Nurses, Sep/Oct '95*

SEE ALSO *Lung Disorders Sourcebook*

Sexually Transmitted Diseases Sourcebook, 3rd Edition

Basic Consumer Health Information about Chlamydial Infections, Gonorrhea, Hepatitis, Herpes, HIV/AIDS, Human Papillomavirus, Pubic Lice, Scabies, Syphilis, Trichomoniasis, Vaginal Infections, and Other Sexually Transmitted Diseases, Including Facts about Risk Factors, Symptoms, Diagnosis, Treatment, and the Prevention of Sexually Transmitted Infections

Along with Updates on Current Research Initiatives, a Glossary of Related Terms, and Resources for Additional Help and Information

Edited by Amy L. Sutton. 629 pages. 2006. 978-0-7808-0824-9.

"Recommended for consumer health collections in public libraries, and secondary school and community college libraries."
—*American Reference Books Annual, 2002*

"Every school and public library should have a copy of this comprehensive and user-friendly reference book."
—*Choice, Association of College & Research Libraries, Sep '01*

"This is a highly recommended book. This is an especially important book for all school and public libraries."
—*AIDS Book Review Journal, Jul-Aug '01*

"Recommended reference source."
—*Booklist, American Library Association, Apr '01*

Sleep Disorders Sourcebook, 2nd Edition

Basic Consumer Health Information about Sleep and Sleep Disorders, Including Insomnia, Sleep Apnea, Restless Legs Syndrome, Narcolepsy, Parasomnias, and Other Health Problems That Affect Sleep, Plus Facts about Diagnostic Procedures, Treatment Strategies, Sleep Medications, and Tips for Improving Sleep Quality

Along with a Glossary of Related Terms and Resources for Additional Help and Information

Edited by Amy L. Sutton. 567 pages. 2005. 978-0-7808-0743-3.

"This book will be useful for just about everybody, especially the 40 million Americans with sleep disorders."
—*American Reference Books Annual, 2006*

"Recommended for public libraries and libraries supporting health care professionals." —*E-Streams, Sep '05*

". . . key medical library acquisition."
—*The Bookwatch, Jun '05*

Smoking Concerns Sourcebook

Basic Consumer Health Information about Nicotine Addiction and Smoking Cessation, Featuring Facts about the Health Effects of Tobacco Use, Including Lung and Other Cancers, Heart Disease, Stroke, and Respiratory Disorders, Such as Emphysema and Chronic Bronchitis

Along with Information about Smoking Prevention Programs, Suggestions for Achieving and Maintaining a Smoke-Free Lifestyle, Statistics about Tobacco Use, Reports on Current Research Initiatives, a Glossary of Related Terms, and Directories of Resources for Additional Help and Information

Edited by Karen Bellenir. 621 pages. 2004. 978-0-7808-0323-7.

"Provides everything needed for the student or general reader seeking practical details on the effects of tobacco use." —*The Bookwatch, Mar '05*

"Public libraries and consumer health care libraries will find this work useful."
—*American Reference Books Annual, 2005*

Sports Injuries Sourcebook, 2nd Edition

Basic Consumer Health Information about the Diagnosis, Treatment, and Rehabilitation of Common Sports-Related Injuries in Children and Adults

Along with Suggestions for Conditioning and Training, Information and Prevention Tips for Injuries Frequently Associated with Specific Sports and Special Populations, a Glossary, and a Directory of Additional Resources

Edited by Joyce Brennfleck Shannon. 614 pages. 2002. 978-0-7808-0604-7.

"This is an excellent reference for consumers and it is recommended for public, community college, and undergraduate libraries."
—*American Reference Books Annual, 2003*

"Recommended reference source."
—*Booklist, American Library Association, Feb '03*

Stress-Related Disorders Sourcebook

Basic Consumer Health Information about Stress and Stress-Related Disorders, Including Stress Origins and Signals, Environmental Stress at Work and Home, Mental and Emotional Stress Associated with Depression, Post-Traumatic Stress Disorder, Panic Disorder, Suicide, and the Physical Effects of Stress on the Cardiovascular, Immune, and Nervous Systems

Along with Stress Management Techniques, a Glossary, and a Listing of Additional Resources

Edited by Joyce Brennfleck Shannon. 610 pages. 2002. 978-0-7808-0560-6.

"Well written for a general readership, the *Stress-Related Disorders Sourcebook* is a useful addition to the health reference literature."
—*American Reference Books Annual, 2003*

"I am impressed by the amount of information. It offers a thorough overview of the causes and consequences of stress for the layperson. . . . A well-done and thorough reference guide for professionals and nonprofessionals alike."
—*Doody's Review Service, Dec '02*

Stroke Sourcebook

Basic Consumer Health Information about Stroke, Including Ischemic, Hemorrhagic, Transient Ischemic Attack (TIA), and Pediatric Stroke, Stroke Triggers and Risks, Diagnostic Tests, Treatments, and Rehabilitation Information

Along with Stroke Prevention Guidelines, Legal and Financial Information, a Glossary, and a Directory of Additional Resources

Edited by Joyce Brennfleck Shannon. 606 pages. 2003. 978-0-7808-0630-6.

"This volume is highly recommended and should be in every medical, hospital, and public library."
—*American Reference Books Annual, 2004*

"Highly recommended for the amount and variety of topics and information covered."
—*Choice, Nov '03*

Surgery Sourcebook

Basic Consumer Health Information about Inpatient and Outpatient Surgeries, Including Cardiac, Vascular, Orthopedic, Ocular, Reconstructive, Cosmetic, Gynecologic, and Ear, Nose, and Throat Procedures and More

Along with Information about Operating Room Policies and Instruments, Laser Surgery Techniques, Hospital Errors, Statistical Data, a Glossary, and Listings of Sources for Further Help and Information

Edited by Annemarie S. Muth and Karen Bellenir. 596 pages. 2002. 978-0-7808-0380-0.

"Large public libraries and medical libraries would benefit from this material in their reference collections."
—*American Reference Books Annual, 2004*

"Invaluable reference for public and school library collections alike."
—*Library Bookwatch, Apr '03*

Thyroid Disorders Sourcebook

Basic Consumer Health Information about Disorders of the Thyroid and Parathyroid Glands, Including Hypothyroidism, Hyperthyroidism, Graves Disease, Hashimoto Thyroiditis, Thyroid Cancer, and Parathyroid Disorders, Featuring Facts about Symptoms, Risk Factors, Tests, and Treatments

Along with Information about the Effects of Thyroid Imbalance on Other Body Systems, Environmental Factors That Affect the Thyroid Gland, a Glossary, and a Directory of Additional Resources

Edited by Joyce Brennfleck Shannon. 599 pages. 2005. 978-0-7808-0745-7.

"Recommended for consumer health collections."
—*American Reference Books Annual, 2006*

"Highly recommended pick for basic consumer health reference holdings at all levels."
—*The Bookwatch, Aug '05*

Transplantation Sourcebook

Basic Consumer Health Information about Organ and Tissue Transplantation, Including Physical and Financial Preparations, Procedures and Issues Relating to Specific Solid Organ and Tissue Transplants, Rehabilitation, Pediatric Transplant Information, the Future of Transplantation, and Organ and Tissue Donation

Along with a Glossary and Listings of Additional Resources

Edited by Joyce Brennfleck Shannon. 628 pages. 2002. 978-0-7808-0322-0.

"Along with these advances [in transplantation technology] have come a number of daunting questions for potential transplant patients, their families, and their health care providers. This reference text is the best single tool to address many of these questions. . . . It will be a much-needed addition to the reference collections in health care, academic, and large public libraries."
—*American Reference Books Annual, 2003*

"Recommended for libraries with an interest in offering consumer health information." —*E-Streams, Jul '02*

"This is a unique and valuable resource for patients facing transplantation and their families." —*Doody's Review Service, Jun '02*

Traveler's Health Sourcebook

Basic Consumer Health Information for Travelers, Including Physical and Medical Preparations, Transportation Health and Safety, Essential Information about Food and Water, Sun Exposure, Insect and Snake Bites, Camping and Wilderness Medicine, and Travel with Physical or Medical Disabilities

Along with International Travel Tips, Vaccination Recommendations, Geographical Health Issues, Disease Risks, a Glossary, and a Listing of Additional Resources

Edited by Joyce Brennfleck Shannon. 613 pages. 2000. 978-0-7808-0384-8.

"Recommended reference source." —*Booklist, American Library Association, Feb '01*

"This book is recommended for any public library, any travel collection, and especially any collection for the physically disabled." —*American Reference Books Annual, 2001*

SEE ALSO *Worldwide Health Sourcebook*

Urinary Tract & Kidney Diseases & Disorders Sourcebook, 2nd Edition

Basic Consumer Health Information about the Urinary System, Including the Bladder, Urethra, Ureters, and Kidneys, with Facts about Urinary Tract Infections, Incontinence, Congenital Disorders, Kidney Stones, Cancers of the Urinary Tract and Kidneys, Kidney Failure, Dialysis, and Kidney Transplantation

Along with Statistical and Demographic Information, Reports on Current Research in Kidney and Urologic Health, a Summary of Commonly Used Diagnostic Tests, a Glossary of Related Terms, and a Directory of Resources for Additional Help and Information

Edited by Ivy L. Alexander. 649 pages. 2005. 978-0-7808-0750-1.

"A good choice for a consumer health information library or for a medical library needing information to refer to their patients." —*American Reference Books Annual, 2006*

Vegetarian Sourcebook

Basic Consumer Health Information about Vegetarian Diets, Lifestyle, and Philosophy, Including Definitions of Vegetarianism and Veganism, Tips about Adopting Vegetarianism, Creating a Vegetarian Pantry, and Meeting Nutritional Needs of Vegetarians, with Facts Regarding Vegetarianism's Effect on Pregnant and Lactating Women, Children, Athletes, and Senior Citizens

Along with a Glossary of Commonly Used Vegetarian Terms and Resources for Additional Help and Information

Edited by Chad T. Kimball. 360 pages. 2002. 978-0-7808-0439-5.

"Organizes into one concise volume the answers to the most common questions concerning vegetarian diets and lifestyles. This title is recommended for public and secondary school libraries." —*E-Streams, Apr '03*

"Invaluable reference for public and school library collections alike." —*Library Bookwatch, Apr '03*

"The articles in this volume are easy to read and come from authoritative sources. The book does not necessarily support the vegetarian diet but instead provides the pros and cons of this important decision. The Vegetarian Sourcebook is recommended for public libraries and consumer health libraries." —*American Reference Books Annual, 2003*

SEE ALSO *Diet & Nutrition Sourcebook*

Women's Health Concerns Sourcebook, 2nd Edition

Basic Consumer Health Information about the Medical and Mental Concerns of Women, Including Maintaining Health and Wellness, Gynecological Concerns, Breast Health, Sexuality and Reproductive Issues, Menopause, Cancer in Women, Leading Causes of Death and Disability among Women, Physical Concerns of Special Significance to Women, and Women's Mental and Emotional Health

Along with a Glossary of Related Terms and Directories of Resources for Additional Help and Information

Edited by Amy L. Sutton. 746 pages. 2004. 978-0-7808-0673-3.

"This is a useful reference book, which makes the reader knowledgeable about several issues that concern women's health. It is recommended for public libraries and home library collections." —*E-Streams, May '05*

"A useful addition to public and consumer health library collections." —*American Reference Books Annual, 2005*

"A highly recommended title." —*The Bookwatch, May '04*

"Handy compilation. There is an impressive range of diseases, devices, disorders, procedures, and other physical and emotional issues covered . . . well organized, illustrated, and indexed." —*Choice, Association of College & Research Libraries, Jan '98*

SEE ALSO *Breast Cancer Sourcebook, Cancer Sourcebook for Women, Healthy Heart Sourcebook for Women, Osteoporosis Sourcebook*

Workplace Health & Safety Sourcebook

Basic Consumer Health Information about Workplace Health and Safety, Including the Effect of Workplace Hazards on the Lungs, Skin, Heart, Ears, Eyes, Brain,

Reproductive Organs, Musculoskeletal System, and Other Organs and Body Parts

Along with Information about Occupational Cancer, Personal Protective Equipment, Toxic and Hazardous Chemicals, Child Labor, Stress, and Workplace Violence

Edited by Chad T. Kimball. 626 pages. 2000. 978-0-7808-0231-5.

"As a reference for the general public, this would be useful in any library." —*E-Streams, Jun '01*

"Provides helpful information for primary care physicians and other caregivers interested in occupational medicine. . . . General readers; professionals."
—*Choice, Association of College & Research Libraries, May '01*

"Recommended reference source."
—*Booklist, American Library Association, Feb '01*

"Highly recommended." —*The Bookwatch, Jan '01*

Worldwide Health Sourcebook

Basic Information about Global Health Issues, Including Malnutrition, Reproductive Health, Disease Dispersion and Prevention, Emerging Diseases, Risky Health Behaviors, and the Leading Causes of Death

Along with Global Health Concerns for Children, Women, and the Elderly, Mental Health Issues, Research and Technology Advancements, and Economic, Environmental, and Political Health Implications, a Glossary, and a Resource Listing for Additional Help and Information

Edited by Joyce Brennfleck Shannon. 614 pages. 2001. 978-0-7808-0330-5.

"Named an Outstanding Academic Title."
—*Choice, Association of College & Research Libraries, Jan '02*

"Yet another handy but also unique compilation in the extensive *Health Reference Series*, this is a useful work because many of the international publications reprinted or excerpted are not readily available. Highly recommended." —*Choice, Association of College & Research Libraries, Nov '01*

"Recommended reference source."
—*Booklist, American Library Association, Oct '01*

SEE ALSO *Traveler's Health Sourcebook*

Teen Health Series

Helping Young Adults Understand, Manage, and Avoid Serious Illness

List price $65 per volume. **School and library price $58 per volume.**

Alcohol Information for Teens

Health Tips about Alcohol and Alcoholism

Including Facts about Underage Drinking, Preventing Teen Alcohol Use, Alcohol's Effects on the Brain and the Body, Alcohol Abuse Treatment, Help for Children of Alcoholics, and More

Edited by Joyce Brennfleck Shannon. 370 pages. 2005. 978-0-7808-0741-9.

"Boxed facts and tips add visual interest to the well-researched and clearly written text."

—*Curriculum Connection, Apr '06*

Allergy Information for Teens

Health Tips about Allergic Reactions Such as Anaphylaxis, Respiratory Problems, and Rashes

Including Facts about Identifying and Managing Allergies to Food, Pollen, Mold, Animals, Chemicals, Drugs, and Other Substances

Edited by Karen Bellenir. 410 pages. 2006. 978-0-7808-0799-0.

Asthma Information for Teens

Health Tips about Managing Asthma and Related Concerns

Including Facts about Asthma Causes, Triggers, Symptoms, Diagnosis, and Treatment

Edited by Karen Bellenir. 386 pages. 2005. 978-0-7808-0770-9.

"Highly recommended for medical libraries, public school libraries, and public libraries."

—*American Reference Books Annual, 2006*

"It is so clearly written and well organized that even hesitant readers will be able to find the facts they need, whether for reports or personal information. . . . A succinct but complete resource."

—*School Library Journal, Sep '05*

Body Information for Teens

Health Tips about Maintaining Well-Being for a Lifetime

Including Facts about the Development and Functioning of the Body's Systems, Organs, and Structures and the Health Impact of Lifestyle Choices

Edited by Sandra Augustyn Lawton. 458 pages. 2007. 978-0-7808-0443-2.

Cancer Information for Teens

Health Tips about Cancer Awareness, Prevention, Diagnosis, and Treatment

Including Facts about Frequently Occurring Cancers, Cancer Risk Factors, and Coping Strategies for Teens Fighting Cancer or Dealing with Cancer in Friends or Family Members

Edited by Wilma R. Caldwell. 428 pages. 2004. 978-0-7808-0678-8.

"Recommended for school libraries, or consumer libraries that see a lot of use by teens."

—*E-Streams, May '05*

"A valuable educational tool."

—*American Reference Books Annual, 2005*

"Young adults and their parents alike will find this new addition to the *Teen Health Series* an important reference to cancer in teens."

—*Children's Bookwatch, Feb '05*

Complementary and Alternative Medicine Information for Teens

Health Tips about Non-Traditional and Non-Western Medical Practices

Including Information about Acupuncture, Chiropractic Medicine, Dietary and Herbal Supplements, Hypnosis, Massage Therapy, Prayer and Spirituality, Reflexology, Yoga, and More

Edited by Sandra Augustyn Lawton. 405 pages. 2006. 978-0-7808-0966-6.

Diabetes Information for Teens

Health Tips about Managing Diabetes and Preventing Related Complications

Including Information about Insulin, Glucose Control, Healthy Eating, Physical Activity, and Learning to Live with Diabetes

Edited by Sandra Augustyn Lawton. 410 pages. 2006. 978-0-7808-0811-9.

Diet Information for Teens, 2nd Edition

Health Tips about Diet and Nutrition

Including Facts about Dietary Guidelines, Food Groups, Nutrients, Healthy Meals, Snacks, Weight Control, Medical Concerns Related to Diet, and More

Edited by Karen Bellenir. 432 pages. 2006. 978-0-7808-0820-1.

"Full of helpful insights and facts throughout the book. . . . An excellent resource to be placed in public libraries or even in personal collections."
—*American Reference Books Annual, 2002*

"Recommended for middle and high school libraries and media centers as well as academic libraries that educate future teachers of teenagers. It is also a suitable addition to health science libraries that serve patrons who are interested in teen health promotion and education." —*E-Streams, Oct '01*

"This comprehensive book would be beneficial to collections that need information about nutrition, dietary guidelines, meal planning, and weight control. . . . This reference is so easy to use that its purchase is recommended." —*The Book Report, Sep-Oct '01*

"This book is written in an easy to understand format describing issues that many teens face every day, and then provides thoughtful explanations so that teens can make informed decisions. This is an interesting book that provides important facts and information for today's teens." —*Doody's Health Sciences Book Review Journal, Jul-Aug '01*

"A comprehensive compendium of diet and nutrition. The information is presented in a straightforward, plain-spoken manner. This title will be useful to those working on reports on a variety of topics, as well as to general readers concerned about their dietary health."
—*School Library Journal, Jun '01*

Drug Information for Teens, 2nd Edition

Health Tips about the Physical and Mental Effects of Substance Abuse

Including Information about Marijuana, Inhalants, Club Drugs, Stimulants, Hallucinogens, Opiates, Prescription and Over-the-Counter Drugs, Herbal Products, Tobacco, Alcohol, and More

Edited by Sandra Augustyn Lawton. 468 pages. 2006. 978-0-7808-0862-1.

"A clearly written resource for general readers and researchers alike." —*School Library Journal*

"This book is well-balanced. . . . a must for public and school libraries."
—*VOYA: Voice of Youth Advocates, Dec '03*

"The chapters are quick to make a connection to their teenage reading audience. The prose is straightforward and the book lends itself to spot reading. It should be useful both for practical information and for research, and it is suitable for public and school libraries."
—*American Reference Books Annual, 2003*

"Recommended reference source."
—*Booklist, American Library Association, Feb '03*

"This is an excellent resource for teens and their parents. Education about drugs and substances is key to discouraging teen drug abuse and this book provides this much needed information in a way that is interesting and factual." —*Doody's Review Service, Dec '02*

Eating Disorders Information for Teens

Health Tips about Anorexia, Bulimia, Binge Eating, and Other Eating Disorders

Including Information on the Causes, Prevention, and Treatment of Eating Disorders, and Such Other Issues as Maintaining Healthy Eating and Exercise Habits

Edited by Sandra Augustyn Lawton. 337 pages. 2005. 978-0-7808-0783-9.

"An excellent resource for teens and those who work with them."
—*VOYA: Voice of Youth Advocates, Apr '06*

"A welcome addition to high school and undergraduate libraries." —*American Reference Books Annual, 2006*

"This book covers the topic in a lucid manner but delves deeper into every aspect of an eating disorder. A solid addition for any nonfiction or reference collection." —*School Library Journal, Dec '05*

Fitness Information for Teens

Health Tips about Exercise, Physical Well-Being, and Health Maintenance

Including Facts about Aerobic and Anaerobic Conditioning, Stretching, Body Shape and Body Image, Sports Training, Nutrition, and Activities for Non-Athletes

Edited by Karen Bellenir. 425 pages. 2004. 978-0-7808-0679-5.

"Another excellent offering from Omnigraphics in their *Teen Health Series*. . . . This book will be a great addition to any public, junior high, senior high, or secondary school library."
—*American Reference Books Annual, 2005*

Learning Disabilities Information for Teens

Health Tips about Academic Skills Disorders and Other Disabilities That Affect Learning

Including Information about Common Signs of Learning Disabilities, School Issues, Learning to Live with a Learning Disability, and Other Related Issues

Edited by Sandra Augustyn Lawton. 337 pages. 2005. 978-0-7808-0796-9.

"This book provides a wealth of information for any reader interested in the signs, causes, and consequences

of learning disabilities, as well as related legal rights and educational interventions. . . . Public and academic libraries should want this title for both students and general readers."

—American Reference Books Annual, 2006

Mental Health Information for Teens, 2nd Edition

Health Tips about Mental Wellness and Mental Illness

Including Facts about Mental and Emotional Health, Depression and Other Mood Disorders, Anxiety Disorders, Behavior Disorders, Self-Injury, Psychosis, Schizophrenia, and More

Edited by Karen Bellenir. 400 pages. 2006. 978-0-7808-0863-8.

"In both language and approach, this user-friendly entry in the *Teen Health Series* is on target for teens needing information on mental health concerns."

—Booklist, American Library Association, Jan '02

"Readers will find the material accessible and informative, with the shaded notes, facts, and embedded glossary insets adding appropriately to the already interesting and succinct presentation."

—School Library Journal, Jan '02

"This title is highly recommended for any library that serves adolescents and parents/caregivers of adolescents." *—E-Streams, Jan '02*

"Recommended for high school libraries and young adult collections in public libraries. Both health professionals and teenagers will find this book useful."

—American Reference Books Annual, 2002

"This is a nice book written to enlighten the society, primarily teenagers, about common teen mental health issues. It is highly recommended to teachers and parents as well as adolescents."

—Doody's Review Service, Dec '01

Sexual Health Information for Teens

Health Tips about Sexual Development, Human Reproduction, and Sexually Transmitted Diseases

Including Facts about Puberty, Reproductive Health, Chlamydia, Human Papillomavirus, Pelvic Inflammatory Disease, Herpes, AIDS, Contraception, Pregnancy, and More

Edited by Deborah A. Stanley. 391 pages. 2003. 978-0-7808-0445-6.

"This work should be included in all high school libraries and many larger public libraries. . . . highly recommended."

—American Reference Books Annual, 2004

"*Sexual Health* approaches its subject with appropriate seriousness and offers easily accessible advice and information." *—School Library Journal, Feb '04*

Skin Health Information for Teens

Health Tips about Dermatological Concerns and Skin Cancer Risks

Including Facts about Acne, Warts, Hives, and Other Conditions and Lifestyle Choices, Such as Tanning, Tattooing, and Piercing, That Affect the Skin, Nails, Scalp, and Hair

Edited by Robert Aquinas McNally. 429 pages. 2003. 978-0-7808-0446-3.

"This volume, as with others in the series, will be a useful addition to school and public library collections." *—American Reference Books Annual, 2004*

"There is no doubt that this reference tool is valuable."

—VOYA: Voice of Youth Advocates, Feb '04

"This volume serves as a one-stop source and should be a necessity for any health collection."

—Library Media Connection

Sports Injuries Information for Teens

Health Tips about Sports Injuries and Injury Protection

Including Facts about Specific Injuries, Emergency Treatment, Rehabilitation, Sports Safety, Competition Stress, Fitness, Sports Nutrition, Steroid Risks, and More

Edited by Joyce Brennfleck Shannon. 405 pages. 2003. 978-0-7808-0447-0.

"This work will be useful in the young adult collections of public libraries as well as high school libraries."

—American Reference Books Annual, 2004

Suicide Information for Teens

Health Tips about Suicide Causes and Prevention

Including Facts about Depression, Risk Factors, Getting Help, Survivor Support, and More

Edited by Joyce Brennfleck Shannon. 368 pages. 2005. 978-0-7808-0737-2.

Tobacco Information for Teens

Health Tips about the Hazards of Using Cigarettes, Smokeless Tobacco, and Other Nicotine Products

Including Facts about Nicotine Addiction, Immediate and Long-Term Health Effects of Tobacco Use, Related Cancers, Smoking Cessation, Tobacco Use Prevention, and Tobacco Use Statistics

Edited by Karen Bellenir. 440 pages. 2007. 978-0-7808-0976-5.

Health Reference Series

Adolescent Health Sourcebook, 2nd Edition
AIDS Sourcebook, 3rd Edition
Alcoholism Sourcebook, 2nd Edition
Allergies Sourcebook, 2nd Edition
Alzheimer's Disease Sourcebook, 3rd Edition
Arthritis Sourcebook, 2nd Edition
Asthma Sourcebook, 2nd Edition
Attention Deficit Disorder Sourcebook
Back & Neck Sourcebook, 2nd Edition
Blood & Circulatory Disorders Sourcebook, 2nd Edition
Brain Disorders Sourcebook, 2nd Edition
Breast Cancer Sourcebook, 2nd Edition
Breastfeeding Sourcebook
Burns Sourcebook
Cancer Sourcebook, 4th Edition
Cancer Sourcebook for Women, 3rd Edition
Cardiovascular Diseases & Disorders Sourcebook, 3rd Edition
Caregiving Sourcebook
Child Abuse Sourcebook
Childhood Diseases & Disorders Sourcebook
Colds, Flu & Other Common Ailments Sourcebook
Communication Disorders Sourcebook
Complementary & Alternative Medicine Sourcebook, 3rd Edition
Congenital Disorders Sourcebook, 2nd Edition
Consumer Issues in Health Care Sourcebook
Contagious Diseases Sourcebook
Contagious & Non-Contagious Infectious Diseases Sourcebook
Death & Dying Sourcebook, 2nd Edition
Dental Care & Oral Health Sourcebook, 2nd Edition
Depression Sourcebook
Dermatological Disorders Sourcebook, 2nd Edition
Diabetes Sourcebook, 3rd Edition
Diet & Nutrition Sourcebook, 3rd Edition
Digestive Diseases & Disorder Sourcebook
Disabilities Sourcebook
Domestic Violence Sourcebook, 2nd Edition
Drug Abuse Sourcebook, 2nd Edition
Ear, Nose & Throat Disorders Sourcebook, 2nd Edition
Eating Disorders Sourcebook
Emergency Medical Services Sourcebook
Endocrine & Metabolic Disorders Sourcebook
Environmentally Health Sourcebook, 2nd Edition
Ethnic Diseases Sourcebook
Eye Care Sourcebook, 2nd Edition
Family Planning Sourcebook
Fitness & Exercise Sourcebook, 3rd Edition
Food & Animal Borne Diseases Sourcebook
Food Safety Sourcebook
Forensic Medicine Sourcebook
Gastrointestinal Diseases & Disorders Sourcebook, 2nd Edition
Genetic Disorders Sourcebook, 3rd Edition
Head Trauma Sourcebook
Headache Sourcebook
Health Insurance Sourcebook
Healthy Aging Sourcebook
Healthy Children Sourcebook
Healthy Heart Sourcebook for Women
Hepatitis Sourcebook
Household Safety Sourcebook
Hypertension Sourcebook
Immune System Disorders Sourcebook, 2nd Edition